Reanimating Regions

Writing regions, undertaking a regional study, was once a standard form of geographic communication and critique. This was until the quantitative revolution in the middle of the previous century and more definitively the critical turn in human geography towards the end of the twentieth century. From then on writing regions as they were experienced phenomenologically, or arguing culturally, historically, and politically with regions, was deemed to be old-fashioned. Yet the region is, and always will be, a central geographical concept, and thinking about regions can tell us a lot about the history of the discipline called geography.

Despite taking up an identifiable place within the geographical imagination in scholarship and beyond, *region* remains a relatively forgotten, under-used, and in part under-theorised term. *Reanimating Regions* marks the continued reinvigoration of a set of disciplinary debates surrounding regions, the regional, and regional geography. Across 18 chapters from international, interdisciplinary scholars, this book writes and performs region as a temporary permanence, something held stable, not fixed and absolute, at different points in time, for different purposes. There is, as this expansive volume outlines, no single reading of a region.

Reanimating Regions collectively rebalances the region within geography and geographical thought. In renewing the geography of regions as not only a site of investigation but also as an analytical framework through which to write the world, what emerges is a powerful reworking of the geographic imagination. Read against one another, the chapters weave together timely commentaries on region and regions across the globe, with a particular emphasis upon the regional as played out in the United Kingdom, and regional worlds both within and beyond Europe, offering chapters from Africa and South America. Addressing both the *political* and the *cultural*, this volume responds to the need for a consolidated and considered reflection on *region*, the regional, and regional geography, speaking directly to broader intellectual concerns with performance, aesthetics, identity, mobilities, the environment, and the body.

James Riding is a Postdoctoral Researcher in the Space and Political Agency Research Group/RELATE Centre of Excellence at the University of Tampere, Finland.

Martin Jones is Professor of Human Geography and Deputy Vice-Chancellor at Staffordshire University, UK.

‘This is a welcome and provocative collection which reveals a resurgence of regional geography, from a spectrum of perspectives. Drawing on a range of detailed case studies, the authors show why regions matter, on the ground, and in the mind, as a locus of social and economic life, a lens on prevailing geographical processes and patterns, and as a resource for imagining alternative, possible worlds.’ — **Stephen Daniels, Professor of Cultural Geography, University of Nottingham and editor of *Envisioning Landscapes, Making Worlds: Geography and the Humanities,* and *The Iconography of Landscape***

‘Through a refreshingly-diverse and contemporary set of chapters, this book fully delivers on its title and its promise. *Reanimating Regions* gathers a distinctive and international set of voices and perspectives. If the fortunes of ‘the region’ as a conceptual frame and substantive topic have risen and fallen through time, then here we see a strong and fresh case made for regionality as cultural form, political crucible and performative inspiration.’ — **John Wylie, Professor of Cultural Geography, University of Exeter and author of *Landscape***

‘Region – both as a generic idea and a tool used in governance, classification and distribution – has become increasingly significant during the last few decades. At the same time regional identities and political regionalism have gained popularity at and across various spatial scales, displaying the meaning of regions for economic and cultural life, social reproduction and related struggles. This exciting book brings together an interdisciplinary and international group of scholars and artists who open novel perspectives on what regions are and do, and how we should understand their functions and power in the contemporary globalizing world.’ — **Anssi Paasi, Professor of Geography, University of Oulu and author of *Territories, boundaries and consciousness: the changing geographies of the Finnish-Russian border,* and *Pure Geography***

Regions and Cities

Series Editor in Chief

Susan M. Christopherson, *Cornell University, USA*

Editors

Maryann Feldman, *University of Georgia, USA*
Gernot Grabher, *HafenCity University Hamburg, Germany*
Ron Martin, *University of Cambridge, UK*
Kieran P. Donaghy, *Cornell University, USA*

In today's globalised, knowledge-driven and networked world, regions and cities have assumed heightened significance as the interconnected nodes of economic, social and cultural production, and as sites of new modes of economic and territorial governance and policy experimentation. This book series brings together incisive and critically engaged international and interdisciplinary research on this resurgence of regions and cities, and should be of interest to geographers, economists, sociologists, political scientists and cultural scholars, as well as to policy-makers involved in regional and urban development.

For more information on the Regional Studies Association visit www.regionalstudies.org

There is a **30% discount** available to RSA members on books in the ***Regions and Cities*** series, and other subject related Taylor and Francis books and e-books including Routledge titles. To order just e-mail Georg Wanek, Georg.Wanek@tandf.co.uk, or phone on +44 (0) 207 017 6364 and declare your RSA membership. You can also visit the series page at www.routledge.com/Regions-and-Cities/book-series/RSA and use the discount code: **RSA0901**

115. Reanimating Regions
Culture, Politics, and Performance
Edited by James Riding and Martin Jones

114. Territorial Policy and Governance
Alternative Paths
Edited by Iain Deas and Stephen Hincks

113. Economics of Planning Policies in China
Infrastructure, Location and Cities
Wen-jie Wu

112. The Empirical and Institutional Dimensions of Smart Specialisation
Edited by Philip McCann, Frank van Oort and John Goddard

111. EU Cohesion Policy
Reassessing performance and direction
Edited by John Bachtler, Peter Berkowitz, Sally Hardy and Tatjana Muravska

110. Geography of Innovation
Edited by Nadine Massard and Corinne Autant-Bernard

109. Rethinking International Skilled Migration
Edited by Micheline van Riemsdijk and Qingfang Wang

108. The EU's New Borderland
Cross-border relations and regional development
Andrzej Jakubowski, Andrzej Miszczuk, Bogdan Kawałko, Tomasz Komornicki and Roman Szul

107. Entrepreneurship in a Regional Context
Edited by Michael Fritsch and David J. Storey

106. Governing Smart Specialisation
Edited by Dimitrios Kyriakou, Manuel Palazuelos Martínez, Inmaculada Periáñez-Forte and Alessandro Rainoldi

105. Innovation, Regional Development and the Life Sciences
Beyond clusters
Kean Birch

104. Unfolding Cluster Evolution
Edited by Fiorenza Belussi and Jose Luis Hervás-Olivier

103. Place-Based Economic Development and the New EU Cohesion Policy
Edited by Philip McCann and Attila Varga

102. Transformation of Resource Towns and Peripheries
Political economy perspectives
Edited by Greg Halseth

101. Approaches to Economic Geography
Towards a geographical political economy
Ray Hudson

100. Secondary Cities and Development
Edited by Lochner Marais, Etienne Nel and Ronnie Donaldson

99. Technology and the City
Systems, applications and implications
Tan Yigitcanlar

98. Smaller Cities in a World of Competitiveness
Peter Karl Kresl and Daniele Ietri

97. Code and the City
Edited by Rob Kitchin and Sung-Yueh Perng

96. The UK Regional–National Economic Problem
Geography, globalisation and governance
Philip McCann

95. Skills and Cities
Edited by Sako Musterd, Marco Bontje and Jan Rouwendal

94. Higher Education and the Creative Economy
Beyond the campus
Edited by Roberta Comunian and Abigail Gilmore

93. Making Cultural Cities in Asia
Mobility, assemblage, and the politics of aspirational urbanism
Edited by Jun Wang, Tim Oakes and Yang Yang

92. Leadership and the City
Power, strategy and networks in the making of knowledge cities
Markku Sotarauta

91. Evolutionary Economic Geography
Theoretical and empirical progress
Edited by Dieter Kogler

90. Cities in Crisis
Socio-spatial impacts of the economic crisis in Southern European cities
Edited by Jörg Knieling and Frank Othengrafen

89. Socio-Economic Segregation in European Capital Cities
East meets West
Edited by Tiit Tammaru, Szymon Marcińczak, Maarten van Ham and Sako Musterd

88. People, Places and Policy
Knowing contemporary Wales through new localities
Edited by Martin Jones, Scott Orford and Victoria Macfarlane

87. The London Olympics and Urban Development
The mega-event city
Edited by Gavin Poynter, Valerie Viehoff and Yang Li

86. Making 21st Century Knowledge Complexes
Technopoles of the world revisited
Edited by Julie Tian Miao, Paul Benneworth and Nicholas A. Phelps

85. Soft Spaces in Europe
Re-negotiating governance, boundaries and borders
Edited by Philip Allmendinger, Graham Haughton, Jörg Knieling and Frank Othengrafen

84. Regional Worlds: Advancing the Geography of Regions
Edited by Martin Jones and Anssi Paasi

83. Place-making and Urban Development
New challenges for contemporary planning and design
Pier Carlo Palermo and Davide Ponzini

82. Knowledge, Networks and Policy
Regional studies in postwar Britain and beyond
James Hopkins

81. Dynamics of Economic Spaces in the Global Knowledge-Based Economy
Theory and East Asian cases
Sam Ock Park

80. Urban Competitiveness
Theory and practice
Daniele Letri and Peter Kresl

79. Smart Specialisation
Opportunities and challenges for regional innovation policy
Dominique Foray

78. The Age of Intelligent Cities
Smart environments and innovation-for-all strategies
Nicos Komninos

77. Space and Place in Central and Eastern Europe
Historical trends and perspectives
Gyula Horváth

76. Territorial Cohesion in Rural Europe
The relational turn in rural development
Edited by Andrew Copus and Philomena de Lima

75. The Global Competitiveness of Regions
Robert Huggins, Hiro Izushi, Daniel Prokop and Piers Thompson

74. The Social Dynamics of Innovation Networks
Edited by Roel Rutten, Paul Benneworth, Dessy Irawati and Frans Boekema

73. The European Territory
From historical roots to global challenges
Jacques Robert

72. Urban Innovation Systems
What makes them tick?
Willem van Winden, Erik Braun, Alexander Otgaar and Jan-Jelle Witte

71. Shrinking Cities
A global perspective
Edited by Harry W. Richardson and Chang Woon Nam

70. Cities, State and Globalization
City-regional governance
Tassilo Herrschel

69. The Creative Class Goes Global
Edited by Charlotta Mellander, Richard Florida, Bjørn Asheim and Meric Gertler

68. Entrepreneurial Knowledge, Technology and the Transformation of Regions
Edited by Charlie Karlsson, Börje Johansson and Roger Stough

67. The Economic Geography of the IT Industry in the Asia Pacific Region
Edited by Philip Cooke, Glen Searle and Kevin O'Connor

66. Working Regions
Reconnecting innovation and production in the knowledge economy
Jennifer Clark

65. Europe's Changing Geography
The impact of inter-regional networks
Edited by Nicola Bellini and Ulrich Hilpert

64. The Value of Arts and Culture for Regional Development
A Scandinavian perspective
Edited by Lisbeth Lindeborg and Lars Lindkvist

63. The University and the City
John Goddard and Paul Vallance

62. Re-framing Regional Development
Evolution, innovation and transition
Edited by Philip Cooke

61. Networking Regionalised Innovative Labour Markets
Edited by Ulrich Hilpert and Helen Lawton Smith

60. Leadership and Change in Sustainable Regional Development
Edited by Markku Sotarauta, Ina Horlings and Joyce Liddle

59. Regional Development Agencies: The Next Generation?
Networking, knowledge and regional policies
Edited by Nicola Bellini, Mike Danson and Henrik Halkier

58. Community-based Entrepreneurship and Rural Development
Creating favourable conditions for small businesses in Central Europe
Matthias Fink, Stephan Loidl and Richard Lang

57. Creative Industries and Innovation in Europe
Concepts, measures and comparative case studies
Edited by Luciana Lazzeretti

56. Innovation Governance in an Open Economy
Shaping regional nodes in a globalized world
Edited by Annika Rickne, Staffan Laestadius and Henry Etzkowitz

55. Complex Adaptive Innovation Systems
Relatedness and transversality in the evolving region
Philip Cooke

54. Creating Knowledge Locations in Cities
Innovation and integration challenges
Willem van Winden, Luis de Carvalho, Erwin van Tujil, Jeroen van Haaren and Leo van den Berg

53. Regional Development in Northern Europe
Peripherality, marginality and border issues
Edited by Mike Danson and Peter De Souza

52. Promoting Silicon Valleys in Latin America
Luciano Ciravegna

51. Industrial Policy Beyond the Crisis
Regional, national and international perspectives
Edited by David Bailey, Helena Lenihan and Josep-Maria Arauzo-Carod

50. Just Growth
Inclusion and prosperity in America's metropolitan regions
Chris Benner and Manuel Pastor

49. Cultural Political Economy of Small Cities
Edited by Anne Lorentzen and Bas van Heur

48. The Recession and Beyond
Local and regional responses to the downturn
Edited by David Bailey and Caroline Chapain

47. Beyond Territory
Edited by Harald Bathelt, Maryann Feldman and Dieter F. Kogler

46. Leadership and Place
Edited by Chris Collinge, John Gibney and Chris Mabey

45. Migration in the 21st Century
Rights, outcomes, and policy
Kim Korinek and Thomas Maloney

44. The Futures of the City Region
Edited by Michael Neuman and Angela Hull

43. The Impacts of Automotive Plant Closures
A tale of two cities
Edited by Andrew Beer and Holli Evans

42. Manufacturing in the New Urban Economy
Willem van Winden, Leo van den Berg, Luis de Carvalho and Erwin van Tuijl

41. Globalizing Regional Development in East Asia
Production networks, clusters, and entrepreneurship
Edited by Henry Wai-chung Yeung

40. China and Europe
The implications of the rise of China as a global economic power for Europe
Edited by Klaus Kunzmann, Willy A Schmid and Martina Koll-Schretzenmayr

39. Business Networks in Clusters and Industrial Districts
The governance of the global value chain
Edited by Fiorenza Belussi and Alessia Sammarra

38. Whither Regional Studies?
Edited by Andy Pike

37. Intelligent Cities and Globalisation of Innovation Networks
Nicos Komninos

36. Devolution, Regionalism and Regional Development
The UK experience
Edited by Jonathan Bradbury

35. Creative Regions
Technology, culture and knowledge entrepreneurship
Edited by Philip Cooke and Dafna Schwartz

34. European Cohesion Policy
Willem Molle

33. Geographies of the New Economy
Critical reflections
Edited by Peter W. Daniels, Andrew Leyshon, Michael J. Bradshaw and Jonathan Beaverstock

32. The Rise of the English Regions?
Edited by Irene Hardill, Paul Benneworth, Mark Baker and Leslie Budd

31. Regional Development in the Knowledge Economy
Edited by Philip Cooke and Andrea Piccaluga

30. Regional Competitiveness
Edited by Ron Martin, Michael Kitson and Peter Tyler

29. Clusters and Regional Development
Critical reflections and explorations
Edited by Bjørn Asheim, Philip Cooke and Ron Martin

28. Regions, Spatial Strategies and Sustainable Development
David Counsell and Graham Haughton

27. Sustainable Cities
Graham Haughton and Colin Hunter

26. Geographies of Labour Market Inequality
Edited by Ron Martin and Philip S. Morrison

25. Regional Innovation Strategies
The challenge for less-favoured regions
Edited by Kevin Morgan and Claire Nauwelaers

24. Out of the Ashes?
The social impact of industrial contraction and regeneration on Britain's mining communities
Chas Critcher, Bella Dicks, David Parry and David Waddington

23. Restructuring Industry and Territory
The experience of Europe's regions
Edited by Anna Giunta, Arnoud Lagendijk and Andy Pike

22. Foreign Direct Investment and the Global Economy
Corporate and institutional dynamics of global-localisation
Edited by Jeremy Alden and Nicholas F. Phelps

21. Community Economic Development
Edited by Graham Haughton

20. Regional Development Agencies in Europe
Edited by Charlotte Damborg, Mike Danson and Henrik Halkier

19. Social Exclusion in European Cities
Processes, experiences and responses
Edited by Judith Allen, Goran Cars and Ali Madanipour

18. Metropolitan Planning in Britain
A comparative study
Edited by Peter Roberts, Kevin Thomas and Gwyndaf Williams

17. Unemployment and Social Exclusion
Landscapes of labour inequality and social exclusion
Edited by Sally Hardy, Paul Lawless and Ron Martin

16. Multinationals and European Integration
Trade, investment and regional development
Edited by Nicholas A. Phelps

15. The Coherence of EU Regional Policy
Contrasting perspectives on the structural funds
Edited by John Bachtler and Ivan Turok

14. New Institutional Spaces
TECs and the remaking of economic governance
Martin Jones, Foreword by Jamie Peck

13. Regional Policy in Europe
S. S. Artobolevskiy

12. Innovation Networks and Learning Regions?
James Simmie

11. British Regionalism and Devolution
The challenges of state reform and European integration
Edited by Jonathan Bradbury and John Mawson

10. Regional Development Strategies
A European perspective
Edited by Jeremy Alden and Philip Boland

9. Union Retreat and the Regions
The shrinking landscape of organised labour
Ron Martin, Peter Sunley and Jane Wills

8. The Regional Dimension of Transformation in Central Europe
Grzegorz Gorzelak

7. The Determinants of Small Firm Growth
An inter-regional study in the United Kingdom 1986–90
Richard Barkham, Graham Gudgin, Mark Hart and Eric Hanvey

6. The Regional Imperative
Regional planning and governance in Britain, Europe and the United States
Urlan A. Wannop

5. An Enlarged Europe
Regions in competition?
Edited by Louis Albrechts, Sally Hardy, Mark Hart and Anastasios Katos

4. Spatial Policy in a Divided Nation
Edited by Richard T. Harrison and Mark Hart

3. Regional Development in the 1990s
The British Isles in transition
Edited by Ron Martin and Peter Townroe

2. Retreat from the Regions
Corporate change and the closure of factories
Stephen Fothergill and Nigel Guy

1. Beyond Green Belts
Managing urban growth in the 21st century
Edited by John Herington

Reanimating Regions

Culture, Politics, and Performance

Edited by James Riding and Martin Jones

Routledge
Taylor & Francis Group
LONDON AND NEW YORK

First published 2017 by Routledge

2 Park Square, Milton Park, Abingdon, Oxfordshire OX14 4RN
52 Vanderbilt Avenue, New York, NY 10017

Routledge is an imprint of the Taylor & Francis Group, an informa business

First issued in paperback 2019

British Library Cataloguing in Publication Data
A catalogue record for this book is available from the British Library

Library of Congress Cataloging in Publication Data
A catalog record for this book has been requested

ISBN: 978-1-138-93153-4 (hbk)
ISBN: 978-0-367-87408-7 (pbk)

Typeset in Times New Roman PS
by diacriTech, Chennai

Contents

Figures

Tables

Contributors

John Agnew is currently Distinguished Professor of Geography at the University of California, Los Angeles (UCLA). From 1975 until 1995 he was a professor at Syracuse University in New York. He has written widely on questions of territory, place and political power. He has also worked on issues of 'science' in geography and how knowledge is created and circulates in and across places. He is best known for his work completely reinventing 'geopolitics' as a field of study and for his theoretical and empirical efforts at showing how national politics is best understood in terms of the geographical dynamics of 'places' and how they are made out of both local and long-distance determinants. One of his best known books is *Place and Politics* (1987). Another is *Geopolitics: Re-Visioning World Politics* (2003). He is now editor-in-chief of the journal *Territory, Politics, Governance*, published by Routledge.

Jess Allen is a dancer and walking artist currently completing her practice-based PhD, 'Tracktivism: Walking and Talking in Rural Landscapes as an Eco-Activist Arts Practice', at the University of Manchester. She uses walking to create unexpected performative encounters in unusual locations. Originally a biologist, she gained her first PhD from Aberystwyth before re-training in contemporary dance, latterly at Coventry with an MA in Dance Making and Performance. Jess has worked as landscape officer for local government, dance lecturer (experiential anatomy/improvisation), arts facilitator (AHRC *Multi-Story Water*) and as an aerial performer for Blue Eyed Soul (UK/US), Full Tilt and everyBODY dance. She was a featured artist in *Playing for Time* (ed. Lucy Neal, 2015) and *Culture Shift* (Emergence, 2014) and a contributor to the Walking Artists Network anthology *Ways to Wander* (Qualmann and Hind, 2015). She has published work in *Research in Dance Education*, *Research in Drama Education* (environmentalism issue), *Journal of Dance and Somatic Practices* and *Contemporary Theatre Review* (activism issue). Jess has recently guest-edited, with Bronwyn Preece and Stephen Bottoms, 'Performing Ecos', the two-part, ecology-themed issue of the Intellect series *Performing Ethos* (2015).

Roger Baars is a Research Fellow at the Faculty of Education and Social Work at the University of Auckland, New Zealand. His research activities are concerned with broader processes of social reproduction and transformation. Central to his work is a critical understanding of social research as investigating the multiple relationships between state, society and citizens to understand how everyday life impacts on and is affected by governmental processes and social developments over time.

David Beel is a Research Associate at the University of Sheffield and the WISERD Civil Society Research Centre, working on the project *Spaces of New Localism – Stakeholder Engagement and Economic Development in Wales and England.* The project is interested in understanding the ways in which New Localism and devolution is being delivered at the City-Regional scale within the UK. He has a varied set of academic interests including urban, rural, social and cultural geographies. This has led to specific interests in cultural repositories such as museums, archives, galleries and libraries and the role they play in creating cultural participation in 'communities'.

Anders Bojen is an independent artist who uses an interdisciplinary and experimental approach. He has an interest in how the relationship between the virtual and mathematical world of the computer and the physical world of the human opens up new opportunities for art. Computer language in the form of code and algorithms is a material that can be modified with an artistic intention, resulting in new aesthetic experiences and tools.

Venetia Congdon recently completed a DPhil at the University of Oxford, in Social and Cultural Anthropology, where she also completed her masters in 2011. Her doctoral thesis, 'Nourishing the Nation: Manifestations of Catalan Identity through Food', studied the ways in which Catalans in north-east Spain use food to express national identity in the context of the pro-independence movement. Her research interests include Catalan culture, the anthropology of food and cooking, national identity, folklore, heritage, tourism, organisational culture, and witchcraft. She has a BSc (Hons) in Business Management from the Royal Agricultural University, where she was top student of the program for three years running. In 2014 she was runner-up in the Linacre Domus Prize, and between 2014 and 2015 was President of the Oxford University Anthropological Society.

Lucy Frears is an Associate Lecturer in BA Digital Media Design and a practice-based doctoral researcher based in the Academy for Innovation & Research (AIR) at Falmouth University supported by ESF (European Social Fund). Lucy's interdisiplinary research focuses on locative technology (smart mobile phones with GPS) and our embodied connection to landscape and community using creative practice. Lucy has received funding for various projects and residencies. Her book based on a community oral history project, *Churks, Clidgy & Doodle-Dashers: Hayle Tales and Trails*, is in its second edition and *Hayle Churks*, her mobile phone app made using AppFurnace by Calvium, won a national Collections Trust Award in 2014. The app is free from iTunes.

Erik Geelhoed is a Research Fellow at Falmouth University working on an EU-funded Framework 7 program called Vconect. In Vconect Erik has conducted requirement studies for mediated performance with actors and dancers; audience research using Galvanic Skin Response sensors; and user evaluations of automated editing (Orchestration) in social media settings. He is currently working with Cornwall-based theatre companies to apply Vconect technology in performance settings.

Rune Graulund is Associate Professor of American Literature and Culture at the Centre for American Studies, University of Southern Denmark. He previously held a Carlsberg Postdoctorate at Stony Brook University, New York, and was also a Lecturer in English Literature at the University of Strathclyde. He is the editor of *Desperately Seeking Authenticity: An Interdisciplinary Approach* (2010) and *Postcolonial Travel Writing: Critical Explorations* (2011), and is the co-author of *Mobility at Large: Globalization, Textuality, Travel Writing* (2012) and *Grotesque* (2013). He has published a range of peer-reviewed articles on postcolonial theory and criticism, and in American studies.

Jesse Heley is a Senior Lecturer in Human Geography at the University of Aberystwyth. Jesse's research is situated within the broad fields of political geography, economic geography and spatial planning, being particularly concerned with rural restructuring and shifting class dynamics in the British countryside. He is Co-Investigator on the project *The Global Countryside: Rural Change and Development in Globalization* (GLOBAL-RURAL) and Project Leader with the ESRC-funded WISERD Civil Society Research Centre.

Rory Hill is a DPhil candidate in the School of Geography and Environment at the University of Oxford, carrying out research into the development, dynamism and sustainability of *terroir* in three regions of France. He is a postgraduate representative of the Rural Geography Research Group of the Royal Geographical Society (with IBG), and an editor of the postgraduate journal *Politics of Place*.

George Jaramillo is a Research Associate at the Glasgow School of Art's Institute of Design Innovation in the Scottish countryside. His experience in rural research, artistic development, and conservation skills is used to support the Scottish Highlands and Islands Enterprises in socially involved design research. He is also completing a PhD in Cultural Geography at the University of Edinburgh. His research interests combine phenomenological and Marxist theories to understand historic industrial mining landscapes and inform heritage conservation of those sites. He has experience in architecture and historic preservation work including adaptive re-use of historic cabins, stone fountain restoration, and cultural site management.

Nicholas James is an Associate Lecturer at the Open University, in Development Policy and Practice and the Faculty of Social Sciences. His research and teaching interests are within the sub-disciplines of development, environment and political ecology. He is working on agrarian change in Africa, the geography of food (especially household food security), livelihoods, water security and place geography within rural Africa. He has also taught at the University of Gloucestershire, University of Wales, Newport and the University of the West of England, Bristol. Recent publications include 'Water Security: A Genealogy of Emerging Discourses' with Chad Staddon, in G Schneier-Madanes (ed) (2014) *Globalized Water. A Question of Governance*.

Philip Johnstone is currently a Research Fellow at the Science Policy Research Unit (SPRU), University of Sussex, UK. He is a Human Geographer interested in the spatial-democratic implications of science and technology, theories of the nation state and understanding political cultures and how they influence the trajectories of policy more broadly. Philip's recent research has explored the nuclear cultures of the UK, particularly in relation to linkages between civilian nuclear power and the renewal of Trident, Britain's submarine-based nuclear weapons system.

Ian Rees Jones was appointed Professor of Sociological Research in 2012 and is Director of the Wales Institute of Social and Economic Research, Data and Methods (WISERD). Previously he was Professor of Sociology and Head of School at Bangor University and Professor of Sociology of Health and Illness at St George's, University of London. His first degree was in History and following work in Hospital Management and Public Health he undertook an MSc at The London School of Hygiene and Tropical Medicine and a PhD at Queen Mary, University of London. He is currently part of the editorial team for *Sociology of Health and Illness* and is the Monograph Series editor. He is interested in theoretical and empirical work on social change and processes of social change and is currently undertaking a series of research projects that addresses processes of social change and their impact on individuals, institutions, communities and civil society.

Martin Jones joined the Department of Geography in September 2013 as Director of the White Rose Social Science Doctoral Training Centre (WRDTC) – an ESRC-funded consortium between the Universities of Sheffield, Leeds and York – and as Professor of Urban and Regional Political Economy. He has produced over 130 publications of all kinds – books, refereed journal publications and significant policy-relevant reports. He has received research funding of over £2 million from a variety of sources (Economic and Social Research Council, Leverhulme Trust, JISC, Welsh Government) and has produced trans-disciplinary knowledge that is theoretically challenging, empirically grounded and philosophically critical. His research has reworked the role of political economy, re-conceptualized the complex interrelationships between state spatiality and political strategy within the social sciences, and brought policy relevance to human geography. He is best known for contributions to debates on geographical political economy, urban and regional studies, advanced capitalism and neoliberalism, economic regulation and governance, local and regional economic and social development, labour market policy, and qualitative data and methods.

David Matless is Professor of Cultural Geography at the University of Nottingham. He is the author of *Landscape and Englishness* (1998), an influential study of cultures of landscape in twentieth-century England, reissued in 2016, and editor of *The Place of Music* (1998) and *Geographies of British Modernity* (2003). His 2014 book, *In the Nature of Landscape: Cultural Geography on the Norfolk Broads*, addresses regional cultural landscape; a related 2015 volume, *The Regional Book*, develops work on geographical description through an account of the Broads region. Other areas of publication include the life and work of ecologist/artist Marietta Pallis (with Laura Cameron), British geographical studies of the Eastern bloc (with Adam Swain and Jonathan Oldfield), geographies of sound, the landscapes of documentary film, and the geography of ghosts. A new area of research considers the ways in which cultural geography might contribute to studies of climatic and environmental change through the theme of the 'Anthroposcenic'.

Misha Myers is a performance researcher and practitioner at Monash University. In both her publications and practice in digital performance she investigates how game design, interactive and location-aware technology and social media enable new forms of participation, storytelling, place-making and civic engagement.

Kristoffer Ørum is an interdisciplinary artist, researcher and organiser based in Copenhagen, Denmark. He spends his time exploring contemporary notions of the everyday, how narratives of lived life are circulated, and what that circulation means for the ways in which we live our daily lives. An example of his net art practice is *Radiant Copenhagen* (2009, in collaboration with Anders Bojen), which uses maps and stories to show a future Copenhagen. At the launch of *Radiant Copenhagen* the web page was linked with a bus tour to the different physical locations in the city. *Recognised Faces* (2016) is an internet application that generates a daily collage of facial parts from images found via Google's lists of top search terms. Homepage: www.oerum.org

James Riding is a Postdoctoral Researcher in the Space and Political Agency Research Group/RELATE Centre of Excellence at the University of Tampere, Finland. He was previously a Leverhulme Trust Early Career Research Fellow, in the Department of Geography at the University of Sheffield, leading the project *New Regional Geographies (For Sarajevo)*. He has written widely on questions of landscape, memory and identity, as well as regional geography.

Antje Schlottmann is Professor of Geography and Education at the Department of Human Geography at the Goethe-University of Frankfurt. Her focus of research lies on processes of communication, both linguistic and visual, that are decisive for the production and reproduction of spatial realities in fields of everyday and political practice. In this respect she is concerned with the making of regions, cities or even nature spaces, and with the possibility of dealing with contingent multidimensional spatialities in education.

Jörn Seemann joined the Department of Geography at Ball State University (Indiana) after teaching cartography at Universidade Regional do Cariri in Northeast Brazil for thirteen years. His main research focus (among many others) is on the relations between maps and society. He is particularly interested in cultural and interdisciplinary perspectives, including mental maps, cartographic education and creative ways of thinking, perceiving and representing space and place. His regional specialty is Latin America, with emphasis on Brazil. Currently, Seemann is member of the Board of Directors of the Conference of Latin Americanist Geographers (CLAG) and associate editor of the *Journal of Latin American Geography*. He received his master's degree in geography from Universität Hamburg in Germany (1994) and his PhD from Louisiana State University (2010).

John Tomaney is Professor of Urban and Regional Planning at University College London. Previously he was Henry Daysh Professor of Regional Development and Director of the Centre for Urban and Regional Development Studies (CURDS), Newcastle University and Professor of Regional Studies at Monash University, Melbourne. He has held visiting positions in Melbourne, Sydney, Dublin, Manchester and Newcastle. John's work has been funded by research councils and foundations, international organisations, national, regional and local governments and non-governmental organisations in the UK and elsewhere. He contributes regularly to the broadcast and print media.

Marc Welsh is a Research Associate at Aberystwyth University. His research and publications are oriented around questions of governance, the state and the production of the subject/citizen, resilience, nature-society relations, rural change and globalisation. He was previously Executive Editor for the journals *Regional Studies* and *Territory, Politics, Governance* and is currently a Research Associate on the project *The Global Countryside: Rural Change and Development in Globalization* (GLOBAL-RURAL).

Kaj Zimmerbauer works as a Postdoctoral Researcher and Coordinator at the University of Oulu (Geography Research Unit) and RELATE Centre of Excellence. His research interests include regional identities, supranational regionalization practices and multilayered borders, particularly in deinstitutionalization processes.

Acknowledgements

In 2014 the editors of this book organised a series of sessions on regions, the regional, and regional geography at the 2014 meeting of the Association of American Geographers in Tampa, Florida, and at the 2014 meeting of the Royal Geographical Society-Institute of British Geographers in Kensington, London. In the short time since the sessions in 2014, which provided the basis for this collection of essays, we have witnessed a series of global events that seem to us to further call into question the end of a regional geography, regions and thinking regionally. And we hope therefore that this timely volume can contribute to the ongoing re-appreciation and critical re-examination of, regions, the regional and regional geography, in the context of current crises in the Middle East, the Balkans, Western and Central Europe and South America.

The editors would like to note here that the journey from the first session to this completed volume would not have been possible without supportive colleagues in the Department of Geography and the Interdisciplinary Centre of the Social Sciences at the University of Sheffield, and also academics at a number of other institutions who provided us with critical, useful and challenging comments. In addition, during the course of our work on this volume we would like to acknowledge that our research has been funded by The Leverhulme Trust and the Economic and Social Research Council, enabling our studies of the regional, regions and regional geography.

Thanks too must go to the authors who have contributed to this volume, John Agnew, Jess Allen, Roger Baars, David Beel, Anders Bojen, Venetia Congdon, Lucy Frears, Erik Geelhoed, Rune Graulund, Jesse Heley, Rory Hill, George Jaramillo, Nicholas James, Philip Johnstone, Ian Rees Jones, David Matless, Misha Myers, Kristoffer Ørum, Antje Schlottmann, Jörn Seemann, John Tomaney, Marc Welsh, and Kaj Zimmerbauer.

The editors and authors would also like to thank those who granted permission to reproduce images, and the artist Mladen Miljanović for allowing us to use a photograph from *I Serve Art* (2006–2007), a nine-month site-specific performance on an ex-military base in Bosnia and Herzegovina, as a cover image.

Foreword

Writing regions, undertaking a regional study, was once a standard form of geographic communication and critique. This was until the quantitative revolution in the middle of the previous century and more definitively the critical turn in human geography towards the end of the twentieth century. From then on writing regions as they were experienced phenomenologically, or arguing culturally, historically and politically with regions, was deemed to be old-fashioned. To describe a region in itself was thought to be a conservative or basic undertaking, which could lead to a simplification or neglect of witnessed peoples and places. And indeed to invoke a regional geography was thought to privilege one region over another, to focus on particularities rather than abstractions, or on the other hand, regional geography seemed simply too rudimentary, unable to describe the modern interconnected and highly networked brave 'new' liberal world. The long-standing subgenre of regional geography was as such seen to be outdated. It apparently missed the everyday and personal specificities of identities and places, and arguably glossed over large swathes of political, cultural and historical landscapes, without ever being able to get at, describe or study the new economic and political spaces of the now globalised world, or indeed to critically examine the existence of these new spaces.

Yet over the past two decades or more there have been attempts to reintroduce a form of regional geography. The new regional geography created in this period was relational, polymorphic and multidimensional, and the new regional geography was as such able to speak of, document and deconstruct an era of late capitalism, neoliberalism and globalisation. It was though an attempt which was undercut by a turn towards landscape, space and place in social and cultural geography, and to flat actor-network geographies beyond regionalism in political and economic geography. As such the region became a forgotten trope through which to write the world, and the new regional geography withered.

With this in mind we sought to gather together both scholars presently interested in writing of regions, culturally, politically and historically, and also the geographers who initially articulated the new regional geography. The discussions that took place during the forum form the basis of this edited volume. *Reanimating Regions*, the first event, was hosted by the 2014 annual meeting of the Association of American Geographers in Tampa, Florida, and the second setting *New Regional Geographies* took place in Kensington, London, at the 2014 annual meeting of the Royal Geographical Society-Institute of British Geographers. Prior to the sessions, we proposed that due to the significance of non-representational and relational approaches to space, place and landscape in human geography, and also the related mobilities and aesthetic turn of recent times, there was a new theoretical and philosophical ground from which to reposition and reanimate a new regional geography, or a new new regional geography.

The journey from those sessions to this published text has meant defining or perhaps more appropriately opening out regional geography. In so doing, this edited volume reanimates regions through critical and creative theoretical approaches, alongside and enfolded around the more popular geographical terms, landscape, space and place. The foreword articulates a new new regional geography within the history of the region and the regional concept in human geography and sets out the methodological basis of this assumption. Here acting as an historical overview, original debates on the region in geography are reframed in order to provide a space from which to reanimate regions. Part 1, *Culture* and Part 2, *Politics* take the reader through a number of regions in order to further articulate what region, the regional and a regional geography might be today, while Part 3, *Performance* writes embodied, subversive and personal accounts of regions. To end, we include a piece on the potential directions regional geography might now take, asking *What's Next for Regional Geography?*

This volume we hope marks the continued reinvigoration of a set of disciplinary debates surrounding regions, the regional and regional geography. For despite taking up an identifiable place within the geographical imagination in scholarship and beyond, *region* remains a relatively forgotten, under-used and in part an under-theorised term. The discipline seemingly lacks, due to the turn elsewhere, an awareness of both the historical role that the region plays in everyday understandings of the world, and via a theoretical reductivism the relationships between region and, place, landscape and space. As such, geographers are rendered blind to the rich possibilities of a newly animated regional geography, and the once deemed old-fashioned, yet fresh potential of writing regions as a way into debates on conflict, identity, environment, borders and injustice. Comprehending the region as animated, relational, performed, lived and in process, as well as documented, described, created and cartographic, is to accept the region is to be best understood and theorised through its tensions. It is on the one hand a geographic idea that is played out every day beyond the geography of writing, and at the same time a region is a constructed world, where regions of the world are seemingly overlaid from above and lived from within.

We find that *region* is either dismissed in scholarly writing as old-hat or included implicitly, as a bounded generalisation of what is understood on the ground experientially or as excessively present but overlooked. Importantly, our aim in this text is neither to fix what a region is, nor to narrate a singular form of regional geography, and to perform an act of disciplinary colonialism.

Instead, we are primarily concerned with reanimating a regional geography and the study of regions – as others have been before – providing an opening for thought on the spatial tensions within and between regions, and deconstructing the apparent disciplinary fault lines between region, place and landscape.

Across its eighteen chapters, *Reanimating Regions* bears witness to the possibilities of thinking amidst the tension between the political and economic version of regional geography and the cultural and social version. Read against one another the eighteen chapters weave together timely commentaries on region and regions across the globe, with a particular emphasis upon the regional as played out in the United Kingdom, and regional worlds both within and beyond Europe, offering chapters from Africa and South America. This is not an exhaustive exploration of regions across the globe, rather our aim is to theorise and perform regions, emboldening those who wish to write of a region and a regional geography.

In sum the eighteen chapters we draw together here collectively rebalance the region within geography and geographical thought. By renewing the geography of regions, as not only a site of investigation but also as an analytical framework through which to write the world, what emerges is a powerful reworking of the geographic imagination. In addressing both the *political* and the *cultural* this edited volume responds to the need for a consolidated and considered reflection on *region* and regional geography, speaking directly to broader intellectual concerns with performance, aesthetics, networks, mobilities, the environment and the body. Written by international, interdisciplinary scholars from different intellectual backgrounds, the chapters are informed by a range of methodological and conceptual preoccupations. The empirical focus ranges from the newly emergent radical politics in the post-socialist states of southeastern Europe, to the politics of regions and the phantom region of Central Germany, from an excursion via regional cultural landscape through a flat wetland region of eastern England, to narratives of regional identity in literature, from a connection between region building and musicality in the British Midlands, to an exploration of new regional geography in the remote Northwest of Zimbabwe, and from an analysis of politically disruptive regions in the United Kingdom, to a reimagining of regions through digital fiction in Denmark. We close this introduction then in the spirit of this text as a whole, shuttling between regions, seeking to take aim at the heart of the region through the opening out of *region*, the regional and a regional geography, collectively *Reanimating Regions*.

Introduction

For a New New Regional Geography

Martin Jones

> Geographical description concentrates attention, gathers experience, observes and inscribes. To account for a region, move across its varieties.
>
> (Matless, 2015: 8)

Regions have been central to geography, and the discipline of geography can be traced through the different ways in which 'the region' has been interpreted (MacLeod and Jones, 2001). Geographers have talked about traditional regional geography, the new regional geography, and the new regionalism. The current 'new new regional geography' debate centres on whether regions can be seen as relational and networked and on territorial and scalar concerns. Thinking about region-making can help to take regional geography forward.

The region is, and always will be, a central concept in geography. So, thinking about regions can tell us a lot about the history of the discipline called geography. Before this though, the perennial question must be addressed: What is a region? For the purposes of this edited volume, a region is a temporary permanence, something held stable, not fixed and absolute, at different points in time, for different purposes. There is, then, no single reading of a region. Regions are multiple entities and we should look at the process of *region-making*.

Regions can have administrative territorial shape through the drawing of borders and boundaries and the making of state spaces. Regions can also delimit economic forms relating to particular functions, for example the spaces of exchange and trading such that we can talk of discrete regional economies in global networks. Regions can also act as symbolic shapes; cultural identifiers and sources of belonging; senses of ownership for political expression and mobilisation. One helpful way of categorising these distinctions is to think about the first two descriptions (the administrative and the economic) as 'regional spaces' and the latter (cultural and political) as 'spaces of regionalism' (see Jones and MacLeod, 2004; Jones, 2004). Again, these distinctions are never out there waiting to be found; they are forged historically through political and policy struggles involving state and nonstate forces. This allows geographers to talk not about 'regional geography', which automatically conjures up fixity and rigidity, but about the 'geography of regions' – the process and practices of making and remaking regions through 'institutionalisation' as Paasi (1996) puts it.

The remaining discussion unpacks this, using four chronological phases, to reveal how geographers have grappled with regional geography. There is a need 'to go back' to go 'forward', as Thrift (1994) has put it.

An era of *traditional regional geography* existed during the long nineteenth century. Here, the region was treated as absolute: as an independent backdrop for, first, conducting geographical inquiry and, second, developing thereafter a world of different regional geographical types. Books such as *Britain and the British Seas* by Mackinder (1902) made assumptions about the interconnected nature of the human and the physical. This regional geography was an 'ethnographical geography' of successive phases and component elements, with (in this case) the physical environment as 'thus analysed'. The work of Herbertson (1905) developed 'climatic regions' from this, and Fleure offered 'human zones' conditioned, rather than entirely governed, by physical circumstances in his *Human Geography in Western Europe* (1919).

The backlash to this came from the likes of Hartshone, whose *The Nature of Geography* (1939), contra Herbertson and Fleure, claimed that none of their regional geographies 'alone' covered a significant number of features to offer an adequate background to regional study, or to provide a tentative system for organising all our regional knowledge of the world. A regional geography of elements (meso-worlds of human–physical interactions) was proposed to produce an elaborate regional geography of 'areal differentiation' – the division of the earth surface by observations that different areas of the world are somehow self-contained and where, extending the work of Vidal de la Blache (1926), relationships between people and land created a distinctive geography or *genre de vie*. The purpose of this regional geography was to understand what these differences are and how they are related. Books such as *One World Divided* (1964) by James summarised the long results of this thinking through offering different areal differentiations.

Regional science, assisted by the power of computation and the desire to study connected variables as part of modernist social sciences dabbling with theories of physics (such as gravity models), logically followed from this. Isard's *Methods of Regional Analysis* (1960) suggested that any general theory of the region, whether this be in relation to locational analysis of industry or population, must be supplemented by techniques of regional analysis, which are operational techniques and which yield estimates of basic magnitudes for the space economy for both the proper understanding of social problems and policy formulation. Isard's work sought to make and model the internal connections between things that flowed through and were seen to actively make regions, albeit in a discrete and bounded way, isolated from external drivers behind the capitalist space economy.

This concern with the structural and strategic forces acting in and on regions could be felt by those critiquing regional science and offering, through regional studies and largely influenced by Marxism, alternatives based around the dynamics and contradictions of capitalism. Books by Massey such as *The Anatomy of Job Loss* (1982) and the 1984 classic *Spatial Divisions of Labour* presented regions as the medium and outcome of economic and political struggles around the geography of production and class struggle. 'Rounds of investment', phases of capital accumulation dealt out like playing cards, as Gregory (1989) put it, acted as waves on a beach, constantly making and remaking regions in geography as a distinctive economic geography of 'localities'.

This emphasis on capital versus the regions, combined with the emphasis on place as a historically contingent process, meant that the mid- to late 1980s was ripe for thinking about a *new regional geography*. Whereas traditional regional geography talked about fixed and bounded territorial and process entities, new regional geography wanted to study regions as produced and transformed through various forms of agency. Gilbert's (1988) classic summary of this position drew attention to regions as varying local responses to capitalist processes; regions as the focus of cultural identification (or senses of place); and regions as the medium for social interaction or meeting places for human agency and social structures. The studies of localities in the United Kingdom, funded by the Economic and Social Research Council (ESRC), offered an economic and social window into this, although they often generated more heat than light (Jones and Woods, 2013).

Authors such as Thrift (1983: 38, 57) took this further and laid down four challenges, derived from what he called a 'reconstructed' or 'reconstituted regional geography', which emerged from a series of 'skirmishes' won by the new regional geography (Thrift, 1990). These were: (1) the contested production of meaning within regions; (2) the changing forms of the 'spaces of regions', most especially their transformation into simulations of other spaces; (3) the relations between people and nature and the deconstruction of landscape; and (4) the problem of 'writing' regions, most especially the chronic problems of description at the nexus between the analytic and the narrative forms. Thrift (1991, 1993) subsequently explicitly placed the subject at the heart of the new regional geography, by calling for a more serious consideration of: (1) the constitution of self and identity; (2) autobiography and memory; (3) the multifarious emotional repertoires available to actors; (4) the forms of knowledge made available through discourse and the shaping of these knowledges; and (5) the importance of context in the becoming of identity, memory (re)construction and regional emotions or structures of feeling.

Globalisation discourses and the politically charged nature of economic development, especially in Europe, overtook these debates, and in the early 1990s geographers and other social scientists were talking about the *new regionalism*. This regional geography saw regions, not nations per se, as the crucibles for both economic success and democratic legitimacy. A rescaling of economic and social life was being witnessed, according to protagonists, who drew much attention to regional things occurring in Emilia-Romagna (Italy), Baden-Württemberg (Germany), Silicon Valley (United States), the Rhône-Alpes (France) and Tokyo (Japan). Storper's *The Regional World* (1997) and Keating's *The New Regionalism in Western Europe* (1998) summarised these trends and speculated variously on their wider applicability.

In short, regional geography was being read through a new economic geography of globalisation and regional development and a new political geography of territorial politics and public policy communities. Critics such as MacLeod (2001) sought to draw attention to three shortcomings of this literature: (1) a 'soft institutionalism' (where institutions are seen as the explanation for economic success, as opposed to looking at the historical geography of institutions); (2) 'thin political economy' (the absence of any analysis of the state and the political economy of territory, scale and region-making); and (3) 'distorted policy' (the inability of some scholars to examine path dependency, the problems of policy transfer and policy borrowing, and how case studies are used to develop both academic and political knowledge).

We are currently witnessing a phase that I would like to call the *new new regional geography*. One aspect of this does not and cannot believe in regions in geography. A group of scholars, following Amin and Thrift (the latter somewhat strangely, as he was a previous advocate of regions in geography) and others advocating a 'thinking space-relationally' approach, envisage a world without regions, where rhizomatic flows and networks dominate and help to promote a new politics of place based on 'propinquity' (the state of being close to someone or something, achieved through the 'folding' of existence, and made possible by globalisation and technological empowerment). Three significant points follow from this position (see Amin, 2004; Amin et al., 2003): regions have no automatic promise of territorial integrity since they are made through the spatiality of relational connectivity; there is a questionable assumption that a regional territory can then be defined and made manageable; and any attempt to fix spatial identities through policy initiatives will be characterised by oversimplification and an inability to capture the ever-changing character of regions. This approach has, in turn, produced a backlash, with scholars seeking to bring regions, territories and geographical scales back onto the agenda. Their argument is not to completely drop regions, but to think about regional geography differently.

Part of the problem is the way the debate is posed, both historically and now, as if the networked worlds of those advocating relational space stand in direct opposition to territories, and, vice versa, those advocating a network positon will also find that these are not without regional geography anchors (MacLeod and Jones, 2007). Geographers are, therefore, seeking a way of reconciling regional geography within a territorial/relational world. In the new new regional geography, where regions remain temporary permanences, the languages of 'bundling', 'assemblage', 'method assemblages', 'spatiotemporal fixing', 'compossibility', 'phase space', 'new localities', 'lengthening of networks' and so on are all being offered as various ways of examining 'region-making' (see Jones, 2009).

A paper by US geographers Murphy and O'Loughlin (2009) outlines the framework and mandate needed for an emerging new new regional geography as a tool for understanding rapid and profound changes in the contemporary world. The authors provide recommendations for, and note the benefits of, a strengthening of regional research and training in geography while, in their case study, mapping out an expanded role for Eurasian geography and economics in disseminating new regional research whose scope extends beyond disciplinary boundaries to embrace current public and political debate. In this sense, then, the important problems that human geographers face today can still be found grounded in the practice of doing regional geography. In doing regional geography though, we should be mindful of the unfinished 'compositional project' that Thrift (1983) charted.

> This involves, first of all, all those geographical determinations that can be grouped under the general heading topography; such things as geology, hydrology, and climatic conditions, which have likely been changed already by the impacts of societies over the years. An account of the organisation of production in a region is then needed, which involves ascertaining the level of the productive forces and the form of the productive relations, concentrating on the labour process. This emphasis on production leads, under capitalism in particular, to an outline of the class structure of a region and to the history of class formation, themes which are inevitably crosscut by other divides; the prevailing sexual division of labour, of course, but also ethnic, racial, and religious divisions. Finally, the local form of the state must be taken into account. Already written into such a compositional analysis is the *possibility* of quite dramatic interactions along the boundaries of one or all these divides .... A compositional account of a region is obviously a difficult enough task in itself, both theoretically and empirically. Perhaps it is for this reason that most analyses stop at this point. But, since the concern here is with developing a (contextual) theory of social action that can interpenetrate and ultimately change the conventional (compositional) theoretical account about social action, it is necessary to go one step further. The process of discourse in which human agency is produced and spun out cannot be reduced to a compositional account without jettisoning the very qualities that make it a discourse; the intricacies of interaction, the specificity of particular times and spaces, the sense of living as meeting, the context .... To constitute a region an interaction structure requires a notion of integration that is mediated by institutional correlations with social structure. The region, initially at least, must not be seen as a place; that is a matter for investigation. Rather, it must be seen as made up of a numbers of different but connected settings for interaction. (Thrift, 1983: 39, 40, emphasis removed)

References

Amin A (2004) Regions unbound: towards a new politics of place. *Geografiska Annaler B* 86: 33–44.

Amin A, Massey D, and Thrift N (2003) Decentering the nation: a radical approach to regional inequality. *Catalyst Paper 8*, London.

Fleure HJ (1919) *Human Geography in Western Europe*. London: Williams and Norgate.

Gilbert A (1988) The new regional geography in English and French-speaking countries. *Progress in Human Geography* 12: 208–228.

Gregory D (1989) Areal differentiation and postmodern human geography, in D Gregory and R Walford (eds) *Horizons in Human Geography*. London: Macmillan, 67–96.

Hartshone R (1939) *The Nature of Geography: A Critical Survey of Current Thought in the Light of the* Past. Washington: Association of American Geographers.
Herbertson AJ (1905) The major natural regions: An essay in systematic geography. *The Geographical Journal* 25 (3): 300–310.
Isard W (1960) *Methods of Regional Analysis*. New York: John Wiley.
James P (1964) *One World Divided*. New York: Blaisdell.
Jones M (2004) Social justice and the region: functional regionalisation and civil society regionalism in England, *Space and Polity* 8: 157–189.
Jones M (2009) Phase space: geography, relational thinking, and beyond. *Progress in Human Geography* 33: 487–506.
Jones M and MacLeod G (2004) Regional spaces, spaces of regionalism: territory, insurgent politics and the English questions. *Transactions of the Institute of British Geographers* 29: 433–452.
Jones M and Woods M (2013) New localities. *Regional Studies* 47: 29–42.
Keating M (1998) *The New Regionalism in Western Europe*. Cheltenham: Elgar.
Mackinder H (1902) *Britain and the British Seas*. New York: D Appleton and Company.
MacLeod G (2001) New regionalism reconsidered: globalisation and the remaking of political economic space. *International Journal of Urban and Regional Research* 25: 804–829.
MacLeod G and Jones M (2001) *Renewing* the geography of regions. *Environment and Planning D: Society and Space* 19: 669–695.
MacLeod G and Jones M (2007) Territorial, scalar, networked, connected: in what sense a 'regional world'? *Regional Studies* 41: 1177–1191.
Massey D (1984) *Spatial Divisions of Labour*. Basingstoke: Macmillan.
Massey D and Meegan R (1982) *The Anatomy of Job Loss*. London: Methuen.
Matless D (2015) *The Regional Book*. Uniformbooks: Axminster.
Murphy AB and O'Loughlin J (2009) New horizons for regional geography. *Eurasian Geography and Economics* 3: 241–251.
Paasi A (1996) *Territories, Boundaries, and Consciousness: The Changing Geographies of the Finnish-Russian Border*. Chichester: Wiley.
Storper M (1997) *The Regional World*. New York: Guilford Press.
Thrift N (1983) On the determination of social action in space and time. *Environment and Planning D: Society and Space* 1: 23–57.
Thrift N (1990) For a new regional geography 1. *Progress in Human Geography* 14: 272–279.
Thrift N (1991) For a new regional geography 2. *Progress in Human Geography* 15: 456–465.
Thrift N (1993) For a new regional geography 3. *Progress in Human Geography* 17: 92–100.
Thrift N (1994) Taking aim at the heart of the region, in D Gregory, R Martin and G Smith (eds) *Human Geography: Society, Space and Social Science*. London: Macmillan, 200–231.
Vidal de la Blache P (1926) *Principles of Human Geography*. London: Constable.

Part I

Culture

1 Writing Regional Cultural Landscape

Cultural Geography on the Norfolk Broads

David Matless

Writing on a Region

This essay reflects on the writing of two books on one region: *In the Nature of Landscape: Cultural Geography on the Norfolk Broads* (2014), and *The Regional Book* (2015). The former is a research monograph published in the Royal Geographical Society-Institute of British Geographers/Wiley-Blackwell book series, the latter a set of geographical descriptions published by Colin Sackett's Uniformbooks. Their common territory is the Norfolk Broads, a wetland region in eastern England. *In the Nature of Landscape* drew together two decades of research on the region, revisiting the idea of regional cultural landscape as an ostensibly old-style geographic theme with new possibilities. *The Regional Book* was a happy offshoot, after Sackett suggested that a particular aspect of the RGS-IBG monograph, the descriptions of regional sites in the opening and closing chapters, might be developed into something more. Having shared various ideas and interests with Sackett over several years, and produced two essays and the cover photograph for *Anticipatory History*, a volume also produced through Uniformbooks (DeSilvey, Naylor and Sackett, 2011), this was a welcome proposal. The second half of this essay considers the production of these two volumes, closely related if different in style, giving a sense of their content and accounting for their regional writing. Both offer excursions in regional cultural landscape, and, given the themes of this edited collection, it is appropriate to begin by reflecting on this term, in its theoretical implications, its resonance in disciplines beyond geography, and its presence in geography's past.

Revisiting Regional Cultural Landscape

In November 2006 I spent two weeks in Melbourne, arriving as Australia turned to summer. The Geography department at the University of Melbourne hosted the visit, and alongside seminars much time was spent with Fraser MacDonald, then a lecturer there, discussing regional cultural landscape. Flying from November England to November Australia neatly underlined the ways in which regions at far distance, but with long interconnection, may depart from and meet one another, the English visitor hit here and there on arrival: bright southern light, oak and eucalyptus, bee-eater and blackbird, Christmas floats in sun, suburban cricket, 'flake' (shark) and chips.

Working on Broadland, but also on the East Anglian region of Breckland (Matless, 2008), had indicated to me the possibilities of regional cultural landscape, and conversations and excursions in Melbourne confirmed these, and suggested other possible lines of enquiry. A projected joint paper never went beyond five subheadings ('Registering the regional cultural landscape', 'Geographical outlines', 'Twentieth century chorographies', 'Retheorisations', 'Five tenets for regional cultural landscape'), but the themes developed would inform *In the Nature of Landscape*, when the opportunity arose to bring together work on the Broads in book form. If the grandly programmatic 'five tenets' never solidified, the notes towards them shaped subsequent work: contested boundaries and history, claims to cultural authority, iconic sites and landscape types, human-animal-vegetable-mineral, and geographical aesthetics.

'Regional cultural landscape' is familiar as a theme, if not always as an exact phrase, from earlier modes of geographical enquiry, and from a wider extra-scholarly topographical literature. One of the aims of *In the Nature of Landscape* was to revisit the term, given the comprehensive retheorisation, across a range of disciplines, of each of its constituent parts: region, culture, landscape. What would happen if region, culture and landscape, in their various ways rethought, were brought together again? If the theme of this collection is region, it is important to consider how that term may spark with others. Conceptually, as well as geographically, regions do not work in isolation.

The 'culture' in a revisited regional cultural landscape may variously indicate ways of life, habits of place, spheres of representation, material objects, forms of media, the province of a 'cultured' elite, that which is popular, that which is not nature, the modes through which nature is valued. The varied capacities and complexities of the term culture, and all the tensions running between such definitions, may be embraced in regional study. Landscape, like culture, entails movement across fields, sometimes obviously adjacent and conversant, sometimes ostensibly living in discrete parallel, thickly hedged. The 'landscape' in regional cultural landscape thus brings with it those qualities of 'duplicity' and 'tension' highlighted in cultural geographic work (Daniels, 1989, Matless, 1998, Wylie, 2007), to which might be added a sense of landscape as colloquial, denoting the presence of different voices: a colloquium of different disciplines, the colloquial voice of the vernacular and everyday. Accents of landscape, expert or common, spoken or written, articulate regional multiplicity.

Bringing region, culture and landscape together again does not make for a newly complex, steady template for empirical application, rather their recombination generates a productive charge, from varieties of cultural baggage and intellectual tradition. As with landscape, we might abide in rather than seek to resolve such instability. Strains of recent work in cultural geography and beyond can indicate some of the possibilities here. Thus Fraser MacDonald's research makes for a Hebridean regional cultural study, with folklore, photography, militarism, geography and archaeology shaping island landscape (MacDonald, 2004, 2006a, 2006b,

2011, 2014). Hayden Lorimer's works on the Cairngorms and wider Highland Scotland effectively combine into regional cultural analysis, encompassing field study and the geographer citizen, landholding and animal killing, natural histories of flora and fauna, and the animal landscapes of herding Cairngorm reindeer (Lorimer, 2000, 2000, 2006; Lorimer and Lund, 2003; Lorimer and Spedding, 2005). Dydia DeLyser's *Ramona Memories* likewise takes a region for scrutiny, the Southern Californian 'Ramona Country', defined touristically following Helen Hunt Jackson's 1884 novel *Ramona* (DeLyser, 2005).

Regional cultural landscape also preoccupies scholarship beyond geography, showing how regional questions may serve to entwine theory and description, and retune tradition. Regional landscape enquiry navigates the historic and experimental in performance studies, as in Mike Pearson's book *"In Comes I": Performance, Memory and Landscape* (Pearson, 2006; Daniels, Pearson and Roms, 2010; Matless and Pearson, 2012). Pearson takes a patch of north Lincolnshire to develop the possibilities of performative engagement with landscape; a parallel 2013 volume, *Marking Time*, offers a Cardiff-based urban companion (Pearson, 2013). Pearson takes region (rather than author, period or genre) as his 'optic' (Pearson, 2006: 3), and his work prompts reflection on disciplinary approaches to regional cultural landscape, made in the spirit of the 2001 invitation in Pearson and Shanks' *Theatre/Archaeology*: 'And the folklorist, the archaeologist, the geographer are most welcome to come and stand in our field. We do not want simply to appropriate their methodologies. We want them to look, and to enable us to look through them, at performance' (Pearson and Shanks, 2001: xiv). If geography and performance studies share regional interest, they perform the region in subtly different fashion. For Pearson region carries novelty, a new term for a relatively new discipline, but for the geographer the word might signal rediscovery, reassertion, reanimation, or an old rut escaped. Performance and geography carry different genealogies to meet over 'region', the word migrating between the novel and familiar, the avant-garde and old hat.

With Regard to the Old Hat

The proposal for this volume suggested of the authors that: 'Importantly they do not argue for a return to an old regional geography of plain description, but rather a relational, co-constitutive understanding of how regions come to be.' The proposal also indicated that recent neglect of regional study might in part be because regional geography had 'struggled to shake off its past: a dangerous, conservative, sub-discipline, which can easily be drawn upon by nationalistic factions, through a simplification of identity politics'. Whatever the virtues of new and reanimating approaches, and the rhetorical conventions of a book proposal, is there a risk here of caricaturing the past? And what are the consequences where a 'reanimation' of regions is established through a deadening of the old? It is as if we must check that the body is dead before trying to reanimate. The history of regional geography might itself however receive a more subtle, relational understanding, and in the process reanimation might appear less as a leaving behind of a moribund past, than something having due regard for former lives, and the lessons they might carry.

A characterisation of an older regional geography as dangerously conservative or nationalistic belies the complexity of earlier work, and in doing so projects an unproblematic and straightforwardly negative quality onto a term such as 'conservative'. The history of regional work cuts across, and sometimes blurs, categories such as radical and conservative, progressive and traditional, cosmopolitan and nationalist, and any reclamation and reanimation of the region might proceed from embracing such a political genealogy (Clout, 2009; Graham, 1994; Livingstone, 1992; Matless, 1992). The aesthetic characterisation of older work as simple and limited might also be questioned. There was more to old regional geography than plain description; and indeed there is always more to plain description than plain description. Even if 'plain description' is an outcome desired and achieved, that denotes an aesthetic accomplishment worthy of appreciative understanding, if not necessarily emulation. And the old hat might even be worth trying on.

Parallel regional questions are raised by recent work in literary studies, where a new 'literary geography' has drawn on cultural geographic work to revisit regional writing. In Ralph Pite's study of Thomas Hardy, *Hardy's Geography*, regionalism becomes central to Hardy's radicalism, challenging any assumed conjunction of regionalism, conservatism and constraint. For Pite the regional geographic sense works in Hardy's novels of character and environment to shape a complex 'clash of registers' (Pite, 2002: 16; Barrell, 1982). The region is also recast as site and scale for literary innovation and experiment through the excavation of a neglected literary conjunction of the regionalist and modernist, resisting a 'metronormativity' aligning modernism with the metropolis (Herring, 2009: 2). Neal Alexander and James Moran's 2013 collection *Regional Modernisms*, whose agenda is informed by work in cultural geography, and by relational understandings of the region, finds regional literary energy. Whether attending to established canonical figures such as James Joyce, DH Lawrence or William Carlos Williams, or lesser-known writers such as Sylvia Townsend Warner or Leo Walmsley, Alexander and Moran note: 'In such instances of regional modernism an internationalist or cosmopolitan sensibility arises, paradoxically, from situations and contexts that are distinctively local or provincial' (Alexander and Moran, 2013: 2; also Alexander and Cooper, 2012). The call in such work is for 'geographically attentive modes of reading' (Alexander and Moran, 2013: 7), exemplified by Alexander's own study of poet Basil Bunting, whose major 1966 work *Briggflatts* (Bunting, 2009), a reference point also for *In the Nature of Landscape*, centres on Northumbria: 'His regional modernism is characterised both by the imaginative centrality of northern landscapes and cultural paradigms to his writing, and by the refraction of such local and regional attachments through a self-consciously international modernist poetics.' In *Briggflatts*, 'Northumbria emerges as a luminous and multi-faceted affective terrain' (Alexander, 2013: 200). Alexander's treatment of Bunting attends to the nuances of geographic scale shaping his work, showing how the regional, national and international are articulated in a nonhierarchical manner, with time and memory enfolded through a dynamic geography. Alexander respects region without seeking to root his subject:

> To speak of the poem's 'rootedness' in place is therefore to neglect its grasp of the dynamism of place itself, its manifestation of change in the here-and-now, and to underestimate the entanglement of regional, national and international affiliations in its representational forms. Indeed, *Briggflatts* eschews the rhetoric of rootedness and dwelling for metaphors of weaving, braiding, and ravelling through which the networks of association and implication that make locations humanly meaningful might be intuited. (217)

If, then, aesthetically and politically, the region carries a past deserving attention, a reanimation of regional geography might benefit from engagement with earlier narratives. The complexities of region's past, and its possibilities for the present, are indicated in the way in which one key figure from the history of regional geography has been subject to recent evaluation. Patrick Geddes, polymathic influence on regional geographic work in many countries in the late 19th and early 20th centuries (Meller, 1990; Welter, 2002), was revisited in the late 20th and early 21st centuries as a pioneer of a radical, ecological Scottish nationalism (Campbell, 1990; MacDonald, 1994), and as a civic urbanist offering 'geographies for the present': 'Prototypically we find, in Geddes, a possibly fruitful point of contact and connection between planning as a governmental, rather than purely technical capacity, and the human sciences' (Mercer, 1997: 224). Geddes' geographical outlook offers for Thomas Osborne and Nicholas Rose a 'spatial phenomenotechnics', with Geddes a 'technician of space' for today:

> Instead of modelling space in terms of morality, Geddes understood space in terms of an ethics of 'outlook'. … In the ethics of outlook, space was conceptualised in terms of the ability of each citizen to find his or her place in the course of evolution. … Such an ethics sought to enable civic action by creating the conditions in which one could insert oneself as a point in smooth space. (Osborne and Rose, 2004: 220)

Osborne and Rose ask: 'Who reads Geddes now? He comes down to us as a maverick figure, straddling many disciplines and many causes: botany, biology, geography, civics, sociology, social reform, town planning' (218).

Not all figures in the history of regional studies are as complex as Geddes, with his planning exhibitions, thinking machines, civic centres and educational charisma, but even in seemingly more prosaic early 20th century works we might find an instructive regional genealogy. Tracing earlier engagements with regional cultural landscape in such work indicates particular ways of attending to culture, and shows how regional work might constitute cultural practice in its own right. Two works, by figures not normally prominent in disciplinary histories, may offer an indicative sample. In 1911 EC Matthews published *The Highlands of South-West Surrey: A Geographical Study in Sand and Clay*, the second of two volumes in the London School of Economics' 'Series of Geographical Studies', developing conventions of map investigation taught at Oxford and LSE under the influence of Mackinder; Matthews' book followed Ellen Smith's *The Reigate Sheet of the One-Inch Ordnance Survey* (Smith, 1910). In 1910 *The Geographical Teacher* had published Matthews' 'Field Work in the Valley of Brent', describing her 'more than a summer's work' in school excursions in outer London (Mathews [sic], 1910), and Matthews' regional geography was indeed cultural practice in its own right, setting out rituals of seeing for teaching citizens. Matthews worked through Surrey Highland geology, climate, rivers, soils, vegetation, population, settlement and transport, with a final tour 'across the region' by rail through the valleys and 'motor-car' over 'the heights', the latter then a rare form of country travel (Matthews, 1911: 114–117). If Matthews did not stretch to culture as object of study, she offered a protopsychogeography:

> It was a very natural feeling, truly, though blindly geographical, that gave rise to a belief in the presence of active forces of kindly or malicious spirits dwelling in hill and stream and rock, which exercise a subtle influence upon the human beings at the mercy of their incomprehensible energies, and whose influence was felt wherever man and Nature came in contact.
>
> The modern geographer, no less than the simple folk of earlier times, recognizes the significance of geographical causes and effects in their bearing, direct or indirect, upon the human activities which come under their influence. So that the life of a region is best interpreted in the light of geographical conditions, using the term in its widest sense to mean the peculiar characteristics which mark any special region – the nature of its soil and its possible uses, the climatic conditions, the forms of vegetation intimately bound up with these, the remoteness or accessibility of any one region as compared with others, and the consequent growth of towns, and distribution and occupations of the inhabitants. (1–2)

Matthews pursued a possibilist geography, echoing that of Geddes, and of Paul Vidal de la Blache in France. In 1933 PW Bryan of University College Leicester extended such themes in *Man's Adaptation of Nature: Studies of the Cultural Landscape*, categorising cultural landscapes in the UK and North America, from the small scale of a Northamptonshire village to Chicago as 'expression of a great world nodal point' (Bryan, 1933: 237; Jones and Bryan, 1924). Bryan evoked geographic variety through exhaustive classification of 'Cultural and Natural Elements', 'Cultural and Natural Units', 'Cultural and Natural Features', 'Cultural and Natural Districts' and 'Cultural and Natural Regions', noting 'that blending, that wholeness, that unity which is of the essence of geographical study and outlook' (Bryan, 1933: 128). Regional geography works its way between the evocative and the categorical; both might continue to offer springboards and traps. Bryan covered landscapes of shelter, farming, urbanisation and transport, and moved to cultural subject matter in a chapter on 'the cultural landscapes of recreation and the gratification of the aesthetic sense', derived from regional field studies on the sand dunes of Michigan and north Norfolk. At Burnham Overy Staithe in Norfolk, Bryan found an Automobile Association hotel, converted from a malthouse:

> It is a unit of the cultural landscape converted and adapted to its new purposes. Stopping at it we find men in shooting-jackets. Others in jerseys and pullovers are starting for the quayside with fishing-tackle and sails. Still others are in plus fours and carry golf-clubs. Girls in khaki shorts are setting out for a long tramp equipped with haversacks. Another group with bathing togs, towels, sandwiches, a rucksack, a tea kettle, and a rough-haired terrier, is moving down the little village street with obvious intent of making a day of it. Let us follow them on the 2-mile tramp to the outer shore. (355)

Knitwear and bags distinguish types of landscape user, aesthetics of dress denoting modes of outdoor conduct. The last party is Bryan's own, gathering holiday knowledge, moving through a landscape of recreation, fishing, farming and science, 'the region a veritable botanical paradise, a Mecca for those whose interests lie in plant ecology' (357). A 'sheltered spot' is found: 'We strip and bathe in the fresh, invigorating salt waves sweeping shoreward over stretches of clean, yellow sand. After a hasty, welcome lunch, we study the dune' (358). The terrier, fresh from swimming, is set 'to work' at dune digging, excavating morphology; a picture of 'Jock' in a dune hole is captioned: 'Evidence of Old Beach Lines, Jock's Researches' (359). Beach pleasures shape geographic analysis.

Revisiting works by Bryan, Matthews and others highlights the ways in which regional cultural landscape might be figured by earlier geographers, and puts current practice in relief: the different formulations of culture deployed to produce different regional geographies, the work to which regional geographic study might be put (for policy, for planning, for teaching, for wide public readership), the ways in which geographic work might connect to, or be cut off from, other fields of enquiry, the undertaking and rendition of field study. It is instructive to put such studies in dialogue with recent works in cultural geography and other disciplines, notably those by Lorimer, Pearson and others seeking a performative recasting of field study: to view old hats in the mirror, to bring ghosts into view, or to re-box old garments, having appreciated their and our difference.

Provision: *In the Nature of Landscape*

The research for *In the Nature of Landscape* was undertaken over two decades or more, moving through projects on specific themes and individuals, and in recent years coming together as a regional monograph. Some elements of research involved collaboration with others, notably work on ecologist and artist Marietta Pallis, with Laura Cameron (Cameron and Matless, 2003, 2011; Matless and Cameron, 2006, 2007). Since the book's publication research has been presented to regional publics, for example at Norwich Castle Museum in July 2014, and in a public lecture in November 2014 for the Broads Authority, marking the 25th anniversary of the Broads achieving national park status.

In geographic outline, Broadland is a region defined by waterways, with six rivers flowing, some into one another, and all waters ending in the North Sea at Great Yarmouth (see map on Figure 1.2). To make up the 'Southern Rivers', the Chet joins the Yare upstream of Reedham, and the Yare and Waveney meet at Breydon Water. For the 'Northern Rivers', the Ant joins the Bure west of Horning, the Thurne and Bure meet north of Acle, and the Bure continues, joining the Yare below Breydon. Only the Yare keeps its name to the sea at Yarmouth. The broads are shallow lakes distinctive to the region, filled-up medieval peat diggings whose artificial industrial origin was figured with some surprise 60 years ago. Some broads sit to one side of the rivers, linked by dug channels, some occupy the river as if it had simply 'broadened' in its flow. The Norfolk Broads made occasional appearance in earlier geographic study, and *In the Nature of Landscape* is set in dialogue with earlier geographical visits to the region. Thus in 1927 Albert Demangeon's *Les Iles Brittaniques* examined the Broads:

> The peaty swamps, the still sheets of water hidden by reeds, the wide channels overhung by willows, and the lonely marshes frequented in winter by

Figure 1.1 Front cover of David Matless, *The Regional Book* (2015).

> water-fowl exhibit Nature in all her wildness, loneliness, and melancholy. But in the summer these solitudes are full of holiday-makers, and the Bure, Ant, and Thurne, together with Wroxham, Salhouse, and Oulton Broads, are dotted with motor cruisers and sailing yachts. Away from the Broads and swamps, the ground is covered with grass and forms a rich pastoral district in which graze thousands of cattle. Green fields, grazing cattle, windmills, willow-lined channels, boats sailing among trees – all these remind one of the scenery in Holland. (Demangeon, 1939: 282–3; Clout 2009)

Demangeon shows an early twentieth century French regional geographic sensibility abroad, his passage signalling lines of enquiry revisited in my own research: the aesthetics of regional description, the geographies of regional discovery, seasonal shifts, and Broadland as a region reminiscent of somewhere else.

In the Nature of Landscape also followed subsequent geographical tours, including a January 1959 excursion from the annual Institute of British Geographers conference in Cambridge. On 6 January 1959, under the headline 'Winter Broads Tour', the Norwich-based newspaper the *Eastern Daily Press* reported a sighting of geographers:

> A BROADS TOURS craft carrying over 60 passengers caused some surprise in the Wroxham, South Walsham, Salhouse and Ranworth areas on Sunday. A familiar sight for half the year, it is rare to see one carrying sightseers in this weather. The passengers were members of the British Institute of Geography who were holding their annual conference at Cambridge and they were taken in the Marchioness through Wroxham and Salhouse Broads to South Walsham Broad and thence to Ranworth Broad.
>
> The party had travelled by diesel rail cars to Wroxham that morning. At Ranworth the Rev. E. D. Everard (vicar) met them and they ascended the 96 ft. high tower which gives an extensive view of Broadland.
>
> Among the party was Dr. Lambert, who has written extensively on the origin of the Broads, and Mr. C. T. Smith, lecturer in the Department of Geography, Cambridge University. The party returned to Wroxham for tea. (Eastern Daily Press, 1959)

Guides Joyce Lambert and Clifford Smith were two of the authors of the 1960 Royal Geographical Society Research Series memoir No. 3, *The Making of the Broads* (Lambert, Jennings, Smith, Green and Hutchinson, 1960). Botanist Lambert had discovered the broads' artificial origins in medieval peat diggings, historical geographer Smith corroborating findings; both were interviewed in the course of my research. It was a pleasant coincidence to publish *In the Nature of Landscape* through an RGS-IBG research series, given the 1960 memoir, not least as Lambert had before her death in 2005 been a very important source of information, research material and commentary for my work.

The Rev. Everard may be gone, but Ranworth Tower continues to be a good spot for an extensive view; the descriptive passages of *In the Nature of Landscape* include Ranworth Church's height alongside lower perspectives of waterway and marsh, street and boardwalk. Regional cultural landscape continues to direct attention to those studies in stratigraphy, botany and history which preoccupied the 1959 IBG tour, but these take their place as cultural practices alongside forms of human conduct which might have passed the earlier discipline by. An expanded sense of culture and landscape, and a contested sense of region, leads regional cultural landscape to a wider compass: natural history, botanic science, landscape history, town and country planning, guidebooks, painting, wildfowling, boat hire, poetry, music, song, film, comedy. Regional cultural landscape demands movement across fields of human conduct often kept apart, a ranging, sometimes trespassing, form of enquiry. Confinement to one region makes study happily rove.

What kind of understanding then follows from thinking of Broadland as regional cultural landscape? Attention is first drawn to the cultural work done by regional definition: the articulation of scale and its political, economic, imaginative, emotional consequences, with the definition of a region an active and mutable component in its life. In Broadland, as in other areas deemed to be of scenic and ecological value, qualities of regional landscape are identified for development or defence. Even the regional name generates rich definitional analysis: the Broads, Broadland, the Norfolk Broads, the Norfolk and Suffolk Broads. The region moved from being an often unlabelled 19th century area whose unusual lakes, locally called broads, drew occasional comment as distinctive features of the district, to being 'The Norfolk Broads', a region newly visited and nationally popular, filling with narrative as other tourist regions before. Broadland also became defined as a distinct region for natural history and field sports, and battles were joined, one interest defending the region against another, leisure against restrictive property, natural history against destructive sightseeing. Regional definition puts cultural landscape at stake, and it is the nature and consequence of such definition that an analysis of regional cultural landscape can highlight.

Origins and histories may also be examined, with historiographic analysis in Broadland finding contested narratives of regional landscape formation. The 1950s discovery that the broads were flooded medieval peat diggings prompted argument over the regional standing of science, and the value of landscape features no longer deemed natural (Matless, 2003). Regional cultural landscape also addresses questions of human conduct. From the leisure 'discovery' of the Broads in the late 19th century, the region has been defined through contested pleasures, the moral geographies of leisure shaping policy debate on practices deemed appropriate to the region (Matless, 1994). Debates over conduct also inform the scales of authority – national, regional, local – deemed appropriate for Broadland governance. Thus the post-1945 possibility of Broadland becoming a national park brought decades of argument over what kind of region this should be, and who should exercise authority over it. The region achieved 'national park status' in 1989, although the duties of the Broads Authority were subtly different to those of other British national parks, with navigation set out as a responsibility equal to that of conservation and recreation. For this reason the area could not formally be termed a national park. Recent proposals by the Broads Authority to label the area as a 'National Park' for tourist and marketing purposes, despite there being no legal change to bring responsibilities into line with other national parks, prompted concern that this might be a move to dilute navigational duties. The Authority has proceeded with the label, but arguments continue.

Regional cultural landscape also demands attention to regional icons, such as the Broadland wherry and windmill. The wherry as river vessel carrying regional cargo, or pleasure craft carrying leisure visitors, has, over 200 years, stood for the regional present and past, and since the mid-twentieth century has been subject to heritage salvage. The windmill, the key mechanism for drainage until the mid-twentieth century, has also since been subject to efforts of preservation and restoration. From their depiction in early nineteenth century 'Norwich School' painting to their restoration by present enthusiasts, the wherry and windmill work as Broadland icons. Regional icons can also encompass animal and plant life, birds such as the bittern, mammals such as the invasive coypu, insects such as the swallowtail butterfly, plants such as milk parsley and reed. Regional cultural landscape indeed demands attention to animal and plant landscapes, human and non-human subjects and objects defined through relation (Head and Atchison, 2009; Matless, Watkins and Merchant, 2005). Specific genres of writing and picturing here convey the non-human such that their practitioners become 'nature voices' (Matless, 2009). Broadland's animal landscapes see mammals and birds variously appearing as objects of biodiverse value, quarry for killing, creatures for careful observation, cherished regional icons, or alien intruders. Broadland plant landscapes see botanical and ecological study finding scientific and cultural value in Broadland flora, while processes of ecological succession, advancing in part through the historical relaxation of human marsh management, inform dispute over what Broadland's plant landscape should be.

Regional cultural landscape also entails consideration of the ends of landscape. Broadland's present is shadowed not only by origin disputes but forebodings of destruction, via overgrowth by wood, aquatic transformation through eutrophication, marsh drainage for cultivation, or flood invasion by the sea. Possible futures haunt the regional present, as threats, or sometimes as opportunities. Prospective climate change concentrates minds on a possible regional end, the Broads making sense in relation to the North Sea, the coast a historically shifting line, the land perhaps under future sea. The possible ends of landscape – undersea, overgrown – haunt the region.

Whether considering threatened futures, contested histories, questions of conduct, animal and plant landscapes, regional icons, or only the regional name, a complex sense of regional identity emerges. Open to dispute, never complete, shaped through relations to elsewhere, and subject to internal variegation, identity carries and is made through regional cultural landscape. In this, regional identity cannot help but be provisional, provision denoting tentativeness, and sustenance.

Description: *The Regional Book*

The Regional Book gives another rendition of Broadland, gathering descriptions of 44 sites around the region (see Figure 1.1). After a short introductory essay, the pieces are ordered alphabetically, with a list of recommended reading and a gazetteer with map at the end. Six of the accounts were first aired at a conference, 'Living Landscapes', on landscape and performance, at Aberystwyth in 2009, and subsequently published in *Performance Research* (Matless, 2010). *In the Nature of Landscape* extended their coverage, with six given at the end of the opening chapter, and six more at the end of the book.

The opportunity to develop such work for publication in a different format was welcome. Colin Sackett's own work has been marked by an inventive reworking of twentieth century British geographical sources, such as works by Geoffrey Hutchings, Dudley Stamp and Alfred Steers (Sackett 2004, 2006), and Uniformbooks also includes in its publication list neglected works of modernist landscape writing (Johnson, 2015). *The Regional Book* is titled in part as a plain description of its content, but also as a nod to earlier regional topographies, notably 'The Regional Books' issued by publisher Robert Hale during the 1950s, including

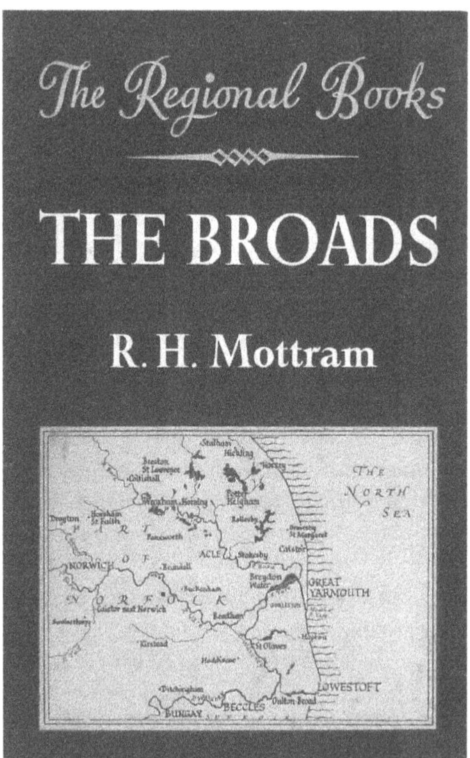

Figure 1.2 Front cover of RH Mottram, *The Broads* (1952).

RH Mottram's *The Broads* (Mottram, 1952) (see Figure 1.2). These guides could be unusually reflexive concerning regional definition; Mottram included a chapter entitled 'The Broads Become Self-Conscious'. Hale also issued a 'County Books' series, but the Regional Books stretched more conventional and administrative units of geographical coverage, with titles including *The Channel Shore*, *The Southern Marches*, *Sedgemoor and Avalon*, and *Holiday Lancashire*.

The Regional Book is an exercise in geographical description. Whatever geography's etymological claim to 'earth writing', 'descriptive' has often been a pejorative term, denoting lack of analysis, a bland surface accounting. HC Darby commented in his 1962 essay on 'The Problem of Geographical Description': 'We look in vain for – to use an oldfashioned word – a "likeness" of, say chalk downlands or clay vales or mountain uplands. What we do sometimes encounter is a kind of verbal cartography, as unattractive as it is unrevealing' (Darby, 1962: 1). Yi-Fu Tuan's 1978 essay on 'Literature and Geography', invoking Balzac, Eliot, Tolstoy and Forster as literary models, similarly reflected:

> It is ironic to note that some of the shoddier specimens of geographical description bear a superficial resemblance to French novels of the 'New Wave'. In geography texts, we have all encountered the dry itemization of streets, shopping centres, and other land use patterns as though they somehow add up to a living portrait of the city. At the other extreme, the interest in viewpoints and perspectives may be carried so far that it dissolves the external world and makes it impossible to depict a unit larger than the fragmented worlds of the committed individual actors.
>
> The model for the regional geographer of humanistic learning is neither Beckett nor Robbe-Grillet but the Victorian novelist who strives to achieve a synthesis of the subjective and the objective. (Tuan, 1978: 204–205)

Description may however carry other cultural possibility. As Svetlana Alpers suggested in her 1983 study of seventeenth century Dutch painting, there is a complex 'art of describing', challenging any distinction between description and narrative action: 'northern images do not disguise meaning or hide it beneath the surface but rather show that meaning by its very nature is lodged in what the eye can take in – however deceptive that might be' (Alpers, 1983: xxiv). Far from being a dull inventory trap, description can offer complex cultural practice, giving an account of landscape in the sense of both itemisation and action proceeding. Description here carries a dual performative sense of, on the one hand, distanced representation – the observer set back, however closely, from a scene – and on the other inscriptive enactment – the instrument describing, engraving, a line.

An outlook more open to modernism might find Darby's lamented 'verbal cartography', or Tuan's 'dry itemization', more intriguing than dull. In his 1974 *Species of Spaces*, Georges Perec, outlining 'practical exercises' for describing a Paris street, proposed exhaustive itemisation to take description beyond expected or conventional forms of notice. Perec states: 'Force yourself to see more flatly' (Perec, 1997: 51). Perec's accounts themselves move between matters of fact, digression, memory and reverie, and show inventories to be neither plain nor simple. The injunction to 'see more flatly' can however serve as a motto for constant notice, respectful looking, the spotting of unlikely material significance. This, and the flatness of Broadland topography (excepting the odd hill or church tower) made Perec's phrase an apt epigram for *The Regional Book.*

Geographical description concentrates attention, gathers experience, observes and inscribes. The accounts in *The Regional Book* are mono-vocal, deliberately singular, responding in part to an assumed request to describe a landscape without reflex resort to the commentary of others. Past accounts can be read, the contrasting answers to questions acknowledged, but what follows if, after all, the plain request is for a description? The pieces range across the Broads' varied constitution: nature reserves, towns, riversides, marshes, seasides, waterways broad and narrow, broads landlocked and connected. Alphabetically ordered varieties practise a cross-regional democracy, with locations treated in non-hierarchical fashion (though with attention to the ways in which hierarchies operate). Descriptions cut against, while also recognising, and occasionally inhabiting, forms of attention, and styles of seeing, claiming conventional authority. If Broadland is a flat landscape, with few rises, it remains possible to see more flatly.

To conclude this chapter, the texts of three entries from *The Regional Book* are reproduced, considering in turn the north shore of the estuarine Breydon Water, inland from the port and resort town of Great Yarmouth; Cockshoot Broad on the south side of the Bure valley, a nature reserve owned by the Norfolk Wildlife Trust where the broad's waters have been isolated from the main river for ecological restoration; and Horning, a village on the north bank of the Bure just upstream from Cockshoot, with river and banks developed for commercial, residential and leisure use. In setting and topic the selection indicates regional variety.

Breydon Water: North Shore

Yare's broadening, an estuary contained. Blue and brown commingle, flats intertidal, waders tapping. Naturalists and wildfowlers co-sponsor signage. Posts channel navigation, warning stakes submerged, dodging mud grounding.

Dyke and river conjoined or aloof by pump and sluice. One capped tower stands for older drainage. Houseboat remains stave shore mud.

Trains follow Breydon west to a divide, the Reedham branch twice more touching shore. Livestock level cross. Rolling stock moves small and flatly under sky.

Yarmouth contains, outflow deflected by two miles of towned spit. Sea blades turn as if landed. Nelson and chimneys, church and rollercoaster, line sky; and sky loops back to water colour.

Cockshoot Broad

No boat to Horning Ferry inn, across the Bure from the marsh road end. Tantalising lights of an evening. Talk crosses water on still days. The southern bank makes other sound; angling shufflings, leaves and calls. Moored craft clunk piling on passing wash.

A five minute path finds another mooring, at Cockshoot Dike. A boardwalk bridges and tracks, to Cockshoot Broad, a hide giving on water for lilies and birds. Loops take in carr.

Notice the water. The footbridge crosses a blockage, river water cloudy, dyke and broad clear. Biomanipulative, mechanical; algae chomped, mud pumped. Boats barred. Plant life viewed in confinements. On flows the river's obscurity.

Horning

Upstream from the Ferry Inn to the west end, northern banks are well appointed. Property as substantial as can be, hard by water, looking across to trees, south bank carr. Public space intrudes awhile at a sharp bend, the Swan Inn and staithe, small grass and moorings.

Parked up, a paddle boat. Cruises leave for Ranworth, spring through fall, incongruous platform for spying wet woodland. Light refreshment and waterborne licence, Mississippi-on-Bure. Jazz swings, a sailor tacks away. Loons display in bobbing wash, blithe to ragtime. A local habitation, use multiple, indifference virtuous.

References

Alexander N (2013) The idea of north: Basil Bunting and regional modernism, in N Alexander and J Moran (eds) *Regional Modernisms*. Edinburgh: Edinburgh University Press, 200–221.

Alexander N and Cooper D (eds) (2012) *Poetry and Geography: Space and Place in Postwar Poetry*. Liverpool: Liverpool University Press.

Alexander N and Moran J (eds) (2013) *Regional Modernisms*. Edinburgh: Edinburgh University press.

Alpers S (1983) *The Art of Describing: Dutch Art in the Seventeenth Century*. London: John Murray.

Barrell J (1982) Geographies of Hardy's Wessex. *Journal of Historical Geography* 8: 347–361.

Bryan PW (1933) *Man's Adaptation of Nature: Studies of the Cultural Landscape*. London: University of London Press.

Bunting B (2009) *Briggflatts*. Tarset: Bloodaxe Books (with DVD of 1982 film by Peter Bell).

Cameron L and Matless D (2003) Benign ecology: Marietta Pallis and the floating fen of the delta of the Danube, 1912–1916. *Cultural Geographies* 10: 253–277.

Cameron L and Matless D (2011) Translocal ecologies: the Norfolk Broads, the "natural," and the international phytogeographical excursion, 1911. *Journal of the History of Biology* 44: 15–41.

Campbell G (1990) Patrick Geddes: a regional nationalist?, *Radical Scotland* 43: 28–29.

Clout H (2009) *Patronage and the Production of Geographical Knowledge in France: The Testimony of the First Hundred Regional Monographs, 1905–1966*. London: Historical Geography Research Group, research series number 41.

Daniels S (1989) Marxism, culture and the duplicity of landscape, in R Peet and N Thrift (eds) *New Models in Geography, vol. II*. London: Unwin Hyman, 196–220.

Daniels S, Pearson M and Roms H (2010) Editorial. *Performance Research* 15: 1–4 (introduction to issue on 'Fieldworks').

Darby HC (1962) The problem of geographical description. *Transactions of the Institute of British Geographers* 30: 1–14.

DeLyser D (2005) *Ramona Memories: Tourism and the Shaping of Southern California*. Minneapolis: University of Minnesota Press.
Demangeon A (1939) *The British Isles*. London: Heinemann.
DeSilvey C, Naylor S and Sackett C (eds) (2011) *Anticipatory History*. Axminster: Uniformbooks.
Eastern Daily Press (1959) *Winter Broads Tour*. 6 January.
Graham B (1994) The search for the common ground: Estyn Evans's Ireland. *Transactions of the Institute of British Geographers* 19: 183–201.
Head L and Atchison J (2009) Cultural ecology: emerging human-plant geographies. *Progress in Human Geography* 33: 236–245.
Herring S (2009) Regional modernism: a reintroduction. *Modern Fiction Studies* 55: 1–10.
Johnson R (2015) *The Book of the Green Man*. Axminster: Uniformbooks (first published 1967).
Jones LR and Bryan PW (1924) *North America*. London: Methuen.
Lambert JM, Jennings JN, Smith CT, Green C and Hutchinson JN (1960) *The Making of The Broads: A Reconsideration of their Origin in the Light of New Evidence*. London: Royal Geographical Society.
Livingstone D (1992) *The Geographical Tradition*. Oxford: Blackwell.
Lorimer H (2000) Guns, game and the grandee: the cultural politics of deerstalking in the Scottish Highlands. *Cultural Geographies* 7: 403–431.
Lorimer H (2006) Herding memories of humans and animals. *Environment and Planning D: Society and Space* 24: 497–518.
Lorimer H and Lund K (2003) Performing facts: finding a way over Scotland's mountains, in B Szerszynski, W Heim and C Waterton (eds) *Nature Performed*. Oxford: Blackwell, 130–144.
Lorimer H and Spedding N (2005) Locating field science: a geographical family expedition to Glen Roy, Scotland. *British Journal for the History of Science* 38: 13–33.
MacDonald M (1994) The Outlook Tower: Patrick Geddes in context: glossing Lewis Mumford in the light of John Hewitt. *The Irish Review* 16: 53–73.
MacDonald F (2004) Paul Strand and the Atlanticist cold war. *History of Photography* 28: 357–374.
MacDonald F (2006a) The last outpost of empire: Rockall and the cold war. *Journal of Historical Geography* 32: 627–647.
MacDonald F (2006b) Geopolitics and 'the vision thing': regarding Britain and America's first nuclear missile. *Transactions of the Institute of British Geographers* 31: 53–71.
MacDonald F (2011) Doomsday fieldwork, or, how to rescue Gaelic culture? The salvage paradigm in geography, archaeology, and folklore. *Environment and Planning D: Society and Space* 29: 309–335.
MacDonald F (2014) The ruins of Erskine Beveridge. *Transactions of the Institute of British Geographers* 39: 477–489.
Mathews EC (1910) Field work in the valley of the Brent. *The Geographical Teacher* 5: 314–318.
Matless D (1992) Regional surveys and local knowledges: the geographical imagination in Britain 1918–39. *Transactions of the Institute of British Geographers* 17: 464–480.
Matless D (1994) Moral geography in Broadland. *Ecumene* 1: 127–156.
Matless D (1998) *Landscape and Englishness*. London: Reaktion.
Matless D (2003) Original theories: science and the currency of the local. *Cultural Geographies* 10: 354–378.
Matless D (2008) Properties of ancient landscape: the present prehistoric in twentieth century Breckland. *Journal of Historical Geography* 34: 68–93.
Matless D (2009) Nature voices. *Journal of Historical Geography* 35: 178–188.
Matless D (2010) Describing landscape: regional sites. *Performance Research* 15: 72–82.
Matless D (2014) *In the Nature of Landscape: Cultural Geography on the Norfolk Broads*. Chichester: Wiley-Blackwell.
Matless D (2015) *The Regional Book*. Axminster: Uniformbooks.

Matless D and Cameron L (2006) Experiment in landscape: the Norfolk excavations of Marietta Pallis. *Journal of Historical Geography* 32: 96–126.

Matless D and Cameron L (2007) Geographies of local life: Marietta Pallis and friends, Long Gores, Hickling, Norfolk. *Environment and Planning D: Society and Space* 25: 75–103.

Matless D and Pearson M (2012) A regional conversation. *Cultural Geographies* 19: 123–129.

Matless D, Watkins C and Merchant P (2005) Animal landscapes: otters and wildfowl in England 1945–1970. *Transactions of the Institute of British Geographers* 30: 191–205.

Matthews EC (1911) *The Highlands of South-West Surrey: A Geographical Study in Sand and Clay*. London: Adam and Charles Black.

Meller H (1990) *Patrick Geddes: Social Evolutionist and City Planner*. London: Routledge.

Mercer C (1997) Geographies for the present: Patrick Geddes, urban planning and the human sciences. *Economy and Society* 26: 211–232.

Mottram RH (1952) *The Broads*. London: Robert Hale.

Osborne T and Rose N (2004) Spatial phenomenotechnics: making space with Charles Booth and Patrick Geddes. *Environment and Planning D: Society and Space* 22: 209–228.

Pearson M (2006) *'In comes I': Performance, Memory and Landscape*. Exeter: University of Exeter press.

Pearson M (2013) *Marking Time: Performance, Archaeology and the City*. Exeter: University of Exeter press.

Pearson M and Shanks M (2001) *Theatre/Archaeology*. London: Routledge.

Perec G (1997) *Species of Spaces and Other Pieces*. London: Penguin.

Pite R (2002) *Hardy's Geography: Wessex and the Regional Novel*. Basingstoke: Palgrave Macmillan.

Sackett C (2004) *Englshpublshing*. Exeter: Spacex.

Sackett C (2006) *The True Line: The Landscape Diagrams of Geoffrey Hutchings*. Axminster: Colin Sackett.

Smith E (1910) *The Reigate Sheet of the One-Inch Ordnance Survey*. London: Adam and Charles Black.

Tuan Y-F (1978) Literature and geography: implications for geographical research, in D Ley and M Samuels (eds) *Humanistic Geography*. London: Croom Helm, 194–206.

Welter V (2002) *Biopolis: Patrick Geddes and the City of Life*. Cambridge: MIT Press.

Wylie J (2007) *Landscape*. Oxford: Blackwell.

2 Regions Rock

Heavy Metal and the Role of Music in the Construction of Regional Identity for the British Midlands

Jesse Heley and Marc Welsh

> Some of us from the Midlands say that we actually breathed in the metal before it came to be a real thing and a real experience. It is that connection, because what metal represents to a lot of people is very tough, hard, working class, honest people form the Midlands in particular. They are part of the psychology – the roots – of metal music.
>
> (Halford, 2015)

Track 1: Intro

In 2012, Jesse Hughes of the California-based band The Eagles of Death Metal delivered a television documentary on the subject of a 'pilgrimage' to the UK to explore the birth of heavy metal. Commissioned by the VICE documentary channel, and sponsored by Marshall Headphones, the first episode charts Hughes' 'metal odyssey' to 'deduce why it all started in the UK, and particular in the Midlands'. Starting in Los Angeles, he interviews Bill Ward, drummer of Black Sabbath, the band who are acknowledged as the 'originators' of the genre. The conversation focuses on how 'Sabbath' formed and the bands' principal influences, both musically and environmentally. Specifically, the manufacturing landscape of the Midlands in the 1960s is given centre-ground in terms of shaping the creative process and harnessing an empathetic fan base to whom the music 'made sense'. In so doing this documentary affirms and reproduces a highly popular 'place myth' with particular cultural and spatial referents. heavy metal music has become a global phenomenon, being produced and consumed internationally, and the Midlands continues to be reified as the 'Home of Metal' in the vein of a modern-day musical mecca.

Reflecting on the rise of heavy metal music, this paper explores construction, affirmation and contestation of regions in the context of musicality. Specifically, we are interested in the associated relations between people, their practices, their multiple identities and the ways in which these interact to produce the region as an imaginary phenomenon with associated material effects and implications, including musical forms. In so doing, we reflect on the limited body of work which explores the connections between music and regional development, which has to date largely considered the actual production of music for consumption, and the role of music as an integral part of urban and regional development strategies (and often as a proxy for cultural industries).

Going beyond the role of music in development policy as the object of analysis, we concern ourselves predominantly with the connection between music and place. In this way music, posited as a cultural artefact, provides a means for interrogating 'the region' as a mutable scale which is constantly coming into being. The region itself becomes the object of analysis through music, not the site through which musical expression may be understood, nor an object of governance developed through musical performance (festivals, venues and attractions etc.) – although such approaches also have their merits. Instead, in this paper we position music as one of many cultural artefacts that bear both the footprint of, and recursively produce the region in a local and global context.

Specifically, we argue that heavy metal music 'works' as one such artefact, bringing together a place, a time and a social context, allowing society to tell a story about its development. Cast in this light, heavy metal constitutes a lens through which to examine the mutability of and relationality of a particular region as constructed internally and (crucially) externally, and the 'region' itself. In short, this chapter is concerned with what might usefully be referred to as the 'regionalisation of metal'. It follows that, in order to explore the relationship between heavy metal music and the construction of regional identity, it is appropriate that we first sketch out the development of the 'region' as an object of analysis and the shifting role of culture within these debates. This is not to suggest that interplays between identity and regional formation have been ignored, but rather that regional analyses have tended to focus on the material manifestations (governments, development agencies) of structured social relations that knit regions together as discretely political-economic entities rather than as emergent cultural referents in a complex socio-political landscape.

Track 2: Lucid Fairytale – Region Building, Performance and Relationality

It is widely accepted that regions emerge and operate in multifaceted ways, taking political forms and having differentiated economic manifestations. They also come into existence insofar as they hold discursive and symbolic influence, and serve as a basis for expressing spatial categories. This perspective is one which has gained traction within regional studies over the past two decades, with regions being widely acknowledged as being expressions of power. They are fluid and far from fixed, with some regional forms having more permanence than others. It follows that regions are often contested, although regional constructs are – as often as not – reproduced with little conscious reflection. This premise was recently described by Joni Vainikka, noting that regions and regional identity 'can become crystallised as part of a reflexive and symbolic meaning system … promoted and realigned through effectual maps, heritage, regional emblems, imageries and representations' (Vainikka, 2013: 27). Regions are, therefore, remade and remodelled through the mundane interactions of everyday life.

The view of regions and regional identity being practically reproduced is now firmly entrenched. This is largely a consequence of the critical impact of a 'performative' turn across the social sciences more broadly from the early 1990s onwards. The relationship between performativity and regional identity is one which is ably set out by Prokkola and colleagues elsewhere (Prokkola et al., 2012). Here they highlight the work of Butler (Butler, 1993, 1997) as being particularly important in laying the conceptual groundwork for this approach, accrediting her as a pivotal inspiration for regional scholars who have extended their analyses beyond the material into the verbal and symbolic politics of everyday life. Here we might include Marston et al. (2005), Paasi (1996, 2010, 2002) and Jones and MacLeod (2004), amongst others. Importantly, Prokkola et al. mark the capacity of performance-orientated analyses to bring out the 'relational' context of region building, wherein regions make sense largely in the context of each other and their apparent attributes, for example, their economic success, language, natural history and ethnic profile (Prokkola et al., 2012: 3).

Primarily concerned with propinquity (as opposed to distance as a measure of closeness) the current vogue for highly relational models of spatiality has challenged the value of 'regions' at all as a basis for characterising and spatial relations. Referring to Ash Amin (2004), connectivity has arguably outstripped territory as a basis for cohesion and this prospect sits neatly within crude narratives on globalisation, global culture and global commerce. However, conceptual and practical application of relational thinking to regional studies has been subject to mounting criticism – and no small amount of scepticism (see, for example, Rodríguez-Pose and Crescenzi, 2008). In short, the relational approach (or at least its more extreme versions) has engendered a critical backlash from those who would argue for the ongoing relevance of regions. Specifically, Jones highlights an evident ambition to 'do' regional geography in more creative ways:

> Part of the problem is the way the contemporary debate is being posed, as if the networked worlds of those advocating relational space stand in direct opposition to territories and vice versa those advocating a networked position will also find that spaces of flows are not without regional geography anchors. (Jones, 2015)

The challenge, so it would seem, is finding a way of integrating territorial and relational sensibilities, and overcoming the notion that that the former is being steadily eclipsed by the latter. What is certain, however, is that 'region' continues to be a meaningful frame of reference for people, both as a means of mediating, managing and imagining a diverse array of policies and practices, and as referent for placing themselves in their world. Undoubtedly, regions are constantly being (re)made, partly on the strength and basis of these culturally-informed 'regional imaginaries'.

With this in mind regions become laboratories for the exploration of empirical and theoretical change in the minds of people living and working within an area, and in the characterisations of those invocating these spaces in policy, academic and media texts. This point has recently been made by Paasi who advocates an 'interpretative geohistorical' approach to regional analysis:

> [Regions] are constructed in contested material and symbolic cultural practices such as regional naming and the choice of other symbols; they come into being in stories, novels, songs, poems, films, and other artefacts that give rise to social classifications, stereotyping and distinctions. Regions 'act' in regional dialects and in collective memories selected for museums, exhibitions and archives. (Paasi, 2010: 2299)

In making the assertion that regions are bound up with material culture and constantly in the process of assembling and finding new spatial extents, this statement resonates with others made elsewhere regarding the time-specific – yet historically-informed – context of regional forms. This particular take on regional development has been put forward and explored by John Allen and colleagues (Allen and Cochrane, 2007; Allen et al., 1998) who collectively ask not only 'where' a region might exist, but also 'when'.

As part of this project Allen and colleagues have focused on the rise and representation of the South East of England as a 'growth region' during the 1980s under the auspices of 'Thatcherism'. Associated with a range of policy mechanisms, these included the internationalisation of the economy, the deregulation of the banking sector, the easing of lending restrictions and the privatisation of national assets. This process further reinforced a two-nation politics (Jessop et al., 1990), where the success of the UK economy as a whole became dependent upon the success of the South East. It was also premised on the rise of a new middle or 'service' class who were largely instituted by this transformation, and who benefitted disproportionally. By comparison the working class became increasingly disenfranchised territorially and structurally, most obviously with the waning of heavy industry and manufacturing in the Midlands and the North which greatly undermined and destabilised the political heartlands of the working class.

For Allen and colleagues, then, the (early) 1980s was 'an exceptional moment, a one-off scenario' (Allen et al., 1998: 14) borne of a neo-liberal project which both secured and championed the South East as the driver of the national economy, and relegated the Midlands and the North to the margins. It was at once political and economic, *and it was distinctly cultural.* In particular, Thatcherism is associated with the rise of a series of left-wing creative processes which were reacting to the dominant, totalising ideology of the time (Short, 1989: 175) inclusive of theatre (Peacock, 1999), film and television (Sterritt, 1993; O'Sullivan, 1993), and music.

Indeed, the influence of the Thatcher Government on the music during the late 1970s and 1980s has been explored to some considerable extent, with its ideals and policies deemed to be a key component shaping the music of this time (Clarke, 2009). For example, the political environment of Britain under Thatcher has been widely acknowledged as a catalyst of punk (Nehring, 2007; Glasper, 2014), but the associated shift in creative direction of other musical genres has also been discussed – including heavy metal. In their recent commentary on the more recent phenomenon of 'Black metal' in the English North, for example, Spracklen and colleagues argue that symbolic boundaries of the heavy metal scene are coterminous with the imagined community of a hard masculinity coming to terms with post-industrial, post-factory environment (Spracklen et al., 2014).

If the relationship between the political climate, economic transitions, social movements and musicality has been discussed in some depth within media studies, sociology and (to a much lesser extent) human geography, a somewhat limited amount of work has been undertaken which focuses on the connection between music, spatial formations and identity within regional studies. Moreover, where regional identity has been considered, it has often been from the perspective of development planning and marketing, and therefore been subsumed into an economic view of the landscape. This stands in contrast to the importance attributed to cultural artefacts and performance within regional theory. That said, some investigations of this kind have been undertaken and are considered in the following section.

Track 3: Into the Void – Musicality and Regional Identity

Of those studies which have explicitly connected regions and musicality, several have focused on the role of the music industry in regional development. These include Ray Hudson's reflections on music in urban regeneration strategies (Hudson, 2006) where he questions the extent to which music can form an even partial basis for regional regeneration efforts. In this discussion he nevertheless highlights the importance of 'music – in both its production and consumption – in shaping the typically hybrid identities of people and places, of engendering a sense of place and deep attachment to place' (ibid.: 633). John Lovering (1998) has also contributed to the growing literature on the political economy of music with his consideration of the global music industry. Taking issue with the reduction of the social significance of music to the 'passive act of consumption', Lovering's work focuses on the concentration of capital and the emergence of music as 'big business', and upon the emergence of corporate strategies and transnational spatial reorganisation. As such, this analysis is distinctly global, but it also gives prominence to the formation of 'local musical spaces'.

Touching on the more emotional and more corporeal aspects of music-making these themes have also been explored in some depth by Watson and Ward (2013) who consider the importance of people and surroundings to the creative process. More precisely they draw on interview data and observation as a means of demonstrating 'performative engineering' in the studio, and the role of studio staff in creating the right 'vibe'. Drawing connections between socio-material environment and music at a micro-scale, other studies have explored this relationship in terms of broader localities (Connell and Gibson, 2003; Gibson and Davidson, 2004) and national identity (Mitchell, 1996; Ramnarine, 2003).

The regional scale, however, remains largely absent from these debates. What is more, where the role of music in the production of regions and regional consciousness is discussed, it is more often than not in tandem with the role of paintings, literature and sculpture – among other forms of artistic expression– in representing spatial experiences and structures of meaning and seldom takes centre-stage in the discussion (see, for example, Kift, 2012; Matless, 2010). Notable exceptions to this scenario are David Russell's work on musical culture and popular politics in Yorkshire's textile districts (Russell, 1983), and Huggins and Gregson's more recent exploration of the interrelationship between songs, sport and northern regional consciousness in nineteenth century England (Huggins and Gregson, 2007). The latter study demonstrates the importance of studying music as a basis for teasing out evolving cultural vocabularies of regional identity over a given period of time. So too does Robert Stradling's (1998) account of the construction and representation of Severn Estuary in the music of the early twentieth century, which collectively defines this region as the 'axial point' of British geography. Lastly, and most significantly in terms of the focus of this chapter, is Andrew Cope's (2010) examination of the relationship between post-war industrial landscape of the Midlands and the development of hard rock music. Advocating the existence of 'musical milieus' (after Webb, 2004) combining musical practises and the dynamics of contemporary political and economic forces, Cope characterises the Midlands of the 1960s and 1970s as holding a unique synthesis of elements necessary for the birth of heavy metal music.

These studies clearly demonstrate the connections that can be made between regional politics, popular culture, time and musical expression, and in the subsequent section we will explore these relationships in regard to the rise of heavy metal music and the British Midlands.[1] As a means of setting the scene (literally and metaphorically) we begin by relating the established narrative on this musical genre and its spatial origins. Often presented unproblematically, the power of this discursive construct is such that the Midlands are continually invoked as the undisputed 'Home of Metal'. This constitutes our empirical setting, and we use heavy metal music as a device to explore the connection between music and discursive acts of region building, and as a lens through which to explore the temporal dimensions of regionalisation (i.e. those moments when regions are deemed to have emerged, transformed and been supplanted).

In this way we take inspiration from Allen et al's (1998) relational approach as a means to theoretically unpack the connections between music and the region, but it also serves as a valuable empirical counterpoint for exploring the socio-spatial aspects of heavy metal music production and consumption in Britain and beyond.[2] Specifically, it provides a context through which to frame the Midlands as a region, the region *itself* as a meaningful social category among those people looking to tell a story about their locality, and also how other people tell their own stories in respect to other localities. Musical culture, therefore, provides another means of analytically 'holding down' *regions* as produced through interior and exterior relations. We also touch on broader debates which consider the role of music as a basis and expression of spatially attuned relationally positioned identity politics, and suggest ways in which such research may be taken forward.

Track 4: Between the Hammer and the Anvil – the Heavy Metal Origin Story

The (British) Midlands is the ancestral home of heavy metal music, or at least as far as countless books, magazine articles, films and television documentaries have, and continue, to claim. This 'fact' is evident in the lyrical content of heavy metal songs – such as those to *Made in Hell* (Halford, 2000) – and arguably in its melodic qualities, perceptible in the volume, beat and phrasing.

> When we were kids walking to school we'd walk past these metal foundries and see the molten metal coming out of the big vats. We were literally breathing in the fumes from these metal works, breathing in metal before heavy metal had even been invented. I'd be in school trying to do English literature and the classroom would be shaking because of the machinery. [Rob Halford of Judas Priest interviewed in 2010] (Wilkinson, 2010)
>
> I've heard people say that it [heavy metal music] is in the water and things like that. There is this steel industry thing that used to be – factories with drop hammers and forges and all that. (Tatler, 2015)
>
> It comes out of the North in swathes. Look at those pictures of people with a cigarette in their mouth and a dark look in their eye. It is inner city music, isn't it? (Lord, 2015)

This association between the Midlands, heavy metal and post-war Britain is persistently voiced by the musicians and fan base responsible for making and consuming this musical form, some of whom come from this locality (including Brian Tatler of the band *Diamond Head*), some of whom do not (including John Lord of *Deep Purple*, for whom the Midlands was 'the North'). Moreover, the mantra that 'Metal was born in the Midlands' has also been regularly asserted within journalistic spheres, historical overviews and scholarly texts, some of which will be considered in the next section. However, we will also seek to unpack this narrative and demonstrate that it is not as clear-cut and incontrovertible as some would have us believe. As with any successful rhetorical device that looks to pinpoint the emergence of a socio-cultural phenomenon it necessarily simplifies, punctuates and homogenises an altogether more messy state of affairs in a persuasive and convincing manner.

Track 5: Victim of Changes – the British Midlands and Heavy Metal – a Time and Place?

> You'd be sitting there with your pint and your fags and your pickled egg, in this yellow-walled shithole of a boozer, [...] with everyone knackered, broke and dying from asbestos poisoning or whatever toxic shit they were breathing in every day. Then, all of a sudden, you'd hear all this hippy crap about 'gentle people' going to love-ins at Haight-Ashbury [...] Who gave a dog's arse about what people were doing in San Francisco anyway? The only flowers anyone

> saw in Aston were the ones they threw in the hole after you when you croaked it at the age of fifty-three 'cos you'd worked yourself to death. I hated those hippy-dippy songs, man. *Really* hated them. (Osbourne, 2009: chapter 2)

Set against a backdrop of significant social and economic turmoil in the UK and US the origins of heavy metal can be traced back to the late 1960s, mixing elements of blues, psychedelia and rock and roll into a form of musical expression noted for its 'crashing guitars, pounding percussion and ear-splitting volume' (Gross, 1990: 119). While American bands such as Steppenwolf, Vanilla Fudge and Grand Funk Railroad, and British bands such as Deep Purple, Uriah Heep, Budgie, the Edgar Broughton Band, Cream and Led Zeppelin were all pioneering a heavier sound in aspects of their work, it is widely accepted that the genre was effectively created and defined by two bands: Black Sabbath and Judas Priest. Both went on to enjoy lasting international success and effectively established a rock phenomenon, both *in* the British Midlands and *of* the British Midlands.

Loud, aggressive and dealing with themes of evil, death and destruction, the music of 'Sabbath' and 'Priest' established the parameters of heavy metal, a working class response to 1960s counter-culture, one dealing directly with the inequities brought forth by the economic realignment of the UK economy.

The 1950s post-war boom had seen the Midlands thrive relative to other regions of the UK. Incomes were above the national average and unemployment below it. The region was characterised by a heavy industry industrial base oriented around metal working (coal, steel and automotive manufacture) with a large array of ancillary factories servicing a small number of key firms. The result was a highly integrated tightly-knit industrial region particularly vulnerable to external economic forces affecting the larger employers cascading throughout the regional economy (Flynn and Taylor, 1986). By the end of the 1960s, while the boom had come to an end, the problem for youth in the region was not so much an inability to find work but the nature of that employment and the livelihood it entailed, of monotonous drudgery, low wages, poor housing and limited opportunities to find alternatives. The economic shocks of the 1970s and 80s would hit the region particularly hard, with factory closures particularly around the automotive industry and a broader decline in manufacturing leading to skyrocketing unemployment. These issues would dominate the political landscape of the region. With similar transformations playing out in parts of Scotland, Humberside, Yorkshire and Wales, rapid industrial decline in these spaces was also in part due to shifting UK government policy on nationalised industries which, in effect, engendered divisions between a northern periphery and southern, economic core (Hudson, 2011).

Inevitably rapid change in the economic fortunes of industrial Britain was accompanied by a sea change in the social fabric of these regions and a rise of antagonistic social-political movements. Making reference to EP Thompson's monumental text, *The Making of the English Working Class* (1964), Moore draws parallels between the rise of heavy metal music and the radical social movements precipitated by the Industrial Revolution.

> Thompson wrote that the Industrial Revolution was a time when men's psychic worlds were filled with violent images from hell-fire and Revelation, and their real world was filled with poverty and oppression. However, he might just as easily be referring to the emergence of heavy metal in a time deindustrialisation was decimating many of the same factory towns in the twentieth century. (Moore, 2009: 143)

Deindustrialisation, then, fundamentally disrupted the link between working class identities, manual labour and masculinity. For young predominately white working class men born into a tradition of manual labour, the retreat of these types of occupation arguably saw the performance of masculinity become disconnected from the sphere of production. As Nayak (2003) argues, under these conditions theatres of leisure and consumption therefore took on a greater significance, and masculine behaviour became centred on such outlets as drinking, sex and emerging forms of creative expression. In this arena feelings of disempowerment became the cornerstone of new dystopian musical subcultures manifesting feelings of dissonance, and helplessness. These included progressive rock (Macan, 1997) and punk (Worley, 2013) and heavy metal.

Leigh Harrison (2010) makes an explicit link between the industrial, working-class geography of post-war Birmingham and the 'birth' of heavy metal music. Black Sabbath and Judas Priest were/are both Birmingham bands, both groups were formed in 1969, and their collective membership all worked in the city's numerous factories and industrial plants. This particular geography and set of experiences, argues Harrison, is reflected in their music in terms of their instrumentation and lyrics. With reference to the creative output of both Black Sabbath and Judas Priest, and interviews undertaken with group members past and present, he draws attention to recurring themes. Specifically, Harrison highlights feelings of anger, frustration and hopelessness concerning their underprivileged, working-class backgrounds, and the function of the bleak, congested and noisy landscape of heavy industry, all of which has been cited by various band members as having a direct impact on the sound and development of their music (Harrison 2010: 1). Indeed, even the fashions of metal music are in some ways influenced by the milieu. For example, the archetypal 'costume' of the 'metaller' includes a certain degree of leather fetishism. This can be wholly attributed to Rob Halford's predilection for cow hide. Coming from Walsall, this is unsurprising given that the town historically served as Britain's leather goods capital. This is reflected by its status as the location of the Walsall Leather Museum which, as part of the 'Home of Metal' event, hosted 'Hell Bent for Leather' featuring stage wear and other leather paraphernalia as donated by members of Judas Priest.

This politics of place as embodied in heavy metal music is, for example, clearly evident in accounts of the making of Judas Priest's *British Steel* album. Released in April 1980 in the wake of an industrial strike, the title demonstrated sympathy with the workforce, as did the lyrical content of such tracks as 'The Rage' and 'Breaking the Law', which remonstrated about the plight of joblessness and the lack of employment opportunities. For Rob Halford, the lead singer of Judas Priest, and Ian Hill the bassist, the influence of the socio-political environment of Britain in the early 1980s on *British Steel* is clear:

> There was a lot of stuff going on in the U.K. — socially/politically, it was in turmoil with the Thatcher government and the unions, street fights with coal miners and the police. It was a really volatile bit of a revolution around the late '70s. I think some of that went into my writing as a lyricist. If you listen to the words and messages on British Steel, it's full of that angst. (Rob Halford interview in *Rolling Stone* magazine, 2009)
>
> At the time of the publication of the album, British Steel workers were on strike. Part of the reason for choosing this particular album title and artwork was sympathetic with what was going on … in the steelworks at the time. (Ian Hill, cited in Moore, 2009: 85)

Connecting class politics and heavy metal, these first-hand accounts correspond with viewpoints expressed by Magnus Nilsson (2009), Liam Dee (2009) and Spracklen et al. (2014), with the former describing this form of aggressive music as an act of working-class resistance in the form of 'cultural' warfare. This phenomenon ties in with the apparent glorification of 'anti-respectability', and with the celebration of 'humble' roots and shared disadvantage between the musicians and their fan base. Indeed, this apparent bond of experience between band and fan is regularly repeated in biographies of Black Sabbath, wherein journalists universally remind readers that 'Sabbath' – as progenitors of heavy metal music – were 'tough' lads shaped by the 'tough' city of Birmingham.

Track 6: Mass Appeal Madness – Metal Comes from the Midlands … and Liverpool, Newcastle, London, Croydon, Los Angeles

The rhetorical connection between heavy metal and the British Midlands is powerful, pervasive and – at least in the popular media – incontrovertible. And yet, we maintain that there is something intrinsically odd about the environmentally determinist view which holds the Midlands as the crucible of this form of music, particularly in light of those musical analyses which trace the aural and melodic qualities of heavy metal music back to earlier rock and blues traditions. Indeed, those accounts which cast the birth of heavy metal in the Midlands – and specifically Birmingham – in the manner of an immaculate conception are in stark contrast to a body of literature which empirically describes the emergence of rock music as a multi-sited, relationally constructed phenomenon. Simply stated, heavy metal did not emerge within a sealed geographic container, and here Cope (2010) goes a significant way in dispelling the myth that heavy metal as a musical genre did and could have only come forth from the Midlands. Why not Manchester, Newcastle, London and Liverpool? In short, it did, and it emerged as a polycentric phenomenon.

The geographical positioning of Birmingham ensured that it played an important role communicating and assimilating a range of musical traditions and styles, both nationally and internationally. The expansion of the English motorway network throughout the 1950s and 1960s was crucial in this regard, and particularly the completion of the M1, M6 and M62 carriageways which positioned Birmingham within easy reach of two of the most important musical centres in the UK. To the North, Liverpool had played host to the 'Merseybeat' phenomenon during the 1960s, with bands such as the Beatles, the Searchers and Gerry and the Pacemakers becoming hugely successful. A brand of music that was shaped by American rock and roll, gospel and Motown influences, Liverpool's particular susceptibility to American sounds can be largely accredited to the city's status as Britain's principal transatlantic port (Inglis, 2000). To the south, Cope draws attention to the significance of the London British Rhythm and Blues (R&B) 'explosion' of the mid-1960s in shaping the development of the Birmingham rock scene. Centred on a number of popular jazz venues in the London metro area, this movement involved a range of musicians who played a key role in transforming electric blues into hard rock as members of such bands as Cream and the Yardbirds (Schwartz, 2007).

The popular press identified R&B as the 'the sound of London' but other cities and other clubs were also centres for the propagation and production of blues-based music. These included the Liberal Club in Newcastle, the Twisted Wheel in Manchester, and Birmingham's Ramblers Club. Moreover, it also had a determinedly international fix. Here we refer not only to the movement of vinyl records and musical scores between the US, the UK and Europe, but also to artists. For example, in 1963 the American Folk Blues Festival Package Tour had a line-up that included various American musicians such as John Lee Hooker, Otis Span, Sonny Boy Williamson, Big Joe Williams and Willie Dixon (see Schwartz 2007: 147). The traffic was not all one way, and from the mid-1960s onwards a wave of British musicians, many of whom were strongly influenced by American blues, toured and met with some success in the US as part of the so-called 'British Invasion'.

Including such groups as the Rolling Stones, the Kinks, the Who and the Yardbirds, these groups have been credited with securing the popularity of electric blues music amongst American youth more broadly, and their success stateside arguably paved the way for other rock acts to break through, including a vast number of American bands (Perone, 2009) and a number of homespun bands who emphasised the heavier, darker elements of this sonic template. At least this is the dominant narrative, one that is particularly apparent, for example, when considering 'The Home of Metal' exhibition, a collection of memorabilia and stories which celebrates (in its own words) 'music from Birmingham and the Black Country'.

Track 7: Heaven and Hell – the Home of Metal?

> If any sound has the rhythm of the factory – the hammering, the drilling and the thumping – it's heavy metal, and Birmingham in the late 60s and 70s had both. The second city hadn't served its denim and leather heritage well until

> Capsule produced a huge Home of Metal exhibition that recreated the factories where members of bands such as Black Sabbath worked. (Bounds, 2013)

Writing in the travel section of *The Guardian* in February 2013 Jon Bounds' article encouraged the readership to pay a visit to the 'Home of Metal' exhibition. Staged between January 2011 and January 2012, the Home of Metal exhibition set out to 'explore the social history of the region, from its metal bashing industries to the post war home life of working class families, beginning the story of Heavy Metal' (Bounds, 2013). The exhibition was launched by Tony Iommi, a founding member of Black Sabbath and identified as the originator of the heavy metal guitar sound,[3] and featured various items of memorabilia relating to the development of the musical genre, including original album artwork, posters and stage costumes. More interestingly, there are walk-in mock-ups of mill settings replete with anvils, lathes and industrial sound effects, and a reproduction of a somewhat dour 1960s front room. The exhibition emphasised the importance of materiality and everyday locations in shaping heavy metal: this affirms what journalist Ben Miller refers to as the 'psycho-musical life of the Midlands' (Miller, 2011).

For Miller, the Home of Metal constituted the 'tale of a region'. More pointedly, the exhibition also represented a long overdue celebration of the Midlands' role as the birthplace of a musical/cultural phenomenon which now enjoys global popularity. Set in contrast to Manchester, forever intertwined with 'arch miserablists' [The Smiths] and 'charismatic bad boys' [including the Happy Mondays and the 'Madchester' scene], and with Liverpool, the home of the 'The Beatles Experience', Miller notes that the 'genre Birmingham spawned bears less umbilical ties with its host city' (ibid.). A critical take, it is one that was echoed by the publicity issued by the event's organisers (a company called Capsule) and other journalists:

> Capsule threw down the gauntlet to the region. Where were the shrines to Heavy Metal? Loved the world over, Heavy Metal in its many forms had its roots in Birmingham and the Black Country. But you wouldn't know to visit it. No plaque, tour or tea towel marked one of the region's most prolific cultural exports.
>
> Heavy Metal was born in the west midlands and has developed a global following matched only in hip-hop. It is time to stop sneering and celebrate this proud cultural heritage. (Trilling, 2007)

These statements testify to the apparent lack of recognition of the role of the Midlands and its artists in creating a lasting an international musical legacy in the form of heavy metal, a discrepancy which the exhibition and associated online memorabilia repository has set out to address. A key artefact in this process is a 'family tree' of heavy metal as produced by the artist Francesca Williams. The chart centres on five key groups originating in the Midlands – Led Zeppelin, Black Sabbath and Judas Priest (all of whom were formed in the late 1960s), and Napalm Death and GodFlesh (both formed in the 1980s). Tracing the membership of these bands and their movements over time and across space, there are a large number of associations with North America alongside a host of other countries, including Germany, Italy, Mexico, Hungary and Scandinavia.

Including groups where there is a direct connection in terms of membership, the heavy metal tree does not include the vast number of other heavy metal bands who have emerged globally; nor does it give reference to a dizzying array of sub-genres which heavy metal incorporates, including (but not restricted to) hair metal, funk metal and black metal. Moreover, it is also important to note that the creative output of these bands is not essentially derivative. It is context dependent – socially, politically and spatially. For example, Los Angeles' Sunset Strip is synonymous with the 'glam' of the 'hair' metal movement of the 1980s, characterised by garish clothing and makeup, debauched lifestyles and the rise of music television, and particularly MTV (Weinstein, 2000). Elsewhere, the phenomenon of black metal has been critically and popularly allied to elements of the heavy metal scene in Norway. Including the likes of Emperor, Burzum and Mayhem, these bands are noted for their use of corpse paint and satanic imagery, misanthropic lyrics and their vocal opposition to organised religion.

Taking Paasi's 'interpretative geohistorical' approach, it might be reasonably argued that heavy metal music has an institutional structure such that the British Midlands represents a central component of its 'territorial shape', with the economic and political fabric of this landscape in the late 1960s being a key, recurring frame of reference. Complimented by a 'symbolic shape' comprised of, for example, a dress code of denim and leather allied to the working-class credentials of its membership, and the consolidation of key institutions such as amplified distortion and the use of musical 'tritones' (creating the so-called Devil's note), these elements come together and effectively institutionalise heavy metal music within the collective consciousness. Alternatively, and coming at this phenomenon from an alternative angle, we might also argue that the institutionalisation of the British Midlands as a region draws, in part, on heavy metal music as part of its symbolic and cultural shape. Heavy metal and the Midlands are, therefore, mutually informed frames of reference.

Track 8: Distorting the Medium – Another Midlands?

> Heavy metal music could only have been born out of the industrial neighbourhoods of Birmingham. The intersection of a changing youth culture in a city dominated by the sounds of heavy industry was a potent mix unique to post-war Birmingham. (Harrison, 2010: 153)

As with all regions, these frames of reference are seldom (if ever) universally acknowledged, stable in time or without contestation and counter-narratives. Here, for example, the sense of environmental and social determinism that is communicated in the notion of the Midlands as the 'Mecca of Metal' can be challenged in light of debates on class and musicality, and with reference to the rise of other musical forms within this territorial context before, during and since the late 1960s.

First, a growing number of studies have highlighted the role of the middle class alongside the working class as key producers and consumers of heavy metal music (Hill et al., 2015; Krenske and McKay, 2000; Verden et al., 1989). For example, Roberta Schwartz (2007) notes the intermixing of art school student and bohemian intellectuals alongside a working-class youth in the nascent UK rock scene of the 1960s. More broadly, other commentators have noted the on-going importance of exclusion from socio-economic and educational opportunities in creating and continuing heavy metal musical subcultures, but that other processes of disaffection also play a part (Arnett, 1996: 441). Second, if metal could only come from the Midlands, then this is not an exclusive relationship as other musical traditions and experiences have emerged and characterised this spatial context (e.g. the 'Brum Beat' in the 1950s, the ska revival and reggae bands of the late 1970s). In particular, the Midlands has strong associations with the 'New Romantics' of the 1980s, and a longstanding tradition of Asian music.

By the early 1960s Midlands cities, like Birmingham and Coventry, were recognised for their large and vibrant music scenes. They were also characterised by increasingly multicultural and musical communities where cross-over, collaboration and experimentation provided a fertile base for the emergence of new musical styles. Emerging at the tail end of the 1970s, the New Romantic movement emerged in both London and Birmingham and within this broad scene a number of Midlands bands emerged which would meet with varying levels of success, including Dexys Midnight Runners, The Human League, and – most iconically – Duran Duran. Indeed, such is the perceived level of connection between the region and the New Romantic movement that there have been calls for a celebration of the genre in Birmingham's Museum and Art Gallery along similar lines to the Home of Metal exhibition. More recently the role of the Midlands as a crucible for Asian music has also come in for considerable critical attention, particularly in regard to Bhangra. A musical form traditionally associated with Punjabi culture, it has played an important role in defining and proclaiming cultural identity for South Asian-British youths from the 1980s onwards. Spawning a number of internationally recognised celebrities (including Golden Star, Malkit Singh and Apache Indian), Bhangra has been described by Dudrah (1998) as a unique form of cultural production and music industry rooted in Birmingham – much in the same terms as heavy metal. And yet, where heavy metal has established a global network of production and consumption, 'Bhangra remains relatively marginalised within the broader music industry, being virtually ignored (or stereotyped) by the mainstream music press and handicapped by poor retail and distribution' (McEwan et al., 2005: 926).

Track 9: Symptom of the Universe – Regions, Music and Other Cultural Moments

In the case of the 'New Romantics' and Bhangra scene we see other forms of musical expression that lay claim to the Midlands, and which play their part in (re) institutionalising a version of this region. Moreover, they both constitute a spatial narrative that centres on a 'moment' within social and political consciousness. This perspective is evident in Rajinder Dudrah's history of Bhangra, where he casts the city of Birmingham in the 1980s as the 'starting point and first co-ordinate' on the map of UK-based Bhangra (Dudrah, 2007). The origin story of the New Romantics is one that is also determinedly spatial and temporal, and one that has been subject to periodic reinvigoration and partial reinvention. Foremost, the rise of the New Romantics is popularly allied to Thatcherism and the shift to a more individualistic, hedonistic culture, summed up by music critic as follows: 'You got the New Romantics, and you got a kind of bright and shiny aspirational pop – a padded-shouldered version of pop – that was about nightclubs, about dressing up, about going out ... a shorthand for the aspirational end of Thatcherism in those years' (Maconie, 2013).

While a number of studies have effectively and forcefully disconnected the ideologies of Thatcherism and the rise of the New Romantics as a cohesive cultural phenomenon (cf. Nehring, 2007), the association between this musical brand and the Conservative politics of the 1980s continues to operate as a seductive frame of popular reference. Moreover, and despite those studies which identify Birmingham as a cradle of the New Romantic genre, it is the London club scene that is often cast as the 'home' of the movement in popular discourse (ibid.). As such, and somewhat ironically, the creative output of New Romantic bands is often characterised as the selective sentiment of the booming South East. In this way the scene plays its part in reproducing a North-South economic, political and cultural divide operating along spatial and social lines. Specifically, the New Romantic genre is critically characterised in opposition to the rise of a series of left-wing cultural products which were reacting to the dominant, totalising ideology of the time (Short, 1989: 175). It could, therefore, be seen as being socially, economically and politically at odds with the Midlands 'of the mind'. Heavy metal, as a voice of angst, decline and dissatisfaction, is a much easier fit with this spatial imaginary.

Track 10: Outro

> From Portugal to the United States to (of course) Norway, metal holds down a spot in the top ten – and usually top five – most listened to genres in every country included in the study [study of Spotify listening trends]. (Kelly, 2015)

To a greater extent, popular culture holds that the British Midlands is the 'home of heavy metal'; or, more explicitly, the British Midlands of the 1970s holds this accolade. This is the popular narrative as espoused worldwide by fans of the genre, the music press and, perhaps, a wider tranche of the public as a form of folklore. Put simply, heavy metal music is a significant – if not intrinsic – part of social constructions of the Midlands as a region by actors who place themselves as *ingroup* members of the metal community, and by some *outgroup* actors who have a commercial or cultural interest in framing discussions of the region (i.e. tourism and media institutions). It should be noted that heavy metal

is a global industry, diversified into a plethora of subgenres, produced in many national socio-political contexts (the politically framed thrash metal of Brazilian band Sepultura, the paganistic black metal of the Nordic band Burzum, the Mongolian folk metal of Tengger Cavalry) and consumed in an even wider array of them. And yet the narratives of metal, its defining features, its various codes (of dress, conduct and performance), however divergent from the template set by Sabbath and Priest and other 1970s metal bands, refer back to their source. For example, Jessie Hughes – as mentioned in the Intro – identifies himself as an American who plays music inspired by the Midlands at concerts in locations all over the world.

However, the home of metal narrative is only a partial (albeit dominant) perspective. It is one that overlooks or excludes other narratives of music and place-making, and one which downplays broader influences and networks. It is at once a product of relational flows, and other sites are key to understanding the rise of this phenomena. Yes heavy metal was fashioned in the Midlands, but it is a form of musical expression which is firmly grounded in the Merseybeat phenomenon and, more so, the broader British Blues Boom of the 1960s. Centred on clubs in London, Newcastle, Liverpool and Birmingham, it was linked by the movement of bands, aficionados and records both nationally and internationally.

As an extension of the above point, a cornerstone of the heavy metal origin story is its connections to class politics and the spatially articulated processes of (de)industrialisation. Here popular accounts of the inception of heavy metal music that portray a very real aura of environmental determinism are highly seductive, coming as they do with allied associations regarding sexuality and gender. And yet, as that body of literature linking musicality and space would remind us, the landscape of musical production and consumption is much more fluid. Here, for example, we are reminded that the Midlands can (and has) laid claim to other musical forms, including British Bhangra and the New Romantic movement. On this basis, we should be wary of imposing overly essentialised narratives which connect shifting social discourses with the cultural artefacts of the period. Nevertheless, these narratives serve a purpose in constructing and capturing social histories and cultural myths regarding space and place. These constructions serve (and are served by) academic debates, which have explored the existence and veracity of these 'origin stories' – inclusive of those that consider the relationship between music, social relations and regional formations.

So in focusing on a 'Midlands region' as the Home of Metal we are able to consider how 'regions' exist, in this case in relation to a particular cultural product and its associated artefacts and narratives. This is revealing of how we conceptualise the region as a concept and social construct because it implies that *other* Midlands regions exist, overlap, reinforce or challenge dominant political economic regional imaginaries. These constructions are not necessarily mutually exclusive, may take alternative territorial shapes around other loci (e.g. Bhangra, ethnic and multi-cultural hybrids, religion, class, place, football etc.) and yet reference a common regional vocabulary. As such we argue that the 'region' is something constantly made and remade by the interaction and negotiation of these plural and pluralistic regional possibilities.

This is in keeping with the accepted status of regions as being historically contingent, and, to paraphrase John Allen and colleagues, we should ask not only 'where' a region might exist, but also 'when'. In accordance with this view, regions 'arrive at the present moment trailing long histories: histories of economics and politics, of gender, class and ethnicities; and histories, too, of the many different stories which have been told about all of these' (Allen et al., 1998: 9). In this way the rapid and locally concentrated deindustrialisation of the UK economy from the 1960s onwards, the resultant economic and political upheavals and the rise of Thatcherism provide(d) an opportunity for people to reflect on change and identity and develop a set of expressions, shared experiences and a collective heritage.

In terms of the Midlands, heavy metal music forms part of this narrative maelstrom, constituting a part of a narrative toolbox that disaggregates the north and the south, the working class and the middle class. Critically, this may contradict the multi-sited origins of rock music and the broader socio-demographic trends apparent in the production and consumption of heavy metal. But, such circumstances unsettle an established, pervasive origin story built around industrial decline, selective social mobility and the entrenching of a two-nation politics (Jessop et al., 1990). In turn this origin story now plays its part in placing the Midlands in an international context, with the region serving as a form of musical mecca, with the international stars of heavy metal music paying homage to their roots when discussing their influences. More often as not making reference to Black Sabbath, Judas Priest and Diamond Head as pioneers of the genre, this connection is consistently invoked. This becomes all the more curious given the time that has elapsed since the 'golden age' of the early 1970s, the kaleidoscope of forms that heavy metal music now takes and the truly international character of its production and consumption. The Midlands has changed greatly since the 1970s, then, and its socio-economic character has altered greatly. It is, however, still the 'Home of Metal'.

Notes

1 In this regard we would note that the historical development of 'hard rock' music into heavy metal music has been thoroughly and deftly set out elsewhere, with the work of Weinstein (2000), Cope (2010) and Harrison (2010) being particularly informative. It is therefore not our intention to cover old ground but rather provide a brief synopsis, and draw out the spatial aspects to this transformation.

2 The international features of heavy metal music are an essential component for any narrative of the region of the Midlands as the Home of Metal and for understanding the social, economic and political significance of this musical form. However, we can only briefly touch on this here.

3 Again, we cannot expand on this point is great detail. However, a key aspect of Iommi's 'sound' is attributed to the loss of some his fingertips in an industrial accident. In overcoming this disability, he experimented with new techniques and equipment, compensating for diminished power and dexterity. This resulted in him forging his distinctive sound, which has provided a sonic template for metal as it would become known.

References

Allen J and Cochrane A (2007) Beyond the territorial fix: regional assemblages, politics and power. *Regional Studies* 41: 1161–1175.

Allen J, Massey DB and Cochrane A (1998) *Rethinking the Region*. New York: Routledge.

Amin A (2004) Regions unbound: towards a new politics of place. *Geografiska Annaler: Series B, Human Geography* 86: 33–44.

Arnett J (1996) *METALheads: Heavy Metal Music and Adolescent Alienation*. London: Westview.

Bounds J (2013) Birmingham travel tips: hear heavy metal on its home ground. *The Guardian,* 4 February 2013.

Butler J (1993) *Bodies That Matter: On the Discursive Limits of "Sex"*. New York: Routledge.

Butler J (1997) *The Psychic Life of Power: Theories in Subjection*. Stanford, Calif.: Stanford University Press.

Clarke L (2009) *An Earthquake Is Erupting: Music and Politics in Thatcher's Britain*. Adelaide: University of Adelaide.

Connell J and Gibson C (2003) *Sound Tracks: Popular Music, Identity, and Place*. London, New York: Routledge.

Cope AL (2010) *Black Sabbath and the Rise of Heavy Metal Music*. Farnham, Surrey: Ashgate.

Dee L (2009) The brutal truth: grindcore as the extreme realism of heavy metal, in G Bayer (ed) *Heavy Metal in Britain*. Aldershot: Ashgate, 53–73.

Dudrah R (2007) *Bhangra: Birmingham and Beyond*. Birmingham: Punch.

Dudrah RK (1998) British Bhangra music in Birmingham: alive, alive — hoi hoi. *Praxis: A Magazine of Contemporary Arts and Culture* 1: 20–22.

Flynn N and Taylor AP (1986) Inside the Rust Belt: an analysis of the decline of the West Midlands economy. 1: International and national economic conditions, *Environment and Planning A*, 18: 865–900.

Gibson C and Davidson D (2004) Tamworth, Australia's 'country music capital': place marketing, rurality, and resident reactions. *Journal of Rural Studies* 20: 387–404.

Glasper I. (2014) *Burning Britain: The History of UK Punk 1980–1984*. Oakland: PM Press.

Gross RL (1990) Heavy metal music: a new subculture in American society. *The Journal of Popular Culture* 24: 119–130.

Halford R (2000) Made in Hell. *Resurrection*. Metal God Records. Recorded 15 August 1998–27 June 2000, produced by Roy Z.

Halford R (2009) The return of "British Steel": Rob Halford Q&A. *Rolling Stone Magazine*, 24 June 2009

Halford R. (2015) *Heavy Metal Britannia*. BBC Four. Produced and directed by C Rodley.

Harrison LM (2010) Factory music: how the industrial geography and working-class environment of post-war Birmingham fostered the birth of heavy metal. *Journal of Social History* 44: 145–158.

Hill R, Lucas C and Riches G (2015) Metal and marginalization: researching at the edges of exteriority. *Metal Music Studies*, 1: 295–301.

Hudson R (2006) Regions and place: music, identity and place. *Progress in Human Geography* 30: 626–634.

Hudson R (2011) Geographies of economic decline, in A Leyshon, R Lee, P Sunley, and L McDowell (eds) *The Sage Handbook of Economic Geography*. London: Sage, 261–273.

Huggins M and Gregson K (2007) Northern songs, sporting heroes and regional consciousness. *Northern History* 44: 141–158.

Hughes J (2012) On the Road. *VICE*,17 July 2012.

Inglis I (2000) 'The Beatles are coming!' Conjecture and conviction in the myth of Kennedy, America, and the Beatles. *Popular Music and Society* 24: 93–108.

Jessop B, Bonnett K and Bromley S (1990) Farewell to Thatcherism? Neoliberalism and "new times". *New Left Review* (January/February): 81–102.

Jones M (Forthcoming) City-region building and geohistorical matters: New new localism and the new new regionalism. *Nordia Geographical Publications* 44: 4, 21–27. So the reference throughout should be Jones (2015) not Jones (forthcoming).

Jones M and MacLeod G (2004) Regional spaces, spaces of regionalism: territory, insurgent politics and the English question. *Transactions of the Institute of British Geographers* 29: 433–452.

Kelly K (2015) Spotify just discovered that heavy metal is more popular than pop music. *Noisey*. http://noisey.vice.com/en_uk/blog/spotify-metal-listeners [Access date 22/1/2016]

Kift D (2012) Brass bands and beat bands, poets and painters: a cross-cultural case study of mining culture and regional identity in the Ruhr area 1947–1966. *International Journal of Heritage Studies* 19(5): 1–16.

Krenske L and McKay J (2000) 'Hard and heavy': gender and power in a heavy metal music subculture. *Gender, Place & Culture* 7: 287–304.

Lord J (2015) Heavy Metal Britannia, in C Rodley (ed). *BBC Four: BBC*.

Lovering J (1998) The global music industry: contradictions in the commodification of the sublime, in A Leyshon, D Matless and G Revill (eds) *The Place of Music*. New York: Guildford Press, 31–57.

Macan E (1997) *Rocking the Classics: English Progressive Rock and the Counterculture*. New York: Oxford University Press.

Maconie S (2013) The Thatcher era's effect on British music. *NPR*. 12 April 2013. http://www.npr.org/2013/04/12/176952013/the-thatcher-eras-effect-on-british-music.

Marston SA, Jones JP and Woodward K (2005) Human geography without scale. *Transactions of the Institute of British Geographers* 30: 416–432.

Matless D (2010) Describing landscape: regional sites. *Performance Research* 15: 72–82.

McEwan C, Pollard J and Henry N (2005) The 'global' in the city economy: multicultural economic development in Birmingham. *International Journal of Urban and Regional Research* 29: 916–933.

Miller B (2011) Home of Metal exhibition rocks Birmingham Museum and Art Gallery's Gas Hall. *Culture24*, 24 June 2011. http://www.culture24.org.uk/history-and-heritage/art359038.

Mitchell T (1996) *Popular Music and Local Identity: Rock, Pop, and Rap in Europe and Oceania*. London: Leicester University Press.

Moore R (2009) The unmaking of the English working class: deindustrialisation, reification and the origins of heavy metal, in G Bayer (ed) *Heavy Metal Music in Britain*. Aldershot: Ashgate, 143–161.

Nayak A (2003) *Race, Place and Globalisation: Youth Cultures in a Changing World*. London: Bloomsbury.

Nehring N (2007) 'Everyone's given up and just wants to go dancing': from punk to rave in the Thatcher era. *Popular Music and Society* 30: 1–18.

Nilsson M (2009) No class? Class and class politics in British HEAVY METAL, in G Bayer (ed) *Heavy Metal in Britain*. Aldershot: Ashgate, 161–181.

O'Sullivan S (1993) No such thing as society: televsion and the apocolypse, in L Friedman (ed) *Fires Were Started: British Cinema and Thatcherism*. London: Wallflower Press, 223–243.

Osbourne O (2009) *I Am Ozzy*. London: Sphere.

Paasi A (1996) *Territories, Boundaries, and Consciousness: The Changing Geographies of the Finnish-Russian Border*. Chichester, England: J. Wiley & Sons.

Paasi A (2002) Place and region: regional worlds and words. *Progress in Human Geography* 26: 802–811.

Paasi A (2010) Regions are social constructs, but who or what 'constructs' them? Agency in question. *Environment and Planning A* 42: 2296–2301.

Peacock DK (1999) *Thatcher's Theatre: British Theatre and Drama in the Eighties*. Westport, Conn.: Greenwood Press.

Perone JE (2009) *Mods, Rockers, and the Music of the British Invasion*. Westport, Conn.: Praeger Publishers.

Prokkola E-K, Zimmerbauer K and Jakola F (2012) Performance of regional identity in the implementation of European cross-border initiatives. *European Urban and Regional Studies* 22(1): 104–117.

Ramnarine TK (2003) *Ilmatar's Inspirations: Nationalism, Globalisation, and the Changing Soundscapes of Finnish Folk Music*. Chicago: University of Chicago Press.

Rodríguez-Pose A and Crescenzi R (2008) Mountains in a flat world: why proximity still matters for the location of economic activity. *Cambridge Journal of Regions, Economy and Society* 1: 371–388.

Russell D (1983) Popular musical culture and popular politics in the Yorkshire textile districts 1880–1914, in J Walvin and J Walton (eds) *Leisure in Britain* pp. 99–116. Manchester Manchester University Press.

Schwartz RF (2007) *How Britain Got the Blues: The Transmission and Reception of American Blues Style in the United Kingdom*. Aldershot, England: Ashgate.

Short JR (1989) Yuppies, Yuffies and the New Urban Order. *Transactions of the Institute of British Geographers* 14: 173–188.

Spracklen K, Lucas C and Deeks M (2014) The construction of heavy metal identity through heritage narratives: a case study of extreme metal bands in the North of England. *Popular Music and Society* 37: 48–64.

Sterritt D (1993) Low hopes: Mike Leigh meets Margaret Thatcher, in L Friedman (ed) *Fires Were Started: British Cinema and Thatcherism* pp. 315–331. London: Wallflower Press.

Stradling R (1998) England's glory: sensibilities of place in English music, 1900–1950, in A Leyshon, D Matless and G Revill (eds) *The Place of Music* pp. 176-196. New York: Guildford Press.

Tatler B (2015) Heavy Metal Britannia, in C Rodley (ed). *BBC Four: BBC*.

Thompson EP (1964) *The Making of the English Working Class*. New York: Pantheon Books.

Trilling D (2007) Midlands should be proud of its heavy metal heritage. *New Statesman*, 30 July 2007.

Vainikka J (2013) The role of identity for regional actors and citizens in a splintered region: the case of Päijät-Häme, Finland. *Fennia* 191: 25–39.

Verden P, Dunleavy K and Powers CH (1989) Heavy metal mania and adolescent delinquency. *Popular Music and Society* 13: 73–82.

Watson A and Ward J (2013) Creating the right 'vibe': emotional labour and musical performance in the recording studio. *Environment and Planning A* 45: 2904–2918.

Webb P (2004) Interrogating the production of sound and place: the Bristol phenomenon, from Lunatic Fringe to worldwide Massive, in S Whiteley, A Bennett and S Hawkins (eds) *Music, Space and Place: Popular Music and Cultural Identity*. Aldershot: Ashgate, 66–89.

Weinstein D (2000) *Heavy Metal: The Music and Its Culture*. New York: Da Capo Press.

Wilkinson R (2010) How Judas Priest invented heavy metal. *The Guardian*, 21 May 2010.

Worley M (2013) Oi! Oi! Oi!: class, locality, and British punk. *Twentieth Century British History* 24(4): 606–636.

3 On Parochialism

John Tomaney

Attachments and Belongings

parochialism, n.

1. Parochial character or tendency; *esp.* confinement of one's interests to the local sphere; lack of global perspective; narrowness of view; petty provincialism.
2. Absorption in parish duties. *Obs. rare.*
3. (*Oxford English Dictionary.* Third edition, June 2005; online version June 2011. <http://www.oed.com/view/Entry/138042>; accessed 12 August 2011.)

Parochialism and provincialism are opposites. The provincial has no mind of his own, he does not trust what his eyes see until he has heard what the great metropolis towards which his eyes are ever turned has to say on any subject. This runs through all his activities. The parochial mentality on the other hand is never in any doubt about the social and artistic validity of his own parish. All great civilisations are based on parochialism: Greek, Israelite, English. Parochialism is a universal and deals with fundamentals (Kavanagh, 1952/2003: 237).

Why do we form attachments to place and develop a sense of local identification and belonging? How are these attachments expressed? What is the moral content of these relationships and their cultural and political implications? Humanistic geographers such as Tuan claim that 'attachment to the homeland appears to be a worldwide phenomenon', expressed in all cultures and economies, wherein, 'The city or land is viewed as mother, and it nourishes; place is an archive of fond memories and splendid achievements that inspire the present; place is permanent and hence reassuring to man, who sees frailty in himself and chance and flux everywhere' (1977: 154). Others object to this characterisation preferring to see place as a 'spatio-temporal event' and see local attachments as containing tendencies to essentialism, 'romanticisation' and reactionary politics (Massey, 1991, 2009). These claims underpin a call for a cosmopolitan ethic to replace national and local attachments as the foundation for political and cultural community (Amin, 2004; Nussbaum, 1996). This chapter addresses these questions in the context of recent debates about the nature of place, 'the local' and 'regionality'. I review the main perspectives in this debate and conclude none offers a satisfactory account of the *formation* and *content* of local identification, attachment and belonging and the role these play in the matter of *dwelling*. I outline why a more convincing treatment of this issue is important and suggest ways we might begin this task.

I seek to rescue local attachments and a sense of belonging from the condescension of the cosmopolites and, instead, to present a defence of *parochialism* as a mode of dwelling. Cosmopolitanism is a kind of provincialism, in Patrick Kavanagh's sense of the term; it doubts the social and artistic value of the parish. A parochial outlook values the local, its culture and solidarities, as a moral starting point and locus of ecological concern and a site for the development of virtues including commitment, fidelity, civility and nurture. I aim to substantiate these claims by reference to the 'art of the local' – that is, by examining the way in which a sense of place and local attachment and belonging are manifest in poetry and literature. I am interested in how poets and novelists, among others, are able to reconcile the role of the universal and the particular in human life in ways that might provide inspiration for social scientists (Saunders, 2010). Some poets, novelists and other artists, I suggest, mark the cultural and ecological bounds of their regions, but in ways that express an imaginative rather than a proprietorial interest in belonging (Bate, 2000: 280). In English-speaking literature I find this quality in works that emerge from the English Romantic tradition (see Stafford, 2010), and especially attempts by those twentieth century English writers and artists – such as Paul Nash, Joh-n and Myfanwy Piper, and Virginia Woolf, the 'Romantic Moderns' (Haycock, 2010; Harris, 2010) and the poet Basil Bunting (Tomaney, 2007) – to reconcile tradition and modernity, topography and topology, home and world. I find it also in much twentieth century Irish literature – notably Joyce, Kavanagh and Heaney (see Tomaney 2010b) – which seeks to reconcile the parish and the universe. In addition, it can be discovered in that twentieth century American poetic tradition that is deeply rooted in place and ecological concerns which includes the Black Mountain poets, Gary Snyder and beyond them Walt Whitman (Rasula, 2002), although of course it exists in many other cultures (see Tomaney 2010a for a treatment of some of these issues in Chinese culture).

In *The Republic*, Plato attributes the opening words in 'the ancient quarrel between philosophy and poetry' to Socrates. In *Poetic Justice*, Martha Nussbaum finds value in the novel as an instrument for generating social sympathy – a means of seeing the world from other perspectives: 'good literature is disturbing in a way that history and social science writing frequently are not' (1997: 5). Richard Rorty argues that cultural and political debates should draw upon 'inspirational value of great works of literature' (1998: 137). The use of literary sources in social science debates is well established. For instance, Shakespeare's history plays have been analysed by political scientists and others for the light they shed on timeless questions of the multi-faceted and contradictory motivations of citizens and leaders in different cultural and institutional contexts, whether in Rome or the Plantagenet court (Lupton, 2011; Murley and Sutton, 2006). There seems no reason not to apply this method to the study of the local. The value of novels and poetry in relation to debates about the local lies in the subtle ways that they can shed light on the uncertainties and possibilities associated human attachments and ask us think imaginatively about them (see Saunders, 2010).

Cosmopolitanism versus Localism

There are currently two predominant understandings of the local and regional in geographical literature (see Entrikin, 2011; Jonas, 2011; Pike, 2007). In the first, regions are understood as open and discontinuous spaces, constituted by social relationships and material, discursive and symbolic forms stretched across and through places, localities and regions. It adopts a topological rather than topographical approach to space and ultimately rejects the notion that regions are territorially bounded. 'Regions' are defined by their momentary place in global networks and by their relationship within and beyond predefined territorial boundaries. Regions are 'unbound' (Amin, 2004). Ideas of stable and clearly demarcated hierarchies of scale are eschewed in this perspective in favour of ideas of a 'throwntogetherness' (Massey, 2005), 'regional assemblage' or, 'multi-actor topological geometry' (Allen and Cochrane, 2007) in which places are produced by relational processes and 'rhizomatic networks' (Painter, 2008), 'an imbroglio of heterogeneous and more or less expansive hybrids' (Thrift, 1999: 317), or even superseded by 'site-based ontologies' (Marston et al., 2005). According to this perspective, the formation of local and regional attachments is a kind of modernist fetish reflecting the influence of Cartesian notions of bounded totalities which are essential to Western social science and find their expression in the 'cartographic anxiety' – i.e. the desire spatially to define and contain social and political processes. This is presented as deeply problematic and particularly associated with the contradictions of the European Enlightenment (Painter, 2008).[1] (If we take this argument further, and reject completely any notion of scale and spatial hierarchy in favour of a flat ontology as do Marston et al. [2005], questions of local attachment and belonging are redundant.) For cosmopolitan critics, local identification expresses 'a tendency to essentialise regional culture, attributing to [regions] a new sort of organic unity' and represents 'the hankering for some model of lasting identity', in which the 'the region presents itself as a trope of a "purer" value – immutable and "persistent identity"' (Dainotto, 1996: 487, 494, 502).

A second perspective abjures the 'discursive of erasure of place' (Escobar, 2001: 141) and claims concerning a 'dramatically delocalised world' (Appadurai, 1995: 204). Instead (shifting) geographies, boundaries and multiple scales – and the identities associated with them – continue to matter 'as expressions of social practice, discourse and power' (Paasi 2004: 541). Boundaries may be porous but abstract notions of globalisation, founded on globally networked forms of social life, neglect the complex ways in which people continue to live locally, albeit in altered ways (Appadurai, 1995; Escobar, 2001). Moreover, 'despite the apparent post-modern fragmentation of identity, discourses of belonging constructed around place remain important' (Graham: 2000: 95). Local attachments that emphasise belonging involve the search for practical solidarities, which emerge 'from the shared ways of life and experiences in place and territory that give individuals a sense being part of a collective' (Claval and Entrikin, 2004: 44).

A concern with the territoriality of human life acknowledges the persistence of 'scalar ontologies' (Jones and McLeod, 2004: 448) and 'the process whereby a space achieves a distinct *identity* as a place', albeit a place understood as 'an imagined state or moral location' (Gupta and Ferguson, 1992: 8, 10; Entrikin, 1999), rather than simply as a physically or administratively bounded territory. In this context, globalisation does not annihilate space by time, but reconstitutes it so that 'People continue to *construct* some sort of boundaries around their places, however permeable, and to be grounded in local socio-natural practices, no matter how changing and hybridised those grounds and practices might turn out to be' (Escobar, 2001: 147). Places are directly experienced phenomena of the lived world and hence are full with meanings, with real objects, on-going activities and intensions (Relph, 1976: 141). Thus, even in the global era, our attention must focus on *dwelling* as well as *movement* (Burawoy, 2000) in the production of human order. The formation of local attachments, however, is a complex process drawing on diverse – and at times contradictory – influences including, 'ideas of nature, landscape, the built environment, culture/ethnicity, dialects, economic success/recession, periphery/centre relations, marginalisation, stereotypic images of a people/community, both of 'us' and 'them', actual/invented histories, utopias and diverging arguments on the identification of people' (Paasi, 2003: 477).

With some notable exceptions (such as the work of Anssi Paasi), recent contributions to the debate about 'the local', on investigation, turn out to contain few systematic analyses or detailed empirical studies of the production of local identities and attachments and modes of local belonging. Despite claims about the importance of 'scalar ontologies', there are very few efforts to specify the formation and content of these. On the other hand, the literature on the 'relational' region builds strongly on a normative commitment to cosmopolitan values in which 'the basic rhetorical opposition between the liberal cosmopolitan and the illiberal local remains influential' (Calhoun, 2003: 532). The working assumption of the cosmopolitan literature is that local attachments produce 'a politics hooked around the myth of a regionalised identity' (Amin, 2004: 37), although there are few empirical studies of this process on which to found such claims.

The assumption here is that local particularisms and attachments are inherently exclusionary. Events such as the break-up of the USSR, the Yugoslav war of the 1990s and tribalism and regionalism in Africa and Asia are offered as evidence (Massey, 2005: 5–8). Cresswell notes how this understanding has come to predominate in human geography:

> the humanistic conception of place, which has been the predominant understanding of place since the 1970s, is simply too fixed, too bounded and too rooted in

> the distant past. As a consequence of these notions of fixity, boundedness, and rootedness, place too often becomes the locus of exclusionary practices. People connect a place with a particular identity and proceed to defend it against the threatening outside with its different identities (Creswell, 2009: 176)

This new approach has 'problematised the notion of local belonging' (Massey, 2006: 35). Amin goes further and proposes 'a new politics of place' free of fixity and boundedness (Amin, 2004). Much of this argument rests on general claims about the porosity of territories in the face of intensifying material and cultural flows ('globalisation'), so that places are understood as 'spatio-temporal events' characterised by 'throwntogetherness' (Massey, 2005: 130, 140). In the face of such processes Amin advocates a 'heterotopic sense of place' which 'assumes no local cultural or economic coherence' (Amin, 2004: 40). In this view local cultural attachments underpin 'a politics of local regard and local defence' and 'a conservationist regional identity that can be profoundly closed and exclusionary' (Amin, 2004: 37, 35). Although Amin professes a desire 'not to diminish the validity of a politics of place or to deny place attachment' (Amin, 2004: 37), in practice, he has nothing positive to say about the content of such attachments. Instead local attachments are treated as a foil against which to measure his progressive cosmopolitanism: 'Many threads are woven in narrating a coherent regional community, from stories of colonisation and common external enemy, to stories of heroism and resistance, as well as the scripting of a regional folk culture' (Amin, 2004: 37).

However, it is possible to think of examples of the representation of the local which do not correspond to this caricature – for instance, we might point to cases of intense local attachments which have produced great art with universal appeal such as Hardy's Wessex novels, Vermeer's paintings of Delft or the Aboriginal art of Emily Kame Kngwarreye. Yet from a cosmopolitan perspective, local cultural attachments are inevitably constraining, while a universal outlook is inherently liberating. Rootedness is essentially problematic. Dainotto contends, for instance, that regionalist literature bequeaths us 'only idyllic regions and their perfect communities' (2000: 17). He goes so far as to suggest that regionalism is part of a continuum with fascism, which seeks to present societies as unproblematically unified and identifies 'the reactionary trait of the literature of place: it tries to take the question away from the space of politics' (Dainotto, 2000: 33). Amin 'rejects an idea of the region as a place of reminiscence and cultural preservation' and offers a politics beyond local attachments proffering, 'a cosmopolitan ethos of solidarity and rights … as a form of local response to global poverty, ethnic intolerance and Empire' (2004: 42). Echoing the Stoic Diogenes, the cosmopolitans offer a world away from the 'comfort of local truths (quoted in Nussbaum, 1996: 15). Nussbaum acknowledges that, culturally, cosmopolitanism may seem dry and abstract because 'it offers only reason and the love of humanity, which may seem at times less colourful than other sources of belonging' (Nussbaum, 1996: 15), but it is nevertheless morally superior to the supposed *Sturm und Drang* of local attachments.

One of the problems of judging the efficacy of the critique of the local and its appeal is that little evidence is brought to bear in support of it. Moreover, epistemologically it operates in relation to binaries it affects to disavow. Amin (2004) makes a contrast, for instance, between the claims of English regionalism (insular/bad) and Scottish nationalism (cosmopolitan/good), although he does not offer any evidential support. (Are local identities in Manchester more closed than those in Glasgow? How do we measure this and what might this mean?) Moreover, there are few clues as to how this new politics of place can be enacted, despite its apparent abstract appeal.

There is an explicit rejection of its cultural and political value in much writing about the local. Massey (2009) acknowledges the role of the local in the construction of the global, but seeks to represent the local as constituted by 'wider processes', while worrying that a local sense of place ends up as 'almost necessarily reactionary' (Massey, 1991: 27). Her account of cosmopolitan Kilburn in inner north-west London presents it as exhibiting a 'global sense of place' characterised by complete cultural openness, a function of its multi-ethnic character (Massey, 1991). Underlying this account, however, is an implicit acknowledgement that although Kilburn is constituted by global flows and constantly being refashioned, nevertheless it exhibits a distinctive character (see also Massey, 2009). It makes sense to think of the local as embodying a distinctive identity – otherwise how could we speak of it? Once we think of Kilburn as a distinctive place we have bounded it imaginatively, albeit notwithstanding the porousness of the boundaries. Moreover, it makes just as much sense to imagine that its residents could develop attachments to it. Implicit in Massey's own analysis, then, is a kind of imaginative boundary-making. It is not my purpose to argue in favour of a 'removal of the local from any implication in wider processes' (Massey, 2009: 412), rather it is to emphasise the way that imaginative boundary-making can take place within the context of these wider process and that this need not be 'inherently reactionary'. Indeed, local identities may provide the conditions for a 'progressive' mode of dwelling within these wider processes. This possibility is either overlooked or rejected by the cosmopolitans, but it is the form and content of this mode of dwelling which interests me and which, I believe, has been given insufficient attention in these debates to date.

As Calhoun (2003) notes, cosmopolitanism generally regards particular attachments as a sort of intellectual error that educated people will move beyond. Local solidarities are seen as inherently sectional, while defence of community and place is seen as irrational, backward looking and reactionary, even if people are being beckoned to futures that are uncertain or threatening. Indeed, as Dirlik complains, 'To speak of places is to invite suspicions of parochialism, reaction and backwardness' (1999: 53). But, local communities and institutions are social achievements created collectively in face of conflict, and roots in 'traditional culture' and 'community' may provide a basis for collective resistance to inequitable social change (Harvey, 1996: 19–45; 2009). Cosmopolitan accounts permit, at best, 'a thin appreciation of the sociological character of group formation and membership, including changes in 'belonging' and efforts to transcend particular solidarities', while such accounts fail to grasp 'the reasons why "thick attachments" to particular solidarities still matter – whether in the forms of nations, ethnicities, local communities, or religions' (Calhoun, 2003: 532; see also Bok, 1996; Barber, 1996; McConnell, 1996).

Our modes of reasoning and our forms of cultural and political action are rooted in particular moral communities and historical traditions as well as in our wider engagements. The cosmopolitan perspective tells us little about why and how attachments are formed, only that they are misguided and reactionary. Yet, there are dangers in preferring a politics 'abstracted from the material world of experience in particular places', an approach which, according to David Harvey, through its promotion of universal considerations 'drove out sensitivity to the particularities of environment, milieu, collective memory, community, myth, built forms', (1996: 314).[2] Moreover, according to Popke: 'Far from instilling a responsibility across distance, a one-size-fits-all cosmopolitan sensibility can be a hindrance to the development of a context-specific ethics' (2007: 514).

Raymond Williams' political and academic writings pointed to a form of politics based on 'militant particularism' that grew out of ordinary culture (Williams, 1988), but his views about the local were best expressed in his novel *Border Country* (Williams, 1962). The local here is imbued with external influences, connections and relationships but nevertheless retains a cultural distinctiveness and moral particularity, which is the basis for wider engagements. This is another version of the cosmopolitan ethos of solidarity, then, but one in which 'the struggle for place in the concrete is a struggle against power and the hegemony of abstractions' (Dirlik, 2001: 23).

Featherstone (2005) though worries about the 'prisonhouse of particularism', which arises when we fail to realise that political struggles must be unbounded. As evidence, Featherstone proffers the case of the 'Newcastle Port Strike of 1768', attributing its relative success in achieving its objective to the relationships that Tyneside workers developed with their fellows on the Thames. The strike is understood as 'place-located event' through which unbounded political identities and agencies were constructed. However the events described by Featherstone can be interpreted with a different emphasis. The strike of 1768 is more commonly known as the Keelmen's Strike. The keelmen were a tightly knit, mutually supportive and self-reliant group of militant workers that operated the keels – flat bottomed boats that transferred coal downriver from staithes to waiting colliers for export (Fewster, 2011). The keelmen inhabited the warren of chares in Sandgate in Newcastle upon Tyne. The strike of 1768 was one of many through the 17th, 18th and 19th centuries which emerged from this tradition of local militancy and were directed at the Company of Hostmen who monopolised the Tyne coal trade. The 1768 strike was certainly significant because it was linked to wider conflicts, although more so perhaps because, for the first time, the keelmen employed a lawyer and sought statutory redress to longstanding grievances. Industrialisation, the introduction of steam tugs and the dredging and embanking of the River Tyne ultimately undermined the position of the keelmen. But their legacy lingers locally and beyond, not least in their contribution to

Tyneside song. (The most famous of these was 'Weel may the keel row', which ended up as a British Army marching tune).[3] In short, a fuller explanation of the 1768 strike needs merely to situate in wider networks, but also to embed it in an account of *local history.*

The attempt to situate the local in wider processes contains its own dangers, mainly failing to account for the persistence of local attachments and neglecting their potential value. We are left with the question of how to arrive at a fuller conception of local commitment and belonging as a basis for culture, politics and dwelling, which recognises 'the inter-relationships between place, self and community' (Entrikin, 1997) and 'the possibility of a world where respect for the validity of every tradition will issue in the creation and maintenance of a salubrious political space' (Heaney, 1995: no page given).

Belonging

Humanistic geographers note that local attachments are persistent and universal. The cosmopolitan critics tell us that these attachments are wrong, but not why they endure. The 'lure of the local', as Lippard (1997) notes, is an enormously powerful cultural and even spiritual force that deserves more than condescension ('scripting of folk culture'). As Seamus Heaney notes, 'We are dwellers, we are namers, we are lovers, we make homes and search for histories' (1981: 148–9). Phenomenological insights stress how our relationship with place determines our identity as human beings (Heidegger, 1934, 1971; Merleau-Ponty, 1962), so that 'it is not merely human identity that is tied to place or locality, but the very possibility of being the sort of creature that can engage with a world (and, more particularly, with the objects and events within it), that can think about that world, and can find itself in the world' (Malpas, 1999: 8).

Belonging is a *task* that requires an individual working to maintain a sense of unity or integrity while engaged in ongoing, dynamic and developing interactions within the physical, historical and social landscape of their being. Belonging, therefore, is not something that is given as a right or bestowed as a privilege or tied to land ownership or length of residency (Miller, 2003: 415–6). Belonging can affect commitment rather than possession and is a means of nurturing 'our capacity for awareness of the myriad histories that constitute a place, and from these rich materials draw inspiration to shape our sense of self and community' (Bunting, 2009: 275). According to bell hooks, reflecting on her identity as a black Kentuckian woman, a sense of belonging concerns 'seeking a fidelity to place' and 'a vital sense of covenant and commitment' (hooks, 2008: 65), what Tuan (1976) calls, 'geopiety'. An ethics of the local may be founded on a recognition of politics of 'becoming' (Gibson-Graham, 2003), but that must also include a process of 'becoming native' to place (Jackson, 1996); uprooting and planting must go hand in hand (Bate, 2000: 275).

An ecological concern is generally absent from discussions of the new politics of place (Dirlik, 2001) – it is barely mentioned by Amin (2004). But, in identifying a 'sense of place', Seamus Heaney notes, 'It is to the stable element, the land itself, that we must look for continuity' (1981: 149). A 'place-based imagination' must be 'grounded' in topography and, as a consequence, in recognition of the persistence of boundaries and boundary-making (Dirlik, 2001). For Massey, in such thinking lies the danger of a romanticisation of 'the eternity of the hills' (2005: 140), which she associates with strong attachments to place. She considers Skiddaw, a mountain in the English Lake District, and asks how its monumental presence can be reconciled with the notion of place as a 'spatio-temporal event' (2005, 2006). She notes that the mountains of the Lake District were laid down 500 million years ago 'and floated about the planet as the continents rearranged themselves' (2005: 134). According to Massey the land is not a stable element – 'the rocks of Skiddaw are immigrant rocks, just passing through' (2005: 137), the Cumbrian massif as evanescence. Even if we find value in this formulation, it does not explain why the mountains contribute to the sense of a bounded place on the part of the people who live (or have lived) beside them. Instead, moving mountains form part of the normative objection to 'groundedness'.

While Nussbaum worries that her abstract cosmopolitanism lacks local colour, Massey insists that the idea of the Lake District as an 'event' should not preclude a sense of wonder; Cumbria, she observes, straddled the Equator in the Ordovician age when Skiddaw was formed. So, we can only wonder at the transience of Skiddaw; to romanticise it is to flirt with the notion of places having timeless qualities and this is a slippery slope to a politics of exclusion. Wordsworth, however, saw the mountain differently:

> What was the great Parnassus' self to Thee
> Mount Skiddaw? In his natural sovereignty
> Our British Hill is nobler far; he shrouds
> His double front among Atlantic clouds,
> And pours forth streams more sweet than Castaly
> ('Pelion and Ossa flourish side by side').[4]

Art of the Local

For Wordsworth Skiddaw is not ephemeral; it is monumental. It is a looming presence shaping lives and cultures. Wordsworth's Lake District is a physical and imaginative world in which he sought to dwell and define a 'scalar ontology':

> A blended holiness of earth and sky,
> Something that makes this individual spot,
> This small abiding-place of many men,
> A termination, and a last retreat,
> A centre, come from wheresoe'er you will,
> A whole without dependence or defect,

Made for itself, and happy in itself,
Perfect contentment, Unity entire.
('Home at Grasmere' or Book I of 'The Recluse' lines 110–151)

Wordsworth then offers a provocation to the 'new politics of space'.[5] In his essay 'Sense of Place', Seamus Heaney identifies how, for Wordsworth, 'the Westmoreland mountains were so much more than a picturesque backdrop', 'they were rather companionable and influential' affecting the psyche of those lived with and beside them and how any 'temperate understanding of the relationship between a person and his place' requires an awareness of 'the way the surface of the earth can be accepted into and be a steadying influence upon the quiet depths of the mind' (1981: 145). For Wordsworth:

Those fields, those hills – what could they less – had laid
Strong hold on his affections, were to him
A pleasurable feeling of blind love,
The pleasure which there is in life itself
('Michael')

Malpas notes, 'the same basic idea of human life as essentially a life of location, of self-identity as a matter of identity found in place, and of places themselves as somehow suffused with the 'human', is common to the work of poets and novelists from all parts of the globe and in relation to all manner of landscapes and localities' (1999: 6). Poets, novelists and artists typically have shown a sustained interested in questions of local belonging and attachment to place and deal with these questions with subtly and depth, avoiding caricature; they seem well equipped to grasp their ambiguities, contradictions, absurdities and comedy, as well as their appeal and potential. Specifically, poetry provides a peculiar articulation of the relationship between history and nature and people and place, 'because it is experiential, not descriptive. Whereas the biologist, the geographer and the Green activist have *narratives* of dwelling, a poem may be a *revelation* of dwelling' (Bate, 2000: 266). Bate coins the term ecopoetics to express this phenomenon: 'Ecopoetics asks in what respects a poem may be a making (Greek *poiesis*) of the dwelling-place – the prefix eco- is derived from Greek *oikos*, 'the home or place of dwelling' (Bate, 2000: 75). Ecopoetry (and other forms of the 'art of the local') contributes critically to defining the 'proprieties of place' (Sanders, 1993: 116).

Often it is an intense engagement with the local than allows the artist to develop insights into the question of how we should live. According to the English novelist, Graham Swift, the cosmopolitan ethos tends to produce poor art and little acumen:

> Writers are always trying to touch, to grasp the universal. And the way not to do this, it seems to me, is to write the avowedly universal, global, cosmopolitan book – the sort book that ought to be written in Esperanto. The key to

> the universal is always the local, if only because all experience is and must be local, all experienced is placed. If I read a book set in China or Peru, or indeed Nice, a great many local references may pass me by, but that doesn't matter, it even helps, because through them I nonetheless sense the true, the genuinely local texture of life as its really lived (2009: 310–11).

Ralph Vaughan Williams, the English composer, concurs with this view: 'I believe it is better to be vitally parochial than to be an emasculate cosmopolitan. The great names in music were at first local and the greatest of all, John Sebastian Bach remained a local musician all his life' (2007: 81). Vaughan Williams (1963) also notes that Bach scarcely left Leipzig during his musical career.

Nineteenth century romantics such as Wordsworth were concerned with a poetic emplacement in search of 'harmony/Home-felt, and Home created' ('Written at Evening') in the face of unsettling urbanisation and industrialisation. But great modernist writers also saw the local (albeit urban rather than pastoral) as the moral starting point. As Patrick Kavanagh noted, James Joyce was a great parishioner and *Ulysses*, among many other things, is a book about life in Dublin. Joyce's attitude to his Irish and Dublin identity was complex and changed over time (Kiberd, 1996, 2009; Gillespie, 2001) but was perennially concerned with 'the complex and mutually dependent relationship between the universal and the particular' (Cheng, 2001: 14). Joyce knew his Irishness – for better or worse – was inescapable:

> 'What do you want to write?' [James] Joyce asked [of Arthur Power[6]]. 'Something on the model of the French satirists.' 'You will never do it', said Joyce decisively, 'You are an Irishman and you must write in your own tradition. Borrowed styles are not good. You must write what is in your blood and not what is your brain.' Power objected, as Joyce might once have done, that he was tired of nationality and wanted to be international, like all great writers. 'They were national first', Joyce contended, 'and it was the intensity of their own nationalism which made them international in the end, as in the case of Turgenev. You remember his *Sportsman's Notebook*, how local it was — and yet out of that germ he became a great international writer. For myself, I always write about Dublin, because if I can get to the heart of Dublin I can get to the heart of all cities of the world. In the particular is contained the universal.' 'But how do you feel about being Irish?' asked Power. Joyce responded, 'I regret it for the temperament it has given me.' (Ellman, 1983: 505)

The tensile relationship between the local and the universal is a recurring theme in modern Irish letters. TS Eliot claimed that for WB Yeats the intensity of his Irishness was critical to the universal appeal of his greatest work (Eliot, 1975: 251–252). Patrick Kavanagh, Seamus Heaney and John McGahern have all explored the relationship directly. According to McGahern: 'Everything interesting begins with one person in one place. … The universal is the local, but with the walls taken away. Out of the particular we come on what is general' (McGahern, 2009: 11). McGahern's Leitrim-set novels – especially *Amongst Women* and *That They May Face the Rising Sun*, with their themes of love and betrayal, family discord, history and myth, home and exile in the context of a deep engagement with the ordinary culture of a particular place, bear witness to his axiom.

If great poets and novelists see the local as the starting point for understanding the world and embed their work in the particularities of place this does not imply a static or timeless view. Wendell Berry's novels and poetry emerge from intense engagement with his Kentucky home-world, but in his poem 'The Sycamore' (Berry, 1987), the tree stands as a metaphor for a place that is far from timeless or idyllic, but nevertheless exhibits a kind of coherence.

It is the intensity of the gaze according to Berry that reveals the distinctiveness of place. Accordingly: 'The better I know my place, the less it looks like other places and the more it looks like itself. It is imagination, and only imagination, that can give standing to these distinctions' (Berry, 2007a: 599). In turn, this places weight on the writer as a guardian of place: 'Without a complex knowledge of one's place, and without the faithfulness to one's place on which such knowledge depends, it is inevitable that the place will be used carelessly, and eventually destroyed. … And so I look upon the sort of regionalism that I am talking about not just as a recurrent literary phenomenon, but as a necessity of civilisation and of survival' (Berry, 2007b: 39). Poetry itself becomes part of the place-making activity: ecopoetics. Berry's poetry is dedicated to this task and invests places with a sacral quality born of devotion (see 'How to be a poet', Berry, 2006).

Like his fellow Kentuckian bell hooks (2009), Berry's relationship with place rests on a call for fidelity (see 'The Current', Berry, 2006). A fidelity to place need not lead to romanticisation or introversion. Places are characterised by disputes which act as a simulacrum of larger conflicts. In his (ironically) titled 'Epic', Patrick Kavanagh, the arch parishioner, captures the petty quarrel between the Duffys and the McCabes over the march (or field boundary) in County Monaghan, but, in truth, asks the poem, is it any different from the larger disputes that history and art judges important? Homer's ghost disturbs the poet: 'He said: I made the Iliad from such/A local row' ('Epic', Kavanagh, 2005; see Tomaney, 2010b for a fuller analysis of Kavanagh's outlook and his place in Irish culture). Similarly, emplacement is the basis for engagement with the world:

> If you are not yourself placed, then you wander the world like a sightseer with no gauge for measuring what you see. Local knowledge is the grounding for global knowledge … those who have no parish, those who navigate ceaselessly among the postal zones and area codes … are a danger not just to their parish, but to the planet. (Sanders, 1993: 114)

Provincialism and Parochialism

> Mr Daedelus was himself a renegade from the Nationalist ranks: he professed cosmopolitanism. But a man that was of all countries was of no country – you must first have a nation before you have art. (James Joyce, *Stephen Hero*, quoted in Richard, 2001: 87)

Parochialism speaks of care for one's parish, including 'the resident alien, settled foreigners and non-native sojourners'. Parochialism is not an end state but one of becoming; we are always becoming native. The poets crucially test the ground between the local and the universal, the particular and the cosmopolitan, in ways that social scientists often struggle to do. Parochialism does not then concern an inherent 'lack of global perspective' or an inevitable disregard for the other. Rather like religious faith, parochialism persists because 'it encodes needs and longings which will not simply evaporate at the touch of tough-minded analysis' (Eagleton, 2009: 90). It provides a means of living in the world and transcending the 'grossly reductive binary opposition between atavistic traditionalism and a liberal, pluralist, enlightened world order on the other' (Eagleton, 1997: 7; see also Gidwani, 2006). Poets and novelists allow us imaginatively to inhabit local worlds through the use of tropes and narrative forms that plausibly thread together complex and particularistic inter-relationships among space, place and environment (Entrikin, 1997) so that 'there is no necessary contradiction between the ideas of the "universal" and the "local" or the "national", but that, on the contrary, there are *only* local universalisms (and for that matter, only "local cosmopolitanisms", where "cosmopolitan" is taken to describe a particular way of registering selfhood in a particular time and place)' (Lazarus, 2011: 133–4).

This has implications for local politics. Václav Havel, poet-politician, provides a good reckoning:

> our country is where it is, its landscape is beautiful in certain ways and devastated in others, its natural resources are structured in such-and-such a way, we speak the languages we speak, we have our own historical traditions and customs, the political right and left are the way they are here and not the way they elsewhere, and no matter how much we might want to, we can scarcely hope to change these things entirely. Why not accept all this as fact? Why not try to understand the inner content of this fact, the potential, the problems and hopes connected with it? And why not deal with it in the most appropriate and adequate way? (Havel, 1992: 125)

The cosmopolites offer a world beyond belonging, shaped by global cultural and material flows. However well intentioned, cosmopolitan appeals typically devalue the ways in which people depend on local solidarities to solve practical problems in their lives (Calhoun, 2003). The obstacles to achieving larger solidarities are formidable and, ultimately, require the generation of abstractions which connect and explain distinctive local experiences but, as Patrick Kavanagh reminds us, that process must begin from an appreciation of the social and artistic value of the parish.

Notes

1 For a critique of the notion of regionality as 'Eurocentric', using evidence from Chinese culture, see Tomaney (2010a).

2 Harvey is concerned with developing a spatialised Marxism founded on an awareness of the place of 'local' politics. Marx himself maintained that aim of the Working Men's International Association was to be a 'bond of union rather than a controlling force', stating that, 'In each part of the world, some special aspect of the problem presents itself, and the workmen there address themselves to its consideration in their own way. Combinations among workmen cannot be absolutely identical in Newcastle and in Barcelona, in London and in Berlin' (Marx, 1871: no page).

3 As I came thro' Sandgate/Thro' Sandgate, thro' Sandgate/As I came thro' Sandgate/I heard a lassie sing:/'O, weel may the keel row/The keel row, the keel row/O weel may the keel row/That my laddie's in.' (Thompson et al., 1827)

4 All quotations are from Wordsworth (2000). Of course Wordsworth also had a global outlook exemplified in poems such as 'French Revolution' ('Not favoured spots alone, but the whole earth') or 'To Toussaint L'Ouverture' ('a breathing of the common wind'). This tension between the universal and particular in the romantic imagination can be identified as an ongoing one in English letters (Tomaney, 2007).

5 See Bate (2000), Cooper (2008) and Kerrigan (1985) for detailed critical studies of Wordsworth's treatment of place. Wordsworth created poetic boundaries around the Lake District. These in turn were challenged by later Cumbrian poets, such as Norman Nicholson, who sought to recast these imaginative limits. This experience is common and provides evidence for McIntyre's contention that membership of communities does not entail self-acceptance of the moral limitations of the particularity of those forms of community. Indeed, 'rebellion against my identity is always one possible mode of expressing it' (1980: 221).

6 Arthur Power (1891–1984): Irish writer and journalist.

References

Allen J and Cochrane A (2007) Beyond the territorial fix: regional assemblages, politics and power. *Regional Studies*, 41(9): 1161–1151.

Amin A (2004) Regions unbound: towards a new politics of place. *Geografiska Annaler* 86B: 33–44.

Appadurai A (1995) The production of the locality, in R Fardon (ed) *Counterworks*. London: Routledge.

Barber B (1996) Constitutional faith, in J Cohen (ed) *For Love of Country*. Boston, MA: Beacon Press.

Bate J (2000) *The Song of the Earth*. London: Picador.

Berry B (2006) *Given: Poems*. Berkeley, Ca: Counterpoint.

Berry W (2007a) American Imagination and the Civil War. *Sewanee Review* 115(4): 587–604.

Berry W (2007b) The regional motive, in VB Canizaro (ed) *Architectural Regionalism. Collected Writings on Place, Identity, Modernity and Tradition*. New York, NY: Princeton Architectural Press.

Berry B (1987) *Collected Poems, 1957–1982*. New York, NY: North Point Press.

Bok S (1996) From part to whole, in J Cohen (ed) *For Love of Country*. Boston, MA: Beacon Press.

Bunting M (2009) *The Plot. A Biography of an English Acre*. London: Granta.
Burawoy M (2000) *Global Ethnography: Forces, Connections and Imaginations in a Postmodern World*. Berkeley: University of California Press.
Calhoun C (2003) Belonging' in the cosmopolitan imaginary. *Ethnicities* 3 (4): 531–568.
Cheng V (2001) 'Terrible queer creatures': Joyce, cosmopolitanism and the inauthentic Irishman, in MP Gillespie (ed) *James Joyce and the Fabrication of an Irish Identity*. (European Joyce Studies 11). Amsterdam: Editions Rodopi.
Claval P and Entrikin JN (2004) Cultural geography: place and landscape between continuity and change, in G Benko and U Strohmayer (eds) *Human Geography: A History for the 21st Century*. London: Arnold.
Cooper D (2008) The poetics of place and space: Wordsworth, Norman Nicholson and the Lake District. *Literature Compass* 5(4): 807–821.
Cresswell T (2009) Place, in R Kitchin and N Thrift (eds) *International Encyclopedia of Human Geography*. Oxford, UK: Elsevier, 169–77.
Dainotto R (1996) 'All the regions do smilingly revolt': The literature of place and region. *Critical Inquiry* 22(3): 486–505.
Dainotto R (2000) *Place in Literature: Regions, Cultures, Communities*. Ithaca: Cornell University Press.
Dirlik A (1999) Globalism and the politics of place, in P Dicken, PF Kelly, L Kong, K Olds, and H Yeung (eds) *Globalisation and the Asia Pacific: Contested Territories*. London: Routledge.
Dirlik A (2001) Place-based imaginations: globalism and the politics of place, in R Prazniak and A Dirlik (eds) *Places and Politics in an Age of Globalisation*. Lanham, MD: Rowan and Littlefield.
Eagleton T (1997) The ideology of Irish studies. *Bullán: An Irish Studies Journal* 3(1): 5–14.
Eagleton T (2009) *Reason, Faith and Revolution. Reflections on the God Debate*. (The Terry Lectures). New Haven, Conn: Yale University Press.
Eliot TS (1975) *Selected Prose*. London: Faber and Faber.
Ellman R (1983) *James Joyce*. Revised Edition. Oxford: Oxford University Press.
Entrikin N (1997) Place and region 3. *Progress in Human Geography*, 21(2): 263–268.
Entrikin N (1999) Political community, identity and place. *International Sociology* 14(3): 269–282.
Entrikin N (2011) Region and regionalism, in J Agnew and D Livingstone (ed) *The Sage Handbook of Geographical Knowledge*. Los Angeles, CA: Sage.
Escobar A (2001) Culture sits in places: reflections on globalism and subaltern strategies of localisation. *Political Geography*, 20(2): 139–174.
Featherstone D (2005) Towards the relational construction of militant particularisms: or why the geographies of past struggles matter for resistance to neoliberal globalisation. *Antipode*, 37(2): 250–271.
Fewster J (2011) *The Keelmen of Tyneside: Labour Organisation and Conflict in the North East Coal Industry, 1600–1830*. Woodbridge: Boydell Press.
Gibson-Graham J-K (2003) An ethics of the local. *Rethinking Marxism* 15(1): 49–74.
Gidwani V (2006) Subaltern cosmopolitanism as politics. *Antipode* 38(1): 7–21.
Gillespie MP (ed) (2011)*James Joyce and the Fabrication of an Irish Identity*. (European Joyce Studies 11). Amsterdam: Editions Rodopi.
Graham B (2000) The past in place: historical geographies of identity, in B Graham and C Nash (eds) *Modern Historical Geographies*. Harlow: Pearson Education.
Gupta A and Ferguson J (1992) Beyond 'culture': space identity and the politics of difference. *Cultural Anthropology* 7(1): 6–23.
Harris A (2010) *Romantic Moderns: English Writers, Artists and the Imagination from Virginia Woolf to John Piper*. London: Thames and Hudson.
Harvey D (1996) *Justice, Nature and the Geography of Difference*. Oxford: Blackwell.

Harvey D (2009) *Cosmopolitanism and the Geographies of Freedom*. New York, NY: Columbia University Press.
Haycock D (2010) *A Crisis of Brilliance*. London: Old Street Publishing.
Havel V (1992). *Summer Meditations. On Politics, Morality and Civility in a Time of Transition*. London: Faber and Faber.
Heaney S (1981) *Preoccupations: Selected Prose, 1968–1978*. New York, NY: Farrar, Straus & Giroux.
Heaney S (1995) *Crediting Poetry*, Nobel Lecture, December 7th, Stockholm. Available at: http://nobelprize.org/nobel_prizes/literature/laureates/1995/heaney-lecture.html (Accessed 04 June 2007).
Heidegger M (1934/1981) Why do i stay in the provinces? in T Sheehan (ed) *Heidegger: The Man and the Thinker*. Chicago: Precedent.
Heidegger M (1971) *Poetry, Language, Thought*. (Trans. Albert Hofstadter). New York, NY: Harper Collins.
hooks b (2008) *Belonging*. London: Routledge.
Jackson W (1996) *Becoming Native to This Place*. Lexington, KY: University of Kentucky Press.
Jonas A (2011) Region and place: regionalism in question. *Progress in Human Geography* 36(2): 1–10.
Jones M and McLeod (2004) Regional spaces, spaces of regionalism: territory, insurgent politics and the English question. *Transactions of the Institute of British Geographers*, 29(4): 433–452.
Kavanagh P (2003 [1952]) The parish and the universe, in A Quinn (ed) *A Poet's Country: Selected Prose*. Dublin: Lilliput Press
Kavanagh P (2005) *Collected Poems*. London: Penguin.
Kerrigan J (1985) Wordsworth and the sonnet: building, dwelling, thinking. *Essays in Criticism* 35: 45–75.
Kiberd D (1996) *Inventing Ireland: The Literature of a Modern Nation*. London: Vintage.
Kiberd D (2009) *Ulysses and Us. The Art of Everyday Living*. London: Faber and Faber.
Lazarus N (2011) Cosmopolitanism and the specificity of the local in world literature. *Journal of Commonwealth Literature* 46(1): 119–137.
Lippard L (1997) *The Lure of the Local*. New York: New Press.
Lupton JR (2011) *Thinking with Shakespeare. Essays on Politics and Life*. Chicago: Chicago University Press.
Malpas J (1999) *Place and Experience: A Philosophical Topography*. Cambridge: Cambridge University Press.
Marston SA, Jones JP and Woodward K (2005) Human geography without scale. *Transactions of the Institute of British Geographers* 30(4): 416–432.
Massey D (1991) A Global Sense of Place. *Marxism Today*, June: 24–29.
Massey D (2005) *For Space*. London: Sage.
Massey D (2006) Landscape as a provocation: reflections on moving mountains. *Journal of Material Culture* 11(1): 33–48.
Massey D (2009) The possibilities of a politics of place beyond place? *Scottish Geographical Journal* 125(3/4): 401–20.
Marx K (1871) Landor R; interview with Karl Marx, head of L'Internationale. *New York World*, 18 July. Available at: http://libcom.org/library/interview-with-marx-landor (Accessed 16 August 2011).
McConnell M (1996) Don't neglect the little platoons, in J Cohen (ed) *For Love of Country*. Boston, MA: Beacon Press.
McGahern J (2009) *Love of the World: Essays*. London: Faber and Faber.
Merleau-Ponty M (1962) *The Phenomenology of Perception*. London: Routledge and Kegan Paul.

Miller L (2003) Longing for Belonging. *Australian Journal of Anthropology* 14(3): 406–17.
Murley J and Sutton S (eds) (2006) *Perspectives on Politics in Shakespeare*. Lanham, MD: Lexington Books.
Nussbaum M (1996) Patriotism and cosmopolitanism, in J Cohen (ed) *For Love of Country*. Boston, MA: Beacon Press.
Nussbaum M (1997) *Poetic Justice. The Literary Imagination and Public Life*. Boston, MA: Beacon Press.
Paasi A (2003) Region and place: regional identity in question. *Progress in Human Geography* 27(4): 475–485.
Paasi A (2004) Place and region: looking through the prism of place. *Progress in Human Geography* 28(4): 536–546.
Painter J (2008) Cartographic anxiety and the search for regionality. *Environment and Planning A* 40(2): 342–361.
Pike A (2007) Whither regional studies? *Regional Studies* 41(9): 1143–1148.
Popke J (2007) Geography and ethics: spaces of cosmopolitan responsibility. *Progress in Human Geography* 31(4): 509–518.
Rasula J (2002) *This Compost: Ecological Imperatives in American Poetry*. Athens, GA: University of Georgia Press.
Relph E (1976) *Place and Placelessness*. London: Pion.
Richard J (2001) A Quaking Sod: hybridity, identity and wandering Irishness, in MP Gillespie (ed) *James Joyce and the Fabrication of an Irish Identity*. (European Joyce Studies 11). Amsterdam: Editions Rodopi.
Rorty R (1998) *Achieving Our Country. The William E. Massey Sr. Lectures in the History of American Civilization*. Cambridge, MA: Harvard University Press.
Sanders SR (1993) *Staying Put. Making a Home in a Restless World*. Boston, MA: Beacon Press.
Saunders A (2010) Literary geography: reforging the connections. *Progress in Human Geography* 34(4): 436–452.
Stafford F (2010) *Local Attachments. The Province of Poetry*. Oxford: Oxford University Press.
Thompson T, Shield J and Milford W (1827) *A Collection of Songs, Comic, Satirical, and Descriptive, Chiefly in the Newcastle Dialect. And Illustrative of the Language and Manners of the Common People on the Banks of the Tyne and Neighbourhood*. Newcastle upon Tyne: John Marshall.
Thrift N (1999) Steps toward an ecology of place, in D Massey, J Allen, and P Sarre (eds) *Human Geography Today*. Cambridge: Polity Press.
Tomaney J (2007) Keeping a beat in the dark: narratives of regional identity in Basil Bunting's *Briggflatts*. *Environment and Planning D: Society and Space* 25(2): 355–375.
Tomaney J (2010a) Eurocentric social science and the Chinese region. *Asian Journal of Political Science* 18(1): 3–19.
Tomaney J (2010b) Parish and universe: the local poetics of Patrick Kavanagh. *Environment and Planning D: Society and Space* 28(2): 311–325.
Tuan YF (1976) Geopiety: a theme in man's attachment to nature, in D Lowenthal and M Bowden (eds) *Geographies of the Mind*. New York: oxford University Press.
Tuan YF (1977) *Space and Place*. Minneapolis: Minnesota University Press
Vaughan Williams R (1963) *National Music and Other Essays*. Oxford: Oxford University Press.
Vaughan Williams R (2007) Local Musicians, in D Manning (ed) *Vaughan Williams on Music*. Oxford: Oxford University Press.
Williams R (1988) *Resources of Hope. Culture, Democracy, Socialism*. London: Verso.
Williams R (1962) *Border Country*. London: Chatto and Windus.
Wordsworth W (2000) *The Major Works*. Oxford: Oxford University Press.

4 Mapping Cultures of Regional Perception and Conception

A Cultural Cartography from Northeast Brazil

Jörn Seemann

Introduction

Under the influence of postmodern theories and post-structuralism, regional geography is experiencing a period of reanimation. The lively debate about a 'new regional geography' in the 1980s has helped to revitalise the idea of region for geographers (Thrift, 1994), shaking off the ghost of descriptive or so-called 'traditional' regional studies and introducing critical political and economic perspectives.[1] However, these new approaches sparsely address the cultural dimensions of the region and its imagined geographies. The central argument of this chapter is that regional geographers should pay more attention to the human and humanistic aspects of regional geography, region-building, and regionalisation and engage more in methodological issues in fieldwork. In this context, maps and mappings could be powerful tools to explore the cultural dimensions of a region. Despite the recent exciting trends to reanimate regional geography, topics such as place, identity, and cultures of region-building and regional perception are still overlooked issues in the subfield. Intentionally misquoting Nigel Thrift (1994), I dare say that regional geographers literally are not aiming at the heart of the region. Their approach is frequently from the top to the bottom, in anthropological terms, etic and not emic, a view from the outside. The geographer appears as an almost omniscient observer. Curiously, research rarely starts with individual regional worldviews and lacks a stronger political and social engagement with regions on a local scale.

The aim of this chapter is to address aspects of these cultures of region (not 'regional cultures'!), with an emphasis on regional perception and conception and interpreted through the lens of humanistic and cultural geography. This approach to regions is through discourse, narratives, and sociocultural representations, taking into consideration that regions are geographically as ill-defined and malleable as other cultural space categories such as place or landscape. They are conceived as mentefacts and produced realities based on perception, imagination, and different worldviews rather than homogeneous spatial units with fixed boundaries.

This chapter is divided into three parts. First, I will briefly discuss the more recent literature on cultural approaches to the region. In the following section,

I present a second important element to the debate, maps and mappings, which should not be regarded as boundary and border markers and makers, but as powerful methodological tools to understand regional worldviews. The third part consists of a case study from Northeast Brazil that I use as an empirical example of cultures of regional perception and conception.

Cultural Approaches to Regions

Sometimes, present-day critical regional geographers are quick to dismiss 'traditional' regional geography as over-empirical and lacking solid theoretical underpinnings. According to these critics, the innumerous *genre-de-vie* studies by French geographers, the historical-geographical investigations by the cultural geographers of the Berkeley school, and the chorological approach used by Richard Hartshorne produce narratives of regional life and focus on facts and processes rather than stimulate a deeper reflection on social agency and constructions. There is a long list of publications proposing a theoretical framework for a new regional geography (for example, Thrift, 1983; Gilbert, 1988; Pudup, 1988; Sayer, 1989). These authors discuss the weak points of traditional approaches and make a plea for a more critical treatment of the concept of region, grounded in solid social theory. In fact, one cannot speak of only one new regional geography (NRG), since this movement entails a set of loosely related thoughts and ideas, an 'ambivalent brand' (Paasi, 2009: 223) that is 'neither something new nor something regional' (Holmén, 1995: 58). Rather, NRG urges for the reconceptualisation of region and place and can be considered 'an umbrella term for research and for reflecting how region and/or place are constituted by and constitutive of social life, social relations and identity' (Paasi, 2009: 223). At the same time, NRG is not a completely new way of thinking and practicing regional geography. The first step for the reading of regional spaces, places, and landscape will always be the solid description of their spatial features and processes.

As in any other field, regional geography is under the influence of academic fashions and competition, combined with the personal desire and professional ambition to present something that other geographers have not done, yet. Regional scholars push forward particular trains of thought including the creation of new terms, concepts, and labels. However, it remains questionable, if one could even speak of a 'new new regional geography' (Thrift, 1998), taking into account the blurry conceptual, theoretical, and methodological boundaries of the subfield itself.[2]

For the purpose of this chapter, I will use Paasi's (2009) definition of regional geography due to its emphasis on cultural identities in the process of creating regions:

> [Regional Geography is a] subfield of human geography whose representatives are interested in the social and cultural construction of regions, in their meanings for individual and social identities and in the power relations that are involved in region-building processes. (Paasi, 2009: 214)

The idea of regional identities as an essential factor in regional studies is nothing new (see, for example, Gilbert, 1988; Murphy 1991; Paasi, 1991). It is an endeavour to steer away from the idea of region as an inflexible container that merely hosts social interactions (Murphy, 1991) and simply exists 'out there' (Agnew, 1999: 92). Geographers recognise now the power of identities in shaping regions on the maps and on the mind.

As a result of this people-bound approach, issues such as culture and regional identification and cultural relations between a specific group and a specific place have been included as important topics in the discourse on regional geography (Gilbert, 1988). But has regional geography become more cultural with these ideas?

Among the earlier contributors to the debate on new regional geography were also humanistic geographers such as Nicholas Entrikin who wrote three essays on place and region for *Progress in Human Geography* (Entrikin, 1994, 1996, 1997). Reviewing the existing literature, he highlights the 'shift away from understanding places in themselves, and towards an appreciation of place as a social and a cultural category', stressing the importance of individual and collective subjects and of self (Entrikin, 1994: 227). Despite the title *Place and Region*, Entrikin limits himself to the concept of place, but does not discuss region. This seems to confirm a trend in NRG: the shift away from the word region itself, giving preference to terms such as place, locale, locality, or even territory (Holmén, 1995: 52) and, at the same time, investigating the tensions between territorial and relations notions of region (Jonas, 2012).

The new concepts in the regional debate are frequently accompanied by key terms such as narrative, performance, and discourse. Geographers have become more interested in how representations and practices produce meanings, constitute identities, and establish social relations (Campbell, 2009: 166). The analysis of narratives, practices, rituals and discourses permits insights into the construction of regional identities and may contain a wide range of topics and elements that address regional perception and belonging, for example, ideas of nature and landscape, ethnicity, language, actual and invented histories, or regional stereotypes (Paasi, 2003: 477). The key issue is not to detect and understand these discourses, but to find out which social actors are the moving forces in this process, how and why these narratives were constructed and how and why they have become part of the 'making' of regions (Paasi, 2003: 481).

The focus on identities and discourse requires new methodological approaches for the study of regions. Surprisingly, the recent literature on regional geography does not include a deeper concern about methodological questions. It seems that the image of the regional geographer as qualitative social scientist is not easily accepted in academic circles. However, if regional identity is a main focus, researchers must address how to approach this topic. Identity is not a taken-for-granted starting point, but an object of investigation itself that must be explained so that 'it is important to ask not what regional identities are but what people mean when they talk or write' (Paasi, 2003: 481). In this context, regional geographers should make use of a variety of unconventional resources to reveal the cultures of regions 'such as films, fiction, photographs, folk art, and grade-school geography texts among many others (...) in an effort to tap popular attachment and imagery for areas' (Price, 1996: 352). In the following section, I will discuss one of these unconventional resources: maps.

Maps and Mappings

A very powerful, but neglected tool to understand regional identities and region-building processes are maps, which should not be conceived as 'technical moment', simple output or mere descriptions, but active elements in shaping a region, both on the mind and on the paper (Gaberell and Debarbieux, 2014: 123). During the last two decades, many new ideas have emerged to rethink cartography: maps can be inscriptions (Pickles, 2004), propositions (Wood and Fels, 2008; Wood, 2010), or processes that, in Deleuzian terms, unfold or are in constant becoming (Kitchin and Dodge, 2007; Kitchin et al., 2013). These approaches go beyond the mere and objective representation of reality and take into account modes, methods, and moments in the form of actions, interests, values, and histories behind the façade of maps (Dodge et al., 2009). The focus is not on products, but on processes (Rundstrom, 1993), with a cultural shift from representation to performance and practices (Perkins, 2009b: 126). It is about mappings and not maps.[3] In broader terms, maps can be any kind of graphic representation to 'facilitate a spatial understanding of things, concepts, conditions, processes, or events in the human world' (Harley and Woodward, 1987: xvi). Mappings are ways of measuring the world that are not restricted to the mathematical, but also include personal emotions, moral values, or political worldviews (Cosgrove, 1999: 1–2).

Maps may be conceived as essential elements of what I call cultural cartography – the critical investigation of the relations between geographical knowledge and representation, and culture and mapping practices. This different angle opens up new possibilities for research in regional geography, since maps and mappings serve as translations and forms of dialogue that link material culture, discourse, and performative ways to understand regions. There are many possibilities to put this cultural cartography into practice, from the reading of historical maps and the drawing of sketch maps on napkins to taking maps on a walk or talking about them at a bar table. These cartographies are everywhere.

This chapter focuses specifically on one of these strategies: the use of mental maps as a qualitative research method for interviews in order to reveal regionally-specific peculiarities such as regional stereotypes, cartographic cultures, ways of perceiving space and place, map biographies, the construction of geographical knowledge, and forms of human relatedness. Visual memory can be disclosed by simultaneously drawing maps and drawing *on* maps (Orlove, 1993). The emphasis is not on cartographic representations themselves, but on how people engage cartographically with their geographies, histories, and identities and how they express their ideas, values, and emotions.

But, what are mental maps? According to the *Dictionary of Geography*, a mental map is:

> A map of the environment within the mind of an individual which reflects the knowledge and prejudices of that individual. Such a map reflects the individual's perceptions of, and preferences for, different places and is the result of the way in which an individual acquires, classifies, stores, retrieves, and decodes information about locations (Mayhew, 2004: 324).

Seen from this perspective, the study of mental maps is not restricted to the drawing and the final product itself, but also includes mental processes to conceive these thoughts and translate them into a material form. Mental maps are not just material structures, but also entail processes of abstract spatial thinking that find their way onto a piece of paper.

These maps 'explore inner space, a little know region of that dark continent inside a man's head ... inner space refers to the representation of the geographical environment as it exists within a person's mind. It is the world as people believe it to be' (Downs and Stea, 1977: 4, original emphasis). Mental maps are personal understandings of the world that may be or may be not maplike, and bear a likeness to real space:

> Most importantly, a cognitive [mental] map is a cross section representing the world at one instant in time. It reflects the world as some people believe it to be; it needs not be correct. In fact, distortions are highly likely. It is *your* understanding of the world, and it may only faintly resemble the world as reflected in cartographic maps or colour photographs (Downs and Stea, 1977: 2, original emphasis).

Research on mental maps tends to give preference either to a local scale (mapping of neighborhoods or smaller administrative units, e.g. Lynch, 1979) or a very small scale (world maps, e.g. Saarinen et al., 1988; Pinheiro, 1998). While a cartographically large scale allows us to map details such as houses, local marks of reference, or even ephemeral phenomena, mental maps in a global scale provide information on different worldviews, political attitudes, and map projections. For studies in regional geography, mental maps may be explored to obtain further insights into how people imagine, think, conceive, and represent their own place.

Region and Geographical Knowledge

In this section, I will present a case study from Northeast Brazil to illustrate this mental-map methodology. The Cariri region is situated in the southern part of the State of Ceará and dominated by the steep slopes of the Araripe tablelands that rise to more than 3000 feet of elevation (Figure 4.1).

Figure 4.1 Location map of the Cariri, indicating the main towns and their major cultural and natural attractions. Retrieved from: https://republicadojasmim.files.wordpress.com/2013/03/mapa_grande.jpg.

Any kind of coloured composite satellite images of the region show a distinct large vegetation 'island' in the middle of the arid backlands of Northeast Brazil that visibly stands out and draws the attention of the image reader. The lands north from the humid flanks of the plateau are fertile valleys that are poetically described as paradise, gift of nature, or even God-sent, in contrast to the desolate dry lands of the *sertão* that surround the area.[4] In poetical terms,

> The valley, always cool and always green, and its perennial water springs that gush from the foot of the mountain are like an assertion that the Cariri is a piece of terrestrial paradise while the entire Northeast is a furnace that crackles through the contact with a scorching sun. (Martins Filho, 1966: 103)

The favorable moisture regime, the existence of more than 300 springs originating from the plateau (Mont'Alverne et al., 1994), and the productive soils of the foothills and valleys have turned the Cariri into an 'island of agriculture in the midst of the *caatinga* [the dry shrub landscape of Northeast Brazil]' (Andrade, 1980: 27) that favours the planting of crops such as sugarcane and coffee. Despite labeling the Cariri as a region, it remains mapless and boundless in geographical terms: there is a strong regional or even regionalist discourse, but regional writing about this place is mainly about names and 'facts', without deeper reference to geographical details. The unique landscapes are not reflected in the local literature, and there are no official maps of the region, because there is no region as such. Historical writing on the Cariri is descriptive and consists of narratives with a constant flow of taken-for-granted selected events and names, from which the 'sense of connection' (Cronon, 1992: 1351) has been removed.

The geography of the region in the writings about the Cariri remains second to the narration of regional history. The geographical setting merely serves as a 'stage space', that is, 'a space that tends to be perceived as a static and neutral category, a pre-political object, and little more than a passive stage upon which historical subjects play assigned roles' (Craib, 2004: 3). The history- and geography-writing of and in the Cariri has lacked a geographical imagination that could turn a place or a region into a visual experience. Many regional constructions begin with maps that solidify the area as an existing place (Price, 1996: 337). However, in the Cariri the opposite has happened: a history-writing with few references to places did not create a spatial image. The regional geographies remained hidden and unexplored.

A strategy to obtain further details about regional identity and mapmindedness is through using interviews to gain a deeper, contextualised understanding of space. A group of about 20 local people who agreed to have a conversation on the region served as sources to discuss regional worldviews. Among these locals with a reputation as regional history and geography buffs were lawyers, medical doctors, university professors, musicians, and retired bankers. Some of them were indicated or recommended by other interviewees. Their ages ranged between 30 to more than 80 years; most of them were male (only five women) and had strong ties to the region.[5]

Qualitative interviewing took place in June and July 2009 to investigate how the interviewees engaged with the geography, history, and the mapping of the Cariri region, how they defined and represented their region, and how they drew their maps, including 'different' or even invisible expressions. The interviews did not only reveal what the interviewees thought about the region, but also what they thought they had to tell about it or what they thought the interviewer expected them to know. As a result of this shifting positionality, there was always the risk of obtaining answers that were not necessarily what the interviewees themselves thought. One example is *Miguel* who answered the initial question about what one should know about the geography of the Cariri in a textbook manner, mentioning facts and figures about the Araripe Plateau such as its dimensions, geology, the number of springs, the regional hospitality, and other run-of-the-mill details. However, during the interview, he went beyond the official discourse and revealed how his own personal biography is intimately related to the region:

> I know that I am an unconditional fan of the foothills, the lowlands, the sugarcane fields, the banana plantations, the springs, especially those with abundant and clean water and I feel happy. I have already lived in the trunk of this Araripe Plateau, at the root of the *chapada* [tablelands] from where I would never leave, if it all depended only on my own decision. Well, I find

> this all a paradise here on Earth because I love this land, I like it, I find it very beautiful. (*Miguel*)

In the Cariri region, geography has been the reproduction rather than the production of knowledge. Research on regional geography has not become a central issue, as *Clara*, another interviewee, affirmed: 'No, nobody did that. We only did what the book told us.' This kind of education could have stalled regional imagination and image production, leading to a lack of historic perspectives and interest in knowing about the region. Details about Mesopotamia and French kings were taught as signifiers without meaning:

> [My teacher] talked about kings, about Mesopotamia, talked about I don't know which place, I don't know, and at that time I lived in a street with the name Tristão Gonçalves. Professor, who was Tristão Gonçalves? And he did not know the answer. But I had already honed [my knowledge] to know why it had that name. There was a resident with that name, who was Tristão Gonçalves? And he [the teacher] told me who was Louis XIV, Louis I-don't-know-his-number, he knew who those old guys were. (*Teresa*)[6]

The initial question was how the interviewees defined the regional boundaries of the Cariri. At first glance, many answers reflected a combination of memorised phrases, official administrative divisions, and stereotypical criteria of delimitation such as climate and vegetation. These replies were given in an almost mechanical way or as a 'machine-gun toting of stereotypes' (*Sandra*) rather than being the result of a deeper reflection and an act of sharing personal knowledge of regional history and geography. However, many interviewees were aware that this delimitation could only serve 'didactic purposes' (*Anderson*). *Hermano*, for example, mentioned the fuzziness of boundaries and limits:

> This is something that I realised here. The landscape is not always a criterion that can differentiate a region from another, a place from another. If there is not a sign saying that from this point onwards it will be that place.

Others proposed a change in the name to indicate that it was not the Cariri valley itself, but the Araripe Plateau that is responsible for the uniqueness of the region. For this reason, 'you should consider the Cariri as all the towns that are embraced by the Araripe Plateau' (*Miguel*). One of the interviewees saw the well-marked horizon of the tablelands as the limits of the world when he was a child:

> I thought that the world would end behind the plateau, as if there was nothing beyond it. That's funny. Until that point we lived, as if it we were in a hole. You tried to look around the mountain to see what was behind it. (*Wellington*)

Asking for details beyond this discourse, several interviewees provided criteria related to culture, language, affect, and feelings. *Anderson* mentioned common cultural origins, aspirations, climate, and the processes of regionalisation. For him, all these elements could serve to delimit an area with common characteristics just for the sake of it. Others such as *Felisberto* referred to the indigenous past of the Cariri. The first inhabitants of the region, the Cariri Indians, and their almost complete erasure from the official history records left space for speculation and mythological musings. *Felisberto* sympathised with the native peoples and believed that the name Cariri itself is a powerful term to define the region:

> See, the best definition of the Cariri that I have heard is the one by the Indians themselves. They defined the Cariri with one word, the word Cariri is theirs and means sad, but at the same time it is not sad, it is to inspire a tranquility so deep that it resembles sadness, you understand? Maybe because they had watched the Cariri from the highest places, in a time when there was no movement such as this town here. So [the view] transmitted tranquility.

The interviewees did not consider the Cariri region as a mere geographic area, but defined it through criteria of human relatedness such as feelings of belonging and cultural and historical identity, shaped by social networks of friends, family, and origins, and their affective boundaries. In *Anderson's* words,

> These are locales I identify with in a certain way, either because I have an ancestor, or because I have a friend, or because I have a cultural reference in that region. So this defines the Cariri for me that is well determined and delimited, geographically speaking, but which is at the same time (…) my maternal lineage.

In the case of *Arlene*, the region can be 'felt': 'There is something, you feel the Cariri when you are in these places.' When asked how exactly she feels the region, she replied that the feeling is transmitted through the people, the popular language, regional expressions, and the accent and concluded with the following words:

> The Cariri for me is in my mind, on my map, when I close my eyes, I imagine the Cariri, I imagine the *chapada* and the towns that surround this plateau, you know, it's like a drawing that I have.

Mapping the Region

What does *Arlene*'s map look like? Her last sentence was an invitation to have her draw a mental map of the Cariri (Figure 4.2). In her map, South is at the top, a view from the Cariri valley (most towns are shown with their initial letters) in the direction of the massive structure of the Araripe Plateau that *Arlene* indicates with wavy lines. She makes clear that the tablelands do not delimit the Cariri, but that the region in her vision must go beyond them reaching into the neighbouring state of Pernambuco. For her, the *chapada* is an identity marker and connector and

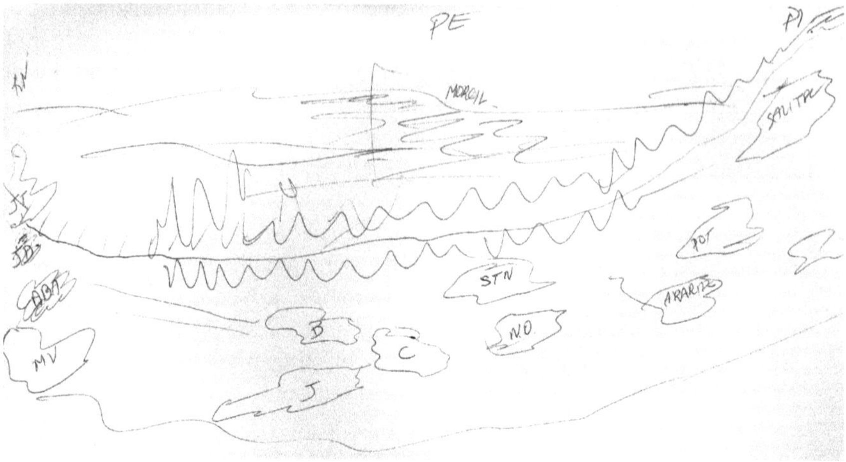

Figure 4.2 A mental map of the Cariri. The zigzagged lines in the centre (divided by the state border) represent the plateau. Town names are abbreviated. The top of the drawing is pointing to the South.

not a cultural barrier and differentiator. *Arlene* affirms that proximity defines the belonging to the region: the further away, the weaker the influence.

Some of the informants felt uncomfortable and even started to drum nervously with their pens on the table. They showed (cartographic) anxiety by admitting that they were simply not good at drawing maps and confessed their cluelessness. This spontaneous reaction was frequently accompanied by a lack of reflexivity and confidence. One of the involuntary draftsmen claimed that it would be too difficult to make a map, while others did not feel like competent mapmakers and tried to talk me out of the mapping exercise, arguing that they lacked cartographical skills and accuracy, as in the following case with *Alfredo*:

> *Alfredo*: Draw a map? Oops, that‘s difficult.
> *Jörn*: I know it‘s difficult, but could you have a try?
> *Alfredo*: No.
> *Jörn*: What would the map look like, if you drew one?

At this point, *Alfredo* referred to the existence of regional maps and town plans that could be bought somewhere and that would solve the problem:

> I think there must be a place here in town where a map of the Cariri exists, I don‘t remember where. If so I would indicate it to you. If I had known that you would ask this question, I would have searched for it around here.

Alfredo preferred to leave the paper blank rather than to add towns and places in inaccurate or wrong positions.

Alfredo: You could imagine how it would be. Putting the towns in their right place. That would be more difficult.
Jörn: Would you like to have a try?
Alfredo: No, and do you know why? For example if I made a map, I would put one town here, put another over there, put yet another here, but it is not here [in this position], it must be there. So it is better not to make it.

For him, there was no need for drawing a map, because there were already other (and better) maps available.

Another example makes clear that these cartographies could have a spiritual or affective nature. *Felisberto* presented a different Cariri and showed that a map does not have to be concrete and accurate. The map he drew did not contain any place names. His drawing in portrait format was an abstract sketch of the Araripe Plateau, representing a geobody (Figure 4.3). The map space was too small for his outline of the tablelands, but this did not matter to him. He simulated the entries, ravines, and runoff riverbeds from the top, but admitted that the ideas in his head were difficult to transfer to a sheet of paper.

He drew an energetic core (a sun symbol) to represent the radiating center in the middle of the plateau and explained: 'The more intense part of the region would be this area around here that resembles an aura.' According to his world-view, there is no exact locality for the centre point:

I suppose that it is in the forest, the densest part of it. You understand? From that point on, it's a place, if you walk through the middle of the forest, you will feel

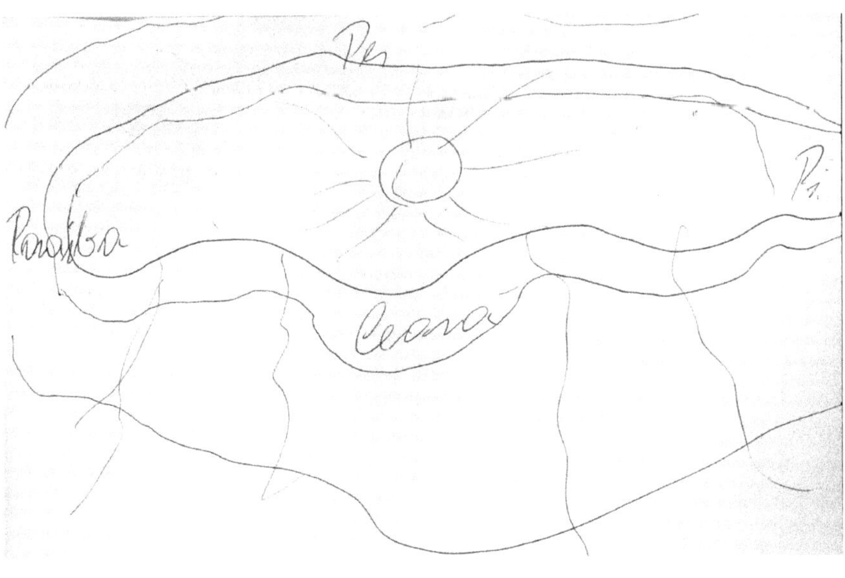

Figure 4.3 A cosmographic drawing of the Cariri (South on top). The sun indicates the energetic centre of the plateau. Some lines continue beyond the paper sheet.

> it. … In some regions where I walk I feel that very strong energy and calm down there, you understand, it recharges me. But this is something very intimate.

Place names and other locations were not relevant for his cosmic philosophy, although he mentioned some places that were under immediate influence of this energy:

> The vertical lines symbolised the water fountains that gush from the Araripe Plateau, they would be like the flowing veins of the Cariri. I don't know, I am very abstract here.

He continues:

> I define the Cariri like this. To be true, a living being, as it is the land itself, a living being, which is also a living being, maybe a cell of the plateau, of the land …. I identify myself more, because I live together with it.

The interviewees produced a variety of different mental maps of the Cariri ranging from simple location maps, simulations, or simulacra to spiritual cartographies of the Araripe Plateau. These mapping samples showed that the act of using a map establishes the connection between space and its representations and helps the map reader and mapmaker to find himself or herself on the map. Map use should not be restricted to the look at maps, but also means engagement with what is represented on the piece of paper by scribbling on the map, following lines, marking places, and initiating a conversation:

> To draw on a sketch map is merely to add the trace of one further gesture to the traces of previous ones. Such a map may be the conversational product of many hands, in which participants take turns to add lines as they describe their various journeys. The map grows line by line as the conversation proceeds, and there is no point at which it can ever be said to be truly complete. (Ingold, 2008: 85)

Maps of Regional Meaning

Most of the maps produced in this regional study were ancillary, and used to express what the interviewees had to say about the region and their own place-boundedness within the Cariri. The maps turned out to be a by-product of the conversation that gave a hint to how each mapmaker situated himself/herself in the region rather than how he or she would draw a map containing his or her regional knowledge. As such, the results of this regional undertaking in Northeast Brazil remained patchy, sketchy, and messy, but at the same time showed the region as a complex universe of worldviews, landscapes, images, and practices that are not static, but in a process of constant becoming and that correspond to regional boundedness rather than to regional boundaries. The idea of the Cariri region in the geographical imagination does not correspond to the concept of region as an area with fixed boundaries.

The interviewees produced a variety of different mental maps of the Cariri ranging from rather official reproductions and simple location maps to spiritual cartographies of the Araripe Plateau, which are not necessarily representational, but could be conceptual, spiritual, and performative – echoing Denis Cosgrove's (1999: 1-2) definition of mapping. For example, *Felisberto*'s map of the Cariri indicated spots of cosmic energy on the Araripe Plateau rather than concrete geographical locations, whereas *Teresa* brought up regional myths that she linked to real places (e.g. a mysterious river under the plateau that emerges on Good Friday). *Joaquim* used his (conceptual) map as a discourse in favor of regional autonomy and a critique of the centralised political structures in the state.

Without a well-defined spatial frame in the form of drawn (out)lines that would give a shape to the Cariri and define which places are inside or outside, the region remained abstract and amorphous. The drawing of the mental map depended on each individual's creativity, imagination, and decisions. The maps, incomplete and imperfect presentations or representations, were not the principal channel to express the interviewees' knowledge of the region, as put by one of the informants:

> I don't know. I made a drawing, so for me it is only a bit, for me this is infinite, you see. It goes on, here it goes on. It was not possible to portray because I don't know … from a cartographic point of view it had to be more, but it is an image that I have. (*Arlene*)

Despite their incomplete and fragmentary character, these images, ideas, and imagined spaces could be considered maps of meaning, alluding to what Peter Jackson wrote about culture's geographies more than 25 years ago: a deeper engagement with 'the way we make sense of the world, rendering our geographical experience intelligible, attaching value to the environment and investing the material world with symbolic significance' (Jackson, 1989: no page). These personal regional mappings are not only mappings of space, but also of subjects. Regions and people are equally difficult to map, since they do not have precise boundaries:

> There is the difficulty of mapping something that cannot be counted as singular but only as a mass of different and sometimes conflicting subject positions. There is the difficulty of mapping something that is always on the move, culturally, and in fact. There is the difficulty of mapping something that is only partially locatable in time-space. Then, finally, there is the difficulty of deploying the representational metaphor of mapping with its history of subordination to an Enlightenment logic in which everything can be surveyed and pinned down. (Pile and Thrift, 1995: 1)

The regional mental maps from this study are not final products, but starting points for further mappings. Traces can be added by many different hands so that 'the map grows line by line as the conversation proceeds, and there is no point at which it can ever be said to be truly complete' (Ingold, 2008: 85). And while the use of mental maps in regional studies is nothing new, it should be pointed out that they could be triggers to stimulate dialogues and conversation and help to outline regional life histories, political discourses, emotions, and other doings that are expressed through drawings, music, dances, poems, or even woodcuts. Curiously, up to now little has been done to study the performative ways of doing these regional geographies, neither by cultural geographers, anthropologists, nor regional geographers themselves, but the door is open for new experiences to reanimate regional geography.

Notes

1 I use the term 'traditional' with quotation marks due to the negative connotation that some geographers have given to regional studies in geography with a strong empirical emphasis. The emergence of a new regional geography does not replace a descriptive geography, since description is an essential step before an interpretation can be done.
2 It is open to debate if one could use the term 'regional geographies' (in allusion to recent trends in cultural geography) to express the pluralism, multivocality, and heterotopia of the subfield.
3 In the literature on culture and maps, it is common to use the singular expression of the term (mapping). I would like to give preference to mappings, the plural form, because it stresses the possibility of different ways of mapping reality. In other words, 'mapping may be angry, boring, celebratory, exciting, happy, painful, persuasive, playful, proud, reassuring, revealing, restless, sad, or wistful. As human practice we can make it what we want. And the limits to what may be known about mapping are similarly boundless' (Perkins, 2009a: 397).
4 The term *sertão* is derived from the Portuguese word *desertão*, big desert, though the *sertão* is not a desert, but an immense arid area with low precipation and predominantly thorny shrub vegetation, the so-called *caatinga*, literally white forest in indigenous language.
5 The quotations from the interviewees are my own translations from the Portuguese. In order to protect the identity and preserve anonymity of my interviewees I used pseudonyms for them that are indicated in italics in the text.
6 This is another promising and overlooked topic for research: how is regional geography taught in educational environments?

References

Agnew J (1999) Regions on the mind does not equal regions of the mind. *Progress in Human Geography* 23(1): 91–96.

Andrade MC de (1980) *The Land and People of Northeast Brazil*. Albuquerque: University of New Mexico Press.

Campbell D (2009) Discourse, in D Gregory et al. (eds) *Dictionary of Human Geography*, 5th edition. Chichester: Wiley-Blackwell, 166–167.

Cosgrove D (1999) Introduction: mapping meaning, in D Cosgrove (ed) *Mappings*. London: Reaktion Books, 1–23.

Craib RB (2004) *Cartographic Mexico. A History of State Fixations and Fugitive Landscapes*. Durham: Duke University Press.

Cronon W (1992) A Place for Stories: Nature, History, and Narrative. *The Journal of American History* 78(4): 1347–1376.

Dodge M, Perkins C and Kitchin R (2009) Mapping modes, methods and moments. A manifesto for map studies, in M Dodge, R Kitchin and C Perkins (eds) *Rethinking Maps. New Frontiers in Cartographic Theory*. London: Routledge, 220–243.
Downs RM and Stea D (1977) *Maps in Minds. Reflections on Cognitive Mapping*. New York: Harper & Row.
Entrikin JN (1994) Place and region. *Progress in Human Geography* 18(2): 227–233.
Entrikin JN (1996) Place and region 2. *Progress in Human Geography* 20(2): 215–221.
Entrikin JN (1997) Place and region 3. *Progress in Human Geography* 21(2): 263–268.
Gaberell S and Debarbieux B (2014) Mapping regions, framing projects: a comparative analysis on the role of mapping in the region-building process of two European regions. *Geoforum* 52: 123–136.
Gilbert A (1988) The new regional geography in English and French speaking countries. *Progress in Human Geography* 12(2): 208–228.
Harley JB and Woodward D (1987) Preface, in JB Harley and D Woodward (eds) *The History of Cartography*. Volume 1. Chicago: University of Chicago Press, xv–xxi.
Holmén H (1995) What's new and what's regional in the 'new regional geography'? *Geografiska Annaler* 77(1): 47–63.
Ingold T (2008) *Lines*. London: Routledge.
Jackson P (1989) *Maps of Meaning. An Introduction to Cultural Geography*. London: Unwin Hyman.
Jonas AEG (2012) Region and place: regionalism in question. *Progress in Human Geography* 36(2): 263–272.
Kitchin R and Dodge M (2007) Rethinking maps. *Progress in Human Geography* 31(3): 331–344.
Kitchin R, Gleeson J and Dodge M (2013) Unfolding mapping practices: a new epistemology for cartography. *Transactions of the Institute of British Geographers* 38(3): 480–496.
Lynch K (1979) *The Image of the City*. Cambridge/MA: M.I.T. Press.
Martins Filho A (1966) O Cariri, in A Martins Filho and R Girão, *O Ceará*. 3rd edition. Fortaleza: Editora Instituto do Ceará, 101–109.
Mayhew S (2004) *A Dictionary of Geography*. 3rd edition. Oxford: Oxford University Press.
Mont'Alverne AAF et al. (1994) *Exutórios naturais do sistema Exu/Arajara na Bacia do Araripe*. Recife: Departamento Nacional da Produção Mineral.
Murphy A (1991) Regions as social constructs: the gap between theory and practice. *Progress in Human Geography* 15(1): 22–35.
Orlove B (1993) The ethnography of maps: the cultural and social contexts of cartographic representation in Peru. *Cartographica* 30(1): 29–46.
Paasi A (1991) Deconstructing regions: notes on the scales of spatial life. *Environment and Planning A* 23(2): 239–256.
Paasi A (2003) Region and place: regional identity in question. *Progress in Human Geography* 27(4): 475–485.
Paasi A (2009) Regional geography I, in R Kitchin and N Thrift (eds) *International Encyclopedia of Human Geography*, Volume 9. Oxford: Elsevier, 214–227.
Perkins C (2009a) Philosophy and mapping, in R Kitchin and N Thrift (eds) *International Encyclopedia of Human Geography*, Volume 8. Oxford: Elsevier, 385–397.
Perkins C (2009b) Performative and embodied mapping, in R Kitchin and N Thrift (eds) *International Encyclopedia of Human Geography*, Volume 8. Oxford: Elsevier, 126–132.
Pickles J (2004) *A History of Spaces. Cartographic Reason, Mapping and the Geo-Coded World*. London: Routledge.
Pile S and Thrift N (1995) Introduction, in S Pile and N Thrift (eds) *Mapping the Subject. Geographies of Cultural Transformation*. London: Routledge, 1–11.
Pinheiro JQ (1998) Determinants of cognitive maps of the world as expressed in sketch maps. *Journal of Environmental Psychology* 18(3): 321–339.

Price M (1996) The Venezuelan Andes and the geographical imagination. *Geographical Review* 86(3): 334–355.
Pudup MB (1988) Arguments within regional geography. *Progress in Human Geography* 12(3): 369–390.
Rundstrom R (1993) The role of ethics, mapping, and the meaning of place in relations between Indians and whites in the United States. *Cartographica* 30(1): 21–28.
Saarinen TF, MacCabe CL and Morehouse B (1988) *Sketch Maps of the World as Surrogates for World Geographic Knowledge* (Discussion paper 83–3). Tucson: University of Arizona.
Sayer A (1989) The 'new' regional geography and problems of narrative. *Environment and Planning D: Society and Space* 7(3): 253–276.
Thrift N (1983) On the determination of social action in space and time. *Environment and Planning D: Society and Space* 1(1): 23–57.
Thrift N (1994) Taking aim at the heart of the region, in D Gregory, R Martin, and G Smith (eds) *Human Geography: Society, Space and Social Science*. London: MacMillan, 200–231.
Thrift N (1998) Towards a new New Regional Geography. *Berichte zur deutschen Landeskunde*, 72(1): 37–46.
Wood D (with J Fels and J Krygier) (2010) *Rethinking the Power of Maps*. New York: Guilford Press.
Wood D and Fels J (2008) *The Natures of Maps: Cartographic Constructions of the Natural World*. Chicago: University of Chicago Press.

5 Regionalists and *Excursionistes*

Catalan 'Regions' and National Identity

Venetia Congdon

The following chapter critically examines how food is used as a means of expressing Catalan identity, and it considers this distinctive culinary heritage alongside the rise in support for the pro-independence movement. The 'Catalonia' that this chapter is concerned with is the Catalan Autonomous Community (CAC) in the north-east of Spain, an area which like the Basque country has had a historically difficult relationship with the Spanish state. This geopolitical situation has come to the forefront recently due to the increased popular support for a vote on independence from Spain. And it continues to be politically fuelled by the Spanish government's refusal to recognise the Catalan Statute of Autonomy of 2010, the main aim of which was to grant greater autonomy to the region, particularly in fiscal matters, and to alter Catalonia's application of Spanish-wide provincial categories. This difficult and complex relationship with the Spanish state has often lead to Catalan attempts to use autochthonous means of self-definition to highlight difference. Here I specifically want to consider the history of factual representations in Catalonia, and their symbolic significance in producing a distinct Catalonia.

The inspiration for this chapter was a comment made by one of my principal informants in the field, a well-known Barcelona chef. He explained to me the centrality of markets in Catalan identity, and that there is a market in the capital of each *comarca* (county) in the CAC. The *comarca* is the principal unit of Catalan local government, and an entity that Catalans can relate to in their everyday lives. He was keen to contrast this with Catalonia's division into four provinces in official Spanish demarcations, one more example, he claimed, of the Spanish government's high-handed treatment of the CAC. This statement made me curious to look further into the issue.

At the start of fieldwork, I was also curious to see whether the regional, *comarcal*[1] identity undermined in any way the sense of Catalan identity, and if there was any conflict or competition between the two. This was confusing to all the Catalans I asked, who saw no contradiction between having a strong identification with their own *comarca* but also an overarching Catalan identity. Indeed, to have pride in one's *comarca* is to express an affiliation with Catalonia as a whole, since the *comarca* is a Catalan-defined unit. My intention here is to explain how this process and identification came about.

Spain is composed of 50 provinces. The four that are in Catalonia are Barcelona, Tarragona, Girona and Lleida, and their names correspond to the four major cities of each of these provinces. Catalonia has 41 *comarques* or counties, each with their own capital. Many of these are based on historic boundaries dating back to the medieval era, then called *vegueries*. This title was resurrected in the twentieth century for groupings of *comarques*[2] as an alternative to provinces. The contemporary *comarcal* map dates largely to research carried out in the Republican period in 1931–36 (*Divisió Territorial)*, although due to the Civil War and anti-Catalan Franco period these were only in practice for three years before being re-enacted in 1987.

Before discussing how maps have been used in Catalan identity construction, I will give a brief overview of how maps have been used in Catalonia and similarly in Basque Country as tools of national identity expression. I will then set out a history of how these units were developed in both Spain and Catalonia, contrasting the externally imposed provincial system with the Catalan-developed system of *comarques* and *vegueries*. I argue in this chapter that maps are a means of identity creation and construction, specifically in relation to the activity of '*excursionisme*', where Catalans use specific food maps to travel and eat on their way through Catalonia.

Maps and Power

Mapmaking is rarely an innocent and simple delineation of land, but frequently an expression of power and dominance. The way in which physical spaces are divided up and reduced to a schematic, choices of what to represent and how, and the physical act of surveying the land, is a means of expressing mastery. Ardener (2006) has recognised that apparently indifferent population statistics can be used by ethnic groups to assert their existence as independent units. In the same way, maps can also be used to assert national existence.

Claims to territory are often central to claims of national identity (Smith, 1986), and this capacity to make maps of a territory act as tacit symbols of ownership on a national scale. As the Catalan anthropologist Josep Llobera has pointed out, 'There is little doubt … that a territory is perhaps one of the most concrete and important phenomena that exists for human beings, as it also reflects their psychological characteristics' (2004: 48). In his work, *Foundations of National Identity*, a detailed ethnography of symbols of Catalan nationalism, he suggests that ideas of national territory (and its associated symbols of landscape, soil etc.) are intrinsically related to ideas of kinship and familial belonging. This is not only expressed in traditional inheritance patterns through houses and land, but also through ideas of 'mother/fatherland'. Susan DiGiacomo (1985: 164) likewise has shown that rural imagery has frequently pervaded Catalan nationalism since its inception, and was used to great effect by the 'home-grown' winning party in Catalonia's first regional elections of Spain's democratic period in 1980. As I will discuss at the end of this chapter, notions of soil and food also come out of this rich nexus of associations.

The interpretation and division of national territory is therefore significant in nationalist movements. A particularly interesting case for the discussion here has been described by Jaqueline Urla (1993) in the Basque country, another nationalist movement within Spain with which Catalonia's has often been compared. In the context of demonstrating how statistics are used (and manipulated) in Basque nationalism, she shows how images of 'floating' (Urla, 1993: 825) maps of the Basque country divorced from the surrounding states (France and Spain) act as 'logo maps' that are 'a constant reminder of the boundaries between the nation and its others' (Urla, 1993: 825). In total, the Basque country is divided into seven provinces, four in Spain and three in France. In Spain, three of these provinces are united under the Basque Autonomous Community, while to the disappointment of many Basque nationalists, the larger province of Navarre was made separate from the Autonomous Community, and any officially recognised relationship between the two was forbidden. In such circumstances 'differences in maps and statistical units of measurement cannot help but resonate with symbolic and political meanings about the integrity of the Basque nation' (Urla, 1993: 826). Also implicit in wider discussions of maps and regional divisions are ideas about land and natural delineations and its connection with Basque language and culture. I shall argue that these are likewise key in Catalonia's mapmaking history.

Geographical Divisions in Spain and Catalonia

The modern division of Spain into fifty provinces goes back to a failed territorial division in 1822, which was resurrected in 1833. This second attempt was a part of a program to modernise the country, and develop Spain into a centralised nation-state, in opposition to the more conservative elements of the Spanish government at that time.[3] Spain was and would continue to be a notoriously disorganised and complicated country to manage (Burgueño, 2011), and this division was an attempt to impose some semblance of unity, while also furthering the power of a weak state. Through provinces, government actions could be applied at local levels. Applying the principles of these new categories in light of Spain's turmoil over the next few decades was a complicated process. By the early years of the twentieth century these were established as the dominant means of Spanish territorial and governmental division. During this period, the *comarques* were not recognised on any official level, although they were a local category for understanding Catalan geography.

In Catalonia and the Basque country, the division seemed arbitrary, a view that continues today. As Catalan geographer Marc-Aureli Vila has said, the 1822 attempt completely ignored Catalonia's *comarcal* system, and the provincial division of 1833 'imposed by decree from the Madrid government, responded to no previous consultation with the most interested parties: the Catalans' (1989: 22). On the contrary, it seemed to wilfully ignore Catalonia's geographic, historic and economic realities, and indeed divided up several *comarques* between provinces, literally overriding Catalan-designated divisions. This was never well accepted by Catalans. Llobera (2004: 60) points out that 'the provinces created by the

Spanish state … are denied any relevance by Catalan nationalism' even though they are now so well entrenched that they are difficult to remove from contemporary Catalan reality. The focus on just four provincial capitals also led to a decline in the official importance of the formerly important county capitals, and administrative problems as citizens had further to travel to their new provincial centre (Llobera, 2004: 60).

Contrasted with the historical associations of the provincial division of 1833, the differences between *comarques* and Spanish provinces could therefore not have been greater. However, in 1834 the Spanish state developed a map for the Judicial Districts (*Partits Judicials*), which was much closer to the contemporary *comarcal* map. Based on local realities, they correspond by 78.9% (Vila, 1989) to the *comarcal* map developed by the Republican government a hundred years later. In contrast to the externally imposed provincial divisions, Judicial Districts had to be centred on practical, local realities of who could move where, since they were the basis for locations of legal courts.

Historian and geographer Jesús Burgueño (2011) has suggested that historic differences in the nature of provinces throughout Spain has also contributed to the contemporary friction. He compares the Castilian versus the Aragonese (Catalan) concept of a provincial area. In territories that were under Catalan-Aragonese control in the medieval period, provinces formed large territorial areas with political and economic powers. Provinces were often equated with individual kingdoms that had come under Catalan-Aragonese rule. During the seventeenth century, in Catalonia in particular, these areas were associated with positive traits and a distinct identity. For example, in the Cortes (the regional government of that time) only inhabitants of the Principat of Catalonia could be members. The boundaries of this Principat coincide remarkably closely with the current CAC three to four hundred years later. This area also functioned as a province in the medieval era as part of the Crown of Aragon, yet even in 1632 outsiders are referred to as being from a different 'nation' (Lluis de Puera, in Burgueño, 2011: 11). In the nineteenth century, this loyalty to a province developed into provincialism, then regionalism, and finally nationalism (see Lluis de Puera, in Burgueño, 2011: 11).

On the other hand, the Castilian notion of provinces saw them as less powerful than in other Iberian kingdoms of the medieval era. An area was owned by feudal overlords but their authority could never destabilise the overall authority of the king. Following the consolidation of Spain after the conquest of the southern Moorish kingdoms in 1492, the Castilian style of government came to dominate Spain. Attitudes to local level control therefore already differed greatly between the former Catalan-Aragonese kingdoms and the newly developed Spanish state. According to Burgueño, these differences have perpetuated into the contemporary era.

The Catalan *Comarcal* System

In contrast to the system of provinces, the Catalan *comarca* was much older and more firmly rooted. They often share the names, if not the boundaries, of historic fiefdoms or '*vegueries*' into which Catalonia was divided in the early medieval period. This historic connection that the contemporary *comarca* has with a medieval concept is significant. Like many nationalist movements (Smith, 1986), central to Catalanism has been the claim to ancient origins and a past 'Golden Age'. Catalan anthropologist Josep Llobera describes it as a need to be 'looking back with relish' (Llobera, 2004: 21), to find the foundation of a nationalism against the state.

For Catalonia, this golden age was the height of the medieval Catalan-Aragonese Empire that ruled over much of the Mediterranean from the twelfth to the fifteenth centuries. Catalan was a language of culture; its capital Barcelona was the prosperous centre of maritime trade in the area. This era was also the inspiration of the nineteenth century Catalan Renaissance (*Renaixença*), which was the origin of today's nationalist movement, through attempts to re-establish Catalan as a literary language.

In light of this, the *comarca* has powerful symbolic value as a descendent or holdover from the medieval *vegueria*. Llobera (2004) has recognised that the most active periods of Catalan mapmaking were those when Catalan nationalism had the greatest freedom. The Catalan Geographic Society was created in 1906, five years after the creation of Catalonia's first political party (Lliga Regionalista). While the current, formal boundaries of the contemporary *comarca* were only established in 1936, the apparent continuity of this self-defined unit of territorial division with a glorified past lends it apparent legitimacy as a long-established structure. Furthering their Catalan nationalist connotations, the end of the period of *vegueries* also coincided with a traumatic moment in Catalan national history: the Decree of the *Nueva Planta* of 1716 (Buergueño, 2003, 2011). At the start of the eighteenth century, there were between twelve and fifteen *vegueries*, which gradually became known as *comarques*. In 1936, when the Republican government brought a new map of Catalonia into force, individual areas became *comarques*, while groupings of these areas became *vegueries*.

In the post-Franco era from 1975 onwards, much greater power devolved to the Autonomous Communities (of which Catalonia is one), rendering the provincial structure less important. This state of affairs has also enforced the provincial system's association with the era of the Franco dictatorship, an era remembered as one of repression of Catalan culture. This provincialisation of Catalonia was also a means of turning Catalonia into a dis-united group of four provinces, or at best a 'region' composed of four provinces, with no difference from the rest of the Spanish areas. Indeed it has been said that in the early years of the dictatorship Franco even suggested renaming Catalonia to give it the name 'North-Eastern Region', though this was never enacted.

Today most Catalans find the use of the word 'region' to describe Catalonia as insulting, as it recalls the Franco era. They much prefer the use of the term 'nation' to describe the Catalan Autonomous Community. In the contemporary era, this rumour of Catalonia's denial as a geographical entity is compared with current politics, for example in a cartoon published in *La Vanguardia* in May 2013, alongside reports on the Spanish Constitutional Court's ruling in March that Catalonia's proposed independence vote was illegal (see Figure 5.1).

Figure 5.1 Cartoon showing how a denial of Catalonia's geographical existence is tantamount to denying its political existence, while also protesting the behaviour of the Spanish Constitutional Court. Source: Toni Batllori. Used with permission of the artist.

In it, a Catalan (obvious by his bright red *barretina*)[4] considers all the outrageous acts against Catalonia that the '*Tribunal Curtitucional*' (a play on 'Tribunal constitucional', suggesting their short-sighted policies) could do. In the following vignettes, he suggests renaming Catalonia the 'Community for Spaniards of the North-East', or reassigning all the election votes amongst anti-Catalanist parties, and finally prohibiting *pa-amb tomàquet*, one of Catalonia's national foods and a gastro-cultural symbol.

It must be said that *comarques* exist throughout Spain, however in each of the different Autonomous Communities they have different roles. In Valencia for example, the *comarca* has no administrative function, and is merely symbolic. In Catalonia however, they have a much more important role as local government areas for voting, census taking, and applying directives from the Catalan autonomous government (Generalitat). The *comarcal* capital was the principal administrative centre, and in the post-Franco era these towns and cities have reclaimed that position. More importantly, county capitals were also the locus of the main market where inhabitants would congregate to buy and sell their goods, making them centres of social life for the area. This role still exists today, and markets held in these historic contexts have become symbolic markers of Catalan identity. This goes back to the comment from one of my informants that I mentioned at the start of this chapter, which combines both the centrality of markets in Catalan gastronational identity with their customary presence in county capitals. These dual associations play off one another, and strengthen both of these different symbols of Catalanism.[5]

The 1936 Development of Catalan Comarques

It is highly pertinent that the present-day delineation of the *comarques* was completed in 1936 by the Generalitat (Catalan Parliament) under the Republic. The Republican period (1931–1939) is remembered as a time of relative freedom, when

Catalan language and culture flourished with the re-establishment of the Generalitat. Creating national maps was part of a modernising drive by the Republican government, and had long been central to the Catalanist agenda. The fact that it was developed by the Republican government, and then reinstated in 1981 by the returning Catalan government-in-exile has furthered the *comarcal* map's historical continuity and nationalist associations in the twentieth century. Attempts to develop cartographic representations of Catalonia had been one other manifestation of Catalan nationalism, and efforts had been made to develop county and regional maps since the mid-nineteenth century (Burgueño, 2003).

In 1931, the newly established Catalan government, the Generalitat, created a committee into the study of Catalonia's territorial division (in Catalan, *La Ponència d'Estudi de la Divisió Territorial de Catalunya*), consisting of eight members. Their aim was to formally standardise the boundaries of the *comarques*, based on surveys within Catalonia. Researchers focused on town halls as the main research unit. The representatives of these town halls would gain a consensus from local inhabitants by asking them the following three questions (Lluch and Nel·lo, 1983):

1 In which *comarca* do you think you are based?
2 What is your principle market?
3 Do you attend any other market?

The findings of this research can be seen in Figure 5.2 and Figure 5.3, published in 1936. The maps produced show a remarkable awareness of clear identification with a *comarca*, and that markets were a clever tool to ascertain this level of identification. The main aim was to use these accurate maps based on the local, practical, everyday realities of Catalans, and their self-identification with a particular region. Developed in this way, such a map had a much greater potential to become a symbol of identity, composed of categories defined by Catalans themselves, and to which all could relate. While this is not recorded, it is possible that upon looking at this map and remembering their part in its construction, ordinary Catalans could feel pride in contributing to a grand scale project uniting other members of the Catalan nation.

Part of the division of Catalonia into *comarques* was also their grouping into *vegueries*, which were presented as an alternative to the Spanish provincial divisions of 1833. It was hoped they would eventually supersede them. The legislature is quite explicit that this was the Generalitat's goal, explaining that the system of provinces in Catalonia is (Diari Oficial de la Generalitat de Catalunya, no. 360, 25 December 1936: 1166):

> A sign of submission to a centralism that repudiates our collective spirit, the four provinces into which Catalonia was divided in 1833, have been superseded to give place to the reconstruction of the Catalan unity.... To govern Catalonia from Barcelona necessitates new divisions adapted to the characteristics of our autonomy and based in the natural and economic realities of the land.

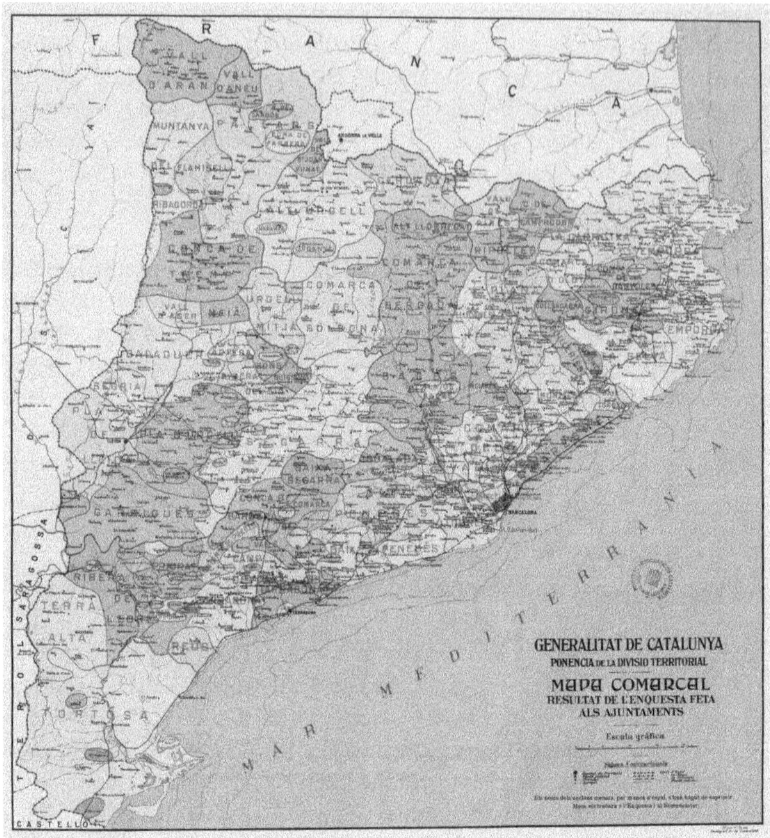

Figure 5.2 Responses to which comarca respondents self-identify with in map form.
Source: Institut Cartogràfic i Geològic de Catalunya. Used with permission of Cartoteca de Catalunya. Institut Cartogràfic i Geològic de Catalunya.

These new divisions will therefore be more suited to a Catalan-based government, now in charge of its own destiny. So the creation of these new divisions is explicitly going against the centralist policies of the Spanish government. The use of the name '*vegueries*' was a significant decision to recognise historic feudal divisions, and update a holdover from Catalonia's historic past to the new Republican era that would allow Catalonia to enter a new Golden Age. An emphasis on naturalness once more underscores how this new map will be based on the realities of Catalonia's varied landscapes, its people and their needs. This emphasis on naturalness is in contrast to the apparently arbitrary provincial divisions that combined contrasting geographies and ignored local morphologies.

Research was completed in 1936, the same year in which the Spanish Civil War broke out. For the following three years, the map was in official use and the provincial model suppressed, with some success despite the wartime situation (Sureda, 2003). A well-known poster promoting the new map can be seen in Figure 5.4. The

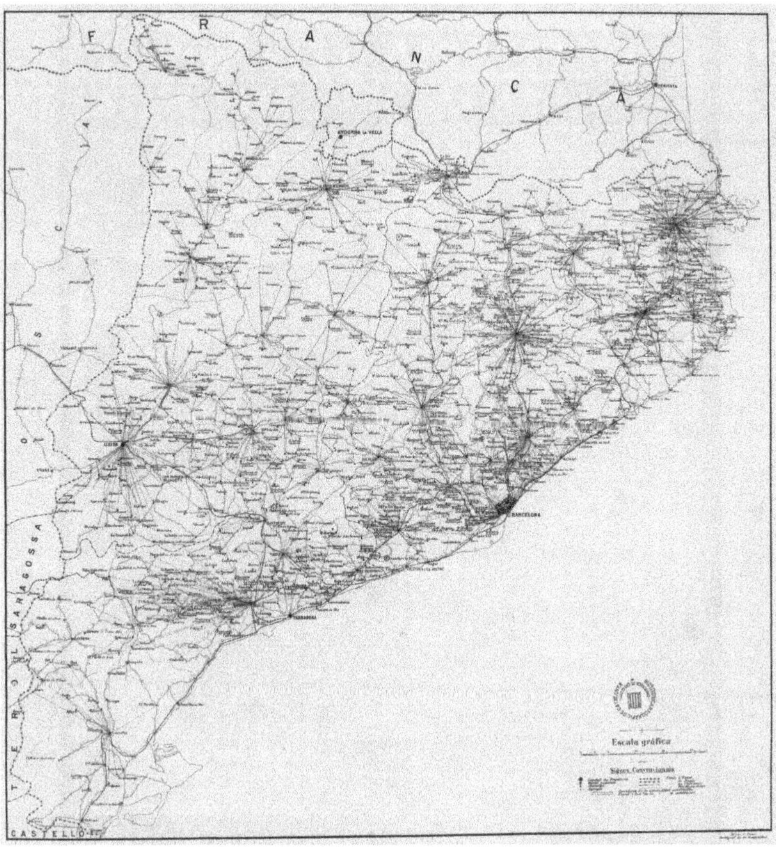

Figure 5.3 Principle markets used by respondents in different towns across Catalonia in map form. Source: Institut Cartogràfic i Geològic de Catalunya. Used with permission of Cartoteca de Catalunya. Institut Cartogràfic i Geològic de Catalunya.

vegueries were not given names, but numbers, though each had their county capitals defined as Barcelona (I), Girona (II), Tarragona (III), Reus (IV), Tortosa (V), Vic (VI), Manresa (VII), Lleida (VIII) and Tremp (IX).

In 1939, Franco's forces defeated the Republican government. The 1936 map of *comarques* and *vegueries* was abolished, and the provincial system re-asserted as the only acceptable cartographic division of Catalonia. Ironically, in the post-war restructuring, the research carried out in Catalonia in 1931–36 was much admired for its approach and thoroughness, and acted as the basis for further mapmaking projects throughout Spain. Even though these maps were banned from official and public use, they were circulated in academic circles (Burgueño, 2003). Even more ironic, as these maps had acquired an academic, scientific status, Catalan geographers could promote a subtle nationalistic bias through their work in the Franco period (Llobera, 2004).

Figure 5.4 1936 poster showing the official territorial division of Catalonia. Source: Cartoteca de Catalunya. Institut Cartogràfic i Geològic de Catalunya. Used with permission of Cartoteca de Catalunya. Institut Cartogràfic i Geològic de Catalunya.

Despite (or perhaps because of) the Francoist suppression, the map itself became an emblem of the Catalan government in exile and of Francoist repression and a symbol of protest against it. Not just the division into *comarques*, but also the regions into which they were divided became significant, as they were a direct contradiction of the provincial system espoused by the central government (Sureda, 2003).

Following Franco's death in 1975, the Catalan government in exile returned in 1977, and the Spanish Constitution of 1978 formally established a democratic system with large-scale devolution of power to the autonomous communities. It would be ten years however before the *comarcal* system was once more established in 1987, and this system continues to this day. The system of *vegueries* is also used, albeit in non-governmental contexts as they have not been formally approved today.

Their application however is still pertinent, and one of the conditions of the 2006 Statute of Autonomy was that the province system would be superseded by these areas, called *Àmbits funcionals territorials* (or 'functional territorial areas'). However, with the 2010 judgement, these plans were put on hold. Once again, the sub-division into these Catalan-defined territorial areas has become a point of contention with the central government.

The recommendations for the 2006 Statute come from a 2000 report into Catalonia's territorial division, the so-called 'Roca report'. According to the report, the motivation is to improve the current territorial organisation of Catalonia, 'which have negative consequences for citizens' (Parlament de Catalunya, 2000: 9). As in 1931–36, stress is placed on respecting local autonomy from town halls, and encouraging individual participation. It encourages the introduction of the *vegueria*, which should take over and replace the Spanish state's provinces system, in order to 'adapt [the system] to the contemporary reality of the country' (Parlament de Catalunya, 2000: 11). Note parallels with statements in 1936. While an early suggestion (in Vila, 1989) involved uniting Catalonia into a single province, the Roca report says time has shown this to be unwise (it does not say why, though a negative reaction from the central government to such a proposal may be the reason). Instead, the provinces themselves should be altered (rather than replaced) to fit better into *vegueries*, thus maintaining the status quo of the Spanish provincial system, but with slight alterations.

The suggested structure of a new territorial division can be seen in Figure 5.5. The *vegueries* would be Barcelona, Catalunya Central, Ponent, Cap de Tarragona, Terres de l'Ebre and Girona. Several of the larger *comarques* would also be divided up into more manageable areas, to recognise the individual characteristics of each area. One of the major differences between the Roca report's suggested map and that of 1936 was that Ponent includes the counties that were formerly of a separate *comarca* (often called unofficially '*Alt Pirineu*', high Pyrenees). This was for population reasons, as this area contained only 1% of Catalonia's population, proof of the Generalitat's awareness and respect for local, contemporary realities.

In suggesting *vegueries* as units for territorial division, the report situates them clearly in the history of the Catalan nation, by justifying their use in the

> long historical tradition in the political-administrative organisation of Catalonia and of the whole Crown of Aragon since the middle ages. Their members and local deputies were figures of territorial representation of the King and the Generalitat until 1714. (Parlament de Catalunya, 2000: 54–55)

These comments once more place emphasis on the *vergueries* as historic units, with ties to Catalonia's historic golden age, and which ended during a traumatic time in Catalonia's history in 1714, a date which has entered Catalan consciousness due to Catalanist celebrations of the tercentenary in 2014. The nationalist sentiment here is therefore implicit. Much like the rhetoric surrounding calls for independence itself, arguments in favour of the Roca report's findings are centred

Figure 5.5 Roca report's proposal for boundaries of comarques and vegueries in a new territorial division. Source: Generalitat de Catalunya. Used with permission of Generalitat de Catalunya.

on rational suggestions for improving the lives of Catalans and contributing to their well-being (economic or otherwise).

Despite their unofficial status, *vegueries* are still used today in everyday parlance, in symbolic contexts, and in tourist guides. For example, it is common when in Vic, Osona, for inhabitants to refer to themselves as being from 'central Catalonia' (*Catalunya central*). They do not really see themselves as from 'Barcelona' in any sense, which they perceived of as purely the city or the *comarca*, despite being in that province. Similarly, one informant who I visited in Terra Alta (in the south-west of Catalonia, on the border with Aragon) felt no affiliation with 'Tarragona' as a province, but much more with the Ebre region. As such, these historic mappings and delineations of space still affect how Catalans perceive themselves today.

Excursionisme, Regional Cuisine and National Knowledge

In 2003, the Generalitat's Department of Agriculture published a work called *Productes de la Terra* (Products of the Land), listing the principal products associated with each different *comarca* of Catalonia, a scheme that imitates the PDO/PGI classifications in the European Union. *Comarques* are divided into the regional groupings, more or less the same as that of the 1936 map. This book is arguably an example of pro-Catalanist propaganda, as much as it is a tourist guide. In his prologue the Catalan President, Artur Mas, explicitly says that the ground base for this book is that food is a sign of a country's identity, and for that reason should be celebrated (Generalitat de Catalunya, 2003).

The different landscapes within Catalonia's borders have led to an unusual culinary richness, as each area is suited to different species of crops, fruit and vegetables, livestock and even cooking styles. In researching food identity in Catalonia, many of my informants used these divisions as frames of reference to perceive other parts of Catalonia. This regional awareness is connected strongly with the *excursionist* ideal of knowing the Catalan territory, land and characteristics intimately. Such knowledge is acquired by travelling around and visiting other areas of Catalonia as internal tourists.

The Pyrenean *comarques* have a mountainous terrain and climate. The high quality pastures have meant the area specialises in cheese and meat production. The central *comarques* are similar to the Pyrenees in that their continental climate and longer winters have produced a preference for starchy vegetables and heavier foods. Wooded and flatter in parts, here mushrooms, truffles and grains are the principal outputs, as well as Protected Denomination of Origin *Llonganissa de Vic*, a cured sausage that results from particular local climate conditions on the Plain of Vic. Girona is a mixture both of the Pyrenees mountains and the Mediterranean seaboard, which, it is said, has led to the development of an interesting cuisine called *mar i muntanya* (or 'mountain and sea'), made up of seafood and meat dishes combined. 'Metropolitan' *comarques* around Barcelona are also known for their seafood, and also fruits and vegetables due to the warm climate and gentle terrain. The climate becomes warmer and dryer further south and west, in Lleida and Tarragona, where Catalonia's primary olive oil producing regions are located. Lleida's flat plain is especially associated with fruit cultivation, and Tarragona with blue fish, and vegetable production in the inland *comarques*. Finally in the south there is the Ebre Delta, a large part of which is wetlands, and also ideal for the growing of rice, which is especially associated with that area. Some Catalan families I knew made a point of travelling once a year to eat rice somewhere in the Terres de l'Ebre.

The physical aspects of the landscape give rise to the produce that is available there, and the food that is subsequently eaten. One phrase that I often heard when in Catalonia was, 'The cuisine of a country is its landscape put into a pot.' The phrase is attributed to Josep Pla, one of the most important Catalan writers of the twentieth century. Pla, along with other Catalan writers under the dictatorship, used his writings to try and preserve a Catalan culture that he and his colleagues saw as being lost. One of the main ways he did this was to emphasise the need to travel through Catalonia, to get to know it, as a means of preserving its unique identity.

This was part of a general trend present in Catalan nationalism since the nineteenth century called *excursionisme*. Llobera (2004: 60) explains that, 'In 1976 hiking (*excursionisme*) became an activity that was not purely a sporting or scientific activity. It acquired a political dimension that was essentially associated with one of the national dimensions of Catalonia.' National poets such as Joan Maragall and Jacint Verdaguer, writing in the late nineteenth and early twentieth century, represented Catalonia's landscapes and landmarks, aware that 'hikers were deeply in love with Catalonia' (see Llobera, 2004).

Excursionisme means more to the people of Catalonia than walking or hiking in the mountains. *Excursionisme* is to travel around and experience different parts of Catalonia. Since the 1930s, tourist posters have encouraged Catalans to spend their time and money in Catalonia (see Figure 5.6). These posters often contained maps, not just as a guide, but also as a 'logo' of the Catalan nation, encouraging nationalist sentiment and loyalty (Urla, 1993). *Excursionisme* is often the act of visiting other parts of Catalonia to taste certain foods, such as the trip to the Terres de l'Ebre in the south, to try their rice dishes. Through *excursionisme* Catalans develop a deep affection and understanding of their land through the experience of eating. Through *excursionisme*, a Catalan can discover things about their nation, and their native land, coming to know it intimately. Indeed one of the activities often included in *excursionisme* is *busca-bolets*, or mushroom hunting. This activity requires an intimate knowledge of the landscape, its landmarks, and its characteristics, in order to find the mushrooms.

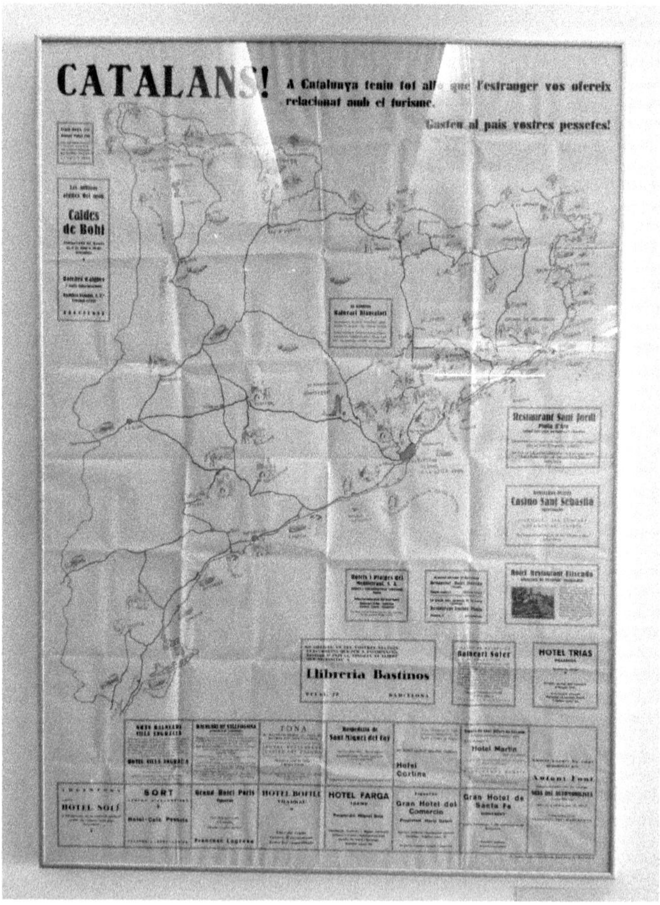

Figure 5.6 Photograph of a 1930 map encouraging internal tourism, held at Barcelona's tourism office. Source: Author. Used with permission of the Barcelona Tourist Board.

Arguably the landscape itself has been preserved through *excursionisme*. There are several instances of *excursionistes* coming across Romanesque churches and monasteries that had been forgotten. These restored ruins became part of the national patrimony and are now Catalanist monuments in their own right. In Josep Pla's later works, from 1950–1970, there are accounts of his own *excursions* through Catalonia, seeking to preserve in writing an identity and way of life he saw as slowly disappearing. Today, Catalans refer to his *excursionisme* as sources of knowledge on their own identity, defining what is Catalan and what is not.

In short *excursionistes* have helped to create a national culture and *excursionisme* remains a common pastime. Catalans are keen to promote the ideal of travel through Catalonia. Two of Catalonia's most popular magazines, *Cuina* and *Descubrir*, stress the need to experience Catalan places through their landscapes, regional foods, and food festivals. *Descrubrir* (literally, 'Discover') is especially active in this regard, acting as a travel magazine for all Catalan-speaking areas. These publications argue that only through physically experiencing Catalonia's geography can Catalans come to solidify their connection with it. They also contribute economically to their nation through tourist spending. In my own personal experience, my Catalan informants encouraged me to get to know different areas of Catalonia, as part of my integration process. *Excursionisme* is thus still a central symbol in creating Catalan identity. It is through contemporary *excursionisme* by Catalans within Catalonia that their nationality becomes reality.

Performing the Map

As with many nationalist causes, the activity of mapmaking has been central to a Catalan nationalism. Mapmaking has allowed the development of an essential national symbol, the map of Catalonia. It has also leant significance to the units involved in that mapmaking, the *comarca* and the *vergueria*, as Catalan defined units that have a long history, like the Catalan nation itself. But most importantly, the development of maps has also been a means of asserting Catalan national identity against that of the Spanish state. This is seen most clearly in Catalan reactions to the provincial system. The provincial system is distinct from the *comarques*, as it is imposed from outside Catalonia's borders, ignores local realities, and is even used to deny Catalonia's existence as a geographic entity.

And, as I have argued in this chapter, whilst maps of Catalonia have become symptomatic of the power play between the Catalan and Spanish central governments, the ideal of *excursionisme* puts a Catalan national identity composed of self-defined regions into practice. By experiencing Catalan regions, and their food ways, one ideally develops a greater knowledge of Catalonia. This behaviour becomes a means of intimately knowing Catalonia's diverse component regions, and strengthens feelings of belonging. *Excursionistes* experience the landscapes that make up Catalan territory, touch them, smell them and in trying regional foods, *excursionistes* can taste them as well. Through visiting the places on the map, the image of the map becomes a means of remembering individual experiences, performing in the landscape a powerful symbol of a greater Catalan nation.

Notes

1 I am using a Catalan adjective '*comarcal*' here to describe anything related to a *comarca*, as it is less unwieldy than an English translation.
2 Plural form of '*comarca*' according to Catalan language rules.
3 These conservative elements were the Carlists, as opposed to the liberals who were tenuously in power. Earlier in 1833, King Ferdinand VII died, leaving only two daughters. The liberal faction supported the daughter's right to rule, while the Carlists supported the King's brother Don Carlos in line with Salic law, and found favour in the more conservative sections of Spanish society.
4 The *barretina* is a type of Phrygian cap originally associated with Catalan peasants, and now part of Catalan national costume.
5 I discuss the connection between Catalan markets and identity in the proceedings from a paper I gave at the 2014 Oxford Symposium of Food and Cookery (Congdon, 2015).

References

Ardener E (2006) *The Voice of Prophesy*. New York, Oxford: Berghahn.
Burgueño J (2003) *Història de la divisió comarcal*. Barcelona: Rafael Dalmau.
Burgueño J (2011) *La Invención de la provincias*. Madrid: Catarata.
Congdon V (2015) Catalan markets: constructing national cuisine and space through the market scene, in M McWilliams (ed) *Oxford Symposium on Food and Cookery: Food and Markets*. London: Prospect Books, 104–113.
Diari Oficial de la Generalitat de Catalunya, no. 360, 25 December 1936: 1166.
Digiacomo S (1985) The politics of identity: Nationalism in Catalonia (symbolism, language, Spain, ideology). Doctoral Dissertations Available from Proquest. AAI8517098. http://scholarworks.umass.edu/dissertations/AAI8517098.
Generalitat de Catalunya: Departament d'Agricultura, Ramaderia i Pesca (2003) *Productes de la Terra*. Barcelona: Generalitat de Catalunya.
Llobera J (2004) *Foundations of National Identity: From Catalonia to Europe*. Oxford and London: Berghan Books.
Lluch E and Nel·lo O (eds) (1983) *La Gènesi de la divisió territorial de Catalunya: edició de documents de l'arxiu de la ponència: 1931–1939*. Barcelona: Diputació de Barcelona.
Parlament de Catalunya (2000) *Informe sobre la revisió del model d'organització territorial de Catalunya*. Available from: www.geosoc.udl.es/professorat/informe_OTC.pdf (accessed 14 November 2015).
Smith AD (1986) *The Ethnic Origin of Nations*. Oxford: Blackwell.
Sureda P (2003) La divisió administrativo-territorial de Catalunya: panoràmica històrica i estat de la question. Available from: https://www.racocatala.cat/ (accessed 14 November 2015).
Urla J (1993) Cultural politics in an age of statistics: numbers, nations, and the making of Basque identity. *American Ethnologist* 20(4): 818–843.
Vila M-A (1989) Les Comarques i els municipis de Catalunya: territori i població. Barcelona: Generalitat de Catalunya.

Part II

Politics

6 A Radical New Regional Geography

Notes on a Revolution

James Riding

> In a world hypnotised by the raptures of the neoliberal moment, the very idea of revolution has, in the global North at least, not just fallen out of fashion but removed itself to the infinite horizon of never-never land.
>
> (Smith, 2010: 51)

The Revolutionary Imperative

Here it is reported that formerly Yugoslav citizens feeling former in the present – a definition of trauma – are currently suffering through the devastating consequences of a twenty-year-old experiment in political, social, and economic engineering – after the collapse of a socialist Yugoslavia – known as 'transition' (see Arsenijević, 2011, 2014; Horvat and Štiks, 2015; see also Fontana, 2013). Yet, as this chapter goes on to describe, perhaps no other post-socialist region in the world can claim to be in such a period of revolution and resistance to the 'transition' period post-1989 than the post-socialist Balkan states. In 2014 to openly question the 'transition' to capitalism became commonplace in Yugoslavia's new states. Resistance sprang from Zagreb to Ljubljana, from Skopje to Sarajevo, as popular movements across the region responded to two common enemies, rapacious neoliberal capitalism and the post-democratic governance of repeatedly corrupt and continually divisive elites (see Arsenijević, 2014; Horvat and Štiks, 2015; see also Fontana, 2013).

Citizen-activists in the post-socialist Yugoslav successor states, as such, undertook a multicultural and multi-ethnic resistance (see Bourdieu, 1998), treading a path towards a future of justice and democracy beyond national borders and territorial disputes (see Campbell, 1999; Crampton, 1996; see also Jeffrey, 2012; Toal and Dahlman, 2011). Entangled within their emancipatory struggle citizen-activists saw a present Yugoslavia, which was bit by bit disappearing. And they sought to retain what remains there were of that older and apparently discredited socialist state, and to reclaim a socialist space in a space of post-socialism. Most of all they sought to rescue the commons, the factories, the museums, the public spaces, indeed everything that the post-socialist 'transition' era had in their eyes diminished (see Fontana, 2013). Occupying space, mobile citizen-activists took to the streets and established self-governed assemblies, and resolved to embed new radically democratic or horizontal forms of governance (see Brookchin, 2014). The most radical of these experiments in non-institutional politics found across the Balkans since the collapse of Yugoslavia is *The Plenum Movement*, the focus of this chapter (see Arsenijević, 2014; Horvat and Štiks, 2015; Kraft, 2015).

Here the cultural raw materials used to open radical spaces, construct new civic discourses, and organise critical citizen-led dialogues are described, in order to give a sense of from where and how *The Plenum Movement* emerged in the desert of post-socialism (see Horvat and Štiks, 2015). The movement began with a revolutionary event, which as Henri Lefebvre (2003: 19) notes, 'generally take place in the street', and then as is often the case the movement crystallised around specific spaces in cities – and in some small towns – across Bosnia-Herzegovina. The event – significant protests after the closure of symbolic factories in the northern Bosnian city of Tuzla – sparked a mass citizen-led mobilisation, with the right to use public space as a site of dissent becoming the initial goal of the movement. Certain objectives were subsequently created, and the uprising coalesced around the formation of citizen-led assemblies or Plenum. The methods through which the movement attempted to force a revolution were at times violent – including the burning of the presidency building in the capital Sarajevo (see Figure 6.1) – though *The Plenum Movement* is largely a force through what it represents symbolically.

In this particular post-socialist, post-conflict region, the movement offers what could be seen as an 'alternative transition' or a 'counter transition' to the

Figure 6.1 Photograph, Sarajevo, February 2014.

'transition' to capitalism after Yugoslavia – or more specifically, an alternative to a toxic nexus of neoliberal capitalism and ethno-nationalist politics, after the collapse of a socialist Yugoslavia (see Arsenijević, 2011, 2014; see also Bieber, 2006). And the multi-local movement deconstructs the overbearing regional schema within which it finds itself without ever arguing for constitutional reform and a tearing up of the Dayton Agreement, signed in 1995 as a territorial peace deal (see Murtagh, 2016). Indeed today Dayton is perhaps the only thing holding the country Bosnia-Herzegovina together, whilst simultaneously separating it into distinct entities (see Campbell, 1999; Crampton, 1996; see also Belloni, 2009; Bieber, 2006; Jeffrey, 2012; Toal and Dahlman, 2011; Gordy, 2015). As such *The Plenum Movement* instead, in an attempt to bypass the entrenched territorial politics of the region, produced radical openings from where neoliberalism is challenged, and created vital multi-ethnic spaces beyond yet within the fixed identitarian and ethno-nationalist regional entities present (see Bieber, 2006; Jeffrey, 2012; Toal and Dahlman, 2011). The movement primarily was about individuals freeing themselves from a toxic nexus of nationalism and neoliberalism, as the revolt enabled citizens to become citizens again and to form bonds and ties beyond their ethnicities, in order to then reimagine society together (see Arsenijević, 2014; see also Anderson, 1983; Brubaker, 2002; Campbell, 1998; Nancy, 2000).

The Plenum Movement is an ideology in its public denial of ethno-nationalism – accepted by the international community for over two decades (see Kennedy and Riga, 2013) – and an imagined future also in its openness to all citizens as individuals, not flattened ethnic-identities (see Touquet, 2015; see also Anderson, 1983; Brubaker, 2002; Campbell, 1998; Nancy, 2000). The movement – transferrable, malleable, and importantly transparent – encouraged citizen-activists to shuttle between mass protests and street moblisations (see Figure 6.2), blockades, sit-ins and direct action taking and occupying public space, manifestos and demands delivered to parliament, remembrance and therapy in order to collectively mourn a traumatic past, and citizens' assemblies where a reimagined socialism was solidified (see Arsenijević, 2014; Kraft, 2015). *The Plenum Movement* was and is, as such, in its horizontal form, in its overall goal to create an alternative to the post-socialist neoliberal 'transition' era, and in its deconstructing of ethno-nationalist divides post-conflict (see Campbell, 1999; Crampton, 1996), a radical *new regional geography* in the state within which it finds itself and also in grand scope a simultaneous opening-on-to and distancing-from the new Europe (see Jeffrey, 2008).

This chapter and the socio-political movement itself are committed to the region out of which they emerged, though the uprising in February 2014 – widely reported as the Bosnian Spring – and the describing of it here extends to and parallels with movements across Europe and the Middle East. After the global financial crisis and the failure of capitalism, there has been a marked upsurge in citizen-led activism across the globe, the Occupy movements and the Arab Spring, the protests in Gezi Park in Istanbul and in the Maidan in Kiev. Such events encompassed the Balkans, from the Aganaktismenoi in Greece to the formation of Plenum in Bosnia-Herzegovina. The scale of dissent in the Balkans was unprecedented in the

Figure 6.2 Photograph, Zenica, March 2014.

post-socialist neoliberal 'transition' era. It was a revolutionary moment in a region where a world that isn't capitalist could be imagined, or more specifically could be re-imagined (see Harvey and Haraway, 1995: 519). In the few years since Neil Smith (2010) penned *The Revolutionary Imperative*, a proliferation of revolt has occurred meaning that revolution is now seemingly less absurd. The story of this attempted heist on capitalism is told in what follows perhaps surprisingly not through the guise of a post-structuralist, Marxist, anarchist, or radical geography; it is instead as the geographer William Bunge (2011: 240) writes, written as 'a call to action, not merely an exercise in abstraction', a study of the regional social and material conditions out of which a revolution could emerge. A never-never land (Smith, 2010: 51).

Deconstructing Territorial Ethno-Politics

The war in Bosnia was eventually brought to an end in December 1995, when the Dayton Agreement was signed. A 'peace' time has lasted to this day, although the framework agreement, which divided the country in roughly half along ethnic lines, has prevented Bosnia-Herzegovina from developing entirely beyond wartime divisions (see Campbell, 1999; Crampton, 1996; see also Belloni, 2009; Bieber, 2006; Jeffrey, 2012; Toal and Dahlman, 2011). Preceded by an agreement between Bosniaks and Bosnian Croats signed in Washington in 1994, the country was separated into two political entities: the predominantly Bosnian Serb, Republika Srpska, and the mainly Bosniak and Bosnian Croat, Federation of Bosnia and Herzegovina, sometimes informally referred to as the

Bosniak-Croat Federation. Locally, the country is further separated out, as the Federation of Bosnia and Herzegovina has 10 autonomous cantons with their own governments. Each canton is known as majority Bosnian Croat, majority Bosniak, or 'mixed' (see Nancy, 2000). Within the cantons are municipalities and homogenous enclaves, which further define the individuals living there (see Campbell, 1999; Crampton, 1996; see also Anderson, 1983; Brubaker, 2002; Campbell, 1998; Nancy, 2000). And while Republika Srpska is led more centrally from the de facto capital Banja Luka, there are still observable geographical divisions between the northern portion and southern portion of 'the state within a state', which is often said to be under threat of being wiped off the map, acting in-place as a nationalising of civic discourse nullifying post-ethnic activism (see Touquet, 2012, 2015).

This cartographic representational idiosyncrasy or more precisely 'apartheid cartography' enforces a nationalist overhaul of space upon individuals in Bosnia-Herzegovina and the wider Yugoslavia (see Campbell, 1999; Crampton, 1996). Cartography has arguably enabled a post-socialist era of never-ending 'transition', diminished democracy, and the continuation of nationalist governance that it was hoped would fade away (see Gordy, 2015). Resembling Berlin after World War II, Sarajevo itself is a meeting point of the different lines that were drawn across Bosnia-Herzegovina and is partly in Republika Srpska and partly in the Federation of Bosnia and Herzegovina. The de jure capital of Republika Srpska is Sarajevo, the de facto capital of the Federation of Bosnia and Herzegovina is Sarajevo, and Sarajevo is the capital of the country Bosnia-Herzegovina, where a weak central government also resides. It is no surprise therefore that protests erupted here, bypassing and dissolving the divisions on the map. Sarajevo is a place that was for Jean-Luc Nancy (2000) a mêlée, due to its long history of multiculturalism in a real and not prescribed sense (see also Rieff, 1995). It was a historical regional focus as bridge between East and West and the old power blocs. Sarajevo is, as such, a non-aligned space, a place where a profoundly anti-capitalist and radically democratic vision of society could form (see Arsenijević, 2014; Horvat and Štiks, 2015; see also Harvey, 2012).

Vitally, as such, this chapter does not seek to simply return to a static, territorial, or mapped regional geography (see e.g., Vidal de La Blache, 1926; Hartshorne, 1939; Sauer, 1925), rather it uses the grounded political intentions of the now old-fashioned regional study to deconstruct the fixed borders of regions from below, speaking back to a relational multi-scalar interconnected new regional geography in radical ambition (see e.g., Agnew, 2013; Elden, 2005, 2009, 2010, 2013; Jonas, 2012; Jones, 2009; Jones and MacLeod, 2001, 2004, 2007; Murphy, 2013; Paasi, 1991, 1999, 2002, 2003; Painter, 2010). The re-writing of regions from below is a vitally important counter-narrative in regions defined and fixed by their traumatic pasts; or indeed regions that seem as if they can only ever be analysed via the gaze of an elevated, distanced, geopolitical eye (see Toal, 1996). As is conveyed in what follows, through a grounded geographical practice it is possible to offer a critically-oriented and intentionally disruptive perspective, documenting the rhythms and affective atmospheres of a social and political movement (see Lefebvre, 2004). And through this practice an attempt is made to re-define and under-cut the stubborn regional schema associated with the implicit identitarian and ethnic territorial geopolitics of this particular region of the world. A region of the world where a simplistic tracing between state and territory, and politics and governance, undergirds the processes involved in the making and unmaking of political subjects and the attachments and detachments of space, politics, and citizens (see Agnew, 2016; Brenner and Elden, 2009; Elden, 2013; Latour, 2007).

Specifically here it is suggested that 'going back to a regional geography' can be a way of tracing the growth of a nascent social and political movement built by citizens previously written out of an orthodox political history (see Thrift, 1994: 200; see also Agnew, 2013). Going back to a grounded, specific, individual, human, regional geography here is particularly worthwhile as it enables a regional writing of the embodied political subjectivities of individuals involved in direct action, and in so doing, importantly, it retains the voice of the individual in a region where it is common to collectivise the individual voice. Meaning a reconstituted regional geography here represents and is of a movement that seeks to deconstruct a fixed identitarian politics, and remove from below and within ethno-nationalist regional borders (see Thrift, 1983; see also Campbell, 1999; Crampton, 1996; see also Murtagh, 2016). In the process 'going back to a regional geography' is, in this chapter argued as such, to be a way of charting an emancipatory struggle, where citizens feel as if they are enabled to become individual political beings again, citizens again (see Thrift, 1994: 200; see also Anderson, 1983; Brubaker, 2002; Nancy, 2000).

As in *Fitzgerald: Geography of a Revolution*, a definitive regional study undertaken by the geographer William Bunge (1971), I will write a regional geography here which considers the view from below, or the view of social groups marginalised in orthodox political history (see Agnew, 2013). It is precisely through studying regions and writing at a regional scale – which unlike the national scale does not represent a privileging of institutions associated with the interests and outlooks of political elites (see Agnew, 2013) – that an emancipatory struggle was once placed and explored geographically in one square mile of Detroit, in a community known as Fitzgerald (see Bunge, 1971).

To write of a revolution as it emerges amidst the streets and squares of cities – where in which freshly political citizens are reclaiming and repairing public space – the chapter embraces the embedded regional geography approach associated with William Bunge (1971), yet updates it and animates it, borrowing from recent geographic work which documents the rhythms of the subject in landscape as it lingers, waits, detours, and ruminates (see Wylie, 2007; Matless, 2014). As such, the experiential narrative produced is reminiscent of a form of non-representational (see Thrift, 2008), embodied, landscape geography, which has emerged in the past decade and a half dealing with performance, affect, and aesthetics in-place, yet it relocates this work to a region of the world where it perhaps seems to some to be out-of-place (see e.g., Daniels, 2006, 2012; DeSilvey, 2007, 2010, 2012; Dubow, 2001, 2011; Edensor, 2005, 2008; Lorimer, 2003, 2006, 2012; Lorimer and Wylie, 2010; Matless, 2008, 2010, 2014; Pearson, 2006; Riding, 2015a, 2016;

Rose, 2012; Wylie, 2002, 2005). This embodied research obliquely refers back to an older form of regional geography, and the on-the-ground regional study, and could be used to refocus a writing of regions, reasserting a view from below (see Riding, 2015b; see also Agnew, 2013).

In the appendix of an article entitled, *On the determination of social action in space and time*, Nigel Thrift (1983) – a driving force behind the non-representational landscape turn in human geography (see Thrift, 2008; see also Wylie, 2007) – offers a similar methodology for a reconstituted regional geography to the one outlined in this chapter. Yet the methodology provided in 1983 was never deployed. Within the appendix Thrift (1983) notes a rich vein to be tapped and reworked, that is the use of autobiographies and diaries, in addition to more typical compositional approaches. Autobiographies and diaries can be used effectively to approach contextual regional issues, and they are 'a useful adjunct to give depth to conventional compositional accounts', while 'even one diary can provide a multitude of information', and can be used 'as a means of posing a series of contextual questions' (Thrift, 1983: 57). Here a life history approach is taken once more to reformulate the regional geography of William Bunge (1971), as oral history is used to investigate in-place, as Thrift (1983: 57) calls it, 'the exact content of sociability', recording how 'personality grows up in a particular region'.

Presently a reconstituted regional geography is perhaps jarringly transported to the region with which this chapter is concerned, as it is common to construct a certain geopolitical narrative in order to write of the former Yugoslavia. Work draws on either ethnographic data collected to explore state-building and post-conflict reconstruction (see e.g., Jeffrey, 2006), or, through a form of discourse analysis work interrogates the loss or dispossession of identity, deconstructing the internal skirmishes of ethnic and identitarian debate (see e.g., Campbell, 1998). Reanimating a regional geography – borrowing from a non-representational, embodied, landscape geography, and channelling the critical methodology and grounded field-work of William Bunge (1971) – this chapter drifts somewhat against the more established geopolitical discourses associated with research on the collapse of Yugoslavia (see e.g., Campbell, 1998; Glenny, 1992; Little and Silber, 1996; Rieff, 1995; Thompson, 1992), the post-socialist transition era after Yugoslavia (see e.g., Horvat and Štiks, 2015; Jeffrey, 2012; Toal and Dahlman, 2011), and the Balkans more widely (see e.g., Glenny, 1999; Goldsworthy, 1998; Mazower, 2002; Todorova, 1997; Žižek, 2000). And in so doing this first-hand account of a political uprising witnessed over three months follows instead the trail of another, more grounded, descriptive, everyday version of the geopolitical (see de Certeau, 1984; see also Bunge, 1971; Toal, 1996).

Clearly the reconstituted regional geography outlined so far seems to be far removed from the radical geography often associated with social and political movements. Defining what sort of a geography must be used to chart and describe a nascent socio-political movement, or indeed what it must look like, what it must represent, what it must build upon, is a constant theme in human geography. In effect David Harvey (2015) and Simon Springer (2014) recently delineated not only what a radical geography must be – anarchist or Marxist, or indeed both, as when closely inspected the distinction drawn somewhat falls apart – but also what kind of geography can be viewed as radical, and used to write of a revolution, of political struggle. Referring to their polemic pieces here is to ask whether an alternative geographical writing of nascent socio-political movements is possible, which considers regions and their everyday processes and affects and the embodied practice of citizen-activists in regional landscapes. Through this reconstituted regional landscape geography an emancipatory struggle is physically placed in the region from which it emerged and a radical fracturing of space is represented on-the-ground. Claiming, occupying, and repairing public space, embedding new spatial links between citizens, and inspiring newly political beings, *The Plenum Movement* is a regional performing of space (see Arsenijević, 2014), a realising of radical regions, and as such it has a regional geography.

The Revolutionary Event

On a television screen are the ice-skaters Torvill and Dean, describing thirty years later their gold medal performance at the Sarajevo 1984 *Winter Olympic Games*. The channel is changed. Flaming buildings and lines of riot police are visible, protesters, Molotov cocktails, rocks, rubber bullets and tear gas. Some of the buildings on the screen look familiar. 'Where are these riots happening?' 'Sarajevo, hell has come to Sarajevo.'

The uprising began on February 4, 2014 in the northern Bosnian city of Tuzla, peacefully to begin with (see Figure 6.3). Many protesters were former workers at recently closed factories, including DITA, Polihem, Guming, and Konjuh. Initially protesters gathered outside the Tuzla cantonal government building, holding the state responsible for the collapse of factories in the region since 2000, when they were covertly privatised. Over the ensuing days the protests spread to other Bosnian towns and cities, including Bihać, Mostar, Zenica, and Sarajevo. The brutality of the police response to the initial protests in Tuzla led to thousands marching on the streets, heading towards the presidency building in the capital Sarajevo. And the protest in Tuzla grew to 10,000 people. Protests in turn spread to the wider region as a reawakening of radical politics on the Balkan Peninsula occurred, almost seventy years after a socialist Yugoslavia was first formed. Protests were held on February 12 in Belgrade, Serbia and on February 13 in Zagreb, Croatia, in support of the political struggle in Bosnia-Herzegovina. And there were also reports of anti-government protests in Montenegro and Kosovo.

Tuzla, the main city in the centre of the northeast of Bosnia was the beating heart of Yugoslav industry (see Singleton, 1985). Indeed Tuzla is named after the extensive salt reserves found underneath the city. The name Tuzla, an important Ottoman garrison, derives from the Turkish for salt mine. Large coal deposits, thermo-electric plants, socialist smokestacks, clouds rolling across concrete cooling towers, endless pipelines, vast grey boxes, produce energy for the rest of the country. The coal mines dotted around the city power the Tuzla Power Station, the largest in Bosnia-Herzegovina. The region is an industrial machine. In the

Figure 6.3 Photograph, Tuzla, February 2014.

past decade five former state-owned companies, including an industrial detergent factory called DITA, were sold to private owners who sold assets, stopped paying workers, and then filed for bankruptcy.

DITA is an industrial detergent factory on the edge of Tuzla. Lorries stand empty in the forecourt, not a soul is about, trees whisper in the wind above the silent machinery, no gravel being crunched by feet, or engines whirring into action, a taxi rank has zero cabs, cavernous peaked hangers contain stopped conveyors, giant domes lay dormant, offices echo without the sound of humans, and lampposts provide light for stray dogs only. The plant has been left to the elements, copper has been stripped, assembly has ceased, pipes, valves, metres, scales, destroyed, costing huge amounts to fix, just jumbles of stuff now, matter without purpose, corrugated metal art forms. 'Nothing is happening here, absolutely nothing, the workers are at home,' Emina, a former worker at DITA, explains. Ministers said production would begin again in 2013. It did not begin.

In a clandestine way, without the workers knowing, factories, such as DITA, were privatised by the cantonal government and sold to new owners (see Arsenijević, 2014). The new owners almost immediately reduced the quality of the product sold, failed to maintain and properly inspect the machinery, and deciding the factory was not profitable enough began to pay the workers less, some not at all, and started to lay off experienced staff. The workers felt they had to do something about it, as they had a stake in the factory, and the city of Tuzla had a stake in the factory. Despite some workers being owed months of wages they continued to show up for work and attempted to keep the factory properly functioning. There were workers who had been working at DITA since the 1970s and saw it as a symbol of a prospering socialist Yugoslavia. So they turned up for work each day, for weeks and months without pay. Until one morning the owners padlocked the gates and refused the workers entry. Backed into a corner and fearing the owners would strip the factory of assets, such as the copper wire, the workers at DITA blockaded the entrance to the factory. Occupying a space around the factory, the workers protested for production to continue, in the hope that they could themselves reopen it. Each day they worried that the machines were slowly decaying, yet they remained hopeful. The protests took various forms, even hunger strikes. The public stood behind the DITA workers, and the small protest outside the factory spread to Tuzla, and other towns and cities across Bosnia-Herzegovina.

Out of this desert of post-socialism, where all remnants of a socialist society were being systematically eroded, *The Plenum Movement* emerged (see Horvat and Štiks, 2015). It is a radical experiment in horizontal democracy. Organised autonomously, citizens' assemblies, or Plenum, articulate socialism beyond the state; Plenum are not aligned to a single political party. Plenum are – as public gatherings open to anyone in spaces outside of the traditional governmental and elite spirals and circles – post-nationalist in a region that remains heavily influenced by nationalist politics during the post-conflict, post-socialist, 'transition' era (see Horvat and Štiks, 2015). Yet their existence required an event – a symbolic moment – to politicise anger, hunger, and frustration, and that is what the closing of DITA, and the other factories, provided. The political potential of space within a post-socialist country was taken up by those first protesters remembering an old Yugoslavia in the present. In so doing bodies were made political and people were given the opportunity to discuss politics beyond nationalism, beyond the municipality, the canton, the entity, beyond yet within the lines that the Dayton Agreement drew across the country (see Campbell, 1999; Crampton, 1996; see also Belloni, 2009; Bieber, 2006; Jeffrey, 2012; Toal and Dahlman, 2011).

A DITA worker stands and defines what her struggle is at the Plenum of Citizens of Tuzla. She connects the collapse of Yugoslavia, the collapse of socialism, to her struggle, the production of a new type of labourer, a wage labourer mercenary. She describes how many young men from Tuzla went to Iraq and Afghanistan to fight in a war. That was the only thing that they could hope for. There is no production that you can do here anymore. 'Bosnia is a testing ground for a new type of labour, a nexus between capitalism and mass atrocity,' Damir, a member of the Plenum of Citizens of Tuzla tells me. He continues to describe how the raw materials of *The Plenum Movement* began with the workers at DITA organising and occupying, and how the movement itself began here in Tuzla:

> That is the marvelous politics in all of this, the workers invented the protest as a new way of protesting for production, rather than going on strike to cease production, they actually protested to keep the commons, that is the most important thing. It took various ways of trying to get the government

to listen. It all congealed when everybody stood behind the workers of those five factories.

The Plenum Movement

The main locus of the uprising switched to the direct democratic Plenum emerging across Bosnia-Herzegovina. The following towns and cities have their own Plenum: Sarajevo, Tuzla, Zenica, Mostar, Travnik, Brčko, Goražde, Konjic, Cazin, Donji Vakuf, Fojnica, Orašje and Bugojno. The demands of the Plenum of Citizens of Sarajevo were distributed widely on social media and were passed around in hard copy. They demonstrate the switching of the movement from street violence to formalised political action. Importantly the demands do not enter *The Plenum Movement* into the usual ethno-nationalist politics of the region, via arguing for constitutional reform and a rewriting of the Dayton Agreement (see Campbell, 1999; Crampton, 1996; see also Belloni, 2009; Bieber, 2006; Jeffrey, 2012; Toal and Dahlman, 2011). Instead each local Plenum created located and concrete social and economic demands for each canton, which sought to open further spaces for dialogue across space, as other cantons reported back with similar socio-economic problems.

In the crucial present redrawing the map was not the aim (see Campbell, 1999; Crampton, 1996; see also Jeffrey, 2012; Toal and Dahlman, 2011). Creating spaces amenable to an alternative politics, within the fixed cantons, municipalities and entities of the Dayton Agreement was the overall goal of *The Plenum Movement*. The political engagement this provided citizens with is not to be downplayed (see Arsenijević, 2011, 2014; Gilbert and Mujanović, 2015; Gordy, 2015; Helms, 2013; Horvat and Štiks, 2015; Hromadžić, 2015; Jansen, 2015; Kurtović, 2015; Kraft, 2015; Majstorović et al., 2015; Mujkić, 2015; Murtagh, 2016; Touquet, 2015). There was, up until the creation of Plenum, no way to voice your own personal political opinion (see Arsenijević, 2011). Through the complicated, corrupt and divisive political system, which encourages a flattening of the self, an individual was forced to first represent their ethnic identity (see Anderson, 1983; Brubaker, 2002; Campbell, 1998; Nancy, 2000). This lack of breathing space, the lack of an ability to speak as an individual voice, is what allowed *The Plenum Movement* to gain a grip over the regional consciousness. It allowed Plenum to become a popular citizen movement without a single institution, non-governmental organisation, international body, or political party on board (see Kraft, 2015).

Citizens felt for the first time as if they had a political voice beyond their ethnicity, and that Plenum was unambiguously, transparently, a forum, an assembly for citizens, a group meeting for all first and foremost. Plenum enabled citizens to become citizens again, and not framed, or flattened ethnic identities (see Anderson, 1983; Brubaker, 2002; Nancy, 2000). This is what gave the movement power, the fact that it represented everyone, and was not interested in working with existing institutions, but rather it sought to demand publically in public space, at Plenum, and through social media as a citizen voice. It demanded action from those who had forced citizens to participate in public life as a Bosniak, Bosnian Croat, or Bosnian Serb. If indeed the movement did eventually slip into the spirals, webs, and spheres of party politics and political structures its power as a citizen voice would be diminished and its force, through ongoing cooperation and in opening dialogue, would be weakened (see Mujkić and Hulsey, 2010; Stojarova and Emerson, 2010). It would lead to the movement losing the very thing which made it different from all of the other political initiatives which seek to re-write the Dayton Agreement for a perceived ethno-political gain. The conquest of state power would be a misguided strategy (see Holloway, 2005). For this reason *The Plenum Movement* remained anti-political, beyond the usual territorial, ethnic, nationalist geopolitics of the state.

> Vignette 1. *The Plenum helps to abolish the multicultural apartheid, and how does it do that, it does that by saying there is one person, there is one vote, so I don't actually participate in the Plenum as a white middle-aged man, or a Bosniak, Bosnian Croat, or Bosnian Serb, but I participate as a political being. The political parties set up the division of public space. This is pretty much about space, and that is why it is important to think about the street and the protest in terms of space. Why is space important and why are people in motion important? That is a strategy. That is a political action. If the political parties divided up the public space, Plenum erased this separation and opened up a proper public space. That is the first thing, and if you enable that, you get an onrush of people who had fled into their private space and were not able to participate in public life.*

Plenum are a *Eulogy for the Mêlée*, they are small eulogies for a Yugoslavia, a Bosnia, a Sarajevo of the certain past, before ethnic cleansing (see Nancy, 2000). They are in a phenomenological sense the spirit of what Jean-Luc Nancy (2000) calls being singular plural. Plenum claim existence is co-existence, they are part of an emancipatory struggle, and they are a vital being-with, which the delineation of a formerly socialist space into nationalist segregation has denied for 20 years or more (see Campbell, 1999; Crampton, 1996; see also Jeffrey, 2012; Toal and Dahlman, 2011). Documenting the morphology of regions and the fracturing of states reveals here a nationalist overhaul of space, which manifests itself locally in the street, the city, the municipality, the canton, the entity, and indeed in the individual (see Elden, 2013; see also Anderson, 1983; Brubaker, 2002; Campbell, 1998; Nancy, 2000).

> Vignette 2. *Plenum is here to stay because increasingly there are Plenum being created in every little town in Bosnia. We are sitting together and thinking about how we can solidify this in order to make it into a movement. Then we will address all of the levels simultaneously. The canton is the key, the canton has all the power, all the power is derogated to the canton. That is*

> *why it is key. The municipality is not the key because the municipality is the garbage, waste disposal, the parks, but they are also important after you claim the space. This is not about occupying, I think it is about claiming and I think there is the difference, it is about taking it and re-taking. You can't perceive this as some kind of interregnum. The space is opened up. The only way is for the industries to be taken out of privatisation and become a public asset again. The whole labour law is the key. We cannot collectively accept to become the slaves again, under a different name. That is going to be the next battle.*

There are core Plenum principles, which translate as openness, transparency, and non-corruption. Plenum opened a space, a possibility into which people can jump. Almost everybody spoke at the Plenum of Citizens of Sarajevo, as the space enabled a kind of collective therapy (see Arsenijević, 2011). Certain performances were demanded from those who attended: no one voice is greater than another and no individual voice is perceived as animal howl. It is, as such, a space for speech beyond prohibition, enabling a disjointed society to collectively mourn a traumatic past and its enduring traces. In the desert of post-socialism, at Plenum, those present imagine a forgotten future, a socialist future beyond the ethno-nationalist divisions of the transition era (see Arsenijević, 2011, 2014; Gilbert and Mujanović, 2015; Gordy, 2015; Helms, 2013; Horvat and Štiks, 2015; Hromadžić, 2015; Jansen, 2015; Kurtović, 2015; Kraft, 2015; Majstorović et al., 2015; Mujkić, 2015; Murtagh, 2016; Touquet, 2015).

> Vignette 3. *The Dayton Agreement set in place a government that is impossible, unwieldy, but actually there is an internal paradox within Dayton. Dayton enabled Plenum. Plenum is the logical contradiction of Dayton taken to the final step. That would be a very productive way of looking at it. Dayton is not the problem, the entities are not a problem, the cantons are not a problem, that is a technical question, it is a political question that it functions, but the question is how do you push the system to its logical conclusion, how you identify the internal paradox within it, so that you can push it. If you want, psychoanalytically speaking, how do you find the symptom, and focus on the symptom.*

In the weeks after the initial uprising politicians resigned, including whole cantonal governments, while many protesters were charged with public disorder, fined, and arrested. Class solidarity was enabled again because people still have a living memory of socialism. Galleries and museums became spaces where working groups of the Plenum are held, a public space for thinking about politics. They got reactivated, empty husks, closed to the public, got reused and reclaimed because of Plenum. The threat of protest continues to give legitimacy to the Plenum. And the abolition of the so-called 'white bread' happened as a result of pressure from Plenum. Other very specific demands continue to be made.

For example, the Plenum of Citizens of Sarajevo calls for a public inquiry into the process of how formerly publically owned factories were privatised, and how that privatisation happened.

Welcome Back to the End of History

It was called *The Plenum of all Plenums*, a symbolic gathering staged in Sarajevo. And it was envisaged that this Plenum of all Plenums would include Plenum participants from across the region. As participants made their way from Mostar, Tuzla, Zenica, and other towns and cities by bus to the capital, they foresaw a pivotal moment in the history of the movement. In an attempt to strengthen and solidify *The Plenum Movement*, Plenum of various places came together to voice a common language of struggle through set demands. Working groups of Plenum had by this time reduced in size; they consisted of citizens sitting indoors working through a manifesto, which they hoped could now be joined into a single document and delivered to parliament. The date was April 9, 2014, over two months after the initial uprising, though here they were in Sarajevo, citizens from different Plenum together, to present a list of concrete demands to the government(s). As they made their way to the meeting site, Plenum realised to their surprise that it was strangely quiet, and a small crowd of activists stood where there should have been active citizenry. It was too late seemingly, the rage had deceased, and the affective atmosphere of the initial uprising was apparently lost. The revolution is over, long live the revolution.

Everything changed on that day in February 2014. February 7, 2014 saw a population unite against perhaps the most complex and contradictory political system in the world, as well as its corrupt leadership. *The Plenum Movement* was brief, but it highlighted the potential of local movements to enact positive change within deeply divided societies. Though it struggled to maintain its initial momentum as a non-institutional alternative to institutional politics, Plenum is unmoved as a mechanism through which citizens can act publically as political beings again beyond playing out an ethno-nationalism. Plenum was never envisaged as a way in to formal politics anyway. Looking back now at those hopeful three months, where power briefly resided with citizens, it is difficult to work out specifically and precisely what did indeed change, and what was achieved. Contradictions become apparent, the street or the Plenum, the street is the Plenum and the Plenum is the street, concrete demands or a plea for a common language of struggle, an institution in itself or a tool for change. Yet this is perhaps to miss the enduring influence of Plenum. It was a movement which altered a public consciousness, discourse, and thinking, and indeed it removed some of the internal borders between citizens. As such, to think of Plenum as a success or a failure is to miss its revolutionary agenda. For a brief moment, people stood together, in cities, on streets, in squares, at Plenum, and that will not be quickly forgotten. Here, in Sarajevo, February 7 has been marked each year since.

With an uncertain future after a period of hope where the region goes from here is unclear. Experimenting with assemblies as a tool of revolt is not over (see Brookchin, 2014; Wainwright, 2003; Webber, 2011). And a trial with direct democracy is not over, as it can now be reanimated at any time. From Macedonia to Slovenia, Kosovo to Montenegro, we are seeing weekly rumblings of discontent and hopeful voices railing against their political situation (see Horvat and Štiks, 2015). *The Plenum Movement* provided a pivotal shift in political discourse, created spaces of dissent within an overbearing political structure, and enabled a traumatised society to collectively mourn what was lost as Yugoslavia collapsed (see Murtagh, 2016; see also Campbell, 1999; Crampton, 1996; Jeffrey, 2012; Toal and Dahlman, 2011). It offers possibilities for future popular movements that seek to change entrenched social structures without seeking constitutional reform, and it provided a transitory hope for citizens feeling former in the present, who could briefly contemplate a forgotten socialist future (see Arsenijević, 2010).

The Plenum Movement was a clear opportunity to engage and develop locally driven solutions to a difficult and complicated regional situation, as it gave a voice to citizens previously unheard and ignored (see Arsenijević, 2011, 2014; Gilbert and Mujanović, 2015; Gordy, 2015; Helms, 2013; Horvat and Štiks, 2015; Hromadžić, 2015; Jansen, 2015; Kurtović, 2015; Kraft, 2015; Majstorović et al., 2015; Mujkić, 2015; Murtagh, 2016; Touquet, 2015). Its power derived from its multi-local nature, chipping away at regional structures, cantons, entities, municipalities – without ever reverting back to a territorial spatial demand and a rewriting of a peace agreement based on ethnic division (see Murtagh, 2016) – and its power was perhaps lost when the movement arrived at a single point in time and space. *The Plenum of all Plenums* reduced a diversity of voices to a small number of demands and in a sense brought about the end of the movement before it had even begun. *The Plenum Movement* melted away in the shadow of the institutional capital as a single, pure, entity in itself, no longer radically diverse and disparate, no longer an anti-apartheid ideology, no longer a hopeful enigma, no longer an opposition to a divisive elite, it instead appeared as a political party, another level or apparatus of government.

Despite the short-lived hope *The Plenum Movement* provided, as this chapter demonstrates, instead of division and fragmentation – the common language of Balkanist literature – the region is in a new era of collective resistance after a recent rebirth of radical politics, as individuals forge a trajectory towards a democratic future (see Arsenijević, 2011, 2014; Gilbert and Mujanović, 2015; Gordy, 2015; Helms, 2013; Horvat and Štiks, 2015; Hromadžić, 2015; Jansen, 2015; Kurtović, 2015; Kraft, 2015; Majstorović, Vućkovac and Pepić, 2015; Mujkić, 2015; Murtagh, 2016; Touquet, 2015). There is, as this chapter contends, now a region of the European continent, that part of the continent that has for so long been defined by its radical politics, which is rebelling against the core. Embraced, subsumed and made dependently peripheral within the 'new' liberal global economy (see Harvey, 2005; Peck, 2010), there are now new reasons to engender a radical politics in this region for a post–Cold War generation.

Beyond the capitalist anarchism associated with certain popular movements – such as Occupy – of recent times, the main charge of this emerging resistance across the Balkans seeks to deconstruct borders and openly questions the new Europe that emerged post-1989 (see Elden, 2013; Snel, 2014). This emerging resistance strives for a revolution (see Smith, 2010). Indeed the new radical politics in the old Yugoslavia – a country which made up a large part of the Balkan Peninsula – aims to reanimate a form of socialism in the desert of post-socialism and states the need for a new radically democratic European project (see Horvat and Štiks, 2015). Decades after a forgotten socialist geographer, Fred Singleton (1985), spoke of a Balkan Federation of Socialist States as a response to Yugoslavia's fracturing, this formerly socialist region, which has exhausted the radical in many guises, once again provides a similarly radical manifesto for a radically democratic future. In order to write what revolution could now mean, after it was rendered ideologically absurd for so long (see Žižek, 1994), we must acknowledge the unique position of *the bastards of utopia* (see Rasza, 2015) – those citizens left adrift after the collapse of Yugoslavia – living radical politics after socialism.

*This research was funded by The Leverhulme Trust. Some sections of this chapter have been published previously, in the journal *Territory, Politics, Governance*.

References

Agnew JA (2013) Arguing with Regions. *Regional Studies* 47(1): 6–17.
Agnew JA (2016) Spatialising Politics. *Territory, Politics, Governance* 4(3): 265–268.
Anderson B (1983) *Imagined Communities: Reflections on the Origin and Spread of Nationalism*. London: Verso.
Arsenijević D (2010) *Forgotten Future: The Politics of Poetry in Bosnia and Herzegovina*. Baden-Baden: Nomos.
Arsenijević D (2011) Mobilising unbribable life, in A Mousley (ed) *Towards a New Literary Humanism*. Basingstoke: Palgrave Macmillan, 166–181.
Arsenijević D (ed) (2014) *Unbribable Bosnia and Herzegovina: The Struggle for the Commons*. Baden-Baden: Nomos.
Belloni R (2009) Bosnia: Dayton is dead! Long live Dayton! *Nationalism and Ethnic Politics* 15(3): 355–375.
Bieber F (2006) *Post-War Bosnia: Ethnicity, Inequality and Public Sector Governance*. Hampshire: Palgrave Macmillan.
Bourdieu P (1998) *Acts of Resistance*. Cambridge: Polity.
Brenner N and Elden S (2009) Henri Lefebvre on state, space and territory. *International Political Sociology* 3(4): 353–377.
Brookchin M (2014) *The Next Revolution: Popular Assemblies and the Promise of Direct Democracy*. London: Verso.
Brubaker R (2002) Ethnicity without groups. *European Journal of Sociology* 43: 163–189.
Bunge W (1971) *Fitzgerald: Geography of a Revolution*. Cambridge, MA: Schenkman Pub. Co,.
Bunge W (2011) *Fitzgerald: Geography of a Revolution*. Athens, Georgia: University of Georgia Press.
Campbell D (1998) *National Deconstruction: Violence, Identity, and Justice in Bosnia*. Minneapolis: University of Minnesota Press.
Campbell D (1999) Apartheid cartography: the political anthropology and spatial effects of international diplomacy in Bosnia. *Political Geography* 18: 395–435.
Crampton J (1996) Bordering on Bosnia. *GeoJournal* 39(4): 353–361.

de Certeau M (1984) *The Practice of Everyday Life*. Berkeley: University of California Press.

Daniels S (2006) Suburban pastoral: Strawberry Fields forever and Sixties memory. *Cultural Geographies* 13(1): 28–54.

Daniels S (2012) To the end of days: narrating landscape and environment. *Cultural Geographies* 19(1): 3–9.

DeSilvey C (2007) Salvage memory: constellating material histories on a hardscrabble homestead. *Cultural Geographies* 14(3): 401–424.

DeSilvey C (2010) Memory in motion: soundings from Milltown, Montana. *Social and Cultural Geography* 11(5): 491–510.

DeSilvey C (2012) Making sense of transience: an anticipatory history. *Cultural Geographies* 19(1): 30–53.

Dubow J (2001) Rites of passage: travel and the materiality of vision at the Cape of Good Hope, in B Bender and M Winer (eds) *Contested Landscapes: Movement, Exile and Place*. Oxford and New York: Berg, 241–255

Dubow J (2011) Still-life, after-life: W.G. Sebald and the demands of landscape, in S Daniels, D DeLyser, JN Entrikin and D Richardson (eds) *Envisioning Landscapes, Making Worlds: Geography and the Humanities*. London: Routledge, 188–198

Edensor T (2005) The ghosts of industrial ruins: ordering and disordering memory in excessive space. *Environment and Planning D: Society and Space* 23: 829–849.

Edensor T (2008) Mundane hauntings: commuting through the phantasmagoric working class spaces of Manchester, England. *Cultural Geographies* 15: 313–333.

Elden S (2005) Missing the point: globalisation, deterritorialisation and the space of the world. *Transactions of the Institute of British Geographers* 30(1): 8–19.

Elden S (2009) *Terror and Territory: The Spatial Extent of Sovereignty*. Minneapolis: University of Minnesota Press.

Elden S (2010) Land, terrain, territory. *Progress in Human Geography* 34(6): 799–817.

Elden S (2013) *The Birth of Territory*. Chicago: University of Chicago Press.

Fontana G (2013) War by other means: Cultural policy and the politics of corporate consociation in Bosnia and Herzegovina. *Nationalism and Ethnic Politics* 19(4): 447–466.

Gilbert A and Mujanović J (2015) Dayton at twenty: towards new politics in Bosnia-Herzegovina. *Southeast European and Black Sea Studies* 15(4): 605–610.

Glenny M (1992) *The Fall of Yugoslavia*. London: Penguin.

Glenny M (1999) *The Balkans, 1804–1999: Nationalism, War and the Great Powers*. London: Granta.

Goldsworthy V (1998) *Inventing Ruritania: The Imperialism of the Imagination*. London: Yale University Press.

Gordy E (2015) Dayton's Annex 4 Constitution at 20: political stalemate, public dissatisfaction and the rebirth of self-organisation. *Southeast European and Black Sea Studies* 15(4): 611–622.

Hartshorne R (1939) *The Nature of Geography*. Lancaster, Penn: Association of American Geographers.

Harvey D (2005) *A Brief History of Neoliberalism*. Oxford: Oxford University Press.

Harvey D (2012) *Rebel Cities*. London: Verso.

Harvey D (2015) 'Listen, anarchist!' A personal response to Simon Springer's 'Why a radical geography must be anarchist.' Available at: http://davidharvey.org/2015/06/listen-anarchist-by-david-harvey/ (accessed July 26, 2016).

Harvey D and Haraway D (1995) Nature, politics, and possibilities: a debate and discussion with David Harvey and Donna Haraway. *Environment and Planning D: Society and Space* 13: 507–527.

Helms E (2013) *Innocence and Victimhood: Gender, Nation, and Women's Activism in Postwar Bosnia-Herzegovina*. Madison: University of Wisconsin Press.

Holloway J (2005) *Change the World without Taking Power*. London: Pluto.

Horvat S and Štiks I (eds) (2015) *Welcome to the Desert of Post-Socialism: Radical Politics after Yugoslavia*. London: Verso.

Hromadžić A (2015) *Citizens of an Empty Nation: Youth and State-Making in Postwar Bosnia-Herzegovina*. Philadelphia: University of Pennsylvania Press.

Jansen S (2015) *Yearning in the Meantime: 'Normal Lives' and the State in a Sarajevo Apartment Complex*. Oxford: Berghahn.

Jeffrey A (2006) Building state capacity in post-conflict Bosnia and Herzegovina: The case of Brčko District. *Political Geography* 25: 203–227.

Jeffrey A (2008) Contesting Europe: the politics of Bosnian integration into European structures. *Environment and Planning D: Society and Space* 26(3): 428–443.

Jeffrey A (2012) *The Improvised State: Sovereignty, Performance and Agency in Dayton Bosnia*. London: Wiley Blackwell.

Jonas AEG (2012) Region and place: regionalism in question. *Progress in Human Geography* 36(2): 263–272.

Jones M (2009) Phase space: geography, relational thinking, and beyond. *Progress in Human Geography* 33(4): 487–506.

Jones M and MacLeod G (2001) Renewing the geography of regions. *Environment and Planning D: Society and Space* 19: 669–695.

Jones M and MacLeod G (2004) Regional spaces, spaces of regionalism: territory, insurgent politics and the English question. *Transactions of the Institute of British Geographers* 29: 433–452.

Jones M and MacLeod G (2007) Territorial, scalar, networked, connected: in what sense a 'regional' world? *Regional Studies* 41: 1171–1191.

Kennedy J and Riga L (2013) A liberal route from homogeneity?: US policymakers and the liberalisation of ethnic nationalists in Bosnia's Dayton Accords. *Nationalism and Ethnic Politics* 19(2): 163–186.

Kraft MG (2015) Insurrections in the Balkans: From workers and students to new political subjectivities, in S Horvat and I Štiks (eds) *Welcome to the Desert of Post-Socialism: Radical Politics after Yugoslavia*. London: Verso, 216–217.

Kurtović L (2015) 'Who sows hunger, reaps rage': on protest, indignation and redistributive justice in post-Dayton Bosnia-Herzegovina. *Southeast European and Black Sea Studies* 15(4): 639–659.

Latour B (2007) *Reassembling the Social*. New York: Oxford University Press.

Lefebvre H (2003) *The Urban Revolution*. Minneapolis: University of Minnesota Press.

Lefebvre H (2004) *Rhythmanalysis: Space, Time, and Everyday Life*. London: Continuum.

Little A and Silber L (1996) *The Death of Yugoslavia*. London: Penguin.

Lorimer H (2003) Telling small stories: spaces of knowledge and the practice of geography. *Transactions of the Institute of British Geographers* 28(2): 197–217.

Lorimer H (2006) Herding memories of humans and animals. *Environment and Planning D: Society and Space* 24: 497–518.

Lorimer H (2012) Memoirs for the Earth: Jacquetta Hawkes's literary experiments in deep time. *Cultural Geographies* 19(1): 87–106.

Lorimer H and Wylie J (2010) Loop (a geography). *Performance Research* 15(4): 6–13.

Majstorović D, Vučkovac Z, and Pepić A (2015) From Dayton to Brussels via Tuzla: post-2014 economic restructuring as Europeanisation discourse/practice in Bosnia and Herzegovina. *Southeast European and Black Sea Studies* 15(4): 661–682.

Matless D (2008) A geography of ghosts: the spectral landscapes of Mary Butts. *Cultural Geographies* 15(3): 335–358.

Matless D (2010) Describing landscape: regional sites. *Performance Research* 15(4): 72–82.

Matless D (2014) *In the Nature of Landscape: Cultural Geography on the Norfolk Broads*. London: Wiley Blackwell.

Mazower M (2002) *The Balkans: From the End of Byzantium to the Present Day*. London: Phoenix.

Mujkić A (2015) In search of a democratic counter-power in Bosnia–Herzegovina. *Southeast European and Black Sea Studies* 15(4): 623–638.

Mujkić A and Hulsey J (2010) Explaining the success of nationalist parties in Bosnia and Herzegovina. *Politička Misao* 47(2): 143–158.

Murphy AB (2013) Territory's continuing allure. *Annals of the Association of American Geographers* 103(5): 1212–1226.

Murtagh C (2016) Civic mobilisation in divided societies and the perils of political engagement: Bosnia and Herzegovina's protest and plenum movement. *Nationalism and Ethnic Politics* 22(2): 149–171.

Nancy J-L (2000) *Being Singular Plural*. Stanford, California: Stanford University Press.

Paasi A (1991) Deconstructing regions: notes on the scales of spatial life. *Environment and Planning A* 23: 239–256.

Paasi A (1999) Boundaries as social practice and discourse: the Finnish-Russian border. *Regional Studies* 33: 669–680.

Paasi A (2002) Place and region: regional worlds and words. *Progress in Human Geography* 28(6): 802–811.

Paasi A (2003) Region and place: regional identity in question. *Progress in Human Geography* 28(4): 475–485.

Painter J (2010) Rethinking territory. *Antipode* 42(5): 1090–1118.

Pearson M (2006) *'In Comes I': Performance, Memory, and Landscape*. Exeter: University of Exeter Press.

Peck J (2010) *Constructions of Neoliberal Reason*. Oxford: Oxford University Press.

Rasza M (2015) *Bastards of Utopia: Living Radical Politics after Socialism*. Bloomington: Indiana University Press.

Riding J (2015a) Death drive: final tracings, in H Hawkins and E Straughan (eds) *Geographical Aesthetics: Imagining Space, Staging Encounters*. Farnham: Ashgate, 181–196.

Riding J (2015b) Landscape, memory, and the shifting regional geographies of northwest Bosnia-Herzegovina. *GeoHumanities* 1(2): 378–397.

Riding J (2016) A geographical biography of a nature writer. *Cultural Geographies* 23(3): 387–399.

Rieff D (1995) *Slaughterhouse: Bosnia and the Failure of the West*. London: Vintage Random House.

Rose M (2012) Dwelling as marking and claiming. *Environment and Planning D: Society and Space* 30(5): 757–771.

Sauer CO (1925) The morphology of landscape. *University of California Publications in Geography* 2(2): 19–53.

Singleton F (1985) *A Short History of the Yugoslav Peoples*. Cambridge: Cambridge University Press.

Smith N (2010) The revolutionary imperative. *Antipode* 41: 50–65.

Snel G (2014) The past is always in the present. Aether and the returns of history and Europe's new post-1989 peripheries. The cases of Mihail Sebastian's diary and Emir Suljagić's Srebrenica memoir. *Neohelicon* 41(1): 241–246.

Springer S (2014) Why a radical geography must be anarchist. *Dialogues in Human Geography* 4(3): 249–270.

Stojarova V and Emerson P (eds) (2010) *Party Politics in the Western Balkans*. London: Routledge.

Thompson M (1992) *A Paper House: The Ending of Yugoslavia*. London: Vintage.

Thrift N (1983) On the determination of social action in time and space. *Environment and Planning D: Society and Space* 1: 23–57.

Thrift N (1994) Taking aim at the heart of the region, in D Gregory, R Martin and G Smith (eds) *Human Geography: Society, Space and Social Science*. London: Macmillan, 200–231.

Thrift N (2008) *Non-Representational Theory: Space, Politics, Affect*. London: Routledge.

Toal G (1996) An anti-geopolitical eye: Maggie O'Kane in Bosnia, 1992–93. *Gender, Place and Culture* 3(2): 171–186.

Toal G and Dahlman C (2011) *Bosnia Remade: Ethnic Cleansing and Its Reversal*. Oxford: Oxford University Press.

Todorova M (1997) *Imagining the Balkans*. Oxford: Oxford University Press.

Touquet H (2012) The Republika Srpska as a strong nationalising state and the consequences for postethnic activism. *Nationalities Papers: The Journal of Nationalism and Ethnicity* 40(2): 203–220.

Touquet H (2015) Non-ethnic mobilisation in deeply divided societies: The case of the Sarajevo Protests. *Europe-Asia Studies* 67(3): 388–408.

Vidal de La Blache P (1926) *Principles of Human Geography*. London: Constable.

Wainwright H (2003) *Reclaim the State: Experiments in Popular Democracy*. London: Verso.

Webber JR (2011) *From Rebellion to Reform in Bolivia*. Chicago, IL: Haymarket Books.

Wylie J (2002) An essay on ascending Glastonbury Tor. *Geoforum* 33: 441–454.

Wylie J (2005) A single days walking: narrating self and landscape on the South West Coast Path. *Transactions of the institute of British Geographers* 30: 37–51.

Wylie J (2007) *Landscape*. London: Routledge.

Žižek S (ed) (1994) *Mapping Ideology*. London: Verso.

Žižek S (2000) *The Fragile Absolute: Or Why Is the Christian Legacy Worth Fighting For?* London: Verso.

7 The Crisis at the Centre of the United Kingdom

Exploring Scottish Independence and Democratically Disruptive Regions

Philip Johnstone

> Scottish independence could be a catalyst for more devolution for England, which I think would really help our region and other regions to rebalance the country with London, which seems to be sucking all the power.
>
> (English folk singer, Billy Bragg, 2014)

> … for the regions, the UK is no longer fit for purpose.
>
> (Poet and playwright, Peter Mortimer, quoted in Henley, 2014)

Introduction: Britain, October 2016. Notes from a Nasty Island …

On the face of it, 'Britishness' is booming. In June 2016, 52% of people who participated in the EU referendum voted to leave the EU. The people have spoken, we are told. Hyped rhetoric of a great success for the UK abounds. Britain has achieved its 'independence day' according to Nigel Farage, leader of the United Kingdom Independence Party (RT, 2016), and a familiar refrain circulates the land: 'we've got our country back'. With some successful displays at the Olympics in Rio and the arrival of a Royal Baby, for many who advocated Brexit, all seems well in England's 'green and pleasant'. The unity of Great Britain is now no longer 'threatened' by the EU, we are told, and Britain is ready to be restored to its former 'greatness'. For the citizens who voted to stay in the EU however, the other 48%, dark clouds seem to be gathering around the resurgent celebration of Britishness. It seems to be constituted by what Billy Bragg refers to as 'England's post-imperial inferiority complex', where Britain resembles 'an old country, whose dotage is portrayed as a matter of crabby resentment, a place where there is a collective wish to lock all the doors' (Harris, 2016).

The ruling Conservative Party overseeing Brexit, led by Teresa May, have fully consolidated an anti-immigrant, anti-EU discourse that formed during Brexit, as an official discourse for the UK. A series of quite extraordinary policies have been suggested, including stopping non-British EU citizens working in the National Health Service (NHS) after 2025, proposing companies 'list' foreign workers, and even banning non-British academics from participating in research on the effects of 'Brexit' (Merrick, 2016). Fundamentally this new British discourse is based on a fear of the other, the desire for walls and fences, a return to an imagined state of unspoilt stability, constituted by an imagined set of 'British' values, ethnic homogeneity, and an increasingly boastful discourse around how 'great' Britain really is in terms of its 'outsized' force and a 'top table' position in world affairs (Coughlin, 2015).

Many claim that Brexit voters were motivated by years of being dismissed or forgotten altogether by a distant centralised political institution that was un-democratic in its very nature. An institution that works through elite networks of power driven by intense corporate lobbying campaigns, or often, the direct placement of corporate interests directly into governmental bureaucracy. This institution usually represents the interests of highly mobile capital rather than place-bound workers: in some of these assessments they were probably right. The targets of that dissatisfaction and anger however, were wrong. In this chapter, the two democratic disruptions under discussion – the rise of the Scottish independence campaign, and the potential increased democratic devolution to England's regions – are discussed in the context of the overly-centralised and arguably democratically deficient *British State*, which is in urgent need of democratic transformation.

Indeed, behind the veil of the resurgent discourse of 'Britishness', all is not well with the Union. The anti-immigrant populist rhetoric of the Conservative government, led by Prime Minster Teresa May, is not a sign of strength but rather a sign of weakness. The more fractured, unequal and divided the United Kingdom has become, the more desperate the rhetoric based around fear of the outside world has to become in order to form unity around 'shared enemies' – a form of Schmitt's (1996) formulation of the political. In so doing, this unification around fear and resentment is a discursive ecology temporarily plastering over the fractured foundations on which the Union is now based. And this thinly veiled fear-mongering constitutes an extremely fragile material from which to hold together a fundamentally disunited country.

Some of the cracks within the foundations of the UK are more visible than others however. For a start, one of the four 'equal' nations of the UK, Scotland, voted in the opposite direction to the rest of the country, voting to remain part of the EU. And Scotland has voted differently to England in the general elections of 1979, 1983, 1987, 1992, 2010 and 2015. What these elections all share in common was that they were won by the Conservative Party. So, a glance at any election map in the UK shows clear political differences between the geographical territory of Scotland and the rest of the country. This longstanding electoral idiosyncrasy is in part what gave rise to Scottish nationalism, and led Scotland to the brink of leaving the UK altogether in 2014. Despite losing in the end, the independence campaign remains and the Scottish National Party (SNP) now occupy 54 out of the 59 Members of the Westminster Parliament in Scotland. In recent years, Scotland has also played the key role in opposing the austerity agenda of David Cameron's Conservative Government, and may continue to do so with an emerging form of authoritarian capitalism on the rise in the UK and across Europe (Žižek, 2014).

Interestingly, what emerged during the referendum campaign for Scottish Independence was innovative forms of cross-party, 'bottom up', political initiatives. The traditional political parties and institutions present did not know how to engage with these movements, which are still very active in Scotland today. These new horizontal initiatives, rather than attempting to battle within the confines of the established assemblages of Westminster, largely bypassed them altogether, creating new democratic polities enacting the disruptive effects of agonistic politics (Featherstone, 2015). And as this chapter contends, this has fundamentally disturbed the 'settled relationships' of the Westminster model, enabling 'new practices, and new people, voices, and ideas [to] enter the public sphere' (Staeheli, 2010: 34).

The second democratically disruptive force in British politics concerns various policies and calls over the previous three decades to distribute more democratic power to England's regions. In 1997, the New Labour Government recognised the overly centralised nature of the British state and the problems this posed for adequate democratic representation. New Labour unleashed an ambitious devolution agenda, with assemblies set up in Northern Ireland, Wales, and London, and a devolved parliament in Scotland. Policies were also put in place to attempt to distribute increasing fiscal and other decision-making powers to the English regions, of which there are nine in total. Assemblies were set up in eight regions, with London opting for a directly elected mayoral system. Regional Development Agencies (RDAs) were established with significant planning powers to make decisions around the economic development of regions, and they also initially became important players in the UK's sustainable development agenda (Goodwin, 2012).

However, the regional assemblies were disbanded between 2008 and 2010, and the Conservative Government dissolved RDAs altogether when they came to power in 2010 (Rodríguez-Pose, 2013). Two movements also took place during this time, one with a greater emphasis upon the centralisation of power in planning in some respects, what was termed National Infrastructure Planning (HM Government, 2008), and the other encouraging more localised forms of engagement, the Conservative Government's localism bill (Communities and Local Government, 2011). The often contradictory governmental policies associated with the distribution of power to English regions over the past three decades has been researched by geographers analysing the rescaling of the nation state, and this work importantly expanded and shifted older topographical understandings of regions (see e.g., Allen and Cochrane, 2007, 2010; Etherington and Jones, 2016; Goodwin, 2012; Jones, 2013; Lobao et al., 2009; MacLeod and Jones, 2001; Martin et al., 2015a Rodríguez-Pose, 2013).

In recent years – especially in the wake of calls for increased autonomy in Scotland – what arguably continues to be the 'elephant in the room' in terms of overall British devolution, remains the fact that the regions of England – with population sizes often larger than Scotland – still do not have devolved decision making and democratic representation. Compared to countries such as Germany which operates under a federalist system, where regions of comparable size to those of England's have significant autonomy and are fully elected (The Economist, 2013), the UK remains remarkably centralised. As the Scottish independence campaign evolved, cross-party progressive movements in English regions campaigning for devolved democracy to be implemented in regions such as the campaign for Northern devolution (Salveson, 2014) and Yorkshire (Yorkshire Devolution Movement, 2016), as well as the Cornish independence movement (Trelawny, 2014), became more pronounced.

Recognising the Scottish independence campaign as first and foremost a democratic rather than nationalist struggle – which has emerged due to the endemic problems with the overly centralised nature of the British state – this chapter also focuses on the potential role that democratic movements for more devolutionary powers in England may play, in the context of the ongoing transformation of UK democracy. This is specifically discussed here, in the context of the spatial manifestation of the 'police order' (Dikec, 2005; Ranciere, 2004) in UK politics, where regional political movements may prove potentially crucial spaces of democratic struggle – similar to the role played by the Scottish independence movement – disrupting the current asymmetrical spatial distribution of Britain's economic and democratic power.

Returning to the present consequences of the recent EU membership referendum in the UK, this chapter outlines a vital spatial response, arguing that the potential role of enhanced democratic English regions – alongside the strength of the ongoing evolution of the Scottish independence movement – will be even more important in the context of Brexit. This is based on the understanding that the displacement of protest has meant feelings of exclusion and marginalisation have been targeted towards the wrong objects, namely the EU and the issue of migration. The marginalisation and inequality felt by many, have more to do with the problematic nature of the British state over the past thirty years than with the EU. I refer to the UK's democratic problem as the ongoing 'crisis at the centre', where five factors, some structural and some more emergent, mean that a meaningful 'rebalancing' of Britain's economic and political power felt necessary by voters of Brexit can only likely be achieved by a transformation and redistribution of the powers of the Westminster model itself. The political centre has managed to displace problems that are internal to the workings of British democracy onto the perceived 'external' factors of the EU. However, these deep-seated problems with British democracy will not be solved by the EU, and hence in future years, the issue of English regional devolution is likely to come to the fore.

The 'crisis at the centre' of the British democratic settlement is discussed throughout this chapter. Five interrelated factors are taken as signposts of the significant problems that sit at the heart of the British institutional democracy. They are important in understanding the 'line of flight' taken by Scotland, and the widespread disenchantment and lack of trust felt by many in the UK of the Westminster model, a model which is increasingly seen as being unable to produce the kinds of redistribution of wealth and representation that there has been calls for a long time. These are as follows:

1 The UK remains one of the most '*centralised*' democracies in Europe and in the OECD more widely (Hall, 2011; BBC News, 2014b).
2 The UK, in terms of 'developed' world countries and certainly in terms of European countries, *ranks poorly in overall ratings of democracy*, and it is considered to be '*one of the most undemocratic countries in Europe*' (Hall, 2011).
3 UK political culture is particularly plagued by '*the distortion and subversion of the public realm in the service of private interests*' (Beetham, 2015). This relates to work investigating institutionally enabled corrupt practice at the heart of the operation of the 'Westminster model' which refers to the political cultures of central government. This work convincingly builds the case related to how politicians increasingly serve the interests of private elites particularly through the 'revolving door' culture that seems to be an endemic feature of how policy making is done in the current Westminster model. Many are aware and disillusioned by such a culture.
4 The UK has recently been *plagued by a range of high profile scandals* involving core institutions of the British establishment. This ranges from the campaign of lies and misinformation coordinated by Yorkshire police around the Hillsborough football disaster, the false premises justifying the Iraq war, the scandals surrounding the hacking practices carried out by the British media, the historic child sex scandals at the BBC, the MPs' expenses scandal, and the various scandals surrounding financial services or 'the city' in London, to name a few. This has created further distance in terms of how connected people feel to the Westminster model because some of the most cherished institutions of British cultural life seem to have been sites of serious malpractice for decades.
5 The UK being *one of the most unequal countries in the world* in terms of distribution of wealth (BBC News, 2016), where the richest 10% of the UK population own over half of the country's total wealth, with the top 1% owning nearly a quarter (23%), and the poorest 20% share just 0.8% of the UK's wealth between them. A Gini-coefficient study conducted by the EU found the UK to be the most unequal country in Europe (Ward, 2015). The regional gaps in where wealth is created is stark: a study found that 24 times as much is invested in infrastructure in London than the North East. Regional inequality has been shown to be bad for the economy over time (OECD, 2014), and many argue the only way to address this is through greater democratic autonomy of regions away from London (Martin et al., 2015b).

Taken together, the legitimacy of the centralised British state to adequately represent people from across its regions, fairly distribute wealth, and the degree to which the Westminster model can be thought to be operating adequately in the public interest as a democracy, is questionable. Many have identified Britain as being a 'post democratic' political system (Crouch, 2004). The question is whether the Westminster model can ever address these problems, or if more regional and national autonomy is required to provide a system of democratic checks and balances to hold the culture of Westminster to account.

As Martin et al. (2015a) argue, the crisis at the centre and in particular, the fundamentally unbalanced nature of the UK's economy, can potentially be solved through increased devolution of real power to regions creating a counter-point to the overpowered, and democratically problematic 'centre' of British political life. Thus the politics of the regions is likely to become an increasingly prominent political fault line in years to come. There are two versions of regionalism that may be enacted however. The first is regions as 'seen by the state' (Scott, 1998), where regions are enrolled in the continuation of a centralised 'spatial fix' of the British state, where they are mapped, calculated, and ordered as a form of spatial policing to keep the centralised Westminster model functioning (Ranciere, 2004; Dikec, 2005). The other sees more bottom-up and democratic forms of regional struggle, which speak in a different language to Westminster, and where progressive alliances work to create new political visions that actively challenge, reshape, and transform the post democratic settlement of the UK. This chapter assesses the emergence of Scottish independence and various calls for more power to regions tracing their emergence over the past few decades. Recognising both as democratically disruptive forces, their future role is discussed in the final section in the context of a more authoritarian form of British capitalism that may be emerging.

Democratic Disruption 1: The Rise of the Scottish Independence Campaign

This section outlines a brief narrative charting the emergence of Scottish independence in relation to the increasingly problematic nature of British democracy over the past thirty years. Scottish independence is understood here as a democratic rather than nationalist movement that has formed in relation to the 'democratic deficit' – which has developed due to the centralised nature of the British state – combined with growing economic inequality and perceived injustice, in terms of the spatial distribution of gains and losses of various economic policies.

It must be pointed out, however, that although in this chapter Scottish independence and the question of the redistribution of power to English regions are discussed as emerging from the crisis at the centre, there are of course important differences between these two democratic disruptions from the start. The United Kingdom of Great Britain and Northern Ireland has only existed in some form since 1801, and the unification between England and Scotland into one kingdom only occurred in 1707. Until then, Scotland was an independent nation.[1] There is not the space here to fully interrogate this history, but the idea of a 'lost nation' has bubbled quietly underneath British life since unification in 1707. While many commentators focused on this nationalist aspect, the real story to be told is why the campaign for independence emerged when it did. By focusing on this important temporal question, the democratic and economic conditions which produced the Scottish independence campaign become clear.

The story begins in the late 1960s and continues through the 1970s. Following the Suez crisis in 1956, and Harold Wilson's 'winds of change' speech, Britain was experiencing an 'existential crisis', as the once great empire was coming to an end. The British manufacturing industry in the 1950s had dominated home markets and 20% of the international market. However, in the 1960s and 1970s, the British manufacturing industry began to experience significant decline, with a lack of firm government policy supporting it. The lack of a change in governmental response to the altered conditions of Britain in relation to its international markets at this point has been referred to as 'imperial overhang', which saw inertia in industrial policy (Skidelsky, 2013). Unable to compete economically, as new manufacturing centres began to emerge around the world, the decline of the British manufacturing industry had begun.

Scotland was the territory where some of the more serious attempts to 'de-industrialise' were being tested by the Westminster government. Many in Scotland were horrified at the perceived disdain displayed by the Conservatives of Westminster in attempting to shut down the shipbuilding industry on the Clydeside in the early 1970s. Here a 'work in' protest coordinated by socialist and later Scottish independence campaigner Jimmy Reid took place. This attracted much public support to the plight of Scottish industry as a perceived result of Westminster policy. The symbolic events that took place on the Clydeside arguably cemented Scotland's 'lurch to the left', which would underpin the nationalist campaign, emphasising the idea of a distant Westminster government, a government that cared little for the suffering inflicted on once useful outposts, such as Glasgow.

In the late 1960s substantial oil reserves were found off the coast of North East Scotland, which proved an important find, especially in the era of the Middle East oil crisis of 1973. During this time the Scottish Nationalist Party (SNP) grew in strength, arguing that oil revenues would be received in Westminster, and Scotland would not receive the benefits it deserved. Destitute factories and damaged communities, suffering due to deindustrialisation, continued to grow. The popular slogan of this period, used by the SNP, was, 'It's our oil!' They foresaw a problem and a political gain. While the majority of the oil lay off the Coast of Scotland, royalty and revenues would be gathered by Westminster. The SNP argued that a Sovereign wealth fund like Norway's should be set up. And public suspicions abounded that Scotland would not see sufficient reinvestment from these revenues, if they were handled by the treasury in London.

Remarkably, decades later, it was revealed that a key report, named the *McCrone Report* – commissioned by government – had shown that Scotland could be a viable independent nation based on these oil reserves. And also, the report provided evidence that the extent of the oil in the North Sea was far greater, and would last longer, than the British government were admitting. The existence of the report was kept top secret by the UK government in the 1970s, until its existence was revealed by a Freedom of Information request (FoI) in 2003 (Russell and Kelbie, 2005). The suspicions the SNP had at the time of the report's writing – that there was more oil than the government admitted – were entirely correct. Yet the question remained, would Scotland see reinvestment and wealth as a result of the oil of its coast?

In the general election of 1979 Labour won a significant majority of seats in Scotland. However, the Conservative Party had won by a significant majority in England. The Conservative vote continued to plummet in Scotland throughout the 1980s. Yet Scotland, like other parts of the UK, suffered considerable hardship due to austerity drives and further de-industrialisation of key industries. David Willets, then an advisor to Margret Thatcher, referred to the Scots as a 'pampered' nation, which was 'ripe for cuts' (Devlin, 2015). Scotland during this decade became one of the poorest places in Europe, dogged by very high unemployment and taking on the unenviable title of the drugs capital of the developed world (Edemariam and Scott, 2009). Author Irvine Welsh (2012: 139), summarises this period as follows:

> During this period one factor remains incontrovertible: hundreds of thousands of working class people in the UK had a lot less money and a lot more time on their hands.

This fact, combined with the flood of cheap heroin onto the streets in Scotland, was a tragic and deadly one.

During these brutal years, a view of the Conservative Government and indeed Westminster was cemented in many Scottish people's minds: Scotland was being punished for something it didn't vote for. And the distant 'centre' of Westminster was inflicting pain and suffering on the region which suffered from destitute communities, drug abuse, mass unemployment, and some of the worse poverty in Europe, without a democratic mandate. Many Scots wondered what could have been done, if like Norway a sovereign wealth fund for Scotland had been set up from the oil revenues, as suggested by the SNP. The Thatcher government set up no such fund.

In 1997 New Labour came to power and by this time the Conservatives were wiped off the electoral map in Scotland completely, failing to win a single seat. New Labour were aware of the desperate reform required in British democracy, in terms of a severe lack of representation at the regional and devolved national level. They outlined a progressive devolution agenda for all parts of the UK. The early years of 'Blairism' were dominated by progressive ideas, participatory forms of governance, the redistribution of power to regions and nations, consultation between central government and the regions, and less central command and control from Westminster (Labour Party, 1997). This was a time of incredible progressive change on a number of issues, including addressing the deep democratic asymmetries at the heart of the Union. The Scottish Parliament was opened, along with assemblies in Wales and Northern Ireland, and it was expected that the opening of a devolved Scottish Parliament would end the question of independence once and for all (Harvey, 2015).

The participatory 'Blair years' did not last long, however. On a range of measures including nuclear power and genetically modified foods, democratic decisions based on participation were increasingly overridden by the decisions of the Blair Government (Johnstone, 2010). Blair increasingly seemed to be stamping authority over decisions reached by participatory measures, withdrawing decision making from participatory forums – which many now saw as window dressing – back into secretive special advisory groups, 'behind closed doors' (Cox et al., 2016). Another turning point in the history of New Labour, as is now so keenly and tragically understood, was the Iraq war. Despite intense public protest, Tony Blair made the decision to go to war. A war opposed by the SNP in Scotland. What was revealed to many in this pivotal moment was the perceived inner mechanisations of Westminster 'democracy', decisions are taken on the part of elite unaccountable networks of power (Wedel, 2014). Or, what we would call, if it were other countries being talked about, written about, analysed, the hidden networks of the 'deep state' (Dale-Scott, 2014).

Partly on the back of this narrative, and the perception of a troublesome, lobbying, and 'war-mongering' culture inside Westminster, in 2007, the SNP made significant gains in the Scottish Parliament. With the 2010 general election, the stark differences between Scotland and the rest of the UK once again became clear: out of 59 seats in Scotland the Conservative Party won just one. In the 2011 Scottish Parliamentary elections, the SNP achieved an overall majority in the Scottish Parliament, with the vote for the Liberal Democrats in Scotland all but totally melting away due to their coalition with the Conservatives (Carrell, 2011). This cleared the way for a referendum on Scottish independence, which was agreed with the signing of the 'Edinburgh agreement' in 2012, between Prime Minster David Cameron and First Minster of Scotland Alex Salmond.

This independence campaign must be understood within a broader set of issues that were apparent at the time. It seemed in Westminster that there was a 'consensus' on austerity, a 'post political' condition (Gill et al., 2012), where Labour failed to provide an alternative political narrative that could counter the Conservatives mantra of, 'There is no alternative'. But there was also a feeling that despite Scotland lurching to the left, the Labour Party had ignored this trend. The SNP occupied a position to the left of Labour and working class voters that were raised to support Labour, and often having a visceral hatred of the Conservative party, began to drift to the SNP. A key saying used by these left-wing 'defectors', as they were seen by the Parliamentary Labour Party, was simply, 'I didn't leave Labour; Labour left me'. During this time Scotland stormed ahead with a progressive agenda, an agenda that seemed to have completely stalled in the UK in the years prior: free prescriptions, no university tuition fees, no to nuclear power, a rejection of the bedroom tax, the legitimisation of gay marriage, more women in politics than any other part of Britain, and of course, strong opposition the renewal of the UK's nuclear weapons system. In short, directions of policy deemed 'impossible' south of the border – in the 'consensus at the centre' – were becoming the signposts of a different political possibility north of it.

The SNP had gained momentum, and the UK government had no choice but to agree to a referendum in 2012. It is important to state here that this was not a reactionary, insular form of nationalism. A progressive move made by the Scottish government regarded those who had a right to vote in the Scottish independence referendum. It had little to do with 'blood', or 'Scottishness', rather it was a referendum for the people of a defined 'region' to articulate their own collective destiny. You could vote in the independence referendum if you had been a resident in Scotland for 2 years or more. The argument for independence was based around a hopeful alternative to austerity, when Westminster dictated that there was none. Migrants and the EU were celebrated not condemned, and renewable energy and climate change formed key priorities. In short, Scottish 'nationalism' could not be further from the discourses perpetuated by UKIP during the EU referendum.

Another key aspect to consider is that while the SNP gained most of the media attention, the Green Party and the Scottish Socialists also formed other key components of the 'Yes to Independence' coalition. However, beneath the terrain of party politics, an unprecedented democratic grassroots movement was also emerging which saw cross-party progressive organisations became equally – if not more important – than the SNP, in driving the democratic argument for independence. As the journalist Fintan O'Toole (2014) described at the time:

> It is impossible to have visited Scotland in recent days and not to have been exhilarated by the sheer vigour of democratic engagement. Scotland at the moment is what a democracy is supposed to be: a buzzing hive of argument and involvement, most of it civil, respectful and deeply intelligent. This energy has been unleashed not by atavistic tribal passions but by a simple realisation: for once, the people have some power.

These political movements were organised in a 'bottom up' fashion, new civic spaces where a range of progressive issues could be articulated, proving to be crucial democratic hubs which were accessible to a range of interest groups, regardless of political experience. Community organising was an essential part of this renewed politicisation, feeding directly into the policy-making process of the SNP. Groups included *The Radical Independence Campaign, The Common Weal, National Collective, Bella Caledonia, Wings Over Scotland, The 1001 Campaign*, some Trade Union branches, including the Edinburgh, Lothians, Fife, Falkirk and Stirling branch of the Communications Workers Union (CWU), the Prison Officers Association, the National Union of Rail, Maritime and Transport Workers (RMT), and other civil society groups, including the Campaign for Nuclear Disarmament (CND), Christians for Independence, and Women for Independence. These horizontally-led movements bypassed and outpaced the traditional framings of party politics, as various issues that had been prohibited for discussion for Westminster 'sparked' publics into political life in Scotland (Marres, 2007). These newly formed social movements, which formed an important part of the independence campaign, were entirely unpredicted, uncalculated, and fundamentally disruptive to the established static model of confined democratic engagement present in the UK over the previous thirty years.

In the end, the vote to remain part of the UK narrowly won. The importance of the media in this result cannot be underestimated. Research indicates that the media coverage of the independence campaign was severely biased towards the 'remain in the UK' camp (Robertson, 2015). Only one newspaper in the whole of the UK, the Herald, was in favour of independence. Compare this to the Brexit vote in which it has been shown that the majority of media coverage was in favour of Brexit (Greenslade, 2016). Put simply, Scottish independence was against 'the establishment', while UK independence *was* the establishment. Prominent journalists in England claimed that the people of Scotland had been 'shafted' through the one-sided nature of the news coverage that verged on, they suggested, propaganda (Monbiot, 2014; Mason quoted in Robertson, 2015). Despite a referendum defeat, the issue of Scottish independence is by no means settled. Scotland voted in a different direction to the rest of the UK in the recent EU referendum, and in response, Nicola Sturgeon, leader of the SNP, published a draft bill calling for a second referendum on Scottish independence (Carrell, 2016).

The everyday ideological substance has arguably been transformed in Scotland. And despite the referendum defeat, the SNP won a historic 54 seats in the Scottish parliament in the 2015 general election. It is now the third biggest political party in the UK. This suggests that though a 'battle' was lost by those that voted to leave the UK, a long-term war of some form continues. The changing nature of politics in Scotland is significant for progressive movements elsewhere in the UK, not just in terms of the number of seats in parliament, but also in terms of the ways in which politics is done. In short, the traditional modes of political engagement along rigid party lines is arguably over. Many of the organisations mentioned above have not disappeared after the referendum vote, but have instead been sustained and continue to campaign on a range of social issues. Their 'bottom up' approach and cross-party, multi-stakeholder coalitions may be of vital relevance to future independence campaigns, and also in terms of the regional politics of England, as UK democracy continues to inevitably transform.

Democratic Disruption 2: The Question of the English Regions

As stated previously, there is a crisis at the centre of UK democracy, identified by five factors. These five factors are the overly centralised nature of the UK nation state, the related poor democratic quality of the UK demonstrated by various ranking systems, a UK political culture represented by a 'Westminster' plagued by 'the distortion and subversion of the public realm in the service of private interests', high profile scandals placing significant doubt on the reliability for honest government from central institutions, and the UK being one of the most unequal countries in the world (Wilkinson, 2005). With regards to the latter, many argue that rebalancing the UK's highly unequal economy will only be possible through further democratisation of England's regions (Martin et al. 2015a).

The Scottish independence campaign, discussed in the previous section, provoked reflection on the role of England's regions within the centralised democracy of the UK. Giovannini and Willett (2014) refer to an 'awakening' that occurred as a result of the Scottish independence campaign, where some campaigns for English devolution were amplified. Progressive devolution campaigns in certain regions of England resembled the kinds of cross-party progressive movements forged north of the border, such as the Yorkshire devolution campaign (Yorkshire Devolution Movement, 2016), and the Hannah Mitchell Foundation, a progressive organisation campaigning to explore devolution options for the North of England (Salveson, 2014).

Increasing calls for regional devolution were made elsewhere too. Cornwall was granted minority status in 2014 and there were renewed calls for a Cornish Assembly (Trelawny, 2014). Campaigns such as 'Devo-Manc' (Gander, 2014), sought increased political power for the devolved city-region of Manchester, taking its name from 'devo-max', a proposed alternative devolution plan to Scottish independence. A 'Devolution deal' for Manchester was announced by Government in November 2014 (House of Commons, 2016), and other 'devolution deals' look set to be implemented in other regions, including the Sheffield City Region, West Yorkshire, Cornwall, North-East, Tees Valley, West Midlands, Liverpool City Region, Cambridgeshire, Norfolk/Suffolk, West of England and Greater Lincolnshire (ibid.). As these developments emerged, some claimed that 'the time for England's regions has come' (Hart, 2016). The *Guardian* newspaper, in the wake of Brexit, recognised the UK's democratic crisis, calling for a new Federalism and an urgent need to 'reimagine the UK', beyond the Westminster model (The Guardian, 2016).

During the Scottish referendum campaign Henley (2014) noted that English regions were 'eyeing up more powers', viewing the power of Scotland to coordinate its own affairs with a certain degree of envy. Arguably the Scottish independence debate, through disrupting the spatial consensus of the centralised British state, contributed to renewed interest in notions of more devolved forms of regional democracy, especially in northern parts of England. Yet, and even if, '[the North's] regional politics are probably about 20 years behind Scotland's' (Paul Salveson quoted in Henley, 2014), a key question geographers must now consider is, what kind of regionalism will emerge out of a new post-Brexit landscape in England?

At the time of writing it is unclear where regional devolution and regional campaigns are headed. Returning to the notion of the crisis at the centre of UK democracy, constituted by five identified signs, it is difficult to see how the 'democratic deficit' (Crouch, 2004) at the heart of the UK political establishment will be solved by exiting the EU. It is likely, therefore, that further regional settlements in the UK are in some ways inevitable in order to rebalance UK democracy. Indeed, there is acknowledgement in some quarters that a driving force behind the Brexit vote was the lack of control that people in certain regions of England felt they had over any part of their lives. Policies were 'set' at Westminster, or 'in Brussels', with little possibility of change or nuance at the regional level. It has been suggested that the feelings of discontent that contributed to Brexit could have been more readily addressed if there had been meaningful political representation in place at the regional level (NESTA, 2016).

It is important to consider the often contradictory ways in which the politics of regions in the UK has developed over the past few decades. An important starting point for understanding the democratic issue at the heart of discussions around regions is to look again at the Thatcher era. Conservatives abolished regional planning frameworks in 1979, replacing them with new local planning frameworks. A potential reason for such a move by Margaret Thatcher was that regional institutional settings were often proving sites of political resistance to the roll out of neoliberalism that was being enacted, for example, the more socially democratic policies pursued by the Greater London Council, as well as their deliberate disruption of Thatcher's policies. New spaces of localism did not seem to have the same resources in providing a balancing force to central government policy. Therefore, taking away regional control was widely seen by many as the 'centralisation' of governmental power to avoid political dissent (Goodwin et al., 1993).

Although there was some progress made by the John Major Government in the 1990s, it was in 1997 with the election of New Labour that substantial moves towards devolution occurred. This saw the creation of nine English Regional Development Agencies (RDAs) implementing regional plans through consultation with a range of stakeholders, as well as non-directly elected Regional Assemblies. These regions include the South East, Greater London, North West, East of England, West Midlands, South West, Yorkshire, the Humber, East Midlands, and the North East. Regional assemblies had little power however, and were not directly elected by people living in the region. There was a push for full democratically elected regional assemblies, however these plans were abolished after the North East rejected proposals for a directly elected assembly in 2004 (Mulholland, 2004).

In 2007 regional governance was put under review, and regional assemblies were abolished between 2008 and 2010. The Conservative government came to power in 2010 and made further changes to England's regions, by abolishing RDAs. New frameworks were created through the Conservatives 'localism' agenda and other reforms. The Enterprise Partnerships that replaced RDAs turned out to be much more limited due to their lack of fiscal power and their limited capacity to articulate long term plans. Unsurprisingly perhaps, calls have been made in some parts for a return of RDAs to enable regions to have more strategic control over their economic direction (Milne, 2016). It must also be added that the movements mentioned above, including the Hannah Mitchell Foundation and campaigns for northern regions to have directly elected assemblies have not gone away, and may well intensify in the coming years.

Scottish Independence and Democratically Disruptive Regions in the Age of Authoritarian Capitalism

The Brexit narrative has led to the successful displacement of concern regarding the democratic deficit at the heart of the 'Westminster model' (Strohmeier, 2006). Brexit has deflected concern regarding the economic inequalities forged through this culture of decision making, towards fear-based concern with exogenous threats, perpetuated through the European Union and particularly, immigration. The Brexit discourse was fully integrated into government in October 2016. Yet it is arguably not a sustainable fabric to hold together an internally fragmented and highly unequal country. There are some reasons to suggest that a Brexit vote will in fact increase inequality and hurt the poorest regions of England because the EU is a vital source of funding for these regions, and there is a lack of coherence regarding regional governance on the part of the Conservative Government (Hetherington, 2016).

Returning to the notion of the crisis at the centre, the overly centralised, scandal-stained, 'revolving-door' based political settlement that many associate with the Westminster model – combined with the lack of substantial change that Brexit will offer in dealing with this culture – will potentially mean that asymmetries in power between Westminster and regions, rather than asymmetries of power between the UK and the EU, will become a key focus. Bringing together the democratically disruptive role of the Scottish independence campaign and the potential for further regional development in the English regions, it is important to also consider wider 'metagovernance' frameworks within which they are continuing to develop (Etherington and Jones, 2016: 4).

This places focus on the UK's evolving nature in the context of the Brexit vote and broader changes in the capitalist economy. Some argue that what the Brexit vote represents is the 'high water mark' of neoliberalism (Mason, 2016), and that a globalised hyper-mobile form of capital accumulation, based around a small non-interventionist state allowing the market to prosper, is, at least rhetorically, over. The financial crisis of 2008, and the lack of substantial growth in the neoliberal model more generally, represents a crisis as a mode of capital accumulation, where it would seem, a stronger state is increasingly required. Neoliberalism has arguably led to widespread dissatisfaction. People have increasingly felt in the past decade as if they lost some form of sovereign control over governmental decisions, through the evolution of 'governance-beyond-the-state' measures (Swyngedouw, 2005). A feeling of powerlessness, and that elected politicians can do little to restrain the revolutionary forces of transnational capital, have come home to roost in the forms of various 'returns of the political', including Brexit (Swyngedouw, 2011).

On top of this, there are some suggestions that the long-held notion that capitalism and democracy go hand-in-hand is not necessarily true (Agamben et al., 2011; Žižek, 2014). In fact Žižek (2014) points towards cases such as China, Singapore, Russia, and Turkey as the signposts towards new regimes of economic growth, where an authoritarian state enables the 'smooth flow' of capital accumulation to occur, often through the silencing of dissenting voices. In short, many theorists are suggesting that one of the main impediments to the continuation of neoliberalism is democracy itself (Agamben et al., 2011; Mason, 2015; Stiglitz, 2013; Varoufakis, 2016). The state, condemned to history by neoliberalism, is returning, but crucially not in a social democratic form, rather as a mere facilitator of even more disruptive forms of capital accumulation, unrestrained from accountability and due democratic process.

In their Party Conference in October 2016, the UK Government signalled a rhetorical sea change in their ideological convictions. Instead of the state being denigrated as a force that is an unnecessary interference to the perfect functioning of the market, the state was talked about in a more positive way. Prime Minster Theresa May talked up a 'strategic role for the state' in enabling economic growth, where 'the winds of change' are 'blowing against the winds of the free market and in favour of intervention' (May quoted in New Statesman, 2016). Considering that this was the same party that initiated neoliberalism and pursued it dogmatically for the past thirty years, it is hard to believe that the ideology of the Conservative party has suddenly changed overnight.

What it may suggest, however, is the advent of an interventionist state designed not to constrain capital and shield people from its excesses as in social democratic systems, but to further unleash a new form of neoliberalism without certain 'barriers'. There are potential signs of an emerging disciplinary and more authoritarian state in the UK, beyond the obvious signalling of such an emergence in the negative rhetoric used by the UK government to describe refugees from Syria and EU migrants. Large state-subsidised projects, such as the proposed nuclear reactor at Hinkley point in Somerset, may offer a clue as to the kind of 'intervention' to expect. The decision-making process around this facility saw a series of secretive 'behind-closed-doors' deals done with the UK government and French and Chinese state-owned industries, with virtually no substantial public scrutiny (Cox et al., 2016). Another revealing moment came in October 2016 when a decision by a local council in Lancashire to refuse a planning application for the 'fracking' of natural gas was overruled by central government (Vaughan, 2016).

If it is true that there may be a more authoritarian form of capitalism developing in the UK, then the British state is potentially in a quandary however. As Martin et al. (2015: 1) highlight, in a paper on 're-spatialising the UK economy', 'no significant or lasting reduction in spatial economic imbalance will be achieved without "decentring" the key institutional structures that make up the UK's national political economy'. On top of this, there are several devolution processes occurring primarily to city regions (Nowles, 2016), and more secessionist movements remain in regions in Northern England (Yorkshire Devolution Movement, 2016; Salveson, 2014) and Cornwall (Trelawny, 2014). There is an impetus for the government to bring further democratic change to the regions, while at the same time also enacting more centrally coordinated state strategies to ensure some form of neoliberalism can continue. There is an apparent tension between these two aims. A danger for the coherence of the centralised British state is that there is no reason that, under the right kind of political conditions where a perceived 'injustice' is collectively sensed, regional political movements cannot transform into forces that have similar organisational and political innovation to the movements that emerged during the Scottish independence campaign.

Therefore the question is, what kind of regional politics can be expected in the coming years? This can be thought of in terms of the ways in which space is a mode of a political thinking (Dikeç, 2012), where there is a difference between how regions are 'seen by the state' (Scott, 1998), and those visions that emerge as a democratic force against a 'perceived injustice' (Barnett, 2012), and grow into powerful political movements. This tension is performed through a 'functional' view of regions (Jones, 2013), where the precise role of the region is defined as part of the 'post-political' spatial mapping of the state (Dikec, 2005), and through regions that create spaces of democratic struggle outside of the post-political map, operating at a 'distance' to the central state apparatus (Critchley, 2007). Such regions could disrupt the stability of the post-political unity of the British state still further.

Some commentators believe it is at the regional level where the Labour Party's best chances of building a coherent movement 'that matters to people's lives', will be forged (Richards, 2016). Put simply, the battle for Westminster is over because it is beyond repair, and times are changing so democratic movements must focus their energies elsewhere. Indeed, the Labour Party in opposition have already made some progressive proposals for devolution to regions and election gains in London (BBC News, 2014a). But crucially, more substantial regional struggles may require cross-party networks to emerge as well as refocussing attention on the democratic deficit of the Westminster model rather than the EU. Enhanced regional political movements could enable the distance that is felt in many neglected parts of the UK, between 'everyday life' and political decision making, to be lessened. This will involve the development of a new democratic culture where instead of answering the questions authorised by the state, which always only have one answer, new questions must be proposed from the bottom up. Or, as Deleuze and Guattari (1987: 128) write, 'to an answer already contained in a question, one should respond with questions from another answer'. The crisis at the centre of UK democracy remains, while the democratically disruptive role of Scottish independence continues. Yet the democratically disruptive role of England's regions may just be beginning.

Notes

1 Before 1707, Scotland was an independent nation with its own parliament. Scotland in the end joined with England, basically because it had bankrupt itself due to the disastrous Darian project where Scotland had attempted to form a colony in what is now Panama. At a poorly attended parliamentary hearing in Scotland, Scottish elites voted to join England, but as poet Robert Burns remarked at the time, Scottish MPs were "… bought and sold for English gold' (quoted in Herman, 2001). The Union was made primarily because Scotland had run out of money, rather than as some sudden desire to be United with its neighbours. Through Education Acts initiated following the unification, the Scots' language was generally banned from being taught in schools in favour of the 'queens English'. Following the battle of Culloden in 1745, a range of other Scottish cultural practices were also banned. The Scots language was only again recognized by the UN as a language in the 1990s after a long campaign. The desire to return to an independent nation resurfaced occasionally such as in 1913 when an independent Scotland (along with Ireland) was proposed by Liberal politicians, but then subsided. What was personally remarkable during the referendum campaign for independence in 2014 living in England was how unaware many English voters seemed to be that the UK was a very recent invention. People also seemed unaware that Scotland had a different legal

and education system. If anything, this resembles the success of the formation of some kind of 'Britishness' where unification in part rests on a certain degree of 'collective forgetting' of previous identity and difference.

References

Agamben G et al. (2011) *Democracy in What State?* New York: Columbia University Press.

Allen J and Cochrane A (2010) Assemblages of state power: topological shifts in the organization of government and politics. *Antipode* 42(5): 1071–1089.

Allen J and Cochrane A (2007) Beyond the territorial fix: regional assemblages, politics and power. *Regional Studies* 41(9): 1161–1175.

Barnett C (2012) Situating the geographies of injustice in democratic theory. *Geoforum* 43(4): 677–686.

BBC News (2014a) Labour plan to give economic power to English cities. *BBC News Online*. Available at: http://www.bbc.co.uk/news/uk-politics-28098586 [Accessed October 12, 2016].

BBC News (2014b) UK 'one of most centralised OECD countries.' *BBC News Online*. Available at: http://www.bbc.co.uk/news/business-25909238 [Accessed July 12, 2016].

BBC News (2016) UK one of the most unequal countries, says Oxfam. *BBC News Online*. Available at: http://www.bbc.co.uk/news/business-37341095 [Accessed October 3, 2016].

Beetham D (2015) Moving beyond a narrow definition of corruption, in D Whyte (ed) *How Corrupt is Britain?* London: Pluto Press, 41–47.

Carrell S (2011) Stunning SNP election victory throws spotlight on Scottish independence. *The Guardian Online*. Available at: https://www.theguardian.com/politics/2011/may/06/snp-election-victory-scottish-independence [Accessed July 12, 2016].

Carrell S (2016) Nicola Sturgeon challenges May with second referendum bill. *The Guardian Online*. Available at: https://www.theguardian.com/politics/2016/oct/13/nicola-sturgeon-challenges-may-with-second-referendum-bill-scottish-independence-snp-conference [Accessed October 15, 2016].

Communities and Local Government (2011) *A Plain English Guide to the Localism Act*. London: The Stationary Office.

Coughlin C (2015) Cameron must save Britain's world-power status. *Gulf News*. Available at: http://gulfnews.com/opinion/thinkers/cameron-must-save-britain-s-world-power-status-1.1511443 [Accessed July 15, 2016].

Cox E, Johnstone P and Stirling A (2016) *Understanding the Intensity of UK Policy Commitments to Nuclear Power*, SPRU Working Paper Series, September 2016, Brighton: University of Sussex

Critchley S (2007) *Infinitely Demanding: Ethics of Commitment, Politics of Resistance*. London: Verso.

Crouch C (2004) *Post Democracy*. Cambridge: Polity Press.

Dale-Scott P (2014) *The American Deep State: Wall Street, Big Oil, and the Attack on U.S Democracy*. London: Rowman and Littlefield.

Deleuze G and Guattari F (1987) *A Thousand Plateaus*. London: Bloomsbury.

Devlin K (2015) Margaret Thatcher archives: Scots were 'pampered' and a 'juicy' target for cuts. *The Scottish Herald*. Available at: http://www.heraldscotland.com/news/14172417.Thatcher_archives__Scots_were__pampered__and_a__juicy__target_for_cuts/ [Accessed July 12, 2016].

Dikec M (2005) Space, politics and the political. *Environment and Planning D: Society and Space* 23(2): 171–188.

Dikeç M (2012) Space as a mode of political thinking. *Geoforum* 43(4): 669–676.

Edemariam A and Scott K (2009) What happened to the Trainspotting generation? *The Guardian Online*. Available at: https://www.theguardian.com/society/2009/aug/15/scotland-trainspotting-generation-dying-fact [Accessed July 12, 2016].

Etherington D and Jones M (2016) The city-region chimera: the political economy of metagovernance failure in Britain. *Cambridge Journal of Regions, Economy and Society*, 9(2): 371–389.

Featherstone D (2015) Revolt on Clydeside? Space, politics and populism. *Geoforum* 62: 193–195. Available at: http://dx.doi.org/10.1016/j.geoforum.2015.04.007.

Gander K (2014) 'Devo-Manc': Manchester should be given devolution powers like Scotland's potential 'devo-max', says think tank. *The Independent Online*. Available at: http://www.independent.co.uk/news/uk/home-news/devo-manc-manchester-should-be-given-devolution-powers-like-scotlands-potential-devo-max-says-think-9734431.html [Accessed June 12, 2016].

Gill N, Johnstone, P and Williams A (2012) Towards a geography of tolerance: post-politics and political forms of toleration. *Political Geography* 31(8): 509–518.

Giovannini A and Willett J (2014) The uneven path of English devolution: will the dog finally bark? *Political Insight*. Available at: https://www.psa.ac.uk/insight-plus/blog/uneven-path-english-devolution-will-dog-finally-bark [Accessed July 12, 2016].

Goodwin M (2012) Regions, territories and relationality: exploring the regional dimensions of political practice. *Regional Studies* 47(8): 1–10.

Goodwin M, Duncan S and Halford S (1993) Regulation theory, the local state, and the transition of urban-politics. *Environment and Planning D: Society and Space* 11(1): 67–88.

Greenslade R (2016) Study confirms that the national press is biased in favour of Brexit. *The Guardian Online*. Available at: https://www.theguardian.com/media/greenslade/2016/may/23/study-confirms-that-the-national-press-is-biased-in-favour-of-brexit [Accessed October 22, 2016].

Hall P (2011) Britain is 'one of most undemocratic countries in Europe.' *Daily Mail*. Available at: http://www.dailymail.co.uk/news/article-1352845/Britain-undemocratic-countries-Europe.html [Accessed October 22, 2016].

Harris J (2016) Don't let England be rebranded as a nation of bigots. *The Guardian Online*. Available at: https://www.theguardian.com/commentisfree/2016/oct/10/england-rebranded-nation-bigots-intolerance [Accessed October 22, 2016].

Hart T (2016) The time has come for Britain's regions. *Prospect*. Available at: http://www.prospectmagazine.co.uk/economics-and-finance/the-time-has-come-for-britains-regions-devolution [Accessed September 21, 2016].

Harvey M (2015) A social democratic future? Political and institutional hurdles in Scotland. *Political Quarterly* 86(2): 249–256.

Henley J (2014) However Scotland votes, UK regions are eyeing up more devolved powers. *The Guardian Online*. Available at: https://www.theguardian.com/politics/2014/sep/11/devolution-regional-powers-scotland-north-east-england [Accessed June 22, 2016].

Herman A (2001) *The Scottish Enlightenment: The Scots' Invention of the Modern World*. London: Harper Collins.

Hetherington P (2016) Brexit would widen the north-south divide as poorest areas stand to lose most. *The Guardian Online*. Available at: https://www.theguardian.com/society/2016/jun/21/brexit-widen-north-south-divide-poorest-areas-lose-most-eu [Accessed June 22, 2016].

HM Government (2008) *Planning Act 2008*, London. Available at: http://www.legislation.gov.uk/ukpga/2008/29/contents [Accessed October 22, 2016].

House of Commons (2016) Devolution to local government in England 2014–2016. *House of Commons Library Research Briefings*. Available at: http://researchbriefings.parliament.uk/ResearchBriefing/Summary/SN07029#fullreport [Accessed June 12, 2016].

Johnstone P (2010) The nuclear power renaissance in the UK: democratic deficiencies within the 'consensus' on sustainability. *Human Geography* 3(2): 91–104.

Jones M (2013) Polymorphic spatial politics: tales from a grassroots regional movement, in W Nicholls, B Miller and J Beaumont (eds) *Spaces of Contention: Spatialisations and Social Movements*. Oxon: Routledge, 103–120.

Labour Party (1997) Labour Party 1997 manifesto. *Labour Party Manifesto*. Available at: http://www.politicsresources.net/area/uk/man/lab97.htm [Accessed September 10, 2015].

Lobao L, Martin R and Rodríguez-Pose A (2009) Editorial: Rescaling the state: new modes of institutional-territorial organization. *Cambridge Journal of Regions, Economy and Society*, 2(1): 3–12.

MacLeod G and Jones M (2001) Renewing the geography of regions. *Environment and Planning D: Society and Space* 19(6): 669–695.

Marres N (2007) The issues deserve more credit: Pragmatist contributions to the study of public involvement in controversy. *Social Studies of Science* 37(5): 759–780.

Martin R et al. (2015a) *Spatially Rebalancing the UK Economy: The Need for a New Policy Model*, London: Regional Studies Association.

Martin R et al. (2015b) Spatially rebalancing the UK economy: the need for a new policy model. *Regional Studies Association* (March): 0–18.

Mason P (2015) *Post-Capitalism: A Guide to Our Future*. Milton Keynes: Penguin Books.

Mason P (2016) The global order is dying. But it's an illusion to think Britain can survive without the EU. *The Guardian Online*. Available at: https://www.theguardian.com/commentisfree/2016/jun/27/global-order-britain-survive-eu-alternative-economic-model [Accessed October 22, 2016].

Merrick R (2016) Brexit: Government 'bars foreign academics from advising on EU withdrawal'. *The Independent Online*. Available at: http://www.independent.co.uk/news/uk/politics/brexit-lse-foreign-academics-barred-banned-government-eu-withdrawal-advisors-a7350691.html [Accessed October 22, 2016].

Milne R (2016) Regional development agencies urged by Plaid Cymru. *The Planner*. Available at: http://www.theplanner.co.uk/news/regional-development-agencies-urged-by-plaid-cymru [Accessed October 22, 2016].

Monbiot G (2014) How the media shafted the people of Scotland. *The Guardian Online*. Available at: https://www.theguardian.com/commentisfree/2014/sep/16/media-shafted-people-scotland-journalists [Accessed October 22, 2016].

Mulholland H (2004) North-east voters reject regional assembly. *The Guardian Online*. Available at: https://www.theguardian.com/society/2004/nov/05/regionalgovernment.politics [Accessed October 22, 2016].

NESTA (2016) Complex places for complex times: An analysis of the complexity of UK local economies, and their future evolution. *NESTA Blog*. Available at: http://www.nesta.org.uk/blog/complex-places-complex-times-analysis-complexity-uk-local-economies-and-their-future-evolution [Accessed October 10, 2016].

New Statesman (2016) Theresa May and the resurgence of the state. *The New Statesman*. Available at: http://www.newstatesman.com/politics/uk/2016/09/theresa-may-and-resurgence-state [Accessed October 22, 2016].

Nowles N (2016) English devolution post-Brexit: Cameron exit stage left, cue Mrs May. *Huffington Post*. Available at: http://www.huffingtonpost.co.uk/nikki-knowles/brexit_b_12132854.html [Accessed October 22, 2016].

O'Toole F (2014) Scotland's vote is not about Braveheart or kilts or tribal nationalism. It's about democracy. *The Guardian Online*. Available at: https://www.theguardian.com/commentisfree/2014/sep/12/scotland-vote-braveheart-nationalism-democracy-independence [Accessed October 22, 2016].

OECD (2014) Inequality hurts economic growth, finds OECD research. *OECD webpages*. Available at: http://www.oecd.org/newsroom/inequality-hurts-economic-growth.htm [Accessed July 12, 2016].

Ranciere J (2004) Introducing disagreement. *Angelaki* 9(3): 3–9.

Richards S (2016) Don't despair – devolution offers Labour a chance. *The Guardian Online*. Available at: https://www.theguardian.com/commentisfree/2016/aug/21/this-is-not-the-1980s-devolution-has-changed-politics [Accessed October 22, 2016].

Robertson J (2015) *Scotland's Propaganda War: The Media and the 2014 Independence Referendum*. Glasgow: Professor John Robertson.

Rodríguez-Pose A (2013) Do institutions matter for regional development? *Regional Studies* 47(7): 1034–1047.

RT (2016) 'June 23rd will go down in history as our independence day' - Nigel Farage. *RT Websites*. Available at: https://www.rt.com/news/348129-farage-brexit-independence-day/ [Accessed July 12, 2016].

Russell B and Kelbie P (2005) How black gold was hijacked: North sea oil and the betrayal of Scotland. *The Independent Online*. Available at: http://www.independent.co.uk/news/uk/this-britain/how-black-gold-was-hijacked-north-sea-oil-and-the-betrayal-of-scotland-518697.html [Accessed October 22, 2016].

Salveson P (2014) Time for a new regional politics: Devolution now? The case for a new progressive Northern politics. *Hannah Mitchell Foundation Webpages*. Available at: http://www.hannahmitchell.org.uk/2014/11/18/time-for-a-new-regional-politics/ [Accessed July 12, 2016].

Schmitt C (1996) *The Concept of the Political*. Chicago: University of Chicago Press.

Scott JC (1998) *Seeing Like a State: How Certain Schemes to Improve the Human Condition have Failed*. New Haven: Yale University Press.

Skidelsky R (2013) Meeting our makers: Britain's long industrial decline. *New Statesman*. Available at: http://www.newstatesman.com/culture/culture/2013/01/meeting-our-makers-britain%E2%80%99s-long-industrial-decline [Accessed July 15, 2016].

Staeheli L (2010) Political geography: democracy and the disorderly public. *Progress in Human Geography* 34(1): 67–78.

Stiglitz J (2013) *The Price of Inequality*. New York: Norton and Company.

Strohmeier G (2006) Consensus politics in Germany versus adversary politics in the United Kingdom? An evaluation of the German and the Westminster model of democracy on the basis of the veto players theory. *Debatte: Journal of Contemporary Central and Eastern Europe* 14(3): 229–245.

Swyngedouw E (2005) Governance innovation and the citizen: The Janus face of governance-beyond-the-state. *Urban Studies* 42(11): 1991–2006.

Swyngedouw E (2011) Interrogating post-democratization: reclaiming egalitarian political spaces. *Political Geography* 30(7): 370–380.

The Economist (2013) How does Germany's electoral system work? *The Economist*. Available at: http://www.economist.com/blogs/economist-explains/2013/09/economist-explains-3 [Accessed July 15, 2016].

The Guardian (2016) The Guardian view on the Act of Union: time to reimagine the United Kingdom. *The Guardian Online*. Available at: https://www.theguardian.com/commentisfree/2016/jul/10/the-guardian-view-on-the-act-of-union-time-to-reimagine-the-united-kingdom [Accessed July 5, 2016].

Trelawny P (2014) Cornwall is far more than just a county – and now it's official. *The Daily Telegraph Online*. Available at: http://www.telegraph.co.uk/comment/10786212/Cornwall-is-far-more-than-just-a-county-and-now-its-official.html [Accessed July 15, 2016].

Varoufakis Y (2016) *And the Weak Suffer What They Must*. London: Random House.

Vaughan A (2016) Fracking given UK go-ahead as Lancashire council rejection overturned. *The Guardian Online*. Available at: https://www.theguardian.com/environment/2016/oct/06/uk-fracking-given-go-ahead-as-lancashire-council-rejection-is-overturned [Accessed October 15, 2016].

Ward A (2015) Report finds that Britain's wages are the most unequal in Europe. *The Indepdendent*. Available at: http://www.independent.co.uk/news/uk/politics/report-finds-that-britains-wages-are-the-most-unequal-in-europe-10259077.html [Accessed July 15, 2016].

Wedel J (2014) *Unaccountable – How Elite Power Brokers Corrupt our Finances, Freedom, and Security*. New York: Pegagus Books.
Welsh I (2012) *Skagboys*. London: Random House.
Wilkinson R (2005) *The Impact of Inequality: How to Make Sick Societies Healthier*. New York: The New Press.
Yorkshire Devolution Movement (2016) Yorkshire devolution movement. *Yorkshire Devolution Movement Webpages*. Available at: https://yorkshiredevolution.co.uk/ [Accessed August 12, 2016].
Žižek S (2014) *Trouble in Paradise: From the End of History to the End of Capitalism*. Milton Keynes: Penguin.

8 From 'Fly Frontier' to 'Cotton Country'

Social Change and Agrarian Transformation in the Northwest of Zimbabwe

Nicholas James

Introduction

The purpose of this chapter is threefold. It is to re-engage with the challenges raised with the adoption of the new regional geography during the 1980s, namely to combine 'practical social action' (Gilbert, 1988: 208) with some scientific enquiry into regions (see Thrift, 1990). I use New Regional Geography as a unifying approach to achieve some synthesis, and the chapter identifies five geographic dynamics that characterise the region as a place to live and make a livelihood. This is achieved through indirect reference to emerging and consolidating theories within geography including agro-ecology (Moore, 2015), political ecology (Peet et al. 2011) and re-invigorated approaches to sustainable development (Polepole, 2015). The primary focus is around depicting and unpicking the dynamic entanglements in the developments in certain parts of Northwest Zimbabwe.

The Northwest of Zimbabwe is a lively political and economic region nevertheless facing unconcealed underdevelopment, neglect and exploitation. Even as recently as 2014, the area was described as cut-off and relatively remote and isolated from other parts of Zimbabwe (Mugugunyeki, 2014). Most people here live in the 'communal lands', others in resettlement areas or 'small-scale commercial farms', and the region has accounted for a sizeable proportion of the nation's cotton, which is the second export earner after tobacco (James, 2006; Mariga, 1994). Harsh conditions, severe political unrest (McGreal, 2002), poverty *and* isolation from the main economy (Worby, 1998) make it a difficult place to live.

The term 'Northwest' refers to a swathe of *frontier* districts skirting the mid-Zambezi River valley. These include Binga, Gokwe North, Gokwe South, Kariba, and Hurungwe (see Figure 8.1). One unifying feature of these districts is that they were very sparsely populated for the larger part of colonial rule and much of the twentieth century, initially because of their exclusion from direct colonial investment and settlement, and later in the 1960s due to the strategic role of the region to absorb displaced Africans and to stimulate cotton production for the home market. Nevertheless, within the region it is crucial to recognise several important differences in context and settings.

Although scholars from several disciplines have examined social and agrarian changes in these frontier districts, what exists thus far remains a collection of well-researched case studies of the experiences from *within* the different districts (Dzingirai, 1998; Brand, 1999; Hammar, 2001; Chmhowu, 2003; Nyambara, 1999; James, 2002b; Worby, 1992). Assembling these findings into a coherent body of understanding on frontier dynamics in Zimbabwe thus provides a broader understanding of the nature and form of transformation in marginal regions (see also McGregor, 2009).

I follow a narrative to identify markers of agrarian change that have characterised the region (see Watts, 1989). An understanding of identity dynamics reveals ongoing changes in cultural and geographical imaginations, from envisaging a hostile and relatively uninhabitable frontier 'fly country' to one of imagined livelihood prospects including riches from cotton growing and the freedom to cultivate on 'virgin' soils within the communal lands. Such imaginations emanate from different perspectives entangled, co-existing and changing over time.

In the first section, I examine the rapid transformation of a largely peasant economy that took place in the lead-up to the introduction of cotton in the 1960s. The following section explores the land use and agrarian characteristics of the region, a discussion based on the notable increase in the total number of commercial smallholder farms following waves of in-migration to the region. A third section explores new institutional developments, particularly in the 1980s, including the incorporation of the region into a wider market. This moves into a discussion of the *de facto* opening up of 'communal lands' and wildlife resources for commercial exploitation and how this poses particular and sometimes contradictory challenges for the Northwest. The chapter ends by highlighting some of the conflict and place-based dynamics that have given the region its uneven and volatile characteristic especially since the late 1990s.

Frontier and Agrarian Livelihood Transformations: Early Commercialisation of a 'Peasant Economy'

Figure 8.1 shows that the districts are located in three provinces: Matebeleland North, Midlands and Mashonaland West. Apart from their location the districts share similar characteristics.

Firstly, they all belong to what was known as the 'Sebungwe Planning Region' (Wekwete, 1989). In 1978, the then head of state in the Zimbabwe-Rhodesia government called on the Regional Town and Country Planning Act of 1976 to declare Sebungwe a 'special planning region' (du Toit, 1985). Under this Act, challenges could be singled out for particular attention by the state.

Secondly, this region was described by the authorities and visitors as a 'frontier area', 'edge of beyond', the 'dark interior' and then, because of cotton, Worby (1992) describes the 'frontier of light' in reference to particular

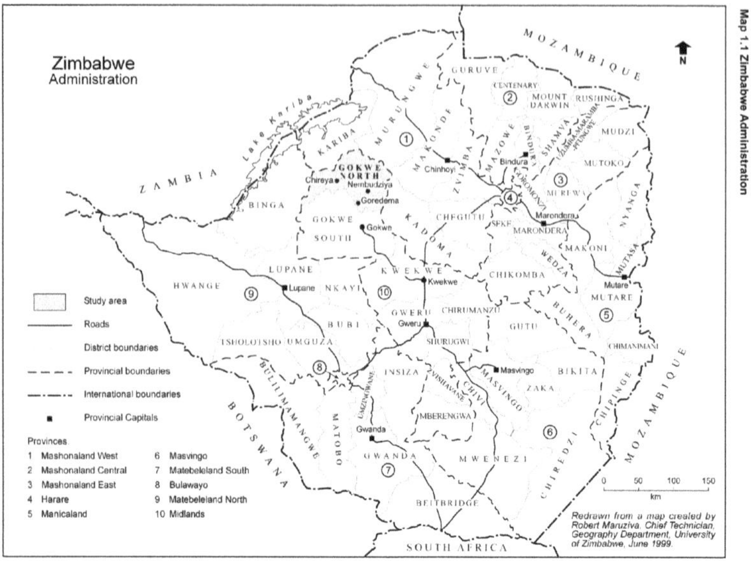

Figure 8.1 Map: Zimbabwe Administration.

optimism in the late 1970s. Most of the areas are classed as Natural Regions IV and V. These are characterised by poor and unreliable rainfall, high temperatures, and relatively infertile soils.[1] The prevalence of tsetse fly (*Glossina spp*.) and malaria-carrying mosquitoes made for notably difficult living conditions throughout the twentieth century. The health risks to cattle including the danger of 'sleeping sickness' (*Trypanosomiasis*) from tsetse fly (*Glossina*) slowed significant movements into the area until after the 1950s (Child and Riney, 1987). In addition to this marginality and remoteness, the region even today conjures images of being very inhospitable and 'culturally backward'. Therefore, throughout the twentieth century, the apparent abundance of land had nevertheless to be considered in light of official verdicts about it. For example, in 1946 it was described by a colonial administrator thus: 'Apart from being full of tsetse fly they [Sebungwe] are for the greater part *unfit at present for human habitation*. When fly has been eliminated and adequate water supplies and irrigation instituted, a reasonable number of natives can be settled' (James, 2002a). Alexander, McGregor and Ranger (2000) discuss similar problems of harsh conditions, malaria and a lack of markets, including the issue of colonial state-organised depopulation in Bubi district.

Thirdly, major developments took place including cotton during the 1960s, agricultural developments in the late 1970s, and several waves of in-migrants to the region. Whilst categorised agro-ecologically as poor, marginal and remote, the Northwest has nonetheless been an important part of the rural and agricultural development of post-independence Zimbabwe.

No 'Reserves' for people to live were demarcated until after 1911. Alexander and Ranger (1998: 4) point out that: '... the whole region was regarded as literally 'reserve' territory – empty land into which African populations could be moved when it became "necessary".' Pashu, Sibaba and Impampa, for example, were Reserves demarcated as drawn circles on a map.

The Sebungwe Reserve was first demarcated in 1914-1915 when the Native Reserves[2] Commission confirmed to the Acting Director of Land Settlement that the Sebungwe area would never be required for European settlement (Palmer, 1977). Moreover, the British South Africa Company Medical Director considered the establishment of Sebungwe Reserve appropriate. The Reserve was then described as 'uninhabited' in 1930 (Palmer, 1977). Following the collapse of the tobacco industry in the area during the 1920s, which I discuss in more detail later, many men migrated to find work and thus may have evaded tax payments, giving the impression that the area was officially unoccupied. Furthermore, the authorities actively moved the people out of these areas during the 1940s in preparation for anti-tsetse fly measures.

The explanation for this noteworthy lack of development in the Northwest has a history. For many years in the twentieth century, it was classed as 'unassigned'. In 1910, the Native Commissioner in Bulawayo described Sebungwe as *a wild district, hidden away and generally unknown to the authorities* (Worby, 1994). Reid (1971) writes: 'Gokwe district is a vast and remote area in the Northwest of Rhodesia. Over one and a quarter million hectares in extent, it is underdeveloped and has poor communications. Railhead and markets in Que Que and Gatooma are 160 kilometres from Gokwe. Tsetse fly infest the entire region.' It became the area for colonial authorities to send Africans forcibly alienated from their land. With its wildlife, and thick miombo woodland, and the presence of tsetse fly, the colonial governments were uncertain what to do with this region until the 1960s. Very few Europeans were willing to settle there.

The region nevertheless had two dynamic phases before the introduction of cotton in the 1960s. After David Livingstone first discovered coal in 1856, it was again explored by the BSA Company in 1894-5, and a small number of white outsiders began to move into the region. However, the absence of roads, the poor quality of the coal discovered, and then the prohibition of aeroplanes flying led to a lapse of interest. In the early twentieth century, 'after the central portion was depopulated following an outbreak of sleeping sickness the area became *terra incognita* except to a few game poachers' (Chorley, 1945: 5).

Secondly, Turkish and Burley tobaccos were grown in many parts of the country prior to the crop being developed commercially by Europeans in the 1920s (Kosmin, 1977: 270). Used for smoking and as a snuff mixture, it was an important local cash crop. Chireya's people living in the area grew significant quantities of tobacco for sale, barter and as tribute gifts for the Ndebele people including those under King Lobengula. Turkish tobacco grew well in the agro-ecological conditions given in Inyoka and surrounding areas in Sebungwe and the people under chiefs including Nemangwe, Neganda and Nebire (now called headman Nembudziya) were able to profit from the finished product. The cones crafted from kneading and pounding the tobacco with ashes from wild *Aloe* (spp.) were significantly superior in quality and thus highly sought after by traders and hawkers.

The indigenous forms of tobacco cropping declined rapidly in the 1920s, and this was significant enough to disrupt livelihoods in the region. This external and commercial undermining of the local industry by the wider commercial introductions of tobacco also damaged social and commercial relations with the Ndebele neighbours to the south (Kosmin, 1977). Based on the evidence of declining benefits from tobacco and the increasing burden of colonial taxes, livelihood conditions became much more of a struggle after the 1930s.

Nevertheless, it remains unclear why this region remained so politically isolated and geographically remote. Worby (1992: 4) discusses the 'gap' on national maps of Zimbabwe suggesting an evocation of emotions for Zimbabweans who do not live there: 'the fear of the unknown and the inhuman, disdain for the uncivilised, and sometimes longing for the unwritten possibilities of a social and economic frontier.' Clyde Mitchell (1961) described the area as *more* distant, in terms of communication and accessibility, than Nyasaland (Malawi).

The colonial state was generally unenthusiastic about African agriculture. However, some individuals were able to note the resourcefulness of African people in the region:

Table 8.1 Summary of environmental and agriculture constraints, Gokwe, Sebungwe District, 1886–1936.

Date	*Nature of problem*	*Other notes*	*Annual rainfall (mm)*	*Days of rain*
1897	Rinderpest outbreak (national)			
1901	Tsetse outbreak			
1903	Drought – Famine (local)	Locust attack on crops		
1907	Drought			
1908	Grain failure			
1912	Smallpox and measles outbreak; mainly noted in the Zambezi Valley			
1913	Bad harvest and increase in tsetse fly		552	49
1914	Tobacco slump leading to failure of Inyoka Company	NRC assign Sebungwe Reserve	585	50

(*continued*)

Table 8.1 (continued)

Date	*Nature of problem*	*Other notes*	*Annual rainfall (mm)*	*Days of rain*
1916	Drought and food shortage in February	Tsetse eradication	440	43
1917	Leprosy outbreak		542	70
1918	Food shortage	Rain adequate nationally	1093	90
1920	Grain failure	European expansion in 'Virginia leaf' tobacco following the opening of export markets	849	64
1922	Drought and famine	Expanded acreage under tobacco in Inyoka Estate, Sebungwe to 1,500 acres; famine relief required	457	47
1924	Drought and food shortage	Bad tobacco year owing to small crop	375	44
1925	Excess rain; tobacco failure		1190	102
1926	Tobacco failure from excessive heat affecting young plants	Yaws disease	925	50
1927	Continued tobacco failure, partly owing to increased migration to find work and partly soil fertility decline		650	53
1930	Famine relief	Rain adequate	801	61
1932	Foot-and-mouth epidemic constraining market for small livestock as alternative to tobacco	Last year in which tobacco could raise enough for the tax bill	818	64
1933	Tobacco failure		584	44
1934	Chief entomologist employed	Difficulties selling tobacco	690	68
1935	Drought	Bad tobacco harvest	1012	64
1936	Grain failure and tobacco revival	Yaws epidemic	660	73

> Necessity, which may largely be attributed to their own improvidence, has recurrently taught them to rely to a great extent on the natural products of the bush and veld. Thus where another native would starve, the average Tonka [Tonga] or Shankwe [Shangwe] – if he does not thrive – manages to subsist wholesomely and moderately well on a diet of wild fruits, roots and grass seeds. (cited in James, 2002a: 135)

The 1921/2 drought showed that nationally the relatively remote areas with forests fared … better (see Table 8.1). Iliffe (1990: 71) nevertheless argues that this was an outstanding drought not only in its extent and intensity, but also in the responses. The use of wild foods from forests was possible in some areas but in other areas (e.g. the Zambezi valley) 'some wild species bore no fruit'. Migrant labour thus became one additional option for survival against drought.

The rapid decline in tobacco farming reduced the commercial opportunities for populations in the region. In 1916, the Chief Native Commissioner (CNC) wrote to the acting Native Commissioner in Sebungwe to recommend suspension of the Game Law Consolidation Ordinance of 1906, which prohibited any hunting of wildlife (Cliggett and Bond, 2013). In a response to severe drought at the time, the interruption was deemed for the benefit of the 'natives only' and *only* for a period of eight months. The correspondence goes on to detail which class of animals could legally be hunted and how armaments should be distributed. The Acting Native Commissioner nevertheless complained that: '… leaving [only] Duiker [*Sylvicapra grimmia*] … would not go far to stave off anything in the shape of even a partial famine.'

The problem of tsetse led to stricter controls and the people of Chireya were moved eastwards to Sanyati an area just outside the region (Chorley, 1945). There are several explanations for this increase in tsetse. One is that, as a result of war and raids from the Ndebele from the mid-nineteenth century, the population of the Northwest fell significantly (Ncube, 1994). This de-population *along* with the strict conservation and hunting laws led to a recovery in wildlife populations, the principle hosts for tsetse fly (Cliggett and Bond, 2013).

The presence of tsetse fly prohibited livestock (cattle and donkeys) from entering the area and this prevented the use of the plough for cultivation. However, donkeys arrived with the people as an alternative draught-power for ploughing and transport. Nevertheless, the donkeys proved not to be as resistant to *trypanosomiasis* as initially thought. Still, they were part of the agrarian landscape in this early period (before cattle were introduced). While coal mining remained mostly uneconomic, some copper was mined in the Copper Queen and Empress Mine areas to the south-east of the region (Chorley, 1945). The combination of this failure of coal mining and limited agricultural investment led to a withdrawal from the region by external investors, including the state, early on in the twentieth century.

The anti-tsetse fly campaigns operated from 1919 to 1964 (Child and Riney, 1987). To keep wild mammals from moving eastwards, a major fence was constructed 'about two metres high and consisted of high-tensile steel wire on wooden posts with wooden droppers. White metal discs suspended along the wires, against which they rattled, were designed to make the fence more conspicuous to animals, but its effectiveness was limited' (Child and Riney, 1987: 49). It was known as the 'Northern Sebungwe Game Fence' and although now defunct, it once enclosed up to half of Gokwe North's land area (Taylor, 1982). The game fence was planned during the 1940s and installed in 1957 (Child and Riney, 1987). The hunting concentrated on small areas aiming to create game-free and cattle-free buffer corridors. Later, hunting was suspended to allow time to build the fences, and 'destroy the tsetse habitats through cutting of riverine vegetation in particular and the use of insecticides such as DDT and deldrin, but was resumed in 1964' (Child and Riney, 1987: 21). The aim in fighting back tsetse was twofold. One, the hunting was co-ordinated nationally to counter and reverse the spread of tsetse fly to protect the large commercial cattle farms and two, to open up land to new settlers.

Elders in Nembudziya recalled a character they called 'Petrol-bomber' who hunted elephants taking the ivory and leaving the meat. This is captured in the place-name 'Musorowenzhou' (Shona for elephant's head). These early 1960s were exciting times. As one new arrival recalled, the hunting effort proved to be both an adventure *and* potentially advantageous for new settlers wishing to farm: 'They [the hunters] were permitted to sell the meat from the animals they shot and this and their poor wages were intended as an inducement to greater hunting effort' (James, 2002a). While commended for their hunting skills, their shooting was hampered by the 'worn state of the ex-military 0.303 rifles with which they were issued' (Child and Riney, 1987: 55).

During the 1960s, once the in-migrants began to settle, large mammals rapidly disappeared from wider parts of the region. The combination of anti-tsetse fly sprays, vegetation removal *and* grass-burning saw the departure certainly of larger vertebrata and led to 'bush encroachment' (Child and Riney, 1987). This purge on the landscape influenced the local environments and altered the quality and diversity of wild foods available. The rapid expansion of fields for cotton cultivation began in 1963, contributing to significant deforestation (Whitlow, 1988).

In-Migration and Demographic Expansion in the Region: The Effect of an Increase in the Total Number of Smallholder Farmers

A combination of in-migration of people from the south of the country *and* the introduction of cotton saw an unprecedented agrarian transformation in the region. Initially, people were moved into the area under the colonial state's direction. However, inflows of migrants increased during the 1960s and intensified after independence in 1980 (Zinyama and Whitlow, 1986). Both the planned and 'spontaneous' migration (Chimhowu and Hulme, 2006) into these frontier districts (Alexander and McGregor, 1997) resulted in significant agrarian transformation of the 'Miombo woodland' region resulting in its rapid incorporation into the national and international agricultural commodity and labour markets.

However, later and especially following independence in 1980, people migrated voluntarily in large numbers (Zinyama and Whitlow, 1986). In this drive for national development, parts of the Northwest experienced economic growth rates described as 'miraculous' (Worby, 1992; Rukuni and Eicher, 1994).

People relocated or were moved into the Northwest for different reasons. The effects of the post-World War II political economy in Rhodesia shaped the settler colonial economy and this led to more than two thousand African families being driven out from several areas on higher land including Rhodesdale. Rhodesdale Estate was bought by the Rhodesian Government from Lonrho and eventually allocated to British ex-servicemen as farms (Nyambara, 1999: 62).[3] In one example, people were coercively moved to Sanyati, the southeastern corner of Gokwe and the Kana area just north of Nkayi District. Worby describes the rapid actions to clear land for new settlers: 'The Rhodesdale residents [from Kwe Kwe] were loaded into lorries at short notice and transported into the hot malarial lowlands of the Sanyati and Sebungwe Districts' (1994: 389).[4] Simultaneously, there were national efforts in Rhodesia to resettle Second World War veterans onto better land on the higher ground but also create Native Reserves to receive the deported people. They nevertheless needed to wait for some infrastructure including water and some clearance in regards to the effort to clear tsetse fly from some buffer zones.

Most significantly, from 1945 to 1955 one hundred thousand Africans described as 'squatters' were moved to these so-called 'unassigned' lands in Sebungwe (Nyambara, 1999). There were nevertheless some Native Reserves which were initially set up to contain and manage labour for the new farms being taken over by colonial settlers. The delay in officially settling people stemmed from difficulties including the lack of surface water. The authorities needed to build boreholes, tank-dams and wells to provide drinking water (Nyambara, 1999).

The region is noted for the lack of surface water and therefore for the authorities, the expense and uncertainty in sourcing water from underground aquifers was considered too much. Furthermore, during the 1930s, the so-called squatters 'alienated' from land that they once occupied helped further the European 'take-off' agriculturally through providing labour, rent *and* crops (Arrighi, 1970). The post-Second World War period saw changing macro-economic priorities with new technologies introduced and bigger capital investments in the agricultural sector.

Despite this move of people into the Northwest based on consequences of the 1951 Native Land Husbandry Act, tsetse fly continued to hamper rural development and officials continued to consider Sebungwe as unfit for human habitation. Moreover, as already indicated by Kosmin (1977), many of the men spent time outside Sebungwe working.

Even by the 1940s, because of the agro-ecological conditions and the isolation, small grains (Sorghum, *Sorghum bicolor* and Millet, *Elusine coracana*) were grown as food crops instead of the increasingly popular maize (*Zea mays*). As a result of the 1947 drought, a nationwide campaign and policy in food production was instituted with an increase in rain-fed maize fields coming under the plough (Scoones, 1997a, 1997b). Although this nationwide drive for increased food production occurred, the Northwest, with tsetse fly, could not take advantage of the situation because of being unable to use the plough. There was no scope for keeping livestock (cattle and donkeys) (James, 2002b).

Instead, two decades later cotton (*Gossypium*) was introduced to combat the sanctions imposed on Rhodesia in 1965 (Nyambara, 1999). The Unilateral Declaration of Independence (UDI) was declared in 1965 based on the imposition of United Nations sanctions. The sanctions compelled the Rhodesian economy to diversify and create many import-substitution processes to compensate for loss of imports. The processing of local raw materials including cotton grew rapidly.

This UDI political period coincided with the movements of people into these relatively remote areas (Ranger, 1998). The 1960s saw a complex entanglement of people becoming small-holder commercial farmers, others moving into the Tribal Trust Lands (which later became the Communal Areas), the growth of nationalist movements as the war for independence began, and emerging relations among in-migrants and the existing settlers, sometimes referred to as *Shangwe*.

The extension effort in the cotton industry required marked effort by the farmers including training, discipline and enterprise (James, 2002b). It was a national imperative for economic reasons. 'One way of "beating" the sanctions was to institute crop-diversification measures and cotton ultimately became one of the most important substitute crops' (Nyambara, 1999: 201).

The colonial government became worried about the swelling numbers of people in the Chidoma area south of the region. 'Farmers are dissatisfied by the locality and wish to change … [The] area is highly politically inclined and trouble brewing in the area will start here first' (cited in Nyambara, 1999: 229). The people that came from Chidoma in the south of Gokwe were in turn the in-migrants from places including Shurugwi, Mberengwa and Gutu. They initially came to settle under Chief Noah. According to Collett's (1963–1965) 'Delineation Report', Chief Noah led the 'Mambo waShaya' movement wishing for the glories of VaRozwi[5] to be re-born.

Chief Noah, under political pressure, decided to expel the new settlers and the District Administrator in Gokwe felt obliged to resettle the people. However, Chief Chireya refused to accommodate them. Nevertheless, the authorities went ahead, ignoring the chief, and resettled them in Goredema, Makore and Nembudziya. The three headmen, in going against Chireya's decree, were later fined heavily for this. However, events moved quickly and in 1963 the number of villages in areas like Nembudziya increased from 8 to 27, leaving Nembudziya the most densely populated area in what was to become Gokwe North.

The point made about nationalist conflicts surrounding early resettlement and objection to the NLHA is that the *madheruka* (in-migrants) were advised to move in to Nembudziya 'on a piecemeal basis, by choice' (Worby, 1994: 390). However, the people gained official permission to settle, and it was Headman Nembudziya's responsibility to allocate each new Kraal-head some land appropriately. Collett argues that as this was a 'large scale movement, each individually did not have to approach Chief Chireya for permission ('uchiri')'. This therefore gave greater power to Headman Nembudziya, and according to the elders, the new settlers were warmly welcomed and there was very little evidence of animosity or friction (James, 2002a). The in-migrants understood local traditions including *chisi* ('farmers' rest day') and they demonstrated their respect for rain-making ceremonies through sending local representatives to the Nevana spirit medium in Chief Nemangwe's area (Alexander and Ranger, 1998). The *Shave yemvura* (rain-spirits including Mbuya Nehova) also received offerings of beer and a black goat.

The early anti-colonial actions involving the Zimbabwe African National Liberation Army (ZANLA) and the Zimbabwe People's Revolutionary Army (ZIPRA) impeded farming which, without livestock, was already extremely difficult. Furthermore, resistance to cotton growing persisted in the 1960s and 1970s in Kana, Nembudziya and Charama (Nyambara, 1999). The opposition was linked to general anti-NLHA stances and out of respect for the views of nationalist agitators. They had no interest in supporting the colonial regime and growing cotton.

The Shangwe people are those loosely associated with living in the area before the arrival of in-migrants from the south of the country. 'Chireya and his associated chiefs established themselves in Shangwe in the eighteenth century' (Alexander and Ranger, 1998: 14). These *vatorwa* (Shona for foreigners) people adapted to the lands and developed a specialised form of tobacco agriculture that tied them commercially and politically to the Ndebele leadership (Kosmin, 1977).

There are unifying themes including the region's peripheral position, both in the important African states of the Ndebele and the VaRozwi *and* in the colonial state. The important influence of *Nevana* among Shona (including the *Shangwe*), the Ndebele and the Tonga people (see Alexander and Ranger, 1998: 4) unifies them in this region noted for empty, culturally idiosyncratic and undeveloped regional features. Worby writes: 'The popular etymology of the noun root Shangwe current in Gokwe today among those to whom the term is applied, suggests that it derives from the word *shangwa*, which for some Shona-speakers conveys the related senses of drought, famine or misery. VaShangwe would then be taken to signify "people of the place of drought"' (1994: 378).

While the cotton industry, directed by the state institutions, saw an 'agrarian revolution' in the Northwest, relative wealth was realised only by a few farmers. The majority struggled at the edges of deprivation (see Reid, 1971; James, 2006). Given two decades since the 1950s to redress the insufficient development, the state continued to provide only minimal infrastructural and financial institutional support. The commercial sector included only minimal marketing, payments for cotton to farmers, and the setting up of collection points, all operated sparsely and cheaply.

The nationalist sentiment felt by the new arrivals in the 1960s and 1970s presented in-migrants with a dilemma. First, engagement with the extension services and the 'disciplined' cotton farming system meant politically giving in to the Rhodesian Front government. Second, any open respect for the local traditional leaders and their local cultures was seen also as giving in to the Tribal Trust Land Act, 1967, which deliberately propped up traditional leaders. 'Traditional land tenure was re-established and the enforcement of land tenure was placed under newly established tribal authorities operating under district commissioners' (Rukuni, 1994: 19).

The 1970s stood out as years of immense trauma for people in the region. The international economic slump in the early 1970s began to undermine the initial cotton farming successes, as did the droughts. New methods of agricultural practice became the norm, although disruption caused by the war was evident. The *derukas* (Shona for people who appeared unexpectedly and were forcibly sent to areas such as Gokwe) continued to arrive throughout the 1970s and a practice of 'gochamupane' (burning the mopane trees) escalated, indicating further expansion of fields and a lack of appreciation for the multipurpose qualities of the tree (James, 2002a).

In summary, the initial reticence about cotton farming transformed to a rapid and frenzied adoption of the crop. This came in part from the desire to earn an income, the evident success in neighbouring areas, the arrival of cattle in the late 1970s *and* a change in the political landscape in the second half of the 1970s. It was contradictory because some people were reluctant or suspicious about growing cotton. Overall, the population of the region increased significantly. Several overlapping interests ensued following the waves of in-migrants to the area. After independence a consolidation and organising of grazing areas was attempted to halt the apparently unstoppable expansion of field areas. Here there is reference to the questions of ethnicity, culture, and socio-politics. Essentially, the contradictory elements refer to the layers of social relations developed from colonial times (i.e. laws and policies in farming methods, and land distribution), following independence (resettlement patterns and 'villagisation'), and in connection to the struggles in relationships between autochthonous cultures and new and modern cultural ways brought by in-migrants since the 1960s.

Institutional and Social Responses on the Frontier: Cotton and the Incorporation of the Northwest into the Global Commodity Market

The institutional changes in the region have been relatively different to other parts of Zimbabwe for reasons already discussed in the opening section. However, cotton arrived along with waves of in-migrants. This happened simultaneously with the war for independence.

Agrarian dynamics were strongly influenced by external state policies, social relations (e.g. local access to resources, tenure arrangements and emerging institutions) as well as cultural factors (loyalty, identity and religious diversity). People's identities were multiple and changing. Some of the customary institutions governing indigenous land use remained including rest days, the headmen's authority and sacred woodlands. Prohibited areas for development included grazing land, areas near dams, sacred woodlands and land adjacent to rivers or wetlands (Nyambara, 1999). With varying details, the rules around sacred places are that entry is restricted and the felling of trees is forbidden. In addition to the traditional respect for local sacred places referred to as *rambotemwa*,[6] some areas have also introduced official fines.

The colonial engagement with cotton was part of economic survival but it also added a dynamic in terms of opportunities for enterprising new arrivals wishing to make a living from farming. Agronomists attested that cotton had been scientifically tested as being agro-ecologically suited to the region. Cotton also became economically relevant once international sanctions were in place following the UDI (Unilateral Declaration of Independence) in 1965. While the cotton industry, directed principally by the state institutions, saw an 'agrarian revolution' in the whole region, relative wealth was realised only by a few households.

The relatively unified social relations among the in-migrants saw them adapt with relative ease to modern farming conditions. However, by contrast the indigenous social and cultural institutions were further eroded in the 1970s because of changes already mentioned including the arrival of cotton cash cropping and the tensions during the war. Given two decades since the 1950s to redress the imbalances, the state continued to provide minimal infrastructural and financial institutional support. The commercial sector included a little marketing, the payments for cotton to the farmers and the setting up of collection points, but all operated meagrely.

The 1980s and independence saw a new dynamic in the regional political economy. New state institutions and local social relations responded to changing environmental conditions observed during the 1970s and 'food security' became a national focus. The Northwest thus fit into the condition of a 'food insecurity paradox' (Jayne et al., 1994) – with economic growth, expansion in cotton cropping and the creation of wealth but with many households and some areas losing out badly. This transformed parts of the local economy, in some cases exacerbating food insecurity (see James, 2002b). After independence, rural development policy aimed expressly at expanding the cotton industry and the economy engaged in a policy of growth and development. The legacy of colonial rule in the region included a significant deficit in investment in the physical and social infrastructure needed to improve welfare and livelihoods (James, 2002a).

The new government in defining 'communal tenure' actively engaged in all facets of rural life by creating Ward Development Committees and Village Development Committees (WADCOs and VIDCOs) (see Nyambara, 1999). They made this explicit through an opposition to the former regime's policy of 'community development' and 'self-reliance' (Munro, 1998).

The populist agenda for 'growth with equity' aimed for rural development. The focus, besides maintaining growth in production and investment in infrastructure, included challenges on environmental degradation, tenure problems, property structures and land pressures. However, the District Councils were dependent on Ministries centrally directing changes from Harare. Moreover, the VIDCO structures remained both weak and unpopular (Nyambara, 1999).

So, while VIDCO structures became effectively branches of ZANU-PF further demonstrating the presence of the state, the traditional village (kraal) heads, headmen and chiefs were neglected. According to Nyambara (2014) 'villagisation' was introduced in communal areas similar to colonial policies of 'centralisation' in the 1920s and 1930s, in which 'going into lines' was part of an administrative attempt to modernise. Ranger (1985) explains the complex process of allocating land, portraying a complex conflict between chiefs and councillors. This lessened slightly when the Ministry of Local Government accorded extra status to the chiefs through the Chiefs and Headman Act, 1988. In the Northwest, most chiefs and traditional leaders such as Njelele in Gokwe South worked with both ZIPRA *and* ZANLA soldiers and also consulted the 'spirit medium' (*mhondoro*) Chindya (Nyambara, 1999). However, this was not always the case and some local leaders were killed as collaborators. Early after independence, the Zimbabwean state undermined the traditional rulers, arguing that they had no rights to control either land or the people. However, although the Chiefs and Headmen Act provided a compromise, it gave developmental powers to the Rural District Councils (RDCs) and significantly omitted mention of the village heads who ultimately know best the people residing in the village. This gave rise to the slogan: '*Hapana Ishe kana sadhunu asina masabhuku*' (Shona for 'there is no chief or headman without village heads').

In the meantime, the area of land devoted to cotton expanded from 23,900 hectares in 1979/80 to 71,600 hectares in the 1980/81 season (Nyambara, 1999), a significant increase with agricultural institutions fully integrated with Agritex, credit provision through Agricultural Finance Corporation and marketing processes developed with a more permanent presence of CMB (Cotton Marketing Board) depots. For example, GMB (Grain Marketing Board) depots in Gokwe increased from 3 to 18 in the first five years of independence (Nyambara, 1999). During the 1980s, both expansion of areas devoted to agriculture and the supporting institutions including infrastructural development helped promote the [second] 'agricultural revolution' in Zimbabwe (Rukuni and Eicher, 1994). In Gokwe, cotton accounted for around 30 percent of the District's cropped area and altogether produces in the range of 31–51 percent of the nation's cotton. Official estimates show that in the 1990s, hectares cultivated with cotton grew from 37,000 to over 70,000 (James, 2002a).

'A revolution is taking place in the rugged, rolling and difficult terrain that encompasses the cotton growing areas of Sebungwe, Munyati, Nemangwe, Goredema, Gandavaroyi, and Masuka – all in the Gokwe District, Midlands' (*Harare Herald*, 17 June 1986 cited in Worby, 1992: 555). The 'revolution' refers to the arrival of Agritex workers on red motorcycles, with the aim of improving farming methods and advising 'communal' farmers. The search for wealth continued as people moved into the region to grow cotton. The 'gochamupane' (started in the 1970s) continued through the 1980s and 1990s. It appears that advice provided by Agritex was to clear fields of all trees. The rationale was that this helped to enhance productivity of cotton (by removing shade) and avoiding harbouring of pests. In addition, the neglect of the grazing land resulted in a major constraint for livestock rearing in some villages. While livestock numbers fell during droughts in the 1980s and 1990s, restocking took place in the late 1990s. Cattle ownership is, however, extremely unequal, with over 40 percent of households owning no cattle (Nyambara, 1999).

Across the region, two main crops (cotton and maize), and the modern farming systems employed required the *total* clearing of the land, including heavy weeding and tree removal, leading to significant transformation of the landscape. Faced with smaller land holdings, increasing use of the plough (Scoones, 1997a), 'expansionist cultivation' (Ranger, 1985), cash cropping *and* 'villagisation' (also communal area reorganisation), it is little wonder that the communal areas have been so intensely cropped. This has led to the decline in soil fertility, poorer and smaller grazing areas, with fewer trees in fields, less woodland and a consequent decline in sources of wild foods (James, 2002a).

The origin and 'invention' of 'communal tenure' is colonial and its precept rests on assumptions about fair and equal access to land (Ranger, 1993). However, research shows that 'land grabbing', expansion of field areas and increasing acquisition of land holdings for political and economic advantage has taken place despite the ideological political motive (Nyambara, 1999). While invented during the colonial period, 'communal' tenure is important in Zimbabwe.

In theory, institutional systems exist for co-operation, co-ordination, redistribution and sharing, but in practice, as Worby (1992) argues, the rapid process of commoditisation, adding to a complex of social relations and contradictory cultural identities, saw the gradual lessening of *both* the traditional and the state socialist-style support systems. The rush to grow cotton continued through the 1980s but it was not always the most lucrative crop. Some enterprising farmers preferred to grow vegetable food crops such as tomatoes that their fellow cotton growers would buy in the markets.

Nyambara (1999) provides examples of farmers able to accumulate resources and diversify their incomes to such an extent that they no longer needed to grow cotton:

> Much of his property such as a good house, TV, radio, refrigerator, two cars including a truck, sola[r] panel and 30 head of cattle were acquired through the sale of tomatoes. (Nyambara, 1999: 423)

By the 1990s, cotton was considered a crop that was labour intensive and time-consuming but also expensive to grow.

During the 1980s and 1990s, rural economies in Zimbabwe faced increasing difficulties arising from the IMF Economic Structural Adjustment Programmes. One effect was to begin the process of administrative and political 'decentralisation' similar to other parts of the world. In the Northwest, the capacity building programme insisted on each district producing a strategic plan to enhance capacity for RDCs to enable them to execute the functions that they are legally obliged to in an efficient, effective, and accountable manner.

The institutions forming in the two decades after independence concentrated on accommodating incomers to the region, developing the cotton industry and to a limited extent establishing the infrastructure that been established already in other parts of the country.

The *De Facto* Opening Up of 'Communal Lands' and Wildlife Resources for Commercial Exploitation

Native Reserves assigned during the colonial period then became referred to as Tribal Trust Lands from 1961 until 1980, after which they became Communal Lands. The Northwest also included Resettlement areas, National and Safari parks and wildlife areas. CAMPFIRE (Communal Areas Management Program for Indigenous Resources) arguably saw the further process of 'privatisation', which was resisted in various conflicts (Hammar, 2001).

During the late 1990s, a violent eviction of a group of small-scale migrant farmers occurred in the Northwest (Hammar, 2001). The local council in Vumba referred to these settlers as 'squatters'. The enthusiasm for CAMPFIRE resulted in various conflicts over land (Dzingirayi, 1998). The local council took control over the locally managed 'wildlife' resources under such policies of community-based natural resource management (CBNRM).[7] The lure of funding from global sources triggered these local political conflicts over land use.

Arguably, since the late 1990s, there have been attempts to diversify and find alternative economic opportunities for the region other than cotton. Simultaneously, decentralisation and marketisation saw new opportunities from 'rewildernising'[8] these margins (Hammar, 2008). From the council's point of view, the forced removal of the migrants was fully justified. They asserted that these were 'illegal squatters, lawless, uncontrollable' (Hammar, 2008: 423). Curiously, as in-migrants, some of the Tonga people joined with the council in describing them as 'foreign' and not authentic. Alexander and McGregor (2000) show how the local attempts to contend with political leadership and the council put all the people in this area in greater danger of being evicted. These settlers growing successful cotton crops were therefore undermined as citizens and in terms of their customary rights.

But according to Hammar, 'what ultimately legitimised the council's violent eviction of the migrant families, which involved burning down houses and full granaries, committing alleged beatings, and forcibly removing people on trucks and dumping them, unprotected, some forty kilometres from their homes, was the consistent interpretation and portrayal of these particular inhabitants of Vumba as already *violent and dangerous*' (Hammar, 2008: 424, emphasis added).

In summary, during the late 1990s and early 2000s some Rural District Councils in the north of the region made steps counter to the rapid agrarian expansion based around cotton farming. The proximity to National Parks in some areas like Vumba as well as the shift in conservation thinking towards community-based natural resource management meant that in these areas people and their livelihoods were less self-determined and more directed by external authorities under CAMPFIRE (see Alexander and McGregor, 2000).

Conclusion: Identity Conflict and Place-Based and Regional Contestations: Re-branding Cultural Characteristics of the Northwest

> If African societies and cultures have exhibited great diversity and fluidity over time, as much scholarship suggests, it is appropriate to shift our analytical focus from structures to processes, from rules and outcomes to ongoing negotiation and debate. (Berry, 1997: 1229)

The dynamic influx of new settlers has meant an unsettling of many old ways. The newcomers brought with them modern sets of aspirations. The conditions, seen as 'primitive', which feature in the Sebungwe before the 1960s, such as lack of infrastructure, schools, clinics, electricity, tap-water and supermarkets, needed development (James, 2008).

However, what this chapter has shown is that there are various layers of cultural complexity with different objectives and many partial resistances to externally driven changes. For example, the relations between the Shangwe people and the Ndebele shifted and varied over many decades. Some colonial engagements during the twentieth century were supportive, e.g. with famines up to and including 1947. Other perspectives on the region and people living there were dismissive, reflecting the overall strategies in colonial governance, for example, the simultaneous attempt to withstand sanctions under UDI in 1965 and also grow cotton to quell any nationalist uprising among people moving into the Northwest. After independence the contests in values arise out of a push for economic growth and modernisation while nevertheless showing respect for some cultural values understandings. More recently in the 2010s, neoliberal market forces have once again exposed the region to an overall lack of infrastructural investment; there are also significant signs of a shift away from cotton and engagement on arguments about the potential economic values of wilderness and community-based natural resource management.

Overall, Northwest Zimbabwe has engaged in dynamic internal and external struggles in social reproduction (Katz, 2002), some material improvements and a search for 'sustainable livelihoods' (Scoones and Wolmer, 2003). Approaches to African rural politics also give greater attention to the complexities of place, culture and the idea of 'multiple modernities' (Mercer et al., 2003). African political geography has raised new questions on the extent of non-western or non-capitalist making of places, and also the two-way relationship between people's livelihoods making places what they are and the qualities and structural make-up of places influencing the way those livelihoods operate. Achieving livelihood and household food security has not been helped by recent political crises in Zimbabwe, as well as the increasingly neoliberal development policies. Many questions have been raised about the so-called advantages of 'mixed farming' and the idea of diversified livelihood approaches (Keeley and Scoones, 2003; James, 2008).

A combination of dynamic livelihood outcomes continue to unfold as different powers to invest into the new social relations or institutions create emergent characteristics of access to food and other livelihood needs. While the cotton industry, directed by the state institutions and international corporations saw one or two so-called 'agricultural revolutions', prosperity was realised by relatively few farmers. In recent years, the price paid by buyers for cotton has fallen significantly.

Notes

1 *Zimbabwe. Natural Regions and Provisional Farming Areas.* Boundaries as of July 1997 compiled and drawn by the Surveyor General, Harare, 1998, Scale 1:1,000,000,000, Third Edition.
2 Native Reserves assigned in the Northwest during the colonial period included Sebungwe, Kana and Gandavaroyi. They then became referred to as Tribal Trust Lands from 1961 until 1980, after which they were called Communal Lands. Since independence in 1980, the Northwest has become communal land, and thus the separate quality of Sebungwe is seldom recognised as distinct.
3 See further discussion of the Rhodesdale and Lonrho story in Worby (1994: 389) and Ranger (1985: 126)
4 This is also described vividly in Shimmer Chinodya's celebrated novel *Dew in the Morning* (1982: 49-56 and *passim*).
5 The Rozvi Empire (1684–1834) was established on the Zimbabwean Plateau by Changamire.
6 The lion spirits would reputedly chase people who flout the taboos of these sacred woodlands.
7 By the 2010s, CAMPFIRE had generated significant revenues for local communities with over 40,000 km squared of communal land being managed.
8 Taken from the earlier paper by Hammar (2001, p. 552), '[The Council] must sustain a certain *il*legibility, blurring particular boundaries and creating a space of violence that will allow it to empty (parts of) Vumba of people, to de-civilise it, to *re-wildernise* it.'

References

Alexander J and McGregor J (1997) Modernity and ethnicity in frontier society: understanding difference in Northwestern Zimbabwe. *Journal of Southern African Studies* 23(2): 187–201.

Alexander J and McGregor J (2000) Wildlife and politics: CAMPFIRE in Zimbabwe. *Development and Change* 31(3): 605–607.

Alexander J, McGregor J and Ranger T (2000) *Violence and Memory. One Hundred Years in the 'Dark Forests' of Matabeleland.* Oxford: James Currey.

Alexander J and Ranger T (1998) Competition and integration in the religious history of North-Western Zimbabwe. *Journal of Religion in Africa* 28(1): 3–31.

Arrighi G (1970) Labour supplies in historical perspective: A study of the proletarianization of the African peasantry in Rhodesia. *Journal of Development Studies*, 6(3):197–234.

Berry S (1997) Tomatoes, land and hearsay: property and history in Asante in the time of Structural Adjustment. *World Development* 25(8): 1225–1241.

Brand C (1999) People of Sengwa. The Gokwe North Community Baseline Study *Unpublished Report.* Rio Tinto-Zimbabwe: July 1999.

Child GFT and Riney T (1987) Tsetse control hunting in Zimbabwe, 1919-1958. *Zambezia* XIV(1): 11–71.

Chimhowu AO (2003) *Land Resettlement and Livelihoods in Rural Zimbabwe: A Study of State Sponsored and Spontaneously Resettled Households in Hurungwe District.*

Unpublished PhD thesis. Institute for Development Policy and Management: University of Manchester.

Chimhowu A and Hulme D (2006) Livelihood dynamics in planned and spontaneous resettlement in Zimbabwe: converging and vulnerable. *World Development* 34(4): 728–750.

Chinodya S (1982) *Dew in the Morning*. Gwelo: Mambo Press.

Chorley JK (1945) The Sebungwe District. *Proceedings of the Rhodesia Scientific Asscociation* 40: 5–16.

Cliggett L and Bond V (eds) (2013) *Tonga Timeline. Appraising Sixty Years of Multidisciplinary Research in Zambia and Zimbabwe*. Lusaka: Lembani Trust.

Collett CW (1963–1965) Delineation of communities. Part two of the report on Gokwe Tribal Trust Lands: Gokwe District. NAZ s2929/7/3.

du Toit R (1985) A middle way for wildlife parks. *New Scientist*, 31 January 1985: 33–36.

Dzingirayi V (1998) Migration, Local Politics and CAMPFIRE. *Centre for Applied Social Sciences Working Paper NRM Series CPN 99/98*. Harare: 1998.

Gilbert A (1988) The new regional geography in English and French speaking countries. *Progress in Human Geography* 12(2): 208–228.

Hammar A (2001) The day of burning: eviction and reinvention in the margins of northwest Zimbabwe. *Journal of Agrarian Change* 1(4): 550–574.

Hammar A (2008) In the name of sovereignty: displacement and state making in post-independence Zimbabwe. *Journal of Contemporary African Studies* 26(4): 417–434.

Iliffe J (1990) *Famine in Zimbabwe 1890-1960*. Harare: Mambo Press.

James N (2002a) *A Geographical Study of Nembudziya, Gokwe North, Zimbabwe. The Relationship between Agrarian Environmental Change and Household Food Security in a Cotton Growing Area*. Unpublished thesis. Lancaster University

James N (2002b) Malnutrition data, food security and the geography of food in a communal area of North West Zimbabwe. *Global and Built Environment Review* 2(3): 42–53.

James N (2006) Factors affecting the sustainability of cotton production: changing rural livelihoods in the north-west region in Zimbabwe, in J Hill, A Terry and W Woodland (eds) *Sustainable Development: National Aspirations, Local Implementation*. Farnham: Ashgate Publishing Limited, 175–204.

James N (2008) Household food security and regional geography. Livelihood prospects in Nembudziya, North West Zimbabwe. *Geography Compass* 2(5): 1337–1362.

Jayne T, Chisvo M and Rukuni M (1994) Zimbabwe's food insecurity paradox: hunger amid abundance, in M Rukuni and C Eicher (eds) *Zimbabwe's Agricultural Revolution*. Harare: University of Zimbabwe Publications, 289–303.

Katz C (2002) Vagabond capitalism and the necessity of social reproduction. *Antipode* 33(4): 709–728.

Keeley J and Scoones I (2003) *Understanding Environmental Policy Processes: Cases from Africa*. London: Earthscan Publishers.

Kosmin B (1977) The Inyoka tobacco industry of the Shangwe People: the displacement of a pre-colonial economy in southern Rhodesia, 1898–1938, in R Palmer and N Parsons (eds) *The Roots of Rural Poverty in Central and Southern Africa*. London: HEB, pp. 268–288.

McGreal C (2002) Zimbabwe struck by new reign of terror. *The Guardian* [Online] http://www.theguardian.com/world/2002/mar/28/zimbabwe.chrismcgreal (Accessed 29 June 2015).

McGregor J (2009) *Crossing the Zambezi. The Politics of Landscape on a Central African Frontier*. Oxford: James Currey.

Mariga IK (1994) Cotton research and development, in M Rukuni and C Eicher (eds) *Zimbabwe's Agricultural Revolution*. Harare: University of Zimbabwe Publications, 219–233.

Mercer C, Mohan G and Power M (2003) Towards a critical political geography of African development. *Geoforum* 34: 419–436.

Mitchell JC (1961) Wage labour and African population movements in Central Africa, in KM Barbour and RM Prothero (eds) *Essays on African Population*. London: Routledge and Kegan Paul, 193–248.

Moore, H (2015) Can agroecology save us from 'scorched earth' agriculture? *The Ecologist* [Online] http://www.theecologist.org/News/news_analysis/2856550/can_agroecology_save_us_from_scorchedearth_agriculture.html (accessed 24 May 2015).

Mugugunyeki M (2014) Development eludes Gokwe North. *The Standard* [Online] http://www.thestandard.co.zw/2014/03/30/development-eludes-gokwe-north/ (Accessed 30 June 2015).

Munro WA (1998) *The Moral Economy of the State. Conservation, Community Development and State Making in Zimbabwe*. Center for International Studies: Ohio University.

Ncube GT (1994) *A History of North West Zimbabwe, 1850-1950s: A Comparative Change in Three Worlds*. Unpublished M.Phil. University of Zimbabwe.

Nyambara PS (1999) *A History of Land Acquisition in Gokwe, Northwestern Zimbabwe, 1945-1997*. Unpublished Ph.D. thesis. Northwestern University, Evanston, Illinois.

Nyambara Pius S (2014) State power, land-use planning, and local responses in northwestern Zimbabwe, 1980s-1990s. *African Studies Quarterly* 14(4): September 2014.

Palmer R (1977) *Land and Racial Domination in Rhodesia*. London: Heinemann.

Peet R, Robbins P and Watts M (eds) (2011) *Global Political Ecology*. London: Routledge.

Polepole H (2015) Sustainable development: challenges and opportunities of an unfinished journey. *Pambazuka News* Issue 728 [online] http://www.pambazuka.net/en/category.php/features/94821 (accessed 31 May 2015).

Ranger T (1985) *Peasant Consciousness and Guerrilla War in Zimbabwe*. Oxford: James Currey.

Ranger T (1993) The communal areas of Zimbabwe, in TJ Bassett and DE Crumney (eds) *Land in African Agrarian Systems*. Wisconsin: University of Wisconsin Press.

Ranger T (1998) Zimbabwe and the long search for independence, in D Birmingham and PM Martin (eds) *History of Central Africa. The Contemporary Years since 1960*. Harlow: Addison Wesley Longman Limited, 202–229.

Reid M (1971) An agricultural programme at Gokwe. *Rhodesia Agricultural Journal* 68(3): 2–8.

Rukuni M (1994) The evolution of agricultural policy: 1890-1990, in M Rukuni and C Eicher (eds) *Zimbabwe's Agricultural Revolution*. Harare: University of Zimbabwe Publications, 15–39.

Rukuni M and Eicher CK (eds) (1994) *Zimbabwe's Agricultural Revolution*. Harare: University of Zimbabwe Publications.

Scoones I (1997a) Landscapes, fields and soils: understanding the history of soil fertility management in southern Zimbabwe. *Journal of Southern African Studies* 23: 617–636.

Scoones I (1997b) The dynamics of soil fertility change: historical perspectives on environmental transformation from Zimbabwe. *Geographical Journal* 163: 161–199.

Scoones I and Wolmer W (eds) (2003) Livelihoods in crisis? New perspectives on governance and rural development in Southern Africa. *IDS Bulletin* 34(3).

Taylor RD (1982) Buffer zones: resolving conflicts between humans and wildlife interests in the Sebungwe, Zimbabwe. *Zimbabwe Agricultural Journal* 79: 179–184.

Thrift N (1990) For a new regional geography 1. *Progress in Human Geography* 14(2): 272–279.

Watts M (1989) The agrarian question in Africa: debating the crisis. *Progress in Human Geography* 13(1): 1–41.

Wekwete KH (1989) Planning laws for urban and regional planning in Zimbabwe - a review. *RUP Occasional Paper* 20: Department of Rural & Urban Planning.

Whitlow JR (1988) *Land Degradation in Zimbabwe: A Geographical Study*. Harare: Department of National Resources, Harare, Zimbabwe.

Worby E (1992) *Remaking Labour, Reshaping Identity: Cotton, Commoditization and the Culture of Modernity in Northwestern Zimbabwe*. McGill University, Canada: Unpublished Ph.D. Thesis.

Worby E (1994) Maps, names and ethnic games: the epistemology and iconography of colonial power in northwestern Zimbabwe. *Journal of Southern African Studies* 20(3): 371–392.

Worby E (1998) Tyranny, parody, and ethnic polarity: ritual engagements with the state in northwestern Zimbabwe. *Journal of Southern African Studies* 24(3): 561–578.

Zinyama L and Whitlow R (1986) Changing patterns of population distribution in Zimbabwe. *GeoJournal* 13(4): 365–384.

9 Intertwined Spatialities

Discursive Construction(s) of Central Germany

Roger Baars and Antje Schlottmann

Introduction

This chapter illustrates the interplay of multiple coexistent and becoming spatialities that constitute polysemic regional spaces. Consequently, we consider such regional spaces as constructed of interrelated material and symbolic processes and structures, as multi-dimensional spatialities in-becoming (Baars and Schlottmann, 2015). As an example, we refer to the everyday use of various spatial concepts in political discourse in the context of both the 'Cultural Region' and the 'Economic Region' of Central Germany. The chapter follows up on research into processes of everyday linguistic regionalisation (see Schlottmann, 2005, 2006, 2007a, 2007b, 2008, 2012, 2013) and on earlier work on the construction of the Central German region in public media and everyday-language use (Felgenhauer, 2007, 2010; Felgenhauer and Schlottmann, 2007; Felegenhauer et al., 2005; Schlottmann et al., 2007). One major finding of this work was that the Central German Broadcast Company MDR succeeded in promoting its version of the Central German entity by constructing a narrative around the history of this particular region. In everyday communication, however, multiple variants and meanings of the region were proven (still) abundant (ibid.). An initial assumption of this research was that irrespective of particular meanings, the linguistic and social constitution of spatial constructs is based on specific spatial concepts and perceptions. This assumption could be evidenced empirically in the narrative construction of the broadcasting council, media content and in common perception. However, the focus of the argument in previous research was founded on the everyday use of the container concept and its essentialisation in everyday language use, while virtually ignoring contemporaneous geographical concepts. The overall objective of ongoing work presented in this chapter, therefore, is rather to reconstruct the spatial multi-dimensionality of regions (and their borders) in-becoming. However, our framework is based on the assumption that particular sub-fields of the cultural and economic politics of regions are dominated by particular spatialities – an approach that aims at capturing the political dimension of the everyday use of spatial concepts (Hannah, 2006; Schlottmann, 2006).

The entity of the Central German Metropolitan Region comprises the three German federal states of Saxony, Saxony-Anhalt, and Thuringia and was established in 2008 as a political alliance between the nine core cities Chemnitz, Dessau-Rosslau, Dresden, Gera, Halle, Jena, Leipzig, Magdeburg, and Zwickau (Central German Metropolitan Region, 2014). Regional cooperation in economic development, business and science, culture and tourism, transport and mobility, and family friendliness weave the fabric of the area. The nine core cities are essential elements of the metropolitan region concept to form the city-network (Figure 9.1). Nevertheless, as will be demonstrated in this chapter, besides the concepts of network, place, and scale, the territorial containers of the three federal states also play an important role in the conception and articulation of the Central German Metropolitan Region. Elucidating the multiple spatialities of the region in specific contexts (and their overlap), we suggest, opens up the possibility of revealing conflicts and frictions between related discourses and practices in the field of regional politics. Such a perspective is crucial to understand the, often contradictory, political processes and motives that are simultaneously translated into, and shaped by, discourses of everyday region-making.

The concept of discourse varies in different strands of scholarly inquiry. In our approach we refer to a pragmatic concept of discourse which is related to the 'Sociology of Knowledge' (Keller, 2005), compatible with actor-oriented micro-analysis used in earlier work on the constitution of Central Germany (Felgenhauer and Schlottmann, 2007; Schlottmann, 2008). Following Hall (1997: 4) we understand discourses as 'ways of referring to or constructing knowledge about a particular topic of practice: a cluster (or formation) of ideas, images and practices, which provide ways of talking about forms of knowledge and conduct associated with a particular topic, social activity or institutional site in society'. These types of pragmatic discourses involve signification rules and normative orientations around ways of saying things as well as resources for action, be they social (actors or actors' positions) and/or material (Keller 2005: 14).

Accordingly, this chapter considers the discourses of Central Germany as a Cultural and Economic Region communicated by the institutional body of the Central German Metropolitan Region and the Industrial Initiative Central Germany, respectively. Publicly available documents (e.g. brochures, maps, press releases) issued by these registered associations were the main source of data. In addition, semi-structured expert interviews with political stakeholders of the Central German Metropolitan Region responsible for culture and tourism and economic development, as well as the official websites (www.mitteldeutschland.com / www.region-mitteldeutschland.com)[1] were used as points of reference. In the subsequent section we first give a brief overview of recent theoretical debates in human geography that are concerned with the material-relational nexus of regional spaces. Subsequently, we utilise the case study of the Central German

Metropolitan Region to demonstrate how regions are constructed in different cultural and economic contexts through the interplay of multiple spatial dimensions (territory, place, scale, and network). This is followed by a critical discussion of spatial multi-dimensionalities before, in the last section, we draw some conclusions to inform current debates on the conceptualisation of regions as polysemic spaces.

Figure 9.1 Germany.

Multi-Dimensionality of Regions

In (political) geography current debates on theoretical conceptualisations of multi-dimensional polysemic spaces illustrate the recent move beyond the long lasting opposition of relational and territorial approaches to regional space and a growing interest in re-animating a new regional geography (cf. Elden, 2005, 2009, 2010; Jonas, 2012a, 2012b, 2013; Jones, 2009; Murphy, 2013; Painter 2010). In their inspiring paper on socio-spatial theory Jessop, Brenner and Jones (2008) identified four distinct spatial lexicons that have been developed by social scientists over the last thirty years to conceptualise space: territory, place, scale, and network (TPSN) (see also Dicken et al., 2001; Leitner et al., 2008; Paasi, 2004, 2012; Sheppard, 2002). Within this TPSN framework, the spatial lexicons are each associated with certain forms of the so-called 'spatial turn', and should be theoretically and empirically considered to be closely intertwined (Leitner et al., 2008), though they problematise partially different topics. Advocates of a given turn, however, are often tempted to focus on one dimension of spatial relations only, so neglecting the role of other forms of socio-spatial organisation (Leitner et al., 2008). Such one-dimensionalism falls into the trap of conflating one part (territory, place, scale, or networks) with the whole (the totality of socio-spatial organisation). In contrast, Jessop et al. (2008) argue that all four (or more) dimensions need to be put into play, albeit not necessarily all at once. Although Jessop et al. (2008) do not discuss the spatial concept of regions explicitly, their proposed TPSN framework informs the conceptual framework of this chapter, considering the idea of regions as the interplay of multiple conceptual spatial dimensions (cf. Jones, 2009).

Terlouw and Weststrate (2013) argue for an overdue shift of attention from the historical evolution of regions to the circumstances in the present in which regions are actually constructed. The starting point, then, is not the social construction of one specific region, but how multiple dimensions of regions are constituted by political stakeholders in different contexts. We call these multi-dimensional spatial effects (Painter, 2010) 'phantom regions' that take different forms of appearance in varied contexts. In other words, when conceptualised as phantoms, regions are ontologically indistinct spatial entities, without clear boundaries. They are spatialities that are constantly (re)emerging in different forms and with different emphasis and meaning. These regions can, however, appear as distinct and bordered entities due to essentialising discursive practices of 'Geography-Making' (Schlottmann, 2008) in particular spatio-temporalities. Regions and socio-spatial relations, thus, can be conceived of as temporarily stabilised spatial phantoms of political action (Metzger, 2013). We observe, however, that Terlouw and Weststrate's (2013) analytic approach is limited to a one-dimensional focus on scale and ignores other important conceptual dimensions of region-making practices. We perceive this as highly problematic as it means that these spatial dimensions are overshadowed by scale as *primus inter pares* – first among equals. This contrasts with the claimed importance of the interplay of different spatial dimensions when conceptualising regions (Jessop et al., 2008) and echoes Jones' (2009) concept of 'phase space' as theoretical middle ground that 'insists on the compatibilities between, rather the mutual exclusivities of, flow-like (networks, etc.) and more fixed (scales, territories, regions, etc.) takes on space' (Jones, 2009: 489). (Regional) space, then, is both territorially anchored and fluid, and perhaps more importantly, framed by the balance between different forces – constantly changing interactions between economic, political and social activities and relationships (Smith, 1995) – which 'can be activated in strategies, practices, and discourses, some of which are bounded and others unbounded' (Jones, 2009: 499).

Though drawing on an empirical case, the social construction of a particular region and its implicit boundaries is not our core interest, but rather the linguistic and discursive actions and instruments through which different regional 'space layers' (Jones, 2009) are made possible in multiple contexts. In the subsequent section, we therefore elucidate in more detail the making of Central Germany as both a 'Cultural' and 'Economic' Region, in order to substantiate how multiple, sometimes contradicting, spatial layers of the region are discursively constituted.

The 'Cultural Region' of Central Germany

In the discourse of Central Germany, shaped by the institutional body of the Central German Metropolitan Region, the region is addressed as a space of long cultural traditions. The Central German Metropolitan Region is a polycentric city-network stretched across three federal states of Eastern Germany. It is institutionalised as a political association (cf. Paasi, 2013) combining the four governmental hierarchies of city, state, nation, and EU to bring together a wide range of energies, identities, potentials and interests in the region. The overriding objective of its activities is the long-term strengthening of the overall region as a location for business and science, as well as a cultural landscape. The principles of voluntary commitment, decision-making on a consensual basis and a variable geometry apply at all levels of the Central German Metropolitan Region. Although the mental map (Downs and Stea, 1977) of Central Germany is most commonly associated with the three federal states of Thuringia, Saxony, and Saxony-Anhalt (Felgenhauer, 2010) the various discursive strands of the region draw on multiple spatial dimensions (e.g. territory, network, place) and create numerous different and temporary spatial layers of the region (Jones, 2009) in the context of Central Germany as a cultural region.

Cultural Discourse of the Central German Region

Within the broad semantic field of Central German cultural heritage, reaching from Martin Luther to the work of Goethe, Schiller, Bach, Kafka, Gropius and Kandinsky to name but a few, arguably seven strands of the Cultural Discourse of Central Germany can be identified (Central German Metropolitan Region, 2014). The Cultural Heritage discourse strand draws on the Garden Kingdom

Dessau-Wörlitz with its historic parks and buildings, the history of modern architecture and the Bauhaus movement in the region, Central Germany's unique medieval towns and its important milestones in German history. The second discourse strand is that of Musical Traditions in the region. Central Germany's famous composers, its orchestras and festivals, and the importance of music from classic to modern times are essential aspects of this discourse of Central Germany. Cultural Routes is a discourse strand stressing the region's pilgrims' ways, its Romanesque Road, and the Martin Luther Way, all of them being cultural routes through Central Germany. Fine arts, in particular, are the focus of the discourse strand of Cultural Locations in Central Germany, involving the creative sites of painting, design, theatre, and literature. Central Germany's eventful past, its medieval treasures, baroque jewels, and contemporary art, which are displayed in various collections and museums in Central Germany, are the focus of a discourse strand that shapes a region of Cultural Treasures. Central Germany's castles, churches, and historic buildings are part of the Cultural Edifices discourse strand and represent another facet of the discursive making of the region. The last discourse strand identified in this study captures Cultural Landscapes drawing on the region's historic gardens, forests, and parks. Due to space limitations in this article, we subsequently limit our analysis of Central Germany's multi-dimensional facets and emergences in a cultural context on the three discourse strands of Cultural Heritage, Cultural Routes, and Musical Traditions.

Cultural Heritage

This discourse strand draws on the region's rich cultural heritage and its historic sites. The Dessau-Wörlitz Garden Kingdom (Figure 9.2) comprises of six castles, seven historic parks and more than 100 smaller architectural edifices that form the heart of this UNESCO Heritage Site. The Wörlitz Gardens, the first landscape garden in continental Europe, are identified as the historic starting point of the UNESCO Heritage Site Dessau-Wörlitz Garden Kingdom (Figure 9.2). Not far from this lies the Bauhaus Building, which was constructed in 1925/26 based on the designs of Walter Gropius. It is known as the creative hub of the world famous 'Hochschule für Gestaltung' (Academy of Design), whose works and ideas influence concepts of modern architecture and design to the present day.

The origins of the Protestant Church are also located in Central Germany, where the birthplace of the Reformation can be viewed at the Luther memorial sites in Eisleben and Wittenberg (Figure 9.2). The Wartburg near Eisenach in Thuringia is known as another significant place of German history and as an outstanding monument of the feudal period in Central Europe. In the year 1521 Martin Luther found refuge in the Wartburg, where he translated the New Testament into German. The historic old town of Quedlinburg is claimed to be an outstanding example of a European medieval town and is under protection of the UNESCO World Heritage programme. In the east of Saxony the joint Polish and German

World Heritage Site Muskau Park (Figure 9.2) represents an important site of cultural cross-border work in Europe.

As a synopsis it can be said that the Cultural Heritage discourse strand involves (and hence produces) six historically significant sites in Central Germany: Bad Muskau (Muskau Park), Dessau (Garden Kingdom), Eisenach (Wartburg), Quedlinburg (Medieval Town), Weimar (Bauhaus), and Wittenberg (Martin Luther Memorial Site). All nine Core Cities of the Central German Metropolitan Region, however, are silenced (with the exception of Dessau) in the cultural discourse. Consequently, in the context of Cultural Heritage the region of Central Germany takes a shape that is different to the one seen above (Figure 9.1). Discursively, a strong focus on the two federal states of Saxony-Anhalt and Thuringia is placed and the region seems somewhat bounded by their territorial borders. Interesting, however, is the heritage site of Bad Muskau, which is the only site administratively located within the federal state of Saxony. It also crosses the national border between Germany and Poland and, in parts, appears as a network of artists and other persons engaged in the cultural sector now and then. Thus, in the Cultural Heritage discourse strand, the region of Central Germany territorially spoken stretches beyond the containers of Saxony, Saxony-Anhalt, and Thuringia.

Figure 9.2 Heritage.

Cultural Routes

The Cultural Routes discourse strand illustrates a network of several walks, from cultural, over historic to religious trails, as constituting the region of Central Germany. The Route of Kings, Merchants and Pilgrims is one example of historic roads linking together people and places and encouraging trade and cultural encounter. The Via Regia, the Ecumenical Pilgrims' Way, and the Way of St. James of Saxony are also part of the regional discourse of Central Germany. The Romanesque Road, which connects over 80 cathedrals, fortresses, cloisters, and churches of Medieval Germany and the Trail of Classic Writers, a track of major literary personalities of Central Germany (e.g. the Goethe Route or the Schiller Trail), are other examples of spatial networks communicated in the discourse. Perhaps the most prominent aspect, however, is the Martin Luther Ways, a network of numerous trails connecting historic sites of the Reformation in Central Germany, thereby following the footsteps of Martin Luther (Figure 9.3).

It is of note that so far all Luther Ways are confined by the territorial borders of Germany's federal states, although for the 500th Luther Anniversary in 2017 one united Central German Luther Way is planned that shall connect all local networks and cross the borders between the three federal states. Hence, it is not surprising that until today only two border-crossing trails are implemented in Central Germany: the

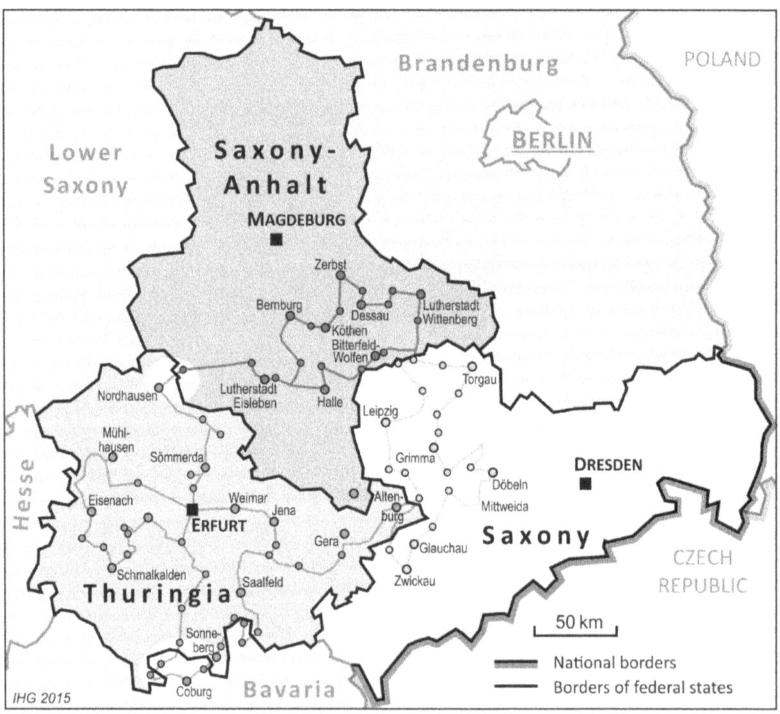

Figure 9.3 Routes.

World Heritage Site Muskau Park (Figure 9.2) represents an important site of cultural cross-border work in Europe.

As a synopsis it can be said that the Cultural Heritage discourse strand involves (and hence produces) six historically significant sites in Central Germany: Bad Muskau (Muskau Park), Dessau (Garden Kingdom), Eisenach (Wartburg), Quedlinburg (Medieval Town), Weimar (Bauhaus), and Wittenberg (Martin Luther Memorial Site). All nine Core Cities of the Central German Metropolitan Region, however, are silenced (with the exception of Dessau) in the cultural discourse. Consequently, in the context of Cultural Heritage the region of Central Germany takes a shape that is different to the one seen above (Figure 9.1). Discursively, a strong focus on the two federal states of Saxony-Anhalt and Thuringia is placed and the region seems somewhat bounded by their territorial borders. Interesting, however, is the heritage site of Bad Muskau, which is the only site administratively located within the federal state of Saxony. It also crosses the national border between Germany and Poland and, in parts, appears as a network of artists and other persons engaged in the cultural sector now and then. Thus, in the Cultural Heritage discourse strand, the region of Central Germany territorially spoken stretches beyond the containers of Saxony, Saxony-Anhalt, and Thuringia.

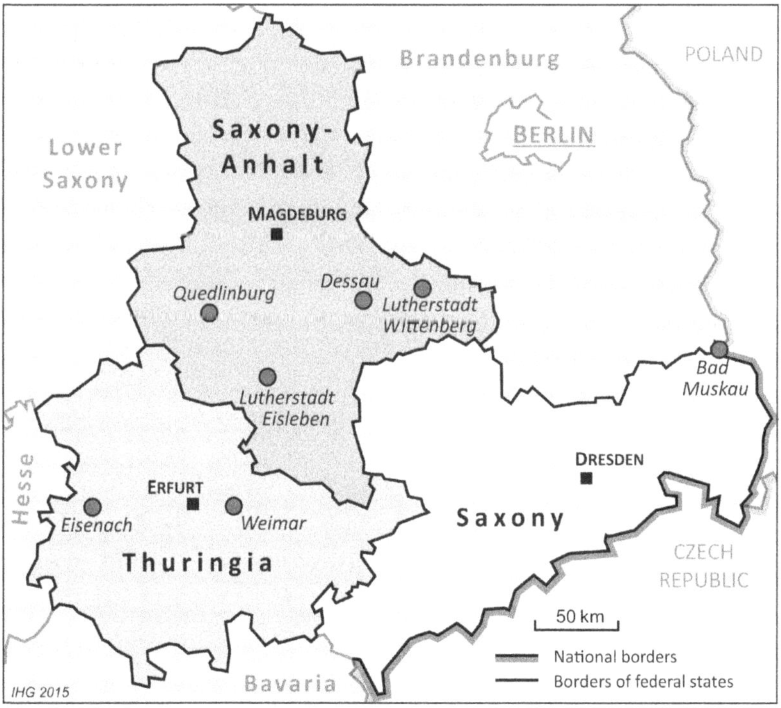

Figure 9.2 Heritage.

Cultural Routes

The Cultural Routes discourse strand illustrates a network of several walks, from cultural, over historic to religious trails, as constituting the region of Central Germany. The Route of Kings, Merchants and Pilgrims is one example of historic roads linking together people and places and encouraging trade and cultural encounter. The Via Regia, the Ecumenical Pilgrims' Way, and the Way of St. James of Saxony are also part of the regional discourse of Central Germany. The Romanesque Road, which connects over 80 cathedrals, fortresses, cloisters, and churches of Medieval Germany and the Trail of Classic Writers, a track of major literary personalities of Central Germany (e.g. the Goethe Route or the Schiller Trail), are other examples of spatial networks communicated in the discourse. Perhaps the most prominent aspect, however, is the Martin Luther Ways, a network of numerous trails connecting historic sites of the Reformation in Central Germany, thereby following the footsteps of Martin Luther (Figure 9.3).

It is of note that so far all Luther Ways are confined by the territorial borders of Germany's federal states, although for the 500th Luther Anniversary in 2017 one united Central German Luther Way is planned that shall connect all local networks and cross the borders between the three federal states. Hence, it is not surprising that until today only two border-crossing trails are implemented in Central Germany: the

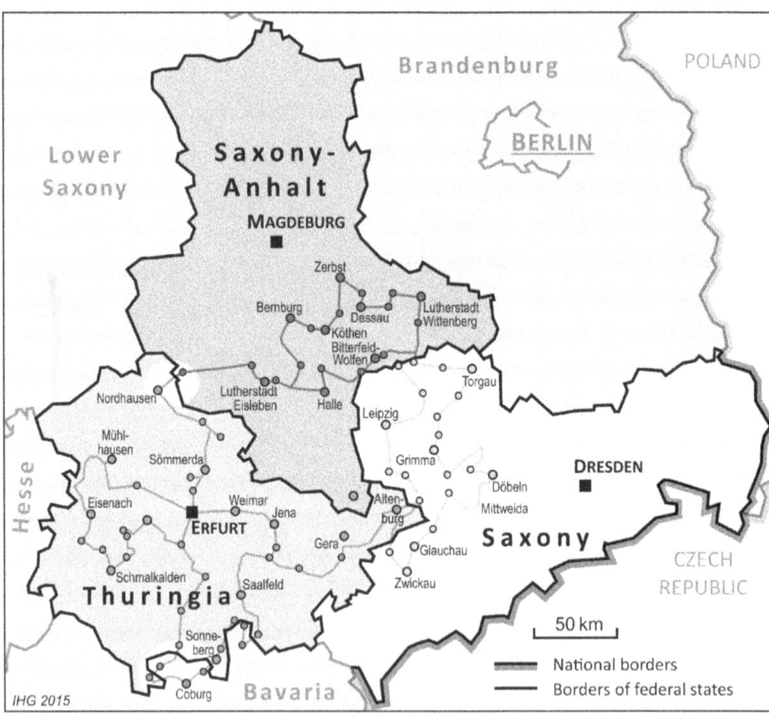

Figure 9.3 Routes.

Luther Way between Nordhausen in Thuringia and Stolberg in Saxony-Anhalt and the Luther Way connecting Eisfled in Thuringia and the city of Coburg in Bavaria, with the latter not only crossing the boundaries of Thuringia, but even exceeding the discursively constructed container of Central Germany (Figure 9.3).

Musical Traditions

The discourse strand Musical Traditions in Central Germany focuses on prominent composers and musical accomplishments of the region. The musical history of the region is closely linked to the two composers Bach and Wagner, who are the main protagonists communicated in the Musical Traditions discourse strand. The name of Johann Sebastian Bach is inseparably linked with the city of Leipzig, where he spent most of his life (Figure 9.4). At the Bach Museum Leipzig original Bach manuscripts and devotional objects from his life are shown. Leipzig's Bach Archive and the Bach House in Eisenach, his birthplace, are other historical sites devoted to the composer's musical legacy. Richard Wagner, the precursor of modern music drama, was born in Leipzig in 1813 where, at a later stage, he was musical director at the Saxon court in Dresden until 1843 and composed some of his masterpieces while visiting his friend Franz Liszt in Weimar (Figure 9.4).

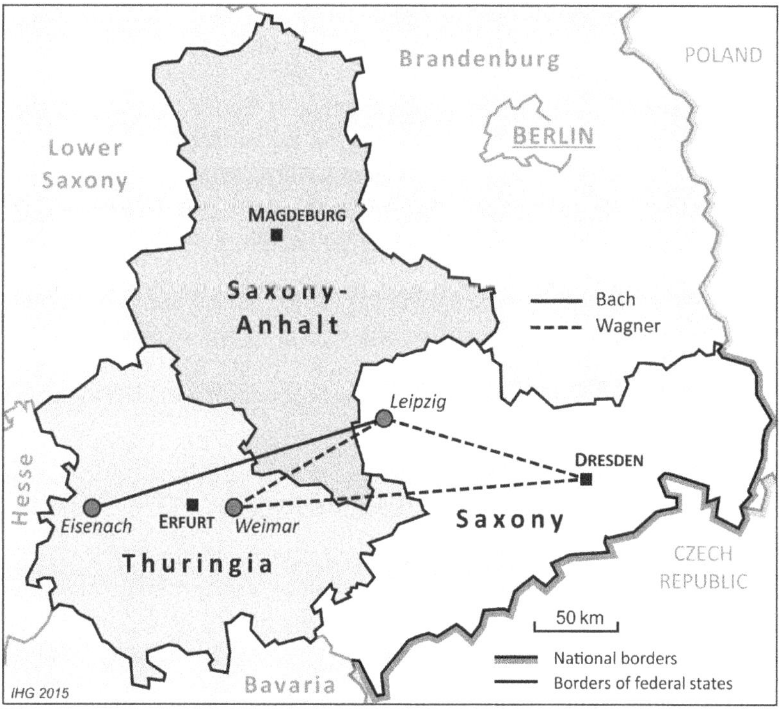

Figure 9.4 Music.

In 1846 in the village of Graupa (near Dresden) Wagner composed large sections of his opera 'Lohengrin'. Here the world's oldest Wagner museum at the Richard Wagner Stätten Graupa was established.

The region of Central Germany communicated in the Musical Traditions discourse strand comprises several historical sites in the states of Saxony and Thuringia. The federal state of Saxony-Anhalt, however, is not integrated into this layer of the spatial dimension of Central Germany. Although the discourse strand illustrates the border-crossing between two federal container spaces, the Musical Traditions discourse strand seems to be somewhat confined by the two territorial containers of Saxony and Thuringia (Figure 9.4) and confirms the territorial characteristic as one important aspect of this spatial layer of Central Germany as observed before (see above).

The 'Economic Region' of Central Germany

Contrary to the cultural discourse of Central Germany which draws frequently on the spatial concept of networks and places, the economic discourse predominantly utilises a cluster metaphor constituting the Central German Economic Region. In the discourse of Central Germany, shaped by the institutional body of the Industrial Initiative Central Germany, the region is addressed as one of the most attractive and innovative economic regions in Europe, combining dynamic growth with a high quality of life. The Industrial Initiative for Central Germany (IICG) brings together key corporations, business chambers and local authorities from Saxony, Saxony-Anhalt and Thuringia with the common aim of promoting the successful development and marketing of the economic region of Central Germany. The IICG's common goal is the sustainable development and marketing of the cross-border business location Central Germany. The initiative aims to strengthen regional competitiveness by developing sustainable cluster organisations in areas such as the chemical industry, optics, automotive production and renewable energies. The Economic Region of Central Germany appears as a polycentric cluster-network comprising the three federal states of Saxony, Saxony-Anhalt and Thuringia. It is characterised by an above-average concentration of interrelated companies and research centres in a number of economic sectors. These 'clusters' are perceived to create regional competitive advantages and to sharpen the region's economic profile.

Economic Discourse of the Central German Region

This section draws on three strands of the Central German Economic Discourse to illustrate the multi-dimensionality of the region in an economic context (Industrial Initiative for Central Germany, 2014). These are the Solar Energy Cluster, the Chemical Industry and Plastics Cluster, and the Transport and Logistic Network. The cluster concept appears to be a dominant spatial reference in the Economic Discourse of Central Germany, referring to flexible networks of complementary businesses along with research, development and training institutes as well as other centres of excellence working together to boost innovation and regional competitiveness and economic growth in Central Germany.

Solar Energy

The Solar Energy discourse strand focuses on the density of photovoltaic industrial enterprises in Thuringia, Saxony and Saxony-Anhalt as being unique throughout the world. The solar industry in Central Germany is organised in the *Solarvalley Mitteldeutschland* cluster. The main goal of this cluster is to increase the industry's competitiveness. Its strategic concept stresses the necessity of businesses, science and education to be closely intertwined and work towards a common goal. The Central German Solar Cluster exhibits a high density of photovoltaic manufacturers. Nearly half of the total revenue in the German photovoltaics industry originates from the Solar Cluster. The close co-operation between photovoltaic manufacturers and their suppliers as well as the dense network of universities and research institutes in this field is seen as a unique quality of the Central German region.

The Solar Cluster has three interconnected foci. The goal of research and technology development is to lower the cost of solar energy by innovation along the whole value chain. In competition with other regions and producers, the cluster is concentrating on a sustainable alliance of production and research. Many production, research and development processes in the photovoltaic industry require highly qualified specialists and leadership personnel. Consequently, an integrated education concept that links education with universities (e.g. Solarvalley Graduate School of Photovoltaics) is crucial for the industry's success. The Solar Cluster office is the central contact point for the solar community in Central Germany. It coordinates photovoltaic activities in the region and supports the expansion of the solar industry network on a national and international level (European Solar Network). With three regional offices in Erfurt, Halle, and Dresden, the Solar Cluster is present in the participating Central German states of Saxony, Saxony-Anhalt and Thuringia. All three associated federal states are active players in Germany's solar industry. Despite the Central German Region being organised around nine core cities (see above), the solar cluster is a matter of federal politics and interests.

The Solar Cluster is institutionalised through the SolarValley body, which consists of multiple sub-regional registered associations. The main locations of the photovoltaic industry in Central Germany centre around three geographical areas of the region (Figure 9.5). First, the Silicon Saxony Association, a cluster of Saxony's photovoltaic economy located in and around the cities of Dresden and Chemnitz. Second, the Thuringian association Solar Input, a solar industry cluster located between Erfurt and Jena. Third, the Association of Renewable Energy Saxony-Anhalt, a solar cluster encompassing production, research and education sites between Halle and Bitterfeld. These three sub-clusters constitute the cluster-network Solar Energy in Central Germany. Interestingly, however, the Central German Solar Cluster also includes the Solar Cluster Baden-Wuerttemberg and

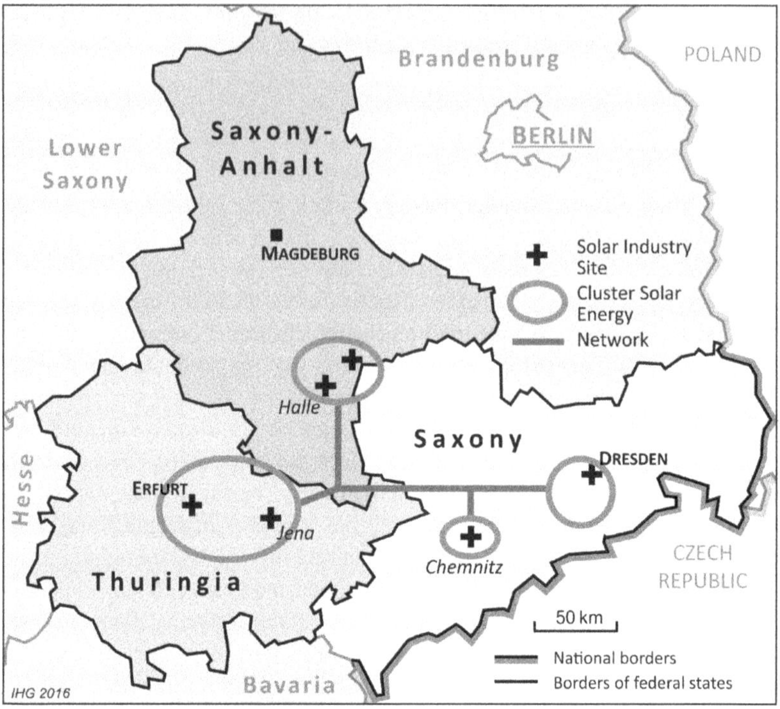

Figure 9.5 Solar energy.

the Berlin Brandenburg Energy Network as part of Central Germany. In this context, Central Germany extends the official boundaries of the three federal states Saxony, Saxony-Anhalt and Thuringia and reaches out to the neighbouring states Baden-Wurttemberg and Brandenburg. Moreover, the networked cluster structure of the solar industry in Central Germany not only crosses administrative boundaries but may also cause frictions with the static federal/territorial container structures of the region inasmuch, for instance, metric administrative and juristic areas of application do not match with the boundaries of the cluster concept.

Central Germany's Chemical Region

The discourse strand Chemical Industry and Plastics communicates the Central German Chemical Region as a trans-regional cluster-network. The cluster is aimed at improving the innovation capacity of small- and medium-sized companies as well as established valued-added production chains within the region. Another declared aim of the cluster lies in strengthening Central Germany as an internationally competitive region of the chemical and plastics industry to attract further businesses and institutions. More than 800 chemical and plastics businesses are organised in the Chemical Industry and Plastics Cluster Central Germany. All three federal state governments actively communicate the chemical industry as the Central German Chemistry Cluster. Central Germany's chemical industry is mainly located at the geographical centre of Central Germany between Halle and Leipzig (Figure 9.6) with the two federal states of Saxony and Thuringia being the main players in Germany's chemical industry. Strikingly, the discourse strand completely disregards Thuringia's chemical industry (e.g. production sites around Jena), although the state is part of the chemical cluster of Central Germany. Interesting here is also the fact that the federal states of Brandenburg and Baden Wurttemberg are discursively incorporated into the Central German Chemical Industry and Plastics Cluster although they are commonly perceived as being located (geographically) 'outside' the regional container. A similar case has been demonstrated in the previous example of the Central German Solar Cluster.

Another interesting fact is that although the discourse strand of Central Germany's Chemical Industry produces the Chemical and Plastics Cluster as part of the European Chemical Regions Network (ECRN), only the federal state of Saxony-Anhalt is institutionally associated and not the other two states of Central Germany. The ECRN network connects the industries' sub-national spatial clusters to the wider European region and blurs the boundaries between and within the

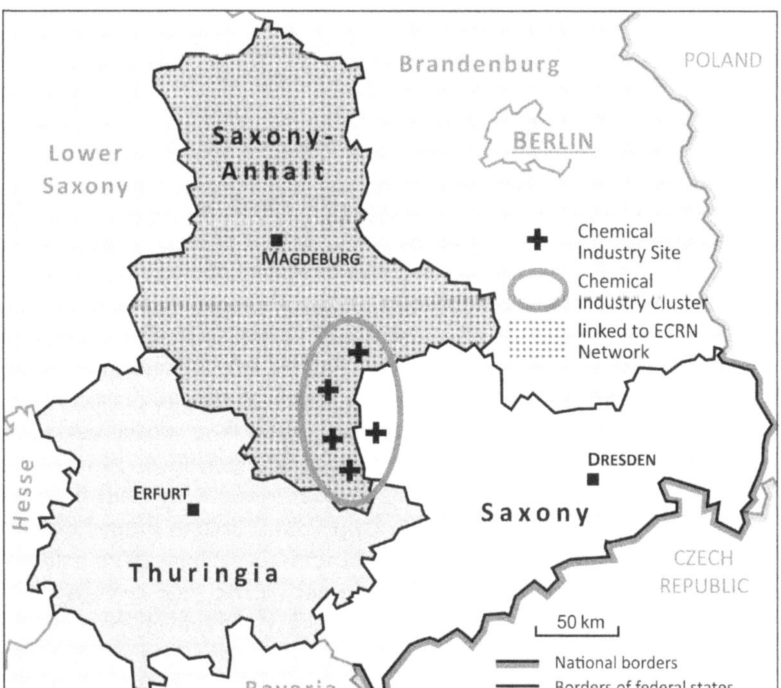

Figure 9.6 Chemical industry.

relational cluster-network of Central Germany. Currently, twenty-one chemical regions from nine countries (Germany, Spain, Italy, the Netherlands, Great Britain, Belgium, Estonia, Czech Republic, and France) cooperate in the ECRN. The network represents the interests of the European chemical regions and facilitates their cooperation and exchange of experience.

Transport and Logistics

The discourse strand Transport and Logistics constitutes the Leipzig-Halle region as one of the top logistics regions in Germany. Both the combination of available logistics-related site factors as well as the number of existing logistics companies are presented as above average compared to the rest of Germany. Logistics companies, public administration and scientific and educational institutions work closely together within the network to enable mutual information sharing and learning. The network was established in 2008 by regional logistics actors and currently is comprised of 144 members. The network combines actors from multiple logistics fields: logistics service providers, suppliers and transporters, public administration, chambers and associations, as well as research and education institutes. The specific objectives of the network are reflected by four objectives. (1) Logistics marketing: To increase the awareness of member companies and the region. (2) Logistics cooperation: Mutual success through logistics cooperation and exchange of experience between logistics companies. (3) Personnel logistics: Member companies cooperate to raise awareness of the region's demands for highly educated and specialised employees. (4) Logistics innovation: Through their participation in the logistic network small- and medium-sized logistics companies can cooperate in IT- and logistics-related research and development projects.

The Central German Logistics Network is seen to play an important role in the region's economic development. It represents the interests of regional actors both internally and externally. The region's logistics industries are mainly located at the geographical centre of the Central German Region between Halle and Leipzig (Figure 9.7). However, within the discourse strand a cross-sectorial logistics and transportation network is communicated exceeding the spatial boundaries of the three federal states with the network discursively and factually (e.g. cash flows, transactions) crossing federal state and national borders. The official discourse strand communicates the Central German Logistics Region as a 'gateway' to Eastern European markets. This connection, however, is explicitly made between the logistics and transportation 'hub' Halle-Leipzig and Eastern Europe but not the Central German Region as a whole. This cluster is an example of an industry network managed and supported on a city and not federal state level as illustrated above. The two city governments of Leipzig and Halle actively promote the transport and logistics industry as the Central German Logistics Cluster-Network. The logistics region is institutionalised through the Network Logistics Leipzig-Halle association, a cross-sector network connecting logistics industry players in Central Germany to improve access to international markets, e.g. Eastern Europe.

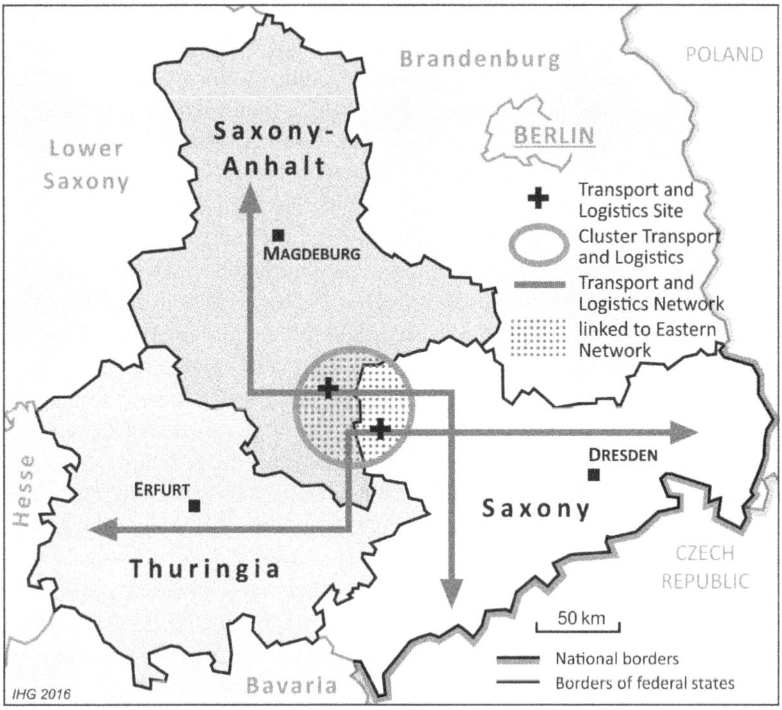

Figure 9.7 Logistic networks.

Discussion and Conclusion

> *The Central German Metropolitan Region network lies at the heart of Europe and brings together [nine core] cities from Saxony, Saxony-Anhalt and Thuringia.*
>
> (Central German Metropolitan Region, 2014)

This quote from the official webpage of the Central German Metropolitan Region illustrates the multi-dimensionality of the Central German Metropolitan Region's coexisting spatialities discussed in this chapter. Different spatial dimensions are drawn upon simultaneously to define the spatial subject of Central Germany, of which only the name is stable, but which turns out to be amorphous and 'phantom-like' in its essence. The relational concept of networks is used as well as the territorial containers of Europe and the federal states Saxony, Saxony-Anhalt and Thuringia. In addition, specific places – core cities – are part of the regional conception of Central Germany in cultural and economic discourse. These cities are territorially located in the three federal states Saxony, Saxony-Anhalt, and Thuringia and discursively constitute the Metropolitan Region of Central Germany. The participating core cities, therefore, can be seen as fundamental elements of the regional concept and form the idea of a regional city-network, which fluctuates in contour and structure according to the multifaceted cultural and economic contexts involved.

The Cultural Heritage discourse strand, for example, designates seven historic sites as important cultural locations in the Central German Metropolitan Region. These historically significant places are Dessau (Saxony-Anhalt) and Weimar (Thuringia), Eisleben and Wittenberg (both Saxony-Anhalt), Eisenach (Thuringia), Quedlinburg (Saxony-Anhalt), and Bad Muskau (Saxony). They constitute the cultural region of Central Germany with the 'modern' core cities mentioned before being completely omitted. Illustrated through the heritage site of Bad Muskau, it was shown that within the discourse strand of Cultural Heritage the region of Central Germany stretches beyond and suspends the territorial container of the three federal states, thereby dissolving borders within and between nation states.

Another consideration is that all cultural locations addressed in the cultural discourse of Central Germany are clustered into thematic groups disregarding their geographical position. Similar to the debates aligned with the economic discourse of Central Germany the territories of the three *Länder* Saxony, Saxony-Anhalt, and Thuringia seem to be blurred in the cultural context, where thematic bridges cross administrative borders and lead to supra-state (i.e. supra-*Länder*) city-networks. One such border-crossing network is the Martin Luther Way – a historic pilgrimage trail through the Central German Metropolitan Region and a cultural and tourism project uniting multiple sites of the Reformation within the region. Although the Luther Way today consists of more or less three separate trails bound by the territories of the three *Länder* Saxony, Saxony-Anhalt, and Thuringia, one continuous city-network is planned to be completed by 2017 – the 500th Reformation anniversary. Other cultural trails in the region, however, are (and most likely continue to be) contained by the federal boundaries. The Musical Tradition discourse strand demonstrates a similar example of border-crossing networks, although comprising only the two federal states of Saxony and Thuringia. Important events/sites in the life of the composer Johann Sebastian Bach are discursively utilised to constitute a city-network of Leipzig (Saxony) and Eisenach (Thuringia), which encompasses cultural places such as the Bach Museum, the Bach Archives, and the Bach House. Similarly, the history of the composer Richard Wagner forms the backdrop for a city-network comprising Dresden, Leipzig (both in Saxony) and Weimar (Thuringia).

The Central German Economic Region was demonstrated to evince similar multi-dimensionalities of the Central German Region. The Solar Energy discourse strand, for example, encompassed cluster-network structures that regularly cross and dissolve rigid territorial borders of the three member states Thuringia, Saxony and Saxony-Anhalt as well as extend the region's spatialities beyond those container images into the federal states of Baden Wurttemberg and Brandenburg. In the case of the discourse strand Chemical Industry and Plastics the Central German region discursively 'shrinks' to the territorial container of Saxony-Anhalt being the only member state of the region to be affiliated with the European Chemical Regions Network (ECRN) but representing the Central German region as a whole at precisely this European scale. Another example of the changing spatialities of Central

Germany was illustrated by the logistics network Halle-Leipzig constituting the Central German Logistics Region on a very different scale. Not only does the Logistics Region's discursive spatiality exclude the federal state of Thuringia, but it also ruptures scalar dimensions of Central Germany by linking the logistics region to a supra-state (European) dimension and, at the same time, anchoring it at the local level of the city-network Halle and Leipzig.

The spatial concept of network is an important constitutive element of the discourse of the Central German Metropolitan Region. However, all three federal states, Saxony, Saxony-Anhalt, and Thuringia, thought of as territorial containers are likewise crucial elements of its constitution. Although the main political stakeholders are located in the administrative core cities of the region, the federal state system of Germany significantly impacts on the cultural and economic discourses in which another dimension of the region is constituted. The fragile and temporary spatialities of the Central German Metropolitan Region incorporate rigid administrative elements on a regular basis and demonstrate the impact of territorial boundaries on the region's changing spatialities. Territorial sub-regional containers are frequently incorporated into the spatial organisation of the Central German region and illustrate the multi-dimensional character as well as the co-existence of relational and territorial dimensions and the temporality of a region ever 'in-becoming'.

This chapter aimed to contribute to current scholarly debates on processes of region building (e.g. Cox, 2013; Crawshaw, 2013; Goodwin, 2013; Harrison, 2013) and to provide a new perspective on the multi-dimensional and prospectively changing character of regional entities that often appear as stable and essentially defined. Using the Central German Metropolitan Region as an example, we illustrated how regional spatialities can be co-constituted by, for example, network and container concepts at the same time, sometimes contradicting each other. Regions understood as products of discursive practices must be conceptualised theoretically as constantly changing and always in-becoming due to the variety of spatial concepts performed in discourse in order to both serve and enable political actions. Hence, they can be conceived as phantoms with contextually changing intertwined spatialities, with the appearance of bounded and stable territorial containers being only one of many others. The co-existence of these different appearances and their conceptual backgrounds in various discourse strands is likely to have an effect on social practices. As a future prospect for our work, it hence seems important to delve deeper into the implications of possible, yet hitherto undiscovered, synergies and frictions between the different shapes of a region over space and time. This would involve, for instance, looking closer at to what extent practices of regulation and governance are affected by the constant concurrence and conflict between territorial, network and fluid spatialities that are involved in the perpetual becoming of a region.

This research was funded by the German Research Foundation (DFG), Individual Grants Programme, 2012–2014. Some sections of this chapter have been published earlier in *Erdkunde* 69(2), 172–186.

Note

1 At the end of 2014 the Central German Metropolitan Region and the Industrial Initiative Central Germany merged into the new European Metropolitan Region Central Germany with their old webpages no longer accessible.

References

Baars R and Schlottmann A (2015) Spatial multidimensionalities in the politics of regions: constituting the 'phamtom region' of Central Germany. *Erdkunde* 69(2): 172–186.

Central German Metropolitan Region (2014) Central German Metropolitan Region - Location. http://region-mitteldeutschland.com/ [Accessed 10 July 2014]

Cox KR (2013) Territory, scale, and why capitalism matters. *Territory, Politics, Governance* 1(1): 46–61.

Crawshaw R (2013) Guest editor's introduction: politics, economics and perception in regional construction. *Regional Studies* 47(8): 1177–1180.

Dicken P, Kelly PF, Olds K, and Yeung, H (2001) Chains and networks, territories and scales: towards a relational framework for analysing the global economy. *Global Networks* 1(2): 89–112.

Downs RM and Stea D (1977) *Maps in Minds: Reflections on Cognitive Mapping*. New York: Harper Collins.

Elden S (2005) Missing the point: globalisation, deterritorialisation and the space of the world. *Transactions of the Institute of British Geographers* 30(1): 8–19.

Elden S (2009) *Terror and Territory: The Spatial Extent of Sovereignty*. Minneapolis: University of Minnesota Press.

Elden S (2010) Land, terrain, territory. *Progress in Human Geography* 34(6): 799–817.

Felgenhauer T (2007) *Geographie als Argument: Eine Untersuchung regionalisierender Begründungspraxis am Beispiel 'Mitteldeutschland'*. Stuttgart: Franz Steiner Verlag.

Felgenhauer T (2010) Regional identity as celebration and routine: 'Mitteldeutschlands' glorification and its taken-for-granted meaning in media content. *European Journal of Cultural Studies* 13(1): 63–80.

Felgenhauer T and Schlottmann A (2007) Schreiben => Senden => Schauen? Medienmacht und Medienohnmacht im Prozess der symbolischen Regionalisierung. *Social Geography* 2: 77–83.

Felgenhauer T, Mihm M and Schlottmann A (2005) The making of Mitteldeutschland: on the function of implicit and explicit symbolic features for implementing regions and regional identity. *Geografiska Annaler: Series B, Human Geography* 87(1): 45–60.

Goodwin M (2013) Regions, territories and relationality: exploring the regional dimensions of political practice. *Regional Studies* 47(8): 1181–1190.

Hall S (1997) Introduction, in S Hall (ed) *Representation: Cultural Representations and Signifying Practices*. London: Sage, 1–12.

Hannah M (2006) Politics in suspenso: reading Antje Schlottmann's raumsprache from the 'North American' container. *ACME* 4(2): 240–248.

Harrison J (2013) Configuring the new 'Regional World': on being caught between territory and networks. *Regional Studies* 47(1): 55–74.

Industrial Initiative for Central Germany (2014) Industrial Initiative for Central Germany – Industry Clusters. http://www.mitteldeutschland.com/de [Accessed 10 July 2014]

Jessop B, Brenner N and Jones M (2008) Theorizing sociospatial relations. *Environment and Planning D: Society and Space* 26(3): 389–401.

Jonas AEG (2012a) Region and place: regionalism in question. *Progress in Human Geography* 36(2): 263–272.

Jonas AEG (2012b) City-regionalism: questions of distribution and politics. *Progress in Human Geography* 36(6): 822–829.
Jonas AEG (2013) Place and region III: alternative regionalisms. *Progress in Human Geography* 37(6): 822–828.
Jones M (2009) Phase space: geography, relational thinking, and beyond. *Progress in Human Geography* 33(4): 487–506.
Keller R (2005) Analysing discourse. An approach from the sociology of knowledge. *Forum Qualitative Sozialforschung / Forum: Qualitative Social Research* 6(3): Art. 32.
Leitner H, Sheppard E and Sziarto, KM (2008) The spatialities of contentious politics. *Transactions of the Institute of British Geographers* 33(2): 157–172.
Metzger J (2013) Raising the regional leviathan: a relational-materialist conceptualisation of regions-in-becoming as publics-in-stabilisation. *International Journal of Urban and Regional Research* 37(4): 1368–1395.
Murphy AB (2013) Territory's continuing allure. *Annals of the Association of American Geographers* 103(5): 1212–1226.
Paasi A (2004) Place and region: looking through the prism of scale. *Progress in Human Geography* 28(4): 536–546.
Paasi A (2012) Border studies reanimated: going beyond the territorial/relational divide. *Environment and Planning A* 44(10): 2303–2309.
Paasi A (2013) Regional planning and the mobilisation of 'regional identity': from bounded spaces to relational complexity. *Regional Studies* 47(8): 1206–1219.
Painter J (2010) Rethinking territory. *Antipode* 42(5): 1090–1118.
Schlottmann A (2005) *RaumSprache – Ost-West-Differenzen in der Berichterstattung zur deutschen Einheit. Eine sozialgeographische Theorie.* Stuttgart: Franz Steiner Verlag.
Schlottmann A (2006) Limited language – linguistic limitations: a reply to the reviews. *ACME* 4(2): 261–268. (Review Symposium on the monograph 'SpaceTalk').
Schlottmann A (2007a) Wie aus Worten orte werden: gehalt und grenzen sprechakttheoretischer sozialgeographie. *Geographische Zeitschrift* 95(1+2): 5–23.
Schlottmann A (2007b): Was ist und wo liegt Mitteldeutschland? Eine etwas andere Länderkunde. *Geographische Rundschau* 59(6): 4–9.
Schlottmann A (2008) Closed spaces: can't live with them, can't live without them. *Environment and Planning D: Society and Space* 26(5): 823–841.
Schlottmann A (2012) Reden vom Raum, der ist. Zur alltäglichen notwendigkeit der ontologisierung räumlicher sachverhalte, in R John (ed) *Ontologien der Moderne*. Wiesbaden, 189–206.
Schlottmann A (2013) Sprache, staat und raum. Zur (neu-)erfindung von nation aus sprachpragmatischer perspektive, in B Belina (ed) *Staat und Raum*. Stuttgart, 59–76.
Schlottmann A, Felgenhauer T, Mihm M, Lenk S, and Schmid M (2007) Wir sind Mitteldeutschland! Konstitution und Verwendung territorialer Bezugseinheiten unter raum-zeitlich entankerten Bedingungen, in B Werlen (ed) *Sozialgeographie alltäglicher Regionalisierungen - Band 3: Ausgangspunkte und Befunde empirischer Forschung*. Stuttgart, 297–336.
Sheppard E (2002) The spaces and times of globalisation: place, scale, networks, and positionality. *Economic Geography* 78(3): 307–330.
Smith N (1995) Remaking scale: competition and cooperation in prenational and postnational Europe, in H Eskelinen and F Snickars (eds) *Competitive European Peripheries*. Berlin: Springer, 123–56.
Terlouw K and Weststrate J (2013) Regions as vehicles for local interests: the spatial strategies of Medieval and modern urban elites in the Netherlands. *Journal of Historical Geography* 40: 24–35.

10 Regions, Regionalisms and Identities

Towards a Regional Mess

Kaj Zimmerbauer

Introduction

Regions have been conceptualized recently as increasingly relational and highly networked, and they are increasingly regarded as distinctively 'soft' spaces, which have at the most, 'fuzzy' boundaries (Amin 2004; Allen and Cochrane, 2007; Haughton et al., 2013; Allmendinger et al., 2014). This understanding of regions is heavily intertwined with the recent emphasis on a global 'quicksilver economy' and a neoliberal global agenda, where interconnectedness and hence competition and competitiveness of all kinds of spaces is typically underlined (Jones and MacLeod, 2004: 435). It is though, as this chapter argues, premature to declare the end of clearly delineated territorial units (Murphy, 2013). At the same time as the flows of all kinds have increased, new boundaries are being drawn and many new regions have emerged (Deas and Lord, 2006). Many old regions have refused to disappear or become any 'softer', and regions are instead increasingly re-institutionalised as highly meaningful bounded spaces both for their inhabitants and – as the current flow of refugees heading to Western Europe has shown – for those who try desperately to enter them (Zimmerbauer and Paasi, 2013). It should be acknowledged that certain regions are distinct from the 'regional spaces' of a neoliberal world, and are not sinuously becoming integral parts of dynamic, global networks, nor are they transforming into hubs of these networks (Jones and MacLeod, 2004). Globalisation is spatially selective and treats certain regions differently, and it also works differently in different spheres of everyday life. While the fast movement of capital has globalised the economy, many places have remained isolated from networks, flows and relational thinking, and the everyday life in them has not substantially changed.

It is true that many regions have transformed and new kinds of regions, such as 'non-standard' or 'unusual' ones have been introduced and are increasingly emphasised (see Deas and Lord, 2006). However, while it is acknowledged that many regions tend to be not as stable or closed as they perhaps were before, they are not totally open or changing similarly either. This 'spatial ambivalence' has caused the need to redefine and re-conceptualise regions. Although spatial change is by no means unique to this time, it cannot be denied that regions and regional systems are in transition, and a better understanding of the processes pushing this transformation forward is needed. Much research in contemporary human geography, planning and urban studies has thus concentrated on the commensurability or incommensurability of territorial and relational understandings of regions (Jones, 2009; Varró and Lagendijk, 2013, Harrison, 2013), and on understanding soft and hard(er) spaces in the now 'globalised' world (Allmendinger and Haughton, 2009).

This chapter builds on this previous work, and seeks to interrogate the transformation of regions, in order to tease out the sometimes paradoxical relationship between various approaches to conceptualising space. It aims to connect discussions on different kinds of regions and regionalisms, considering both deinstitutionalisation and institutionalisation processes. It questions in particular the mismatch between regions in everyday life and regions in planning literature. It does this by studying one old region and one new region, highlighting processes of deinstitutionalisation and institutionalisation in relation to ideas of new (or new new) and old regionalism. The aim is also to focus through the lens of two distinctive regions, upon the relations between the key ideas of regionalism and the contemporary understandings of a 'new new regional geography' (Jones, in this volume). The chapter concludes by arguing that a spatial system is simultaneously softening and hardening and regions have a certain amount of inertia, while penumbral regions and the idea of a regional mess is also introduced here. Specifically, the two regions analysed in this chapter, to demonstrate the links, gaps and fissures between different approaches to regions and regionalisms, are the municipality of Nurmo in western Finland and the supranational Barents Euro Arctic region in the northernmost Europe.

Relational/Territorial

It is common to make analytical distinctions in order to gain a better understanding of regions and their transitions. For example, new regionalism has become defined in relation to the old regionalism (e.g. Keating, 1998; Harrison, 2006), relational space is defined in relation to the territorial (e.g. Paasi, 2013), and soft spaces are defined in relation to hard spaces (e.g. Allmendinger et al., 2014). These distinctions have been widely reproduced in literature on regions and often in a particular way: a new spatial vision is followed by a critical reaction and then an aim to synthesise, placing emphasis upon contextuality or on the commensurability of the original seemingly distant approaches. For this reason, it is argued that the debate was in fact was a 'non-debate' (see Varró and Lagendijk, 2013). One particular example of this type of 'non-debate' is the examination of nation states and the controversial idea of 'hollowing out' (see Jessop, 2004). The 'borderless world' thesis – nurtured mostly by economic geographers – stemmed from the notion that in a gigantic 'global village' with a single global market, nation states have become increasingly powerless in their capacity to control their economic affairs (Ohmae, 1990). The initial response was that states have nevertheless an important role in providing public services, controlling migration, regulating markets, and serving as a 'last resort' if markets fail. While the 'relationists' envisaged a world of rhizomatic flows and networks without regions, the 'territorialists' highlighted the fact that even though the emphasis might be on networks, soft spaces and fuzzy boundaries, it should be stressed that many spheres of society operate within established administrative structures that tend to have clear spatial borders (cf. Allen and Cochrane, 2007).

Highlighting contextuality and specificity has reduced the juxtaposition of approaches, but it has perhaps also downplayed the debate unnecessarily by underlining contextuality too greatly. In other words, are we belittling the different theoretical arguments by viewing the world contextually and in a sense in isolation? There can be ontological or fundamental changes in society that call for new openings and understandings of space. Analytical distinctions are not unnecessary or irrelevant; their co-existence, and understanding their commensurability and particularly incommensurability, is necessary. This means that it is the tensions and contestations between different conceptualisations and understandings of space that are key to understanding the nature of regions. More often we should ask what does it actually mean when the territorial confronts relational, soft confronts the hard, or new regionalism confronts old regionalism, and we should ask: what are the real-world effects that these tensions cause?

To respond to these issues, it is useful to conceptualise regions as processes. This means that transformations of regions over time are acknowledged: they become institutionalised, re- and de-institutionalised, usually with respect to more general socio-spatial restructuring processes. Typically, institutionalisation theories have conceptualised regions as evolving through various 'stages', such as naming, symbolising and bordering (see Paasi, 1986). Through these processes, regions 'solidify' or 'harden' to become uncontested parts of the acknowledged spatial structure (Metzger and Schmitt, 2012; Metzger, 2013).

Deinstitutionalisation as a process has been understudied, but it usually refers to a process where a region loses its acknowledged status and ceases to be part of a legal/administrative structure (Raagmaa, 2002). This conceptualisation of deinstitutionalisation tells us that a region gradually disappears from all collective consciousness, and deinstitutionalisation is therefore a reverse process of institutionalisation. The German reunification though suggests that this is not the case, as the closure of borders for a quarter of a century provoked only a 2 to 3 percent difference between the East and West German vocabularies (Lindeborg, 1999, 94–97; Fernández Manjón, 2010, 72), which through present re-institutionalising will lead to retaining an old regional consciousness and also collective spatial identities (see Metzger and Schmitt, 2012). Similarly, a study of municipality mergers in Finland showed that there was some concern about a weakening of regional identity in the merged municipalities. Currently though, over 40 years after the amalgamations, such concerns have disappeared, as merged regions exist in various manifestations, alongside and outside of the former merged regions in the consciousness of their inhabitants (Leinamo, 2004).

Deinstitutionalising Old Regions

Regional structure must understandably change due to several reasons. Yet the justifications for structural change have been lately centered mostly on economies of scale, as bigger spatial units are argued to work better, are more powerful and attract more flows of all kinds. The ideas of streamlining, increasing competitiveness and producing services more economically fit nicely with the idea of metropolis policy, where sub-national urban regions are created and municipalities are being amalgamated. On the other hand, demographic changes, urbanisation and aging populations also give rise to regional restructuring. These justifications are particularly relevant in Nordic 'welfare' states, where governments seek to both cut the costs of public sector, and also boost the competitiveness of (city)regions (Zimmerbauer et al., 2012). This has led to waves of municipality mergers and regional restructuring in Scandinavian countries. Heavily influenced by calculations aiming to convince inhabitants about cost-savings, what is missing from this rhetoric is an understanding of regional culture, local democracy and proximity of services, and how they should be valued in an economic restructuring process (Laamanen, 2007). The emphasis on economies of scale has meant that regional identities, a sense of belonging and a will to maintain an old region have been muted and labelled as emotional idealism, regressive and a relic of past times (Zimmerbauer and Paasi, 2013).

Municipalities present in Nordic countries are typical examples of old regions. In Finland, the municipality structure was officially established in 1865 when the municipal statute was given by the central authority. At that time, municipalities were separated from the church. Currently, the just over 300 municipalities have many responsibilities and statutory tasks, such as child care services, as well as providing education, rescue services and road maintenance (Kuusi, 2011). They have also traditionally been responsible for organising healthcare and social services, but these services will soon be withdrawn from local authorities and joint municipal consortiums, to be controlled instead by a smaller number of autonomous regions. Municipalities are also major bodies of local democracy. Municipality councils are elected every four years by inhabitants and they have considerable decision-making power. To be able to organise the statutory tasks, municipalities have a legal right to collect taxes from their citizens. Due to their long history and their strong role in the everyday life of citizens, municipalities are unsurprisingly the regional units that people identify most beyond the state (see Oinonen et al., 2005; Pekola-Sjöblom et al., 2006).

Municipalities have been a part of the politico-administrative space for about 150 years and were actually established some 50 years before Finland gained independence. Their deinstitutionalisation does not simply occur with a single decision to remove (administrative) borders. Resistance can be expected. This was particularly apparent in the case of Nurmo, western Finland, where opposition was severe. Nurmo, a relatively rural and small municipality with 12,000 inhabitants, was merged with Seinäjoki on the first of January 2009. As studies on the amalgamation illustrate, resistance was explained by concerns on proximity and availability or public services and local democracy (Zimmerbauer et al., 2012; Zimmerbauer and Paasi, 2013; Zimmerbauer, 2016). Much resistance was also linked to a regional identity that can be described as geo-historical (cf. van Houtum and Lagendijk, 2001), attached to territoriality and a territory-based 'imagined community' (Anderson, 1991). It can be argued that this kind of resistance has its roots in old regionalism, as the spatial is based on fixity and a clear demarcation of lines, inclusiveness/exclusiveness, and not on fluidity, interconnectedness, or an idea of fuzzy boundaries. Thus regional restructuring, or the deinstitutionalisation of regions, is not just a technical process of streamlining administration, but is a complex process where new and old forms of regionalism collide.

The mass resistance in Nurmo has been experienced in other amalgamation processes too. These resistances are not wholly due to the centralising of decision-making or the losing of statutory services, but rather with concerns about losing *the territorial basis* of identity, as some of the regional institutions and symbols disappear. Quotations from the *ProNurmo* anti-merger bulletin board illustrate this:

> *The fact is, simply, that our municipality was stolen, and now we are asked to forget it. To start co-operating with the thief!*
>
> *You supporters of the merger ... You did it after all: ruined our dream of the independent municipality and trampled over all the foundation pillars of democracy. We, the inhabitants, will never forget this day, we will never forget you who did not give any value to our municipality. What you did can be never made up. Never. You just could not let this be as the people wanted it to be. I am speechless and feel tremendous hatred because of you traitors ... I want that ProNurmo will continue, because if ever, now such movement is needed. There is a clear will. We should not let that will wane and let the time dilute this bottomless sadness and anger.*

These quotations summarise initial feelings just after the Nurmo municipality council decided upon the merger by a margin of one vote (18-17), after a referendum in which 63.1% of inhabitants voted against the amalgamation. While it is difficult to extract the meaning of identity from other anti-merger arguments (identity as a word was in fact only rarely mentioned in the 358 bulletin board messages), the quotations show that the amalgamation was about much more than just re-organising services. Losing a region that was meaningful to its inhabitants was evident here, and a will to stay 'independent' is clear. The arguments resonate with an old regionalism, where fixity, territory, historical-cultural identity and local scale are commonly emphasised.

Conflicting regionalisms become even more visible when looking at the arguments of those who supported the merger. Those supporting the merger stated for example that the citizens who were anti-merger, 'Voted more with their emotions than with their reason,' or that, 'A merger is not for immediate benefits, but for the advantages in the more distant future'. It was also mentioned that 'while the inhabitants of Nurmo will witness some increased costs immediately after the merger, in a long run the inhabitants will benefit economically'. These statements speak to an argument that old regionalism is 'regressive' and not future-oriented. They also illustrate that the citizens who were pro-merger emphasised economic arguments when justifying the municipality amalgamation.

While regional identity is invariably linked to an old regionalism and bounded space, it also needs to be emphasised that borders are multilayered social constructs and they typically have an identity layer as well (Schack, 2000). Borders affect perceptions of geographical space and an emotional and cognitive identification with regions. Identity can also be highly durable, and can in fact strengthen after political or administrative institutions have been removed. As Schack (2000: 203) states, 'borders do not come and go, but they persist in people's minds even if the political agenda changes'. This means that regardless of an official agenda, in which administrative borders are constructed and deconstructed, established regional divisions tend to be preserved and an idea of a region remains (Zimmerbauer, 2016).

Institutionalising New Regions

While Nurmo is an example of an old region and the amalgamation process illustrates the relationship and division between old and new regionalism, through regional restructuring or deinstitutionalising, Barents Euro Arctic Region is an example of a new region and region-building. Covering 13 sub-regions in 4 countries, Barents was officially established in 1993, when the Kirkenes Declaration was signed by the foreign ministers of Norway, Russia, Sweden and Finland (Svensson, 1998). The primary goal of co-operation was to promote sustainable economic and social development and thus contribute to peaceful development in the northernmost part of Europe. Barents though has been increasingly characterised by cross-border trade, and ensuring stability and security in the region has been replaced by business opportunities and economic networks (Zimmerbauer, 2014). A shift from geopolitics to geoeconomics was evident in Barents. Yet recently due to the crisis in Ukraine and the recent tensions between Russia and European Union, geopolitics has again returned and plays a role in co-operation (cf. Moisio and Paasi, 2013). Even in this sense, discussions have focused on trade, and concerns over EU sanctions against Russia which hit the co-operation badly, as 'big geopolitics' impacts the 'small' nations and their subnational regions.

Due to its top-down origin and relatively young age, the Barents region is not a region that is very well known, let alone identified with. Although there have been some grassroots projects with good results, Barents' public, or regional, consciousness has remained rather weak. This is something that the 'regional elite' responsible for developing the supranational region acknowledge. Yet it is not known what could be done in order to change this and to grow the region and its nascent identity. A regional advocate illustrates this well:

> *There are these structures and institutions, but if it (Barents) has become genuinely established or not depends who you talk to. We who are very much in this job of developing the region probably say it has, but if we ask someone else, somebody who is not directly involved with these issues, he/she does not necessarily see it as institutionalised. Or is not even familiar with the name.*

Regional 'elites' are participating in regionalisation as administrators and stakeholders, but the 'general population' has yet to become involved. For those involved in promoting the Barents region, or other such newly conceived 'territorial assemblages', a sense of regional consciousness is beneficial, as it creates active citizenship that can be highly supportive of the dominant planning and development ideology (see Allmendinger et al., 2014). Although a strong regional identity can also make citizens increasingly resistant to prevailing ideologies, as seen in Nurmo, it nevertheless creates also a sense of cohesion. The current planning agenda often emphasises regional initiativeness, or the devolution of state power to regions, and cites a regional activism as highly significant to this restructuring. Regional consciousness and identity is something that administrators seek to use, but they do not understand here what the Barents region could be identified with or could be imagined as:

> *I don't know what the use is, if people know they belong to Barents region. Knowledge as such has no meaning, I guess. Probably. I don't know. Maybe it has.*

Regional consciousness is related not only to cohesion and initiativeness, but also legitimises regional advocates and institutions. This means that stakeholders are eager to emphasise the viability of supranational regions through visibility. Many of the newly conceived supranational regions are linked with various regional programmes, such as the EU. And some could simply disappear altogether if external funding stops, as they are not widely known and referred to by the general public. Thus regional advocates are keen to promote new regions to Eurocrats in order to create an idea of a coherent region that deserves to be supported. Some kind of an 'imagined community' is thus brought into being, via branding and other representational means, to illustrate that the region does in fact exist – it may indeed exist wholly in the imaginary and on paper yet it does exist – and the allocating of funds accordingly gives it an institutional, political, or 'real' life.

Developing regionalism and regional identity based on an imagined supranational community in the context of Barents region is troublesome. It was felt that the administrators and stakeholders have limited means to promote an identity based on cohesion, or a sense of common history and culture. Barents as a territorial idea has a long history that dates back to the Pomor trade era of the early nineteenth century. Yet it is not regarded as an old region which people identify with or as a historical region known to outsiders (Zimmerbauer, 2014). Instead, it is arguably a little known soft space that has been molded and has already taken up several different spaces and shapes after negotiations amongst regional elites.

Despite its role as a 'soft tool', supranational identity is not something that is actively or consciously developed or utilised in region-building. Contemporary or newly-conceived of (soft) spaces, as such, sometimes 'jar against established territorially bounded bodies' (Deas and Lord, 2006: 1848). There is a reason for this. Newly-conceived regions are often only 'regions on paper' and people identify instead with older regions. The institutions that create and develop such regions are typically institutional rather than identity-building. They are interested in networks, branding and competitiveness, rather than in a regional consciousness and identity (see Blatter, 2004).

'New New Regionalism' and Old and New Regions as Processes

Looking at Nurmo and Barents, it is easy to see a paradox: at the same time as old, meaningful regions that people identify with are being deinstitutionalised, new regions that are top down and insignificant to most – except perhaps regional elites – are being established. The situation where new regions are being established only to remain 'regions on paper' while old regions are being deinstitutionalised against the will of their inhabitants is certainly not an ideal one, as little cohesion between regions and initiativeness in regions can be expected. Yet the demolishing of significant regions and the construction of insignificant regions is unlikely to be changed anytime soon, as often old regions are regarded as unsuitable or uncompetitive spaces for regional elites – or at least their boundaries are experienced as problematic in many practices associated with the global neoliberal economy. So it remains important to critically interrogate this paradox, and to ask whether 'regions on paper' are actually deterring regional development and active citizenship.

The new regional geography created to understand and theorise these paradoxes is largely concerned with 'thinking space relationally' and emphasising networks, flows and fluidity. It is less concerned with understanding space territorially and underlining boundaries, inclusiveness/exclusiveness, rigidity and fixity. And while many scholars have lately stressed that these are analytical 'extremes' – the question of relationality and territoriality is a contextual rather than ontological question – it is nevertheless clear that traditional understandings of space have been challenged. Indeed, we have witnessed scale-bending and scale-jumping, and we have observed and documented processes beyond the control of individual states or other such territories (Smith, 2004). These processes require thinking via networks and through soft spaces that are often temporary and created only for limited often economic purposes. In other words, spaces are not as hard as they used to be. Despite a softening of space, we not living in a highly networked world of flows, where boundaries have lost all their meaning either. As the case of Nurmo illustrates, territory and boundaries matter. This does not mean that they matter in all practices, however. In Nurmo, parts of the municipality have knitted together with Seinäjoki over time, and many people commuted across the municipality border in the past without acknowledging its existence. The process of deinstitutionalisation – or more precisely the threat of deinstitutionalisation – triggered a resistance, and the inhabitants of Nurmo sought to re-institutionalise their municipality as a bounded region.

Understanding space as relational or territorial is not only matter of context. An 'old regionalism' has not disappeared. Regions, borders and communities, imagined or not, are highly significant, and although they are not pivotal continually in all practices, territory has a certain allure, particularly when under threat. Old regionalism is not replaced by new regionalism. They continue to exist in parallel, albeit often manifested in different social, political and cultural practices. Old regionalism should not be regarded as regressive or as a relic from a (territorial) past. It may in fact ignite initiativeness far more powerfully than a vague promise of a new, fuzzily bounded competitive 'regional space' (cf. Jones and MacLeod, 2004). Acknowledging existing regions and interrogating the regional restructuring process via a relational and territorial approach is as such valuable, serving the purposes of regional elites and advocates. Planning spaces and lived spaces should not be pulled apart, as often seems to be the case.

As regions are conceived of here as processes, it is important to note that old regions were once new. And as such certain new regions might eventually become as meaningful as old regions to their inhabitants and become something to be identified with. Nurmo and Barents were selected in this chapter as they illustrate starkly that not all regions are alike. Some regions are experienced by citizens as more significant and important than others. The answer is not to only set territory against networks or the relational against the territorial, but perhaps the answer here is to study different regions, their histories and regionalisms, and their contested 'forms' of agency. The answer is perhaps to move beyond a 'regional fetishism', foregrounding instead regional activists and advocates who contribute to and reveal what are often contested regional processes (Paasi and Metzger, 2016).

Highlighting agency

To discuss whether different regionalisms are linked to different kinds of agency, a distinction between activists and advocates is useful. In short, activists are actors who struggle actively over specific meanings which are often distinctively 'regional'. Advocates, on the other hand, are more often actors responsible for what can be described as 'soft region work' (Paasi, 2010). This means that advocates operate in institutionalised positions that have continuity. Also advocacy is not embedded within an emotional attachment to territory, but to a position that can be filled by another actor, given the advocate moves elsewhere. Advocates are often 'professionals', such as regional planners and consultants, whereas activists are often 'amateurs' in the very original meaning of the word,[1] as they have a strong emotional attachment to a region and are thereby strongly 'rooted' in the region. A sense of regional identity fuels their endeavor, and the work they do in promoting and maintaining a region is typically unpaid.

This distinction suggests implicitly that activists operate more often in the context of bounded space, and understand a boundary as a line of demarcation, while advocates are often region builders and therefore conceptualise spaces as more open, as distinctively relational. The case of Nurmo illustrates activism is often connected to the territorial, or an old regionalism, whereas the pro-merger advocates emphasise ideas of soft spaces and relationality, more typical aligned with a new regionalism. Accordingly, old regionalism, territoriality and regional identity, built upon the idea of boundedness, are often placed in contrast to ideas of relational thinking in current planning ethos, which emphasises competitiveness and economies of scale.

Seeing agency as played out through territorially-oriented activists hanging on to fixity and network-oriented advocates emphasising relationality would be an oversimplification. This is by no means always the case, as activist movements can occur within softer spaces and can in fact find territorial structures legitimised and maintained by advocates as restrictive or harmful in their politico-spatial aspirations. It is often the case that activists and advocates operate in an intertwined manner, negotiating and renegotiating spatial transformations from both territorial and relational standpoints simultaneously. It should be noted that no matter how far advocates, such as planners, emphasise fluidity and relationality in their work, they still have to operate within systems of bounded spaces, thinking relationally and territorially at the same time (Paasi and Zimmerbauer, 2016).

Regions are often constructed and deconstructed 'top-down', and agency should be distinguished not only on an individual level, but also understood through various institutions wherein advocacy is responsible for constructing regions and regional identities. As originally outlined by Blatter (2004), an analytical distinction between identity providing and instrumental institutions is particularly useful here. Blatter's conceptualisation starts with an assumption that institutions are created to serve specific public and private purposes. An identity dimension stresses a certain 'ritualism' and 'symbolism', creating mutual obligations among social actors who have 'objective' interdependence. An instrumental dimension emphasises that institutions are mechanisms of power and control. Identity-providing institutions seek to decrease ambiguity while the key objective of instrumental institutions is to reduce uncertainty (Blatter, 2004). The former builds on emotional symbols for citizen mobilisation whereas the latter focuses on the establishment of clearly defined regulations. The two dimensions are complementary and are embraced by almost every regional (political) institution. Constructed simultaneously through various governance structures, they are, however, not totally commensurable, and according to Blatter (2004) a holistic assumption should be avoided in order to make analytical differentiations between various institutions and their objectives.

Penumbral Regions and Regional Mess

As stated earlier, 'regions on paper' do not necessarily stay that way, but – depending on agency (both at an individual and institutional level) – can also harden and become 'regions with identities' or at least regions that are widely known. There is a body of literature that has studied how soft regions emerge and how they are hardened or 'solidified'. In much of this literature, regions have been seen to be built or institutionalised through various phases or as becoming hardened through speech acts by regional spokespersons (Paasi, 1986). Similarly, institutionalisation has been connected to the emergence and stabilisation of a regional public and to singularisation – or hegemonisation – of regionalisation discourses through political struggles (Metzger and Schmitt, 2012; Metzger, 2013).

While these conceptualisations are suitable for region-building processes, more research is needed on how spatial structure is changed by the simultaneous hardening of soft regions and softening of hard ones. As can be seen, old, hard regions will not always remain hard, but may become softened in order to overcome the 'problem' of borders. This two-way process of concurrent hardening of soft spaces and softening of hard ones calls for new understandings on the transformations of regions, understandings that go beyond the institutionalisation process, where spaces are often seen merely as 'regions-in-becoming', which will be eventually fully institutionalised. What are the outcomes of institutionalisation processes – in terms of spatial understandings, definitions and manifestations – and what real-world effects do these processes have and cause? As both soft and hard spaces become renegotiated or (re)performed (cf. Kaiser and Nikiforova, 2008; Haughton and Allmendinger, 2015), will regions become less hard and less soft at the same time, and simultaneous multiple imaginaries overlap partly but not exhaustively, causing a regional mess and contested regional identities? The idea of penumbral borders and regions seeks to answer that question by serving as a conceptual tool to understand some of the multiplicity of bounded spaces.

The idea of penumbral borders/regions is an alternative way of conceptualising regions as processes, and steps beyond the usual institutionalisation theory with stages that lead eventually into a fully institutionalised region that has an uncontested status in the official spatial structure. Accordingly, the idea of penumbral borders/regions does not understand the deinstitutionalisation of regions as a complete deconstruction, where regions disappear altogether from the collective consciousness. The idea of penumbral region emphasises the 'contextuality of things' by capturing the multilayered roles of borders. It underlines that the various layers of borders have an effect only when 'the light is cast from a certain angle', i.e. in certain practices and discourses. Penumbral regions have multilayered borders and some layers can be highlighted and meaningful at one time. The concept underscores the temporal aspect of the issue (cf. Walsh et al., 2012). A penumbral region may be visible and meaningful – that is, relevant – only for a relatively short time, for instance when funding is applied for the newly conceived unusual or non-standard regions, or when such regions are promoted in various advertising campaigns with supporting cartographic representations. Penumbral regions and borders alike are highly selective in terms of flows and closures, and they are activated in both context – and time – contingent junctures. The notion does not imply that these borders would be fuzzy, wavering or illusory, instead they are typically clear-cut.

Penumbral regions are regions with definite borders, yet they occur only in certain times and spaces, possibly remaining in the background for most of the time. They are not particularly soft, but their borders define insides and outsides clearly. They can be understood as 'ghost' or 'shadow' regions too. While they may not have confirmed administrative or legal boundaries, they have boundaries that are present in the public consciousness and in speech acts. Accordingly, they represent a kind of in-betweenness. They can be soft regions that are in the process of becoming hardened or – perhaps more typically – hard regions that become softened through the vanishing of layers of borders. They can be regions constructed for statistical use (NUTS) or for EU programmes, such as Interreg, and they can be regions with borders of one sort or another that 'are now dispersed a little everywhere' (Axford, 2006).

If regions are understood as penumbral, it is possible to view a spatial system metaphorically as a palimpsest, a parchment from which writings become occasionally partially or completely erased to make room for another text (Mitin, 2007). However, this is not to say that all the (old) layers of texts are completely washed off, but only certain layers (depending greatly on power structures), leaving limited space for new layers. In the context of this chapter, old regions and territorial notions of space do not disappear, but remain as one layer of many in the palimpsest of spatial systems. A palimpsest is filled with transforming and penumbral regions of all kinds, and they have various amounts of stickiness and inertia. Inertia works both ways. Regional systems have a certain inertia, which decelerates the institutionalisation of newly-conceived regions, as can be seen in the case of Barents. And regions have a certain stickiness when they are deinstitutionalised, as seen in the case of Nurmo.

Conclusion

Table 10.1 illustrates the analytical distinctions between different regionalisms and emerges out of the arguments that I have put forward in this chapter. It seeks to go beyond the conventional new/old dichotomy, outlining key features of a 'new new regional geography'. This is done in terms of spatial form, organisation, agency, purpose, time and scale, placing them alongside each other in order to critically interrogate competing regionalisms, as I have done throughout this chapter. While old regionalism has served as a lens through which to interrogate newer regionalisms here, it is, significantly, not argued to be an intrinsically regressive category.

Table 10.1 Analytical distinctions between different regionalisms.

	Old regionalism	*New regionalism*	*"Hybrid" regionalism, New new regional geography*
Spatial form	Closed Hard	Open Soft	Relational and territorial "Penumbral"
Organization	Institutionalized	Project	Mixed
Agency	General population	Administrators and stakeholders	Interplay of activists and advocates
Purpose	Multiple Culture	Single Economy	Multiple, cohesion and competition
Time	Historically oriented Stable Old	Future oriented Fluid New	Palimpsest (layers of assemblages that vary over time)
Scale focus	Local and national	Supranational, global	Cross-scalar

In a period of fuzzy regions, soft spaces and unclear spatial imaginaries, a territory with definitive boundaries reveals structures within which identities are built. Territory holds a continuing allure, and boundedness should not be regarded as problematic by default. Despite the increasing attention placed upon themes such as flows and nodes, many processes work within the realities and complexities of bounded space (Allmendinger and Haughton, 2010: 813). Many operations and processes, especially in planning and development, take place within and through administrative boundaries which fundamentally are not fuzzy, but are instead clear cut. As Allmendinger and Haughton (2010: 813) state, 'there are multiple spaces and scales that must be negotiated in everyday life, some of which are more fixed and formal than others'. It should be recognised that there are regions with specific histories and identities, and these regions react sometimes rebelliously to regional change. And while new regions may start out as soft spaces with fuzzy boundaries due to the 'territory-effect', regions become solidified through various spokespersons and speech acts (Metzger, 2013). The boundaries of newly-conceived regions harden as the region in question becomes gradually embedded through various spatial strategies and regional promotion, where the idea of boundedness and distinctions between inclusiveness and exclusiveness are pivotal.

Different regionalisms, as well as institutionalisation and deinstitutionalisation processes, need to be understood in relation to universal changes in societies and ideologies. Deinstitutionalisation, and the softening of borders, stems from a general need to increase competitiveness and to adapt to demographic changes. It can also be seen as a mechanism of de-politicisation where clear insides and outsides are not needed to be defined. Vague or fuzzy spatial definitions leave open 'whether a particular area or place is included in a policy framework or not' (Haughton et al., 2013: 218). Olesen and Richardson (2011) state that 'fuzzy spatial representations become an effective means to camouflage spatial politics and depoliticise strategic spatial planning processes'. As such, deinstitutionalising bounded spaces may be seen as a way to avoid conflicts that concrete borders of inclusion and exclusion might cause.

It is, as this chapter argues, therefore politically pertinent to question and seek to halt the constructing of new regions – perhaps particularly if they remain only 'regions on paper' – when old, meaningful regions are being top-down deinstitutionalised. These new regionalisms and regional transformations are often manifestations of policy transfer – a process 'in which knowledge about policies, administrative arrangements, institutions, etc. in one time and space are used in the development of policies, administrative arrangements and institutions, in another time and space' (Dolowitz and Marsh, 1996: 334). Relating to the themes highlighted in this chapter, policy transfer can mean 'bringing together the diffusion of currently dominant ideas on "relational space" and the normative planning ideals of national ministries, the EU or the OECD, for instance' (Paasi and Zimmerbauer, 2016). This can be read as a diffusion of largely Western spatial ideas to a non-Anglo-American spatial context. These 'solidified paradigms' have colonising effects upon spatial practices and vocabularies elsewhere. Indeed various post-communist countries have attempted to emulate the West, as it has been seen as 'the quickest solution to many problems without having to reinvent the wheel' (Stead, 2012: 107; Randma-Liiv, 2005). Accordingly, Prince (2012) argues that the circulation of policy agendas does not simply mean their transfer from one bounded state territory to another. Policy transfer is instead crucially related to institutional formations both 'above' and 'below' the national scale.

As such, regions – when understood – as ongoing processes are influenced by prevailing and dominant ideologies, which are often adapted locally somewhat uncritically. Allen and Cochrane (2007:1162) note, 'Rightly or wrongly ... political institutions lend themselves to the language of territory, fixity and boundaries ... territorial focus has remained much the same, despite a more flexible spatial vocabulary that speaks about regionalisation and the re-scaling of the state', while at the same time the emergence of 'fuzzy spatial representations' has led to changing geographical understandings of regions among planning practitioners (Paasi and Zimmerbauer, 2016), and new relational concepts of space are now brought into a 'discursive melting-pot' full of various spatial conceptions (see Healey and Underwood, 1978). This is the ongoing paradox of regions, regionalisms and identities; it is a regional mess.

Note

1 The word *amateur* comes from the Latin *amator* which means *lover* (Oxford Dictionaries, 2016)

References

Allen J and Cochrane A (2007) Beyond the territorial fix: regional assemblages, politics and power. *Regional Studies* 41: 1161–1175.

Allmendinger P and Haughton G (2009) Soft spaces, fuzzy boundaries and metagovernance: the new spatial planning in the Thames Gateway. *Environment and Planning A* 41: 6017–633.

Allmendinger P and Haughton G (2010) Spatial planning, devolution, and new planning spaces. *Environment and Planning C* 28(5): 803–18.

Allmendinger P, Chilla T and Sielker F (2014) Europeanising territoriality – towards soft spaces. *Environment and Planning A* 46: 2703–2718.

Amin A (2004) Regions unbound: towards a new politics of place. *Geografiska Annaler B* 86: 33–44.

Anderson B (1991) *Imagined Communities. Reflections on the Origin and Spread of Nationalism*. London: Verso.

Axford B (2006) The dialectic of borders and networks in Europe: reviewing 'topological presuppositions'. *Comparative European Politics* 4: 160–182.

Blatter J (2004) From 'spaces of place' to 'spaces of flows'? Territorial and functional governance in cross-border regions in Europe and North America. *International Journal of Urban and Regional Research* 28(3): 530–548.

Deas I and Lord A (2006) From new regionalism to an unusual regionalism? The emergence of non-standard regional spaces and lessons for the territorial reorganisation of the state. *Urban Studies* 43(10): 1847–1877.

Dolowitz D and Marsh D (1996) Who learns what from whom: a review of the policy transfer literature. *Political Studies* 44: 343–357.

Fernández Manjón D (2010) *La identidad humana y los territorios. El caso de Castilla y León*. Madrid: Vision Libros.

Harrison J (2006) Re-reading the new regionalism: a sympathetic critique. *Space and Polity* 10(1): 21–46.

Harrison J (2013) Configuring the new 'regional world': on being caught between territory and networks. *Regional Studies* 47(1): 55–74.

Haughton G and Allmendinger P (2015) Fluid spatial imaginaries: evolving estuarial city-regional spaces. *International Journal of Urban and Regional Research* 39(5): 857–873

Haughton G, Allmendinger P and Oosterlynck S (2013) Spaces of neoliberal experimentation: soft spaces, postpolitics and neoliberal governmentality. *Environment and Planning A* 45: 217–234.

Healey P and Underwood J (1978) Professional ideals and planning practice. *Progress in Planning* 9: 73–127.

Houtum H and Lagendijk A (2001) Contextualising regional identity and imagination in the construction of polycentric urban regions: the cases of the Ruhr area and the Basque country. *Urban Studies* 38(4): 747–767.

Jessop B (2004) Hollowing out the nation-state and multilevel governance, in P Kennett (ed) *Handbook of Comparative Social Policy*. Cheltenham: Edward Elgar, 11–25.

Jones M (2009) Phase space: geography, relational thinking, and beyond. *Progress in Human Geography* 33: 487–506.

Jones M and MacLeod G (2004) Regional spaces, spaces of regionalism: territory, insurgent politics and the English question. *Transactions of the Institute of British Geographers* 29: 433–452.

Kaiser R and Nikiforova E (2008) The performativity of scale: the social construction of scale effects in Narva, Estonia. *Environment and Planning D: Society and Space* 26: 537–562.

Keating M (1998) *The New Regionalism in Western Europe: Territorial Restructuring and Political Change*. Cheltenham: Edward Elgar.

Kuusi S (2011) *The Local Government System in Finland*. Helsinki: Kuntaliitto.

Laamanen E (2007) *Vapaaehtoiset pakkoliitokset. Diskurssianalyyttinen tutkimus kuntarakennetta koskevasta julkisesta keskustelusta*. Helsinki: Tampereen yliopisto, Suomen kuntaliitto.

Leinamo K (2004) *Kuntaliitoksen jälkeen. Kuntien yhdistymisen vaikutukset liitosalueiden näkökulmasta*. Vaasa: Vaasan yliopisto, Levon Institute, publication 111.

Lindeborg L (1999) Regional deep structures in the German cultural space, in S Tägil (ed) *Regions in Central Europe. The Legacy of History*. London: Hurst & Co.

Metzger J (2013) Raising the regional Leviathan: a relational-materialist conceptualisation of regions-in-becoming as publics-in-stabilisation. *International Journal of Urban and Regional Research* 37: 1368–1395.

Metzger J and Schmitt P (2012) When soft spaces harden: the EU strategy for the Baltic Sea Region. *Environment and Planning A* 44(2): 263–280.

Mitin I (2007) Mythogeography: region as a palimpsest of identities, in L Elenius and C Karlsson (eds) *Cross-Cultural Communication and Ethnic Identities*. Lulea: Lulea University of Technology.

Moisio S and Paasi A (2013) From geopolitical to geoeconomic? The changing political rationalities of state space. *Geopolitics* 18(2): 267–283.

Murphy AB (2013) Territory's continuing allure. *Annals of the Association of American Geographers* 103(5): 1212–1226.

Ohmae K (1990) *The Borderless World*. Harper Collins: New York.

Oinonen E, Blom R and Melin H (2005) *Onni on olla suomalainen? Kansallinen identiteetti ja kansalaisuus*. Helsinki: Yhteiskuntatieteellisen tietoarkiston julkaisuja 1.

Olesen K and Richardson T (2011) The spatial politics of spatial representation: relationality as a medium for depoliticization? *International Planning Studies* 16: 355–375.

Oxford Dictionaries (2016) Amateur. http://www.oxforddictionaries.com/definition/english/amateur (accessed 20 May 2016).

Paasi A (1986) The institutionalisation of regions: a theoretical framework for understanding the emergence of regions and the constitution of regional identity. *Fennia* 164(1): 105–146.

Paasi A (2010) Regions are social constructs, but who or what 'constructs' them? Agency in question. *Environment and Planning A*, 42: 2296–2301.

Paasi A (2013) Regional planning and the mobilisation of 'regional identity': from bounded spaces to relational complexity. *Regional Studies* 47: 1206–1219.

Paasi A and Metzger J (2016) Foregrounding the region. *Regional Studies*, 51(1): 19–30.

Paasi A and Zimmerbauer K (2016) Penumbral borders and planning paradoxes: relational thinking and the question of borders in spatial planning. *Environment and Planning A* 48(1): 75–93.

Pekola-Sjöblom M, Helander V and Sjöblom S (2006) *Kuntalainen – kansalainen. Tutkimus kuntalaisten asenteista ja osallistumisesta 1996–2004.* Suomen kuntaliitto, KuntaSuomi 2004 – tutkimuksia nro 56. Acta Nro 182, Helsinki.

Prince R (2012) Policy transfer, consultants and the geographies of governance. *Progress in Human Geography* 36: 188–203.

Raagmaa G (2002) Regional identity in regional development and planning. *European Planning Studies* 10(1): 55–76.

Randma-Liiv T (2005) Demand- and supply-based policy transfer in Estonian public administration. *Journal of Baltic Studies* 36: 467–487.

Schack M (2000) On the multicontextual character of border regions, in M van der Velde and H van Houtum (eds) *Borders, Regions and People.* London: Pion, 202–219.

Smith N (2004) Scale bending and the fate of the national, in E Sheppard and RB McMaster (eds) *Scale and Geographic Inquiry: Nature, Society and Method.* Oxford: Blackwell, 192–212.

Stead D (2012) Best practices and policy transfer in spatial planning. *Planning Practice and Research* 27 103–116.

Svensson B (1998) *Politics and Business in the Barents Region.* Stockholm: Fritzes.

Varró K and Lagendijk A (2013) Conceptualising the region. In what sense relational. *Regional Studies* 47(1): 18–28.

Walsh C, Jacuniak-Suda M, Knieling J and Othengrafen F (2012) *Soft Spaces in Spatial Planning and Governance: Theoretical Reflections and Definitional Issues.* Regional Studies conference proceeding. http://www.regionalstudies.org/uploads/funding/conferences/presentations/european-conference-2012/presentations/walsh-et-al.pdf (accessed 3 February 2016).

Zimmerbauer K (2014) Constructing peripheral cross-border regions in planning: territory–network interplay in the Barents region. *Environment and Planning A* 46: 2718–2734.

Zimmerbauer K (2016) Alueiden sekamelska. Vanhaa ja uutta regionalismia aluejärjestelmän muutoksessa, in S Riukulehto (ed) *Kunnat, rajat, kulttuuri. Muutoskokemuksia.* Helsinki: Suomalaisen Kirjallisuuden Seura, 23–45.

Zimmerbauer K and Paasi A (2013) When old and new regionalism collide. Deinstitutionalization of regions and resistance identity in municipality amalgamations. *Journal of Rural Studies* 30: 31–40

Zimmerbauer K, Suutari T and Saartenoja A (2012) Resistance in deinstitutionalization of a region. Boundaries, identity and activism in municipality merger. *Geoforum* 43: 1065–1075.

11 City-Region Building and Geohistorical Matters

David Beel, Martin Jones and Ian Rees Jones

Introduction

In an article published nearly 15 years ago, MacLeod and Jones (2001) carefully reviewed, situated, extended, and above all celebrated the enormous intellectual contributions of Anssi Paasi to the scholarly project of doing 'regions in geography'. Situated within, and going beyond, the 'new regional geography' movement in human geography and the social sciences more broadly, they looked at Paasi's thinking on regionalization processes, abstracted in four stages, which collectively allowed them to advance (as they claimed) a meaningful understanding of regional change. Rolling forward the research clock to the likes of the Northern Powerhouse and other 'devolution deals' and events across the UK, the authors of this chapter maintain that Passi's framework *remains* a cutting-edge theoretical framework in and through which to examine region-building processes and practices. This chapter accordingly looks at the 'new new localism' and suggests the need to now think about the dawn of a 'new new regional geography' (see Jones, in this volume).

New New Localism

City-region-based agglomerations are currently riding high on the political and policy agenda across the world. Their emergence is not accidental; they are being built in direct response to the deep ideological and thinking exposed in key documents such as the World Bank's *Word Development Report 2009: Reshaping Economic Geography*. This set in train a series of 'new economic geography' influenced arguments closely following the work of policy advisors such as Krugman and Glaeser (Peck, 2016). These collectively claim that, firstly, urbanization is a global phenomenon to be embraced at all costs and within this, city-regions are the principal scale at which this happens and people experience lived reality. Secondly, somewhat provocatively, the economic basis of city-regions rests on concentration and specialization, which allows spatial agglomeration to take place. Thirdly, cosmopolitan policy management is required with a bold and confident voice, working with the grain of market logistics and new 'spatial orderings' (such as governance frameworks) to lubricate agglomeration and provide efficiency by lowering transaction costs and promoting proximity, thereby liberating growth and allowing it to spread geographically (for an overview, see Storper, 2013).

In the UK, this motif is clearly evident in interventions over the last few years in the wake of RSA's City Growth Commission, which argued for the unleashing of metro growth, through a series of city-regions, or 'metros' – defined as the '*larger constellation of cities and towns that constitute a functional economy within build up areas*' – as the main drivers of economic growth in an increasingly knowledge-driven, global economy (RSA, 2014). The UK Conservative Government, through policy discourses and narratives of devolution, localism, rebalancing, and the Northern Powerhouse, is currently taking these agendas forward as a response to hold down the global and also finding a way around the messy nature of austerity and local state restructuring (see Conservative Party, 2015).

The authors are currently involved in a three-year research project based at the Universities of Sheffield and Cardiff. It is probing on the missing socially and spatially disembedded sphere of these competitive relationships, equilibrating tendencies, and critically the vacuum around the policies and politics of assembling city-regions. In short, there is little research being undertaken on *City-Region Building*, i.e. which civil society stakeholders are involved and what the motives are for engagement or a lack of engagement. Added to this, there is no critical assessment of whether and how marginalisation (by interest groups and by geographical location) and uneven development (the relationship between regions, cities and places) operates, and in turn whether this fuels, sustains or destroys economic agglomeration, development and growth. The project is therefore addressing this gap within the research field of human geography and the social sciences more broadly.

The authors are deploying case study research – based on three sites in Wales (Cardiff Capital Region, Swansea Bay City-Region, and the North East of Wales) and two sites in England (Sheffield City-Region and Greater Manchester City-Region). This involves interviews with around 20–25 stakeholders in each location – and we are currently undertaking a comparative study of stakeholder and civil society organizational involvement in the *City-Region Building* agenda. By focusing on the institutions of economic governance, the project is specifically looking at those involved in Local Enterprise Partnerships, various City Deals, Enterprise Zones and city-region development in general. The following research questions are being asked: what policy, strategy, and institutional changes have taken place, and are currently taking place, in the landscape of economic development since 2010 in England and Wales? How do these changes affect and involve civil society organizations? What are the narratives of devolution and community engagement in the LEPs, EZs, City Deals and City-Regions? How are these being worked into policies and procedures for stakeholder engagement? Who is involved in the new localism and how does this relate to forms of associational life and political engagement? In turn, what are the compositions of LEP, EZ, City Deal and City-Region boards, and their sub-groups and other structures of engagement? And, how successful are the *City-Region Builders* and the new localism in realizing the objectives of agglomeration, economic development and growth, and social empowerment?

Geographers have positioned the above as part of a 'new localist' political and policy discourse, given the arguments around the reanimation of civil society as a means of stimulating localist economic development (see Clarke and Cochrane, 2013; Clark, 2014). This localism is not new though: it is a reworked policy narrative (see Peck, 1995), and one that will doubtless recur again, and I prefer to note this as an instance of 'new new localism' (Jones and Jessop, 2010). This is because the latest variant of localist thinking draws extensively on some key antecedents. According to the 'Big Society' guru, Norman, localism '*is a coherent and logistical expression of a conservative tradition which goes back to the 18th century*' (Norman, 2011: 201). Edmund Burke's '*little platoons*' pepper this literature and are presented as progressive enablers for a democratic form of civil society-centred economic and social policy. The Conservative's new localism, then, stresses a '*three-way relationship between individuals, institutions and the state. It is when this relationship is functioning well that societies flourish. This requires each element in the triad to be active and energised in its own right …. Societies should be thought of as ecosystems*' (ibid.: 201). We would like to suggest in this short chapter that Paasi's treatise on regions increasingly allows a window into the study of such new new localist ecosystems.

New New Regional Geography

If the new regional geography (Gilbert, 1988) was launched to capture a coalescing concern with local responses to capitalist processes, cultural identifications, and identifying the region as a medium for social interaction, then Anssi Paasi's has clearly gone well beyond this; hence the suggested label of a 'new new regional geography'. As noted previously (MacLeod and Jones, 2001), Paasi (1986: 110) sought to transcend the dualism between Marxism and humanism by seeing regions 'not as static frameworks for social relations but as concrete, dynamic manifestations of the development of a society'. Areal extent though is a misnomer, as regions are to be analysed reflexively within the context of their very cultural, political, and academic conception (Paasi, 1991, 1996, 2010). Notions of *institutionalization* come into play here, which is not a shorthand with the study of institutions; instead, attention is paid to *geohistorical* socio-spatial processes during which territorial units emerge as part of the spatial structure of a society and become established and clearly identified in different spheres of social action and social consciousness. They are at once lines on the map and also geographical reference points in popular and political culture. This is operationalised through a methodology of abstraction: abstract to concrete and simple to complex in the identification of phenomenon (cf. Brenner et al., 2004; Sayer, 1992).

Stage 1

Paasi has deconstructed the regionalisation process by abstracting four stages, which rather than implying a linear sequence, of course, are to be understood as mutually constituting, reciprocal and recursive processes of structuration only distinguishable from each other analytically for the purposes of grounded research, hence why they are abstractions. The first of these concerns the assumption of territorial awareness and shape, where a territory assumes some bounded configuration in individual and collective consciousness and becomes identified as a distinct unit in the spatial structure of society. At the heart of this stage one can point to a series of struggles relating to cognitive mapping and the hegemony of one geographical imagination over others, the politics of scale, difference, identity and subjectivity, and the stretching and bounding of power relations (MacLeod and Jones, 2001).

Rolling things forward, this clearly connects with the drawing of, and designation of, the city-region boundaries of Sheffield, Manchester, Swansea and Cardiff noted above, where power-holding actors in a territory (or outside it even) have defined and symbolised the spatial and social limits of membership and create the discourses and practices for inclusion and exclusion, to the extent that territorial shaping refers not only to the creation of boundaries but also to their representation, to their roles both as social institutions and symbols of territory. Relatedly, territorial awareness and shape can be used to shine light on the ongoing and somewhat cul-de-sac debate in English-speaking human geography on territorial (seemingly bounded) versus relational conceptions (networked and mosaic) notions of space and statehood (see Jones and MacLeod, 2011). The illuminated perspective is that these processes are co-constituted: not either/or, but and/both, and the balance between them depends on institutionalisation practices and the balance and roles of those actors involved and their geographical dependency (see Jones and Paasi, 2013, 2015; Paasi, 2010, 2013).

In following Paasi's first stage, Figure 11.1 highlights well both the bounded, mapped nature of producing city-regions but also the ways in which this can be contested. The city-region as a whole is largely based upon what it termed the 'functional economic area' surrounding Sheffield which in turn focusses upon commute work patterns and employment opportunities (see Etherington and Jones, 2016). This represents the city-region as a whole but as Figure 11.1 suggests, this is far from simple when trying to create a contiguous city-region. Here, the economic geography of the region has been contested by the cultural and historical identities of the different Local Authorities. This means that only Chesterfield and Bassetlaw (Derbyshire and Nottinghamshire originally and respectively) have chosen to constitute themselves within the SCR and be part of the 2017 Mayoral elections, whereas the remaining local authorities have chosen to wait for a possible future devolution deal with their historic county regions. In Chesterfield, these overlapping senses of 'regionality' (Painter, 2008) became set against the regionalisation of the city-region within the context of austerity. The following letter represents the deep geohistory of Derbyshire in Chesterfield:

> *What on earth is our council thinking? Chesterfield is in Derbyshire. What a plan, live in Derbyshire and be controlled by Sheffield ... I do hope, fingers and toes crossed, they choose the Derbyshire and Nottinghamshire path.* (Derbyshire Times Letters, 3 March 2016)

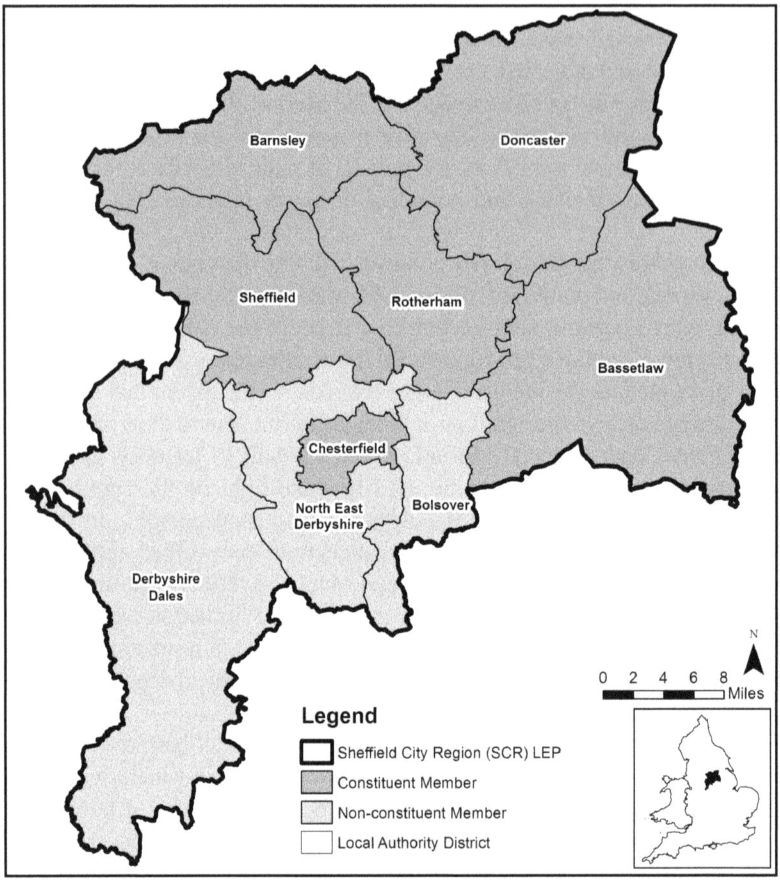

Figure 11.1 Sheffield City-Region membership.

Whereas the response from the Chesterfield Borough Council took a different approach choosing to follow the potential offer of the city-region, emphasising the economic necessity of the decision:

> *Full membership would align with Chesterfield's economic geography and provide opportunities for new and existing businesses on a footprint that makes sense to them … Chesterfield would be able to benefit fully from the two existing SCR devolution deals, including the £30m p.a. additional funding over 30 years, and continuing negotiations with government for further devolution.* (Chief Exec. Unit, 25 Feb 2016)

Therefore, the cognitive mapping and the economic hegemony of the city-region is disrupted by the pre-existing geohistory; this in part contests the processes of regionalisation in play with by SCR. It causes the SCR to split, as Figure 11.1 highlights, creating an uneven geography moving forward.

Stage 2

For Paasi, of course, this leads to the second stage, the formation of the conceptual and symbolic shape of regions, which is neither pure nor uncontested but is instead subject to continuous negotiation, translation and a hybridity of cultural expression. That said, power holding elites will endeavour to press that such negotiations and translation manifest in a hegemonic territorial grid of meaning whereby only a selection of invented traditions, histories, and remembrances are established and creatively implicated in the constitution of a territory's social relations. Paasi's work mentions the importance here of power-laden symbols such as cartographies, flags, memorabilia, histories etc. (Paasi 1996, 2013). Attention is drawn to the very naming of a region, which helps to connect its image to a place consciousness for both insiders and outsiders. The case of city-region building in South Wales is important in this regard.

In 2011, the Welsh Government established a task and finish group to consider the potential role of city-regions in future economic development. The task was to decide, on the basis of objective evidence, whether a spatially focused city-region approach to economic development, as opposed to the (national) Wales Spatial Plan, could deliver an increase in jobs and prosperity for Wales. Drawing on evidence mainly from Europe and North America, three arguments for adopting a city-region approach were made: improving the planning system; improving connectivity; and driving investment through a stronger and more visible offering from an agglomerated wider region (see Jones and Jones, 2015). Two distinctive city-regions were proposed – the South East Wales City-Region and the Swansea Bay City-Region – with the proviso being that all this has to be about creating urban engines and power-houses of growth by harnessing the beneficiaries of transport, housing, inward investment and funding opportunities. In following Paasi's tract, the South East Wales City-Region naming history is illuminating as over time it has morphed to being called the Cardiff Capital Region (see Figure 11.2).

Cardiff
Capital
Region

Figure 11.2 Cardiff Capital Region logo.

This was initially to purposefully distinguish Cardiff from neighbouring Newport for external promotion purposes, then later to the full renaming of the city-region in order to acknowledge both capital city power status and the stretched-out variegated geography of city-region building. This points to a metro centric focus upon Cardiff, as the agglomerative centre to the region, and highlights the way in which city-region governance is funnelled with regards to the future growth of the city-region.

Stage 3

These processes are constituted in particular structures of expectation, themselves critical in facilitating the third stage, the emergence of institutions, where Paasi sought and still seeks to capture the identity-framing vehicles of education, law, local politics, and organisations rooted in civil society (local media, working clubs, arts and literature organisations), as well as informal conventions such as economic ties or proximity and social mores. The entrenchment of these processes into the spatial matrix of society can also foster symbolic shape. For example, as more city-regional scale organisations are instituted into an activity such as economic development, the very consciousness of some place-based agendas may be intensified (MacLeod and Jones, 2001). All of which helps in providing an effective means of reproducing the material and mental existence of the territories in question.

This, again, closely connects to the city-region research agenda noted above, particularly the roles played by key activists (either those involved or outside the representational institutional governance structures of the four city-regions) in colouring the territorial consciousness and at the same time reproducing the very power assigned to such institutional roles. Indeed, for Paasi (1986, 1996, 2013), it is the institutions of a territory (and associated infrastructural power as state theorists would put it) that eventually become the most important factors in the macro-reproduction of the region. Within the context of England, there have been attempts to create new soft spaces of governance for city-regions through the creation of Local Enterprise Partnerships (LEPs). These have sought to bring business into the processes of producing a growth coalition for the city-region. This strategically places economic interest at the centre of the regionalisation process, framing the way in which sub-national devolution and growth will take place. Within the context of city-regions, this can make LEPs powerful institutions that enable business elites to have a stronger voice whilst at the same time pushing other voices to the periphery:

> *Trickle down doesn't work for the most vulnerable and disadvantaged and you have to have strategies around social regeneration (for want of a better word) alongside economic regeneration. Those two things should come together and I don't think they do because the LEP is very purely focused on the economic policy .... Feels like I'm in a rowing boat and my colleagues are in a rowing boat and we're trying to turn round this big tanker*. (Interview 1, Sheffield, 2015)

The local civil society actor in the quote above highlights how the governance structures and actors involved in the Sheffield City-Region shape the processes in a purely economic direction. This means two things for the respondent: one, it fails to address the social problems existing in the city-region and two, the civil society actor has little voice in addressing this through the current structures of governance put in place. Hence, a place-based agenda for growth is intensified which territorialises the strategic interest of the LEP towards an agglomerative growth model, as it reshapes the representational regime of the city-region.

Stage 4

Every theory has its limitations and previously MacLeod and Jones (2001) noted it was only fair to acknowledge that Paasi's key research objective has been to uncover the more localised or bottom-up articulations involved in the reproduction of socio-spatial consciousness and regional shaping of society (though see emerging research on spatial planning, Paasi, 2013; Paasi and Zimmerbauer, 2016). The final stage in this latter process concerns the establishment of a region in the spatial structure and popular consciousness, where it assumes the form of an institutionalised 'territorial unit' and as an identifiable constituent in the regional division of society. In practical terms, the region is ready to be mobilised for such purposes as place marketing or as a weapon in an ideological struggle over resources and power. Further, if provided with administrative status, it comes to assume the material expression of the end to which state power is applied (Paasi, 1991).

The last few years in England demonstrates the relevance of Paasi's thinking. The full map of Local Enterprise Partnerships (LEPs) is now complete, is becoming embedded, and is now being superimposed by further voluntary arrangements of local authorities through City Deals and Local Growth Deals with government and proposals for devolution to five initial (indirectly elected but legally-recognised as strategic coordinating bodies) Combined Authorities. Whilst the result is complex, these point towards the endurance of a *de facto* city-region scalar and institutional fix. Indeed, each of the three main political parties appears to be wedded to such a fix, subject to proposing modifications. The South Yorkshire Sheffield City-Region (SCR), which straddles the 'traditional' administrative geography of counties and regions and internalises a new scale of policymaking, is becoming an established region. As part of the 'Northern Powerhouse' movement, which has been emerging in the past 12 months as a means of addressing austerity and rebalanced development, Sheffield has recently secured a deal with the UK Government to transfer more powers over transport, housing and economic growth to the city-region. The Sheffield city devolution deal, only the second to be agreed in England, although not involving additional money, is being presented as a shift in power from Whitehall to the Combined Authorities in the region. This will include responsibility for the majority of the adult skills budget, greater control over transport schemes and greater power to decide which assets to sell for development (compare Etherington and Jones 2016; HM Government 2014).

These processes go against the grain of Paasi's fourth stage, as a form of central government localism is created, not a bottom-up flourishing of local and regional identity. This has significant impact to the processes of city-regional regionalisation because the scalar jumps in governance from the local authority to the combined authority circumvents existing institutions, coalitions, popular identities and civil society actors working at the local authority scale:

> *At one point they talk about localism but if you look at regionalisation, it's huge, it's huge and actually the local voluntary community sector can't even hope to engage with, let alone deliver against that agenda. Therefore, civil society is finding itself squeezed behind/between a rhetoric that emphasises its importance but a reality which mitigates against its ability to capture the resources to deliver against that agenda.* (Interview 12, Bolsover, 2016)

The Bolsover respondent above highlights how the scalar change in governance marginalises both their ability to work at the local level (to address the needs of the communities they serve) and their ability to have influence upon processes of governance at a combined authority level. This is further reflected below in Cardiff also:

> *All of a sudden we become completely insignificant so whereas at the moment locally we can lobby quite hard and push the direction on certain things, all of that power would go away and how to influence rather than power. So that for us would cause quite a significant problem. If we start working more collaboratively with other similar organisations then greatw, we can form a nice little consortium and then we can retain the same level of perceived power and all will be well with the world. But it doesn't fit well with how any of us work really; we work with quite defined communities, we do quite tailored things for them.* (Interview 2, Cardiff, 2015)

The respondent identifies how changes in the scalar relationship to governmental structures deeply weakens their position as an actor in the local community and state. This means that despite the language of localism being threaded through the centralised processes of devolution there is in fact a further distancing of the local from the structures of governance created by the introduction of city-regions and their combined authority governmental structures.

Conclusion

In following Paasi's treatise on regions in geography, we feel this can provide (once again) fresh thinking for today, even 30 years after the original argument was put down in *Fennia*, and in doing so still offer powerful methodological means and conceptual tools with which to advance an imaginative and progressive understanding of regional change. In particular, as MacLeod and Jones (2001) argued previously, Paasi's geohistorial approach still provides much scope with which to unravel the political, economic and cultural process that enable individual and institutional place-based biographies to coalesce in the form of a distinctive territorial unit with the overall regionalisation of society (MacLeod and Jones, 2001). Moreover, by placing the institutionalisation process, its multiple and overlapping 'stage', and the critical role played by discourse and symbolic orderings of space at the centre of his treatise, Paasi still enables us to locate many of the complex forces at work in constructing the regionalisation of society.

Further, and in the context of city-region building research, Paasi's framework permits us to problematise the reciprocal relationships that can exist between the whole gamut of institutional forms relating to economic behaviour (LEPs, EZs, City-Region Boards, Combined Authorities etc.), the politics of representation, political power geometries, scale, and identity, and the sedimentation of these practices into regions. In most accounts of city-regions, questions pertaining to the social construction of boundaries, territorial shape, and the very becoming of region and their associated institutional fixes remain hidden from view (compare Storper 2013; RSA 2014; HM Government 2014). In contrast, Paasi's stress on region building as an active and ongoing processes, rich in political strategy and cultural expression, still sanctions useful insights for researchers and regional strategies alike to uncover the very formation of economic and political life. Perhaps, then, it is time to think about a 'new new regional geography'.

References

Brenner N, Jessop B, Jones M and MacLeod G (2004) Introduction: state space in question, in N Brenner, B Jessop, M Jones and G MacLeod (eds) *State/Space: A Reader*. Oxford: Blackwell.

Clark N (2014) Locality and localism: a view from British human geography. *Policy Studies* 34: 492–507.

Clark J and Cochrane A (2013) Geographies and politics of localism: the localism of the United Kingdom's coalition government. *Political Geography* 34: 10–23.

Conservative Party (2015) *The Conservative Party Manifesto 2015: Strong Leaderships, a Clear Economic Plan, a Brighter, More Secure Future*. London: Conservative Party.

Etherington D and Jones M (2016) The city-region chimera: the political economy of metagovernance failure in Britain. *Cambridge Journal of Regions, Economy and Society* 9: 371–389.

Gilbert A (1988) The new regional geography in English and French-speaking countries. *Progress in Human Geography* 12: 208–228.

HM Government (2014) *Sheffield City Region Agreement on Devolution*. London: HM Government.

Jones M and Jessop B (2010) Thinking state/space incompossibly. *Antipode* 42: 1119–1149.

Jones M and Jones IR (2015) Spaces of new localism: stakeholder engagement and economic development in Wales and England. *WISERD News* 10: 13.

Jones M and MacLeod G (2011) Territorial/relational: conceptualising spatial economic governance, in A Pike, A Rodrigues-Pose and J Tomaney (eds) *Handbook of Local and Regional Development*. London: Routledge.

Jones M and Paasi A (2013) Guest editorial: regional world(s): advancing the geography of regions. *Regional Studies* 47: 1–5.

Jones M and Paasi A (eds) (2015) *Regional Worlds: Advancing the Geography of Regions*. London: Routledge.

MacLeod G and Jones M (2001) Renewing the geography of regions. *Environment and Planning D: Society and Space* 19: 669–695.

Norman J (2011) *The Big Society*. Buckingham: Buckingham University Press.

Paasi A (1986) The institutionalisation of regions: a theoretical framework for understanding the emergence of regions and regional identity. *Fennia* 164: 105–146.

Paasi A (1991) Deconstructing regions: notes on the scale of spatial life. *Environment and Planning A* 23: 239–256.

Paasi A (1996) *Territories, Boundaries and Consciousness: The Changing Geographies of the Finnish-Russian* Border. Chichester: Wiley.

Paasi A (2010) Regions are social constructs, but who or what 'constructs' them? Agency in question. *Environment and Planning A* 42: 2296–2301.

Paasi A (2013) Regional planning and the mobilisation of 'regional identity: from bounded spaces to relational complexity. *Regional Studies* 47: 1206–1219.

Paasi A and Zimmerbauer K (2016) Penumbral borders and planning paradoxes: relational thinking and the questions of borders in spatial planning. *Environment and Planning A* 48(1): 75–93.

Painter J (2008) Cartographic anxiety and the search for regionality. *Environment and planning A* 40: 342–361.

Peck J (1995) Moving and shaking: business elites, state localism and urban privatism. *Progress in Human Geography* 19: 16–46.

Peck J (2016) Economic rationality meets celebrity urbanology: exploring Edward Glaeser's city. *International Journal of Urban and Regional Research* (forthcoming).

RSA (2014) *Unleashing Metro Growth: Final Recommendations of the City Growth Commission*. London: Royal Society of Arts.

Sayer A (1992) *Method in Social Science: A Realist Approach*. London: Routledge.

Storper M (2013) *Keys to the City: How Economics, Institutions, Social Interaction, and Politics Shape* Development. New Jersey: Princeton University Press.

Part III

Performance

12 Radiant Copenhagen

Reimagining Regions through Digital Fiction

Rune Graulund, Kristoffer Ørum and Anders Bojen

> The best way to predict the future is to create it.
>
> Abraham Lincoln

In March 2009 the collective art project *Radiant Copenhagen* launched the vision of a future Copenhagen that is as yet to be. As an intermingling of present, past and future, of the everyday and the fantastic, of lived experience and digitally crafted worlds, *Radiant Copenhagen* intended to challenge preconceived ideas not only of what the city of Copenhagen is today, but also of what it might become. Covering a wide variety of activities ranging from performance art over guided bus tours, conventional art exhibits in established galleries on to spontaneous action in the streets, *Radiant Copenhagen* presented a playful intervention with a range of different territories, media and spatial practices. As such, the project was ephemeral, existing only in the days and weeks during which the physical activities and exhibitions were active. And yet the project continues to live on in the digital footprint left behind, primarily in the interactive website radiantcopenhagen.net. Accordingly, while the physical aspects of the project are now gone, digital remnants of the project still exist, continuing to exert an influence on the city of Copenhagen in both its present and future tense(s).

In the following, we will provide an overview primarily of the digital project and discuss its original intent as well as what it did in fact (and did not) achieve. Specifically, we will attempt to examine to what extent the project succeeded in reanimating, and reimagining, Copenhagen as a city as well as a region. In this, we will query whether the project effectively challenged more traditional notions of single, or at most a few, authoritative narratives governing a given region. Indeed, *Radiant Copenhagen* suggests, regions should be viewed in the manner that social geographer Doreen Massey views place, namely as 'the product of interrelations; as constituted through interactions, from the immensity of the global to the intimately tiny' (Massey, 2005: 9). In this, the regional space of Copenhagen is not a set, fixed physical entity but 'constructed out of a particular constellation of social relations, meeting and weaving together at a particular locus' (Massey, 1994: 154).

In *Radiant Copenhagen*, such loci were continually challenged by a variety of very different, and sometimes clashing, constellations of relations.

As a collective artistic vision including contributions from architects, artists, designers, journalists, engineers and musicians, this was precisely the sensation that *Radiant Copenhagen* attempted to invoke. *Radiant Copenhagen* was by design constructed so as to obstruct any absolute or singular vision of Copenhagen to appear. While a creative framework was provided by the core members of the collective, primarily through the website (to be described and discussed in detail below), the individual contributors to the project were encouraged to alter the material created by other contributors as they saw fit. Accordingly, by far the majority of the material uploaded to the website can be said to be multi-authored in the full extent of the word. Indeed, so successful was this process that the contributors themselves can no longer recall precisely how much of a given entry constitute their own original contribution. In this, the site engages with the region as a multi-layered, and ever-changing, process rather than as a fixed and confined presence.

The argument to follow consists of five sections. First, we give a short introduction to the authors of this text, all of whom worked on the project itself. Second, we introduce the basic functionality of the website itself, as well as explain the decisions that led to the design and style of the site. Third, we explain how the site attempted to mimic the manner in which we in general appropriate and construct knowledge through digital media. Fourth, we cover the impact the site and the project overall had on the world outside the digital platform itself. And finally, we attempt to briefly evaluate the manner in which arguably whimsical projects like *Radiant Copenhagen* impact on the hard and jagged nature of everyday reality.

We, Ours, Us: The Artist Collective and the Artistic Process

For any individual or group of individuals to write about a collective artistic project like *Radiant Copenhagen* is inadvertently to force an authoritative perspective on what was in both intent and practice a deliberately chaotic and multi-strained cacophony of voices. In presenting the project in essayistic form, as we are attempting here, it is therefore necessary to qualify this 'we' in the first place. When we refer to what 'we' believe 'the intent' of *Radiant Copenhagen* to be, what is presented in the following is the opinion of but a fraction of the contributors to the project.

With Anders Bojen, Kristoffer Ørum and Rune Graulund constituting three out of four members of the original core group of the project (Kaspar Bonnén being the fourth original member), the 'we' of this text cannot entirely evade claims at authorial hierarchy. With the origin and early stages of the project primarily in our hands, we undoubtedly had a greater say in the overall design than the majority of contributors to the project. However, seeing as the remaining contributors come from very different disciplinary backgrounds and that the project was eventually opened up through a truly non-hierarchical creative process, it would be naïve to claim that the following is anything but one of several interpretations of what *Radiant Copenhagen* was intended to accomplish. When we in this text write 'we', what we are referring to is thus an amalgam, and to some extent an uneasy compromise, of the opinions of Bojen, Ørum and Graulund, but with a clear appreciation that we cannot claim even this to represent anything like full authorial intent. Before we proceed any further, it is perhaps therefore fitting to shortly delineate two distinct positions of this we, namely that of the visual artists Bojen and Ørum, and the literary scholar Graulund.

Bojen and Ørum: Concluding a three-month residency in Seoul, South Korea, in 2008, we returned to our home country Denmark with a sense of having only encountered our own, preconceived ideas of what Seoul was supposed to be. We had hoped that Seoul, as one of the iconic mega-cities of a new and radically novel Asia, would act a window to the future. Yet we never really felt we had managed to move much further than the image we had set off with when we first left Copenhagen. The city we saw in South Korea was the city we expected to see. Hence our visit to the actual, physical locality of Seoul left the future as uncharted a territory as ever. As a consequence, we eventually came to the realisation that we needed to anchor our visions of the future in something that was familiar rather than something strange. Copenhagen, our hometown, seemed the perfect testing ground. As so many other old European cities, Copenhagen is a largely 'museal [city] in which preservation reigns supreme' (Huyssen, 2008: 9). Accordingly, visions of the future are hard to come by in Copenhagen, but precisely therefore all the more alluring. Indeed, as the Italian futurist Antonio Sant'Elia proclaimed in his 'Manifesto of Futurist Architecture of 1914', 'EVERY GENERATION MUST BUILD ITS OWN CITY' (Sant'Elia, 2009: 172), a motto we took on as our own. The result of this attempt at building our own city all over again – at reanimating our local region through a radical reimagining of it – was *Radiant Copenhagen*.

Tellingly, we borrowed the title of our project from yet another Asian mega-city. Like the exuberant urban renewal project *Radiant Shanghai*, which we had encountered on a trip to China, we wanted our new version of Copenhagen to constitute a radical break with the past. What is more, we wanted to ensure that in the process leading to our city of the future there would be no sense of individual ownership or copyright to any of the material provided for the project. This in practice meant that all contributors had the access and the right to alter, add or delete the material provided by other contributors. The technical decision to employ Google Maps and Wikipedia as the base technology of the site however provided a range of restrictions and rules as to what was possible in terms of individual and/or collaborative contributions. Within the boundaries of this non-hierarchical system, we invited a range of people to join us on equal footing in our pursuit to explore and challenge the future of Copenhagen. We intentionally opted for a strategy that would allow for a group of people to be inspired by each other's ideas, but also to challenge them. Finally, it was important for us that the project was to gain a size and an autonomy that lay beyond the capabilities of any single individual, including our own preconceived ideas of what the project was and what it might turn into. The core rules of the project therefore present themselves as a template for a manner in which self-organised groups can act in (divided) unison in an attempt to challenge and alter predetermined ideas of how a given regional geography is perceived and acted upon.

Graulund: As the third member of the group, I was invited to participate in the second visionary phase rather than the initial technical and strategic phase of the project. While some of the technology had at this stage already been developed by Bojen and Ørum, primarily through a tweaking of the existing technologies of Google Maps and Wikipedia, our overall idea of what *Radiant Copenhagen* was to be was at this point (and to some extent still is) hazy. Similarly, the chaotic but productive misunderstanding and misinterpretation that much of the future creative process was to rely on was already present even at this early stage of development. With both a professional and personal interest in urban studies, science fiction, computer games and the avant garde, I shared common ground with Bojen and Ørum when it came to joint discussions of our inspirations for the project. Nevertheless, the very title of the project, 'Radiant Copenhagen', set us off in different directions almost from day one. As mentioned in the above, Bojen and Ørum had been inspired by the actual and present-day project *Radiant Shanghai*, whereas I inevitably thought of Le Corbusier's utopian and never realised project *The Radiant City* (La Ville Radieuse). Simply presuming this to be the case, I set to work on my first entry for the project, 'La Voisin II', directly referencing Le Corbusier's plans for a more efficient, contemporary city (Corbusier, 1933), but situating it in a Copenhagen and at a much more ambitious scale.

One of the early first entries to the site was thus based on a misunderstanding, or at least a reinterpretation, of already existing material, namely the title of the project itself. This minor yet nevertheless telling misprision neatly illustrates the larger and far more chaotic processes of similarly creative, yet also confusing, re-/misinterpretations that were to follow once the project opened up to an even larger 'we'. What is more, as the project developed further, it became increasingly clear that 'our' respective focal points were not exactly aligned. Whereas my focus was primarily on text and description, Bojen and Ørum had a more holistic approach, not only in their focus on the visual and auditive experience of the website, but also in their involvement in the activities taking place in the physical city of Copenhagen. In this, our different backgrounds, training and interests played out yet another early schism of a creative process that would expand and fragment even further the more members were included in our collective but also disjointed 'we'.

Site and Interface: The Digital in the Everyday

The core of *Radiant Copenhagen* is radiantcopenhagen.net, a fictitious version of Copenhagen in digital format. While the interactions with the physical geography of Copenhagen were important, the digital platform was always intended as the anchor point to which the many divergent activities of the project were to be tied. In this, the project would from its very conception subvert the notion of the digital as an appendix to the physical rather than vice versa. As an arts project that intentionally engaged the city of Copenhagen through a mix of guided bus tours, performances, lectures, exhibitions, manipulation of news media and more,

Radiant Copenhagen did not intend to prioritise digital space over physical space. It did however intend to question traditional hierarchies of what does and does not 'matter' when it comes to the manner in which we perceive, move through, and imagine, a region like the city of Copenhagen.

In terms of the information presented on the website, the project combined a wide variety of artistic and academic disciplines and practices. Ranging from visualisations of new fantastic architecture to manifestos for radical social change, the site also presented already existing proposals for novel means of transportation that could in fact potentially become a reality in the not too distant future. In addition to these grander plans for radical social and physical change, including fantastic suggestions like 'whale dominion', 'reversed gravity' and 'rotating tectonic plates', the site also included descriptions of personal walking tours that diverged only slightly from what one could experience on any given day in the present-day city. In mixing the spectacularly fantastic with mundane experiences of the everyday, it was thus the intent of the project to engage the powers of imagination as active and critical tools for engaging with the city as a collectively imagined space and as a social practice rather than as a physical entity only. Specifically, we wanted to examine whether the imaginary and the digital could have any meaningful impact on the manner in which we experience and shape our present, lived, and everyday experience of the city, as well as its possible future manifestation(s) (Figure 12.1).

Radiant Copenhagen presents itself as a modified Google Map on which a range of data points allow access to textual entries. Many of these texts are accompanied by images, video, diagrams, music, and visual additions to the Google map itself, and all are interconnected in a Wiki-structure that leads to a far larger amount of entries than those presented on the map itself. At first sight the interface of the webpage thus seems to signal usability and functionality. Most people versed in everyday digital communication will instinctively know how to navigate

Figure 12.1 Welcome to *Radiant Copenhagen*.

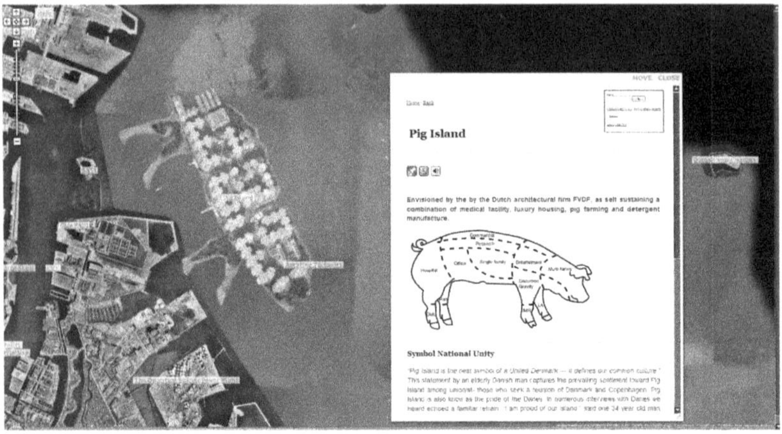

Figure 12.2 Pig Island.

the site with no further introduction. The site offers no useful explanation for how to navigate it, nor does it explain what the project is about. A list of contributors' names is provided, but no credits are given for individual entries. Most important of all, it is not made clear exactly what *Radiant Copenhagen* is about. A short introductory text alludes to potential uses of the site, but the suggestions of where to begin are randomised and the nature of the site kept vague (Figure 12.2).

With this relatively simple and low-tech approach to already existing technologies, *Radiant Copenhagen* was able to develop and evolve as a self-funded project that required no institutional funding or support. The decision to employ already familiar digital frameworks like Google Earth and Wikipedia rather than inventing new technologies were however not solely a question of producing a low-cost framework (even though that was certainly also a factor in allowing the project to unfold independently of the limitations posed by established arts networks and institutions, or funding bodies). As important, if not more so, was the need to appropriate already existing digital discourses and platforms so as to provide the users of the site a sense of the ordinary and the everyday. In this, *Radiant Copenhagen* was an attempt at eliding some of the standard mechanisms of the art world. *Radiant Copenhagen* can thus be seen as a continuation of the avant garde movement's belief in art as an independent and socially redemptive force with the potential to reflect and change our everyday lives. *Radiant Copenhagen* however diverged from the early avant garde movements' desire to act outside the normative and outside the lives of the masses. On the contrary, *Radiant Copenhagen* was envisioned as a phenomenon with mass appeal. It is thus significant that the project was by design intended to be widely and freely accessible via the internet rather than via art institutions and galleries, as is it important that the accessibility of the interface was designed to appeal to as many users as possible.

Open Work and Thick Description: Constructing Knowledge through Confusion

The content of the website was, like the majority of the content on the internet, dominated by text supplemented by sound, video and a range of interactive elements. The site consists of a closed system of hyperlinks connecting various locations in the city in a manner akin to the process described by Umberto Eco's *The Open Work* (1989). Eco recounts how contemporary mid-twentieth century compositional music had begun using partially undecided compositional aspects that did not provide a unitary and predictable course for the further form and direction of a given composition, thus leaving the arrangement of parts of a given work open to the public or to accident. Subsequently, this is what we have seen in the development of hypertext on the internet, ensuring that this kind of openness and interconnectivity prophesised by Eco has in many ways become the dominant way of structuring and employing knowledge. 'The open work' has accordingly shifted from being an artistic and academic ideal to becoming part of our common and everyday manner of perceiving and explaining the world. Indeed, as Ted Nelson, the American sociologist and philosopher who invented the term hypertext in 1963, the year after the publication of Eco's text, recently phrased it: 'HTML [the core structure of the internet] is precisely what we were trying to PREVENT – ever-breaking links, links going outward only, quotes you can't follow to their origins, no version management, no rights management' (Nelson, 1999). Yet what Nelson here critiques, namely the opaque and often perplexing nature of the internet, was one of the major strategies of *Radiant Copenhagen*. With over 400 individual entries interconnected in a myriad of ways, the possibilities of navigating the website are, if not exactly infinite, then at least multifarious. In addition, many of the individual entries openly contradict former entries, a deliberate strategy intended to evoke and make visible just how diverse and often dissimilar these entries really are (Figure 12.3).

Figure 12.3 The Quantum Suicide Power Plant.

Yet another example of an early and pre-digital inspiration for the project's unpredictable and non-linear structure can be found in *Topographie Anecdotée du Hasard* (1962) by artist Daniel Spoerri. Where Eco's text is important for its stress on openness and interconnectivity, Spoerri's is significant for its deliberate and meticulous emphasis on the seemingly trivial. Despite being several hundred pages long, the entirety of the book is devoted to a meticulous mapping and description of the objects on Spoerri's work desk. Accordingly, the book presents itself as a number of spatially related anecdotes, all of which take as their point of departure otherwise unrelated everyday objects. Nevertheless, while the different objects described have very little in common other than that they happen to be present on Spoerri's desk on a given day in the author's life, the flights of fancy elicited by the attempts at describing the objects eventually begin to connect radically different subjects through the book's own peculiar internal logic.

In much the same manner as *Topographie Anecdotée*, it was our intention that *Radiant Copenhagen* should present itself with 'a mass' large enough that its size and depth would allow its users to create an autonomous, internal logic specific to whatever path they might happen to choose, that is to say an amount of text sufficiently large that it would be difficult for any one person to accumulate, read and make sense of the entire site, and for any of the contributors (including the original core members) to survey, comprehend and control the project as a whole. The hope was for an imaginary Copenhagen to evolve independent of our control. We anticipated a city whose individual elements would seem strange and surprising even to us, its nominal creators. And indeed, this process succeeded to a degree that we are even now, half a decade after the completion of the first edition of the project, discovering entries we have not seen before.

In this, *Radiant Copenhagen* has deliberately mimicked Wikipedia. This is obviously the case structurally and technically, seeing as the site is partially constructed via retrofitted wiki-technologies. Yet even more importantly, *Radiant Copenhagen* deliberately copies the manner in which Wikipedia establish authority in terms of knowledge. For Wikipedia does not, as was traditionally the case in the sort of knowledge production familiar to us from, say, academia, the medical sciences or politics, establish authority through the status of the writer as an individual of expertise and of stature (the professor, the doctor, the statesman). Nor is it validated by the prestige of external textual references located outside the site itself (in the manner that for instance academic peer-review tends to validate its knowledge production through reference to a range of officially accepted sources). Rather, the informative authority of Wikipedia relies on an interconnected and collaborative community of a closed loop in which an individual point of reference is solely to be verified by the recognition provided by a similar point of reference in the same system. What is more, the internal validity of the knowledge provided on Wikipedia is bolstered even further by external use, simply because the site has become the first and increasingly only site through which a wide range of people gather their factual knowledge.[1]

The information provided by Wikipedia is however by definition always open, mutable and unstable. Open to revision by the entirety of users on the internet, and despite various safeguards and the conscientious and high standards of the majority of contributors to the site, the core structure of Wikipedia inevitably opens up for digression and manipulation. In some instances such manipulations are discovered, as when Walmart was proven to edit their own entries in order to present themselves in a better light. But often such changes go unnoticed. Accordingly, Wikipedia is often a political battlefield, a fact that has resulted in the decision of a range of splinter groups to create their own Wiki-sites over recent years. Regardless of their intent, these alternate Wiki-sites doubtlessly profit from the authority and supposed sincerity of the original Wiki-format, even as they constitute a revolt against the authority claimed by the original platform itself. It is in the vein of this tradition that *Radiant Copenhagen*'s co-option of the Wiki-style and structure should be read. In part-revolt and part-acceptance, *Radiant Copenhagen* deliberately copied – but also parodied – the semblance of authenticity, integrity and consistency that Wikipedia so convincingly present us with in the chaos of unauthorised voices that otherwise dominate the internet (Figure 12.4).

The ever-present map service Google Maps provided the second major technical and conceptual framework for *Radiant Copenhagen*. As opposed to Wikipedia, a site that strives for precise knowledge governed by a variety of internal checks and safeguards, the philosophy of Google is founded on a belief of an entirely individualised and free, which is to say pluralistic and non-exclusive, internet. Accordingly, Google's open API (Application Programming Interface) gives everybody access to integrate and remix maps and information from Google Maps on their own websites. Such information is frequently employed for commercial, academic or media purposes, but it is also employed in the mashup-culture of sites like Google Maps Mania (http://googlemapsmania.blogspot.com/). Sites like Google Maps Mania draw on the tradition of 'modding' commercial products such as, for instance, computer games, in order to create new and radically different versions than the original copy. Even as these modified Google Maps consciously

Figure 12.4 New Dyrehaven.

attempt to deviate from the normalcy of 'official maps', they nevertheless also rely on the authority engendered by the regular employment of Google Maps for commercial and academic purposes. Once again, and as it is often the case with alternate Wiki-sites as mentioned in the above, the status of modded Google Maps are not always apparent, hence the authority and provenance of such maps can be difficult to trace. In much the same way, users of *Radiant Copenhagen* will inadvertently be confused as they try to navigate the site for the first time, wondering whether it is an art project, a viral gimmick intended to promote a commercial brand, or perhaps an official site promoting the city of Copenhagen.

Out/site: *Radiant Copenhagen* in Media and in Public Life

Radiant Copenhagen has since its release lived a parasitic life. It has been discussed on many different fora and platforms, nationally and internationally. Opinions have differed as to whether it is a useful tool for city planning, whether it is a form of architecture, if it is science fiction, and so on. With *Radiant Copenhagen* appearing on academically inspired blogs like BLDGBLOG and sci-fi blogs like IO9, it has in its reception proven difficult to classify exactly what *Radiant Copenhagen* is, and what its intended use might be.

On the occasions when *Radiant Copenhagen* was mentioned by the mainstream media, such appearances were often linked to the fictionalising aspects of the project's ability to infuse the fantastic into contemporary debates about present-day Copenhagen. For instance, in the press releases sent out prior to the launch of the site, *Radiant Copenhagen* falsely presented itself as a subsection of *Wonderful Copenhagen*, the actual and official tourist organisation of the city of Copenhagen. One of these press releases described how a giant skull would take the place of the Little Mermaid sculpture, a reproduction of the heroine of Hans Christian Andersen's fairy tale of the same name and Copenhagen's most famous tourist attraction. The story of the giant skull was inspired by debates in the media about the decision to temporarily relocate the Little Mermaid to the World Expo in Shanghai in 2010 (which also happened to be the year following the launch of *Radiant Copenhagen*). Although the press release was but a minor part of a much larger whole, the story turned out to be sufficiently sensational – and apparently also sufficiently credible – that it ended up on the front page of the digital edition of Jyllands Posten, one of the largest national Danish newspapers. As other major national media outlets got wind of the fact that Jyllands Posten had been fooled, the story took on a life of its own. *Wonderful Copenhagen*, the tourist organisation with which *Radiant Copenhagen* claimed to be affiliated, subsequently released their own press release as a response to the non-event of the giant skull. Denying not only the veracity of the story itself, but also any and all affiliation with *Radiant Copenhagen*, it was for a time considered whether *Wonderful Copenhagen* should sue *Radiant Copenhagen* for disseminating false information (although this threat was never carried out). Strategies like these helped create a bridge between the inner and self-contained fantastic logic of the site itself, and the actual, contemporary world to which it was supposed to act as a comment on (Figure 12.5).

Figure 12.5 Copenhagen Skull.

As the incident of the giant skull illustrates, the imaginary does on occasion have a tendency to become real. While the press release was intended as a comment on the news media's tendency to uncritically reproduce press releases of a given story of the region's 'actuality' without further background checks as to their veracity, this minor and frankly speaking ridiculous prank ended up being taken absolutely serious. In this, the project proved even more successful than we could initially have hoped for. Envisioned as an attempt to reanimate the region of Copenhagen by inventing a new regional geography, *Radiant Copenhagen* was intended as a means to offer alternate visions of what Copenhagen is and could be. *Radiant Copenhagen* was an attempt at a manifold restructuring of the development through fantastic and, as the story of the giant skull exemplifies, often silly yet thought-provoking additions to the imaginary geography of the city of Copenhagen. While it would be naïve to think that a prank like the giant skull would alter much in the actual politics of the decision to ship off the Little Mermaid to Shanghai for the World Expo (she dutifully went as planned), it nevertheless managed to pose a range of important questions. Not only did it question the status of the Little Mermaid as national heritage, it also critiqued the status of institutions like the tourist organisation *Wonderful Copenhagen*. As self-appointed guardians of the reputation of the Little Mermaid, as of the official tale of Copenhagen as a city ('No Giant Skulls Here!'), *Wonderful Copenhagen's* aggressive attempt to control and repudiate any alternative narrative of Copenhagen proved a reminder that the imaginary of a given region is rarely entirely free.

The project's basic premise of letting the contributors come up with anything whatsoever for the project, no matter how ridiculous, fantastic or seemingly unrealisable, was an experiment in allowing the imagination to run wild. Nevertheless, such imaginative roaming was precisely intended as a means to set the collective vision of Copenhagen free from established patterns and entrenched ideas of what is fitting or not for the 'actual' and lived-in city of Copenhagen. The internet format made it easy for many contributors from a range of backgrounds to either describe or visualise fantastic and sometimes nonsensical ideas through the website, while at the same time anchoring these visions not only with a range of other equally fantastic visions, but with actual local geographies and already existing tales of these. In this, a project like *Radiant Copenhagen* acts as a counterpoint to the far more serious yet equally utopian pretenses at citizens' participation in a given region through public hearings. Such hearings are supposed to give voice to local citizens' concerns regarding new major alterations in a given region (the construction of a mall, the demolition of historic buildings, the construction of a new highway, the closure of a park), but are in fact all too often sham operations masquerading as democracy. It is of course debatable to what extent the project helped alter anything whatsoever in the actual streets of Copenhagen. Still, or so at least we hoped, our often provocative and sometimes ludicrous alternatives to present-day Copenhagen were intended to make both local citizens and visitors view the city as a new and open geography unbound by centuries of tradition. In addition, we attempted to set the city free from contemporary commercial and public interests trying to streamline and control any single and hegemonic narrative of the city.

Radiant Futures: Reanimating Regions in the Light of the Present

As a conclusion, it is fitting to question whether a project like *Radiant Copenhagen* had any lasting impact on the bricks and mortar, the streets and the squares, or the manner in which people live in the city of Copenhagen. The most immediate answer is likely no. Half a decade after the website was first launched, the cityscape continues to present itself much as it did before, a mix of Romantic 19th century ideals and contemporary concrete structures. On a lesser scale, however, we nevertheless claim the project to have had a tangible impact. At the very least, the project had an impact in terms of the manner in which we can view the city from alternate perspectives, as indeed on how such alternate perspectives can be established in the first place. To pick one example out of many, in a special issue on public space in the Danish architectural magazine *Arkitekten*, 'Who's Afraid of Public Space?', the editors employed an entry from *Radiant Copenhagen* about the disappearance of public space as the platform from which the remainder of the articles related. The entry from *Radiant Copenhagen* recounts how:

> In the period between 2060 and 2100, sidewalks, squares and other public spaces ceased to have a function. They became simply obstacles, areas that had to be traversed in order to reach private spaces similar to the ones one had left behind. There was little or no resistance as the government of Copenhagen sold off all public space.
>
> *Radiant Copenhagen*, 'The Fall of Public Transport.'

This is a vision that, despite its connotations of the fantastic, apparently struck a note in contemporary concerns about the specifics of present-day public space in the city of Copenhagen.

Finally, when we ourselves, the contributors to the project, look upon Copenhagen today, we cannot help but recall the alternative visions engendered by *Radiant Copenhagen*. In the place of the Black Diamond (the national library), we tend to see the Red Ruby, a brilliant reconstruction of the present-day building 'covered in red rubies from Myanmar' ('Red Ruby'). When we look at Frederiksberg City Hall, the monumental solemnity of the present-day building becomes a little less serious when we see not just the contemporary building and its function as a municipal building, but also its future manifestation as the Church of Soapology, the result of a religious awakening due to the mysterious phenomenon of 'a bubble 16 or 17 meters in diameter, all blindingly white, with a blue halo' ('Soapology'). And when we pass by parliament, the reverberations of the Underground Labyrinth makes themselves felt too. As the refuge of thousands of homeless who have taken up residence in the Under-River, a place partly controlled by 'divers clad in a neoprene variant of the characteristic khaki and red uniform of the Marxist splinter group Under-River Liberation Front (URLF)' ('Underground Labyrinth'), the often grim reality of the politics emerging from the nearby parliament become a little easier to bear.

Arguably, this novel and to some extent bizarre regional geography of Copenhagen is perhaps not quite here, not quite yet. But in imagining alternatives to the status quo, it is always on the cusp of becoming. For as Alastair Bonnett remarks in his investigation of *Off the Map: Lost Spaces, Invisible Cities, Forgotten Islands, Feral Places, and What They Tell Us about the World* (2014): 'When the world has been fully codified and collated, when ambivalences and ambiguities have been so sponged away that we know exactly and objectively where everything is and what it is called, a sense of loss arises' (4). *Radiant Copenhagen*, an example of an invisible city if ever there were one, tries to make such ambivalences and ambiguities visible in order to make us see not just the future, but also the present.

*Participants in *Radiant Copenhagen*: Rune Graulund, Maja Zander Fisker, Kaspar Bonnén, Stig W. Jørgensen, Palle R. Jensen, Ida Marie Hede Bertelsen, Peter Rasmussen, Kasper Hesselbjerg, Ulrik Nørgaard, Daphne Bidstrup, Andreas Pallisgaard, Kristian Haarløv, Anders Bojen, Kristoffer Ørum.

Note

1 An example of this is the manner in which journalists routinely employ Wikipedia uncritically. For with no further cross-referencing and/or with no fact-checking of the information provided on the site, such unsuspecting reproduction of wiki-knowledge in digital, print and visual media further legitimises aforesaid information in a closed loop in which Wikipedia both provides and affirms its contributors' claims.

References

Bonnett A (2014) *Off the Map: Lost Spaces, Invisible Cities, Forgotten Islands, Feral Places, and What They Tell Us about the World*. London: Aurum Press.

Corbusier L (1933) *La Ville Radieuse*. Boulogne-sur-Seine: Éditions de l'Architecture d'Aujourd'hui.

Eco U (1989) *The Open Work*. Trans. Anna Cancogni. Harvard: Harvard University Press.

Huyssen A (2008) Introduction: world cultures, world cities, in A Huyssen (ed) *Other Cities, Other Worlds: Urban Imaginaries in a Globalising Age*. Durham: Duke University, 1–23.

Massey D (1994) A global sense of place, in *Space,* in D Massey (ed) *Place and Gender*. Cambridge: Polity Press, 146–156.

Massey D (2005) *For Space*. London: Sage Press.

Nelson T (1999) *Ted Nelson's Computer Paradigms Expressed as One-Liners*. http://xanadu.com.au/ted/TN/WRITINGS/TCOMPARADIGM/tedCompOneLiners.html [accessed 31 July 2015].

Sant'Elia A (2009) Manifesto of Futurist Architecture of 1914, in U Apollonio (ed) *Futurist Manifestos*. London: Tate Publishing, 160–172.

13 *Tracktivist Topographies*

Mapping in the Marches and Marching on the Map in Rural Activist Walking Performance

Jess Allen

Tracktivism is a neologism that describes my nascent eco-activist performance practice in rural landscapes: walking along *tracks* with *activist* intent. The term was conceived as a tongue-in-cheek antidote to 'slacktivism': the sedentary practice of half-heartedly participating in political campaigns on the internet. In contrast, I wondered how the demonstrable, embodied commitment to walking alone on long-distance routes – with an overarching aesthetic borrowed from the tradition of walking art, but tempered with an ecological theme – might render activist commitment legible and ecological problems tangible. To this end, I wanted these walks to become a means of facilitating unexpected conversational encounters with the strangers I met. My hope was that by encountering others transiently and non-confrontationally on foot – whilst committed to the intriguing trajectory of a wider, unseen performance – it might be possible to create a space where conversations about troubling ecological concerns could unfold more freely. In this sense, I wondered how walking might be used as a means to slip through a gateway to a conversational territory where the dialogue itself can be free to meander, safely or subversively.

The geographical territory that I have been walking across for the past three years is the English county of Herefordshire, which lies on the border with Wales – the 'Welsh Marches' – between the counties of Shropshire to the north, Gloucestershire to the south and Worcestershire to the east, in the West Midlands region. It is here, in this richly fertile agricultural county that tracktivism has come of age: perhaps an unlikely location for performance art to flourish in the red clay soils, alongside the cider orchards and eponymous beef cattle, but a fruitful one nonetheless. The three very different pieces that comprise the body of work have been performed at a variety of different scales, durations and contexts: from month-long 'life performance' in my local parishes, to the week-long walking performances for the county-wide sustainability festival h.Energy week, and the nationally-promoted Herefordshire Walking Festival. The work has been made in conjunction with community craft groups, performed from a farm, and installed at a church café and in a commercial orchard. It is performance art that has been rain-drenched, nettle-stung and sunburnt; that has been fed cake and cider; that has got mud on its boots, and dirt under its fingernails.

Figure 13.1 'Here you can ...': a county boundary road sign with the Visit Herefordshire branding, Retrieved from http://www.hereyoucan.co.uk.

In the chapter that follows, I begin by offering a partial overview of Herefordshire as a county through the lens of my own particular relationship with it, both as a resident and a former local government landscape officer. I then go on to compare and contrast the three tracktivist performance pieces I have devised and performed here as an artist, in order that I might map the learning of my practice-as-research journey through these landscapes. At the same time, I hope to examine the reciprocal topographic imprint this 'region' has left on my own practice. Working and walking here has forced me to question how contemporary performance can both challenge and sit within rural communities, and what it might reveal about place. Here, I document and discuss what is emerging from this multi-layered 'mapping' in the Marches, in order to consider how a walking practice might 'perform' a cartographic imbrication of the regional and the personal, in turn revealing that the parochial is political (Figure 13.1).

Here You Can ...

> [In] Herefordshire ... we have the England of hamlets, medieval farms in hollows of the hills, lonely moats and great barns in the clay-lands, pollards and ancient trees, holloways and many footpaths, fords, irregularly shaped groves with thick hedges colourful with maple, dogwood and spindle – an intricate land of mystery and surprise. (Rackham, 1986/2000: 4)

One of the most rural counties in England, Herefordshire is a complex, ancient and multi-functional landscape that supports a great diversity of agriculture. There are five market towns – Kington, Leominster, Bromyard, Ledbury and Ross-on-Wye – arrayed around the central city of Hereford. The flood plains and meadows of the county's main rivers – the Wye, Lugg, Teme, Frome and Arrow – now support large tracts of arable crops and potatoes, alongside their (now diminishing) traditional use for stock-grazing. Hop-growing was once widespread, and is now more localised. Cider orchards – both traditional standard and commercial bush – are still a valuable part of the county's habitat, economy and identity. Until recently, the apple was the 'brand' symbol of the county, now replaced by a Hereford bull: the white-faced breed of beef cattle which is the county's best known international export. Increasingly, land is being given over to polytunnel-growing, predominantly of soft fruit. This makes the growing economically viable, but raises concerns at the substantial visual impact of so many hectares of plastic, which, in certain lights, gives the uncanny illusion of vast areas of flooding. True fluvial flooding *is* a significant, seasonal problem here, particularly along the River Wye, which can rise rapidly in response to high rainfall in the Welsh uplands. A dramatic change in weather patterns has given rise to a number of 1 in 100 year flood events even within the past decade: for those who choose to make the connection, climate change is tangible even in this seemingly immune, idyllic region of lowland England.

Environmentally, and for all its bountiful, bucolic appearance, Herefordshire suffers from the same denuded ecological functionality as many other lowland counties: an increase in the scale and intensity of agricultural practices has given rise to widespread fragmentation of semi-natural habitat. Socio-economically too, the local unitary authority, Herefordshire Council, recognises a number of key problems in the county including the second lowest earnings in Britain after Blaenau Gwent; one of the highest gender pay gaps in the UK; and one of the poorest provisions of affordable housing. Due to the dispersed nature of the rural population, social isolation and loneliness are significant problems, especially for older people without their own vehicle and/or living in remoter areas with limited access to bus transport and other public services. Demographically there is an ageing population, and also an ethnically and culturally homogenous one, though during the spring and summer months, the county plays host to several thousand migrant agricultural workers, the majority from Eastern Europe. Their presence here is generally welcomed, but pernicious 'rural' racism occasionally also surfaces, roadsign graffiti signposting a minority unease and reluctance to acknowledge that the 'foreigners' come here to do the work that locals are now infamously reluctant to take on (Anon, 2014) (Figure 13.2).

After agriculture, tourism has always provided a significant income for Herefordshire, largely due to the appeal and accessibility of the landscape to walkers, from the gentle undulations of its interior, to the more dramatic topography along its edges, the Black Mountains to the west, the Malvern Hills to the east and the Wye Gorge to the south. Indeed, the latter is arguably the birthplace of British tourism, being the dominant inspiration for William Gilpin's Picturesque movement in the late eighteenth century. This gave rise to a new enthusiasm for

Figure 13.2 'Poland/Moreton': a vandalised signpost between Burghill and Moreton.

appreciating landscapes for their scenic beauty, greatly popularising the British countryside as a destination for bracing aesthetic encounters with the natural world, often when accessed or appreciated on foot (Crane, 2007).

In 2001, the county was badly affected by the foot and mouth disease crisis and the Herefordshire Walking Festival was instituted the following year to signal that the county was once again 'open for walking'. This now-annual midsummer festival – which works alongside the smaller, seasonal, satellite festivals around the self-styled 'Walkers Are Welcome' market towns of Ross, Kington, Leominster and Bromyard – hosts over 30 themed and graded walks, devised and led by local volunteers. It is advertised nationally through its website and print brochure (Herefordshire Walking Festival, 2015).

The Personal Is Political

Of course, in spite of these pedestrian lures, I did not move to Herefordshire to become a walking artist. Originally from the west coast of Mid-Wales and fresh from a PhD in biological sciences at Aberystwyth University, I came here in 2003 to work for Herefordshire Council, mapping opportunities for landscape-scale habitat restoration. Later, following vocational and postgraduate degrees in contemporary dance performance, I went on to combine dance work with employment as landscape officer for neighbouring authority Worcestershire County Council. The opportunity to embark on a second PhD arose from my 2010 piece *Tilting at Windmills*, in which I had sought to reconcile these seemingly disparate interests, constructing a pedestrian performance that used long-distance walking between the wind farms of my native Mid-Wales as a vehicle to facilitate conversations about changing landscapes in a changing climate. It was in this way that I stumbled on a nascent methodology for eco-activism through the oblique medium of a rural, relational walking arts practice, one that I have gone on to develop through doctoral research in the Herefordshire landscape.

I describe this chronology to make it clear that my creative practice has grown with and is firmly embedded in my understanding of this particular place, informed by my acquired 'professional' awareness of the social, economic and environmental pressures and peculiarities of these landscapes. When US feminist Carol Hanisch wrote her famous essay *The Personal is Political* in 1969, she was defending the possibility that women sharing and talking about their everyday experiences – of domesticity, discrimination and oppression – could still be a valid, and validating, political act. She meant this in the broadest sense of 'politics' as being about power relationships and 'liberation' arising from the exposure of inequality within them (Hanisch, 1969/2006).

In developing my own eco-activist practice, I have, it turns out, unconsciously borrowed from Hanisch a great deal. Beginning in the domestic sphere and working outwards, I have been motivated to expose, through performance, the ecological imbalances and behavioural absurdities that personally concern me. In doing so lies the hope that they may also concern others, if made gently and creatively more apparent. And in providing a container for open discussion that is expressly artistic rather than overtly political lies the still more intangible hope that the work could somehow, ultimately, slowly or cumulatively motivate action. As part of my practice, I *also* aim to expose or challenge the ways in which I live – to share my own ecological 'ignorances' or successes – with the intention of demonstrating, as non-didactically as possible, how living sustainably might be 'tractable, pleasurable, and meaningful' (O'Shaughnessy and Kennedy, 2010: 566).

These characteristics situate tracktivism loosely between 'relational activism' (ibid.) and 'slow activism' (Heim, 2003). The former is the almost exclusively female practice of celebrating daily, domestic acts of environmental responsibility – the 'acts behind activism' – through openly sharing them with/in the wider community (O'Shaughnessy and Kennedy, 2010: 555). The latter, a coinage by performance theorist Wallace Heim, describes a field of activist performance that constructs situations to facilitate conversation between (an activist) performer and participant. They may be more or less open-ended, discursive and reciprocal but are also intended to be subliminally persuasive: the subsequent transformative potential of these encounters Heim describes evocatively as a 'slow contagion' (2003: 187).

Triangulating Tracktivism

The three Herefordshire-based performance works that comprise the current oeuvre of tracktivism are *All in a Day's Walk* (2012-13), *Drop in the Ocean* (2013-15) and *Trans-missions* (2015). Each has its own elemental theme: food, water and power, respectively. And each has a distinctive shape, scale, duration and season, collectively revealing how the form and timing of performance can unearth something different about and *from* place. The conception of each tracktivist performance is marked by the formulation of a score. Here I use the term 'score' according to the conventions of contemporary performance practice to describe a set of rules or instructions that are adhered to (occasionally subverted) by the performer(s). In the section that follows, I describe the scores for each work, then go on to offer some reflections on my own, specific experience of performing them and in doing so, walking a personal conception of 'region' into being.

1. All in a Day's Walk

All in a Day's Walk is a score for a month-long performance, in which I must live entirely within the distance I can walk away from home in a day, eating only the food that is grown, processed and obtainable within this distance. I must only travel on foot, accepting no lifts, using no public transport, walking for six days a week. I can accept no hospitality or food from hosts or visitors that does not meet these criteria. And wherever possible, I must cook only on locally-sourced wood. My walks are a means of fetching (rarely foraging) food, facilitating conversation with others – farmers and growers, shopkeepers, walkers, woodsmen, butchers, bakers, artisan cider-makers – in the process. We talk about the weather and the walking, but, invariably, we also talk about food, hunger and the space in between. The score has been performed twice: first in the frosts and floods of winter 2012 from my then caravan home on a mixed farm in the upper Wye Valley AONB; and six months later in the heatwave of summer 2013, from a cottage on the northern edge of the Forest of Dean.

The score derived purely from a concatenation of circumstance and curiosity; the need to establish a walking art-research practice that was consciously activist and could foreground the political in the rural; my desire to embed myself as an artist-activist within the landscape and local community; and a simple curiosity about what might happen when I walk from home. It was intended as a frame to draw attention to loss – of rural food infrastructure, seasonality, knowledge and connection. But also, as a female walking artist with a stereotypically male, 'heroic' solo practice (Heddon and Turner, 2010) I was really curious to explore exactly how far I *could* walk away from home in a day, measuring my own version of what J. G. Ballard called his personal horizon (Nicholson, 2011). Ballard's was determined purely by sightlines – how far he could see away from home – but mine would be determined by 'effortlines', with a metabolic twist: determinedly beating the bounds of the area that sustained me nutritionally.

It is curious to me now, given my deep-seated awareness of the vulnerability and complexity of agricultural food systems, that I naively thought the principal limitations I would encounter in the first winter performance were daylight and topography. But of course, in coupling an acutely local eating practice with a walking one – where calories consumed are perfectly coupled to those expended – my personal horizon contracted dramatically. Far from being a boundary I anticipated finding out in the fields, it snapped back like elastic to the shrinking contours of my own body. I quickly became hedged in by hunger; metabolically constrained by a seriously illogical food infrastructure – one that sees the oats, wheat and oil-seed rape grown on the farm where I lived – hauled as far away as Birmingham and Manchester to be milled or otherwise processed, and thus inaccessible to me.

In that first, winter performance – and as a lifelong vegetarian – I was entirely restricted to a diet of root vegetables from Aconbury and Stoke Edith; apple juice and cider from Putley; and eggs and honey from Brockhampton, supplemented with the sourdough bread, from Woolhope grain, that I learnt to cook on top of my woodburner with logs from Howle Hill. In the summer, I found myself largely subsisting on the indigestible combination of berries from Newent, duck eggs from Aston Crews and cheese from Dymock and Huntley, after the same wet winter I'd floundered through gave way to a delayed vegetable harvest. So the personal and political – topography, weather, physiology and metabolism – collided spectacularly within my own body, causing a dramatic implosion: the loss of over a stone in winter, and crippling stomach cramps in summer. In this way, a dysfunctional local food infrastructure was giving rise to a dysfunctional metabolic and digestive one.

Both performances became less about walking, and more about crawling my way back to an understanding of how to feed myself from what *was* available. How could I re-enter into a dietary duet, and a functional working relationship, exclusively with this region? Curiously too, with my rule to walk almost daily, it was also about making food that was *portable*, that could be taken with me and consumed while walking over the land that produced it, and that was sufficiently calorific to support that walking. (Boiled duck eggs, raw carrot, dry sourdough and improvised fatless beetroot-honey 'cake' were the best combination, I discovered.) The shape of the walks became an important part of this choreography;

walking daily to and from my home – in this radial, Tolkienesque 'There and Back Again' way – and to and from the farmers and vegetable growers arrayed around me, I was daily ricocheted into conversation with what was revealed to be a lively network of actors. Those I met shared their knowledge, with and through me, a viscerally embodied knowledge that was passed each night through the hub of my hearth. 'Region' thus started to become an alimentary assemblage of both produce and people, connected through the inextricable processes of my walking and eating.

The performances made curiously apparent how a bio-regional food infrastructure operates out of an eccentric range of spaces: improvised structures, sheds, kitchens, porches, milking parlours and honesty systems that seem ideally encountered on foot, being often unintentionally camouflaged, or at the end of torturous driveways and rural cul-de-sacs. These are places that might be unsuitable to the limited speed of noticing afforded by motor transport, but their dispersal would (normally) make the distance of walking between them (and the calories expended in doing so) impractical, reinforcing the oft-cited excuse for the rural necessity of a car. And also demonstrating how it was only the necessity of intense hunger that was revealing my own ignorance. After a decade of already ecologically-conscious, vegetarian eating in this place, I had not known there were cheap organic vegetables at Aconbury, duck eggs at Woolhope, apple juice at Aylton. When landscape historian Oliver Rackham describes (in the section epigraph) these landscapes as intricate, mysterious and surprising he could also be describing how that topography might be inadvertently obscuring the liveliness and the burgeoning functionality of newly emerging local food networks.

Throughout these performances, I maintained an internal – and sometimes external, expletive-laden – dialogue with place that shifted from the animistic to the anthropomorphic: I found myself becoming furious with what I perceived as the relentless and deliberate slipperiness of mud, that 'made me' so often slip and fall, and with the gradients (Marcle Ridge, May Hill, Harechurch Wood) that used up too much energy, too many calories. Or even in the delayed harvest of the summer performance, I got furious with the intractable, willful unavailability of the unripe, sometimes head-high crops I was having ironically to battle through (oats, maize, oilseed rape). In Tim Ingolds's taxonomy of linear travel he makes a binary distinction between the wayfarer, who mindfully travels *along* a path dwelling in the moment of moving, and the navigator who territorially travels *across* space with an omniscience granted by the map (2007). But, I would add that the hungry walker moves *through* – ankle-deep mud, waist-high crops – using energy she does not have to push through things she cannot eat.

The relationship between walking and eating was, of course, once a logically linear one. Walking to eat is unquestionably embedded in our evolutionary history and anthropological studies confirm that pedestrian foraging practices are still very much a way of life for tribal peoples: for the Foi of Papua New Guinea, 'journeying on foot "is never a means of getting from one point to another". Always on the look out for fruiting trees, quality rattan or edible insect larvae, [they] *work* their paths' (Weiner, 1991: 38, in Ingold, 2007). Far from exercising skill or ingenuity as a forager, I was demonstrating, through an almost clownish failure to thrive, just how far we have farmed out our responsibility for where our food comes from. And in doing so, how we have farmed ourselves away from the rich knowledge of our hunter-gathering roots and the practices of consumption it supported. Gary Snyder observes that 'our distance from the source of our food enables us to be superficially more comfortable and distinctly more ignorant' (1990: 184). By literally pacing out the distance of my own ignorance – of food producers even within my own parish – I was unravelling that comfort.

And so, *through* a walking-eating practice, my sense of what comprises this 'thing' called region shifted too. Sometimes it was people who were the dominant signifier, sometimes the terrain and crops, and occasionally something altogether older, larger and more complex: the geological, or the hydrological. And it was my interest in the latter – and how our nebulous understanding of 'water' intersects with our ecological responsibility towards it – that shaped the subsequent tracktivist performance piece that followed that autumn.

2. Drop in the Ocean

Drop in the Ocean is a score for a six-day walk in six concentric circles of daily increasing diameter, performed around an accompanying, interactive installation: the ripples around a drop ((((((.)))))). As the solo performer, I carry water in two buckets on a milkmaid's yoke: a visual provocation to encourage (literally) immersive one-to-one encounters with others. Trying to indicate that this is just strange enough to be interesting, but not so strange as to be threatening, I walk until someone looks or sounds curious, amused or bemused enough at the anachronistic sight to allow me to invite them to make a wish, placing their hand in the water of one bucket, taking a stone and transferring it to the other. In between, I ask them to hold the stone in their wet hand for at least 30 seconds, while I offer poetic instructions for how they might think about water in all its guises from the domestic to the political to the sublime: first memory of swimming to last cup of tea, the sound of the sea or the click of the kettle. The title of the work is of course a reference to its aesthetic, but also to its ethical pretensions: the dichotomies of scale apparent in how we use or need water; how we abstract it; how, in a changing climate, we increasingly have too little or too much; how impotent we feel in the face of ecological crisis; how 'small acts' of care nevertheless have cumulative power.

Drop was first performed in October 2013 around an installation housed at All Saints Church and Café in Hereford.[1] My walks began – uncomfortably for a 'rural' performer – in the pedestrianized city centre. Here, for all the squeak of my buckets and the yoke's bite into my neck, my first sense was, perversely, of blending in, merging with all the people similarly burdened with plastic shopping bags. My very first encounter was with a toddler and his grandparents; the little boy was so enthusiastic to make a wish, he plunged his whole arm into the water and got his sleeve wet. Menacingly, however, a security guard immediately materialised, asking me to move on. I later discovered that, unbeknownst to us, this open, city street we were on had become private property. In lending its shape to the walks, water was at the outset 'performing' as an activist provocateur; finding its way through the cracks in awareness that apparently public, civic, open-air spaces are becoming commercialised places where our freedoms – even the innocent act of carrying water, offering a free wish – are restricted.

Eliciting encounters in the city centre was problematic in other ways too: the incongruity of the yoke was a draw, but people's faces flickered quickly from amusement to uncertainty. This was not my stage, I realised: it was already too crowded and confused by the agendas of others – the charity fundraisers with clipboards, the Big Issue seller, or the silent girl dressed as a forlorn bunch of grapes, advertising the pub of the same name – making people too nervous of what they feared I might ask of them. But as I curved off into side streets, parks or onto the banks of River Wye, there was a palpable shift in the frequency and readiness with which people would stop, and engage fully – as if here they had 'permission' away from surveillance, control or expectation. The wishing process then took on rhythmic pattern of its own: a reassurance from me that it was free; the acceptance of the offer; the immersion of the hand; the choosing of the stone; the holding in the wet palm, as they listened and internally responded to the litany of aquatic 'thought provocations' I offered. After a moment's silence, they made their wish and almost invariably shared something with me – a story, anecdote, comment – about water, more or less political, more or less personal:

> *'Hm. We use too much water, don't we? Yeah'* – Hereford City Centre, three teenage boys outside Game whose heckling, after wishing, gave way to a sudden, quiet seriousness.
>
> *'Balancing the needs of recreation and navigation on the river is difficult'* – a bailiff of the River Wye fishing on a slippery bank in the rain, this conversation after he'd eyed up the yoke, looked up and down stream suspiciously and asked: '*This isn't for* You've Been Framed *is it?*'
>
> *'I think about water a lot. It floods off the fields and breaks up the road. But in future there might not be enough'* – homeowner, Upper Lyde.
>
> *'Sometimes I worry about water'* – walker on footpath at Shelwick Green
>
> *'I respect water'* – young mother on Walnut Tree Avenue, Hinton, Hereford
>
> *'We think about water a lot, don't we?* [father to young daughter] *Living next to a river that floods – sometimes it comes up to bite you'* – Greyfriars Avenue, Hereford City
>
> *'I rescued a thirteen-year-old boy from drowning in the Wye at Victoria Bridge: years later I moved house and it turns out his sister lived next door. She remembered me: "You're the man who pulled my little brother out of the river"'* – a man at Castle Green, Hereford City.
>
> *'You don't see those every day'* – a farmer commenting on my yoke as I walk through her farmyard. I realise it is as anachronistic and out of place here now, as it was in the city centre.

Of course, the routes were not, and were never going to be, perfectly circular. Walking in circles around a city bisected by a major river is an impossibility, given the paucity of even pedestrian river crossings. (In order to 'draw' the requisite circles on the map, I found I had to walk half circles on alternate days, mushrooming north and south of the Wye, out and back through the narrow conduit of proximal bridges Wye, Greyfriars and Victoria – vehicular and pedestrian, respectively – linking north and south of the city). Nevertheless, even the attempt at walking a circle became significant to what they revealed about this place, at least to me as the walker. Far from being *about* water, the piece came to reveal more *through* its symbolic form, the circular ripples of the walking challenging my long-held misperception of a rural-urban binary. Acting as virtual contour lines, the routes strode indiscriminately across arbitrary administrative boundaries, trespassed over thresholds of perception. Repeatedly entering, leaving, circling and tangenting with the city served to dissolve any sense of a boundary that might form a city-country binary. Instead it was replaced with a continuum of meetings – people, cows, terrain, traffic – and crossings – water, roads, stiles. In this way walks were revealing in their wake a plethora of micro-political minutiae, though no less significant for their 'smallness' (Figure 13.3).

Figure 13.3 'Where the only bovine left is a hollow bronze bull (outside Starbucks)': the life-size sculpture of a Hereford bull, installed in the city centre.

In my circumambulating routes, I was struck by the olfactory irony of walking the smell of cow manure on my boots back to a city that has just lost its livestock market to the construction of a shopping centre. Builders on the scaffolding around Debenhams took pictures of me on their phones as I walked past with my yoke. Coincidentally this on a day when my trajectory would take me miles out to the new purpose-built, sanitised, manicured, out-of-town livestock market, divorced from the city which had sprung up around it. There I noted that, with arid poignancy, the displaced drinking water trough – 'erected by public subscription in 1883' – is full of flowers. This, too, was on the same isobaric trajectory that brought me back to a city centre where the only bovine left is a hollow bronze bull (outside Starbucks). The orbiting nature of the walks thus delivered me repeatedly back to the city centre and to a neat full-circle realisation that, divorced from functional relationships with landscape and each other, now it was the *people* who'd become the nervous, skittish livestock: just like the herd of dairy cows I walked through that same day on their way to milking, goggling, snorting and curious at the slosh and clank of my buckets and the possibility I might have something for them, but too suspicious and wary to approach.

3. Trans-missions

Following on two years after *Drop*, *Trans-missions* was very much a walk for and of Herefordshire, or more specifically its people, and what my cumulative experiences of public engagement here had revealed to me about human disconnection at the root of ecological dysfunction. Taking place over five days during and for the annual county Walking Festival in June 2015, the route followed the electricity transmission lines that cross the county border to border, west to east. The rules of the score dictated that I must speak to or otherwise acknowledge every person I randomly encountered, forming an unbroken line of transmission. Carrying a rucksack of 50 low-energy lightbulbs, I gave one to each person who offered me a message to pass on to the next person I met, in exchange for, or response to, a message they had similarly received. Tied to each lightbulb was a hand-written invitation to a celebratory gathering – a midsummer picnic and outdoor art event with local food, apple juice and cider – that took place at the end of the walk, in the orchard where I live. There, a festoon string of 50 empty lightbulb holders awaited the hopeful return of each bulb that had been handed out.

The form of the performance was inspired in part by Herefordian eccentric Alfred Watkins, the amateur archaeologist whose 1925 book *The Old Straight Track* introduced the beguiling notion of leys or ley lines. These were the networks of linear trackways that Watkins identified by the alignment of ancient features [mounds, barrows, hill forts] in the landscape, and along which he proposed Prehistoric man would have navigated by sightlines. Very likely erroneous, they 'extend[ed] archaeology's lunatic fringes for decades' as Robert Macfarlane puts it (2013: n.p.). Nevertheless, I was interested in overcoming their subsequent and embarrassing mis-appropriation as mystical New Age 'energy pathways' by returning to Watkins's original (albeit flawed) thesis, which suggested leys were significant – and those who knew how to identify them 'powerful' – because of the navigational knowledge they 'embody' topographically. In ancient landscapes, such knowledge *was* power (Figure 13.4).

Now, of course, the landscape is covered and crossed by very tangible powerlines and I had long been interested in electricity pylons as highly visual landscape features that we have largely become immune to noticing. Our habitual blindness towards pylons seems emblematic of a more pernicious myopia about the future and a failure to take responsibility for what we consume, because of the collective amnesia of distance from where it is produced. And yet what powerlines serve to illustrate very effectively is *connection* – the idea that stretching into the distance is a continuous, purposeful 'thread' of transmission supported by the 'arms' of uncannily anthropomorphic pylons. So I hoped that a walking performance that followed the route of electricity powerlines could illuminate the pathways of energy infrastructure in rural landscapes, at the same time optimistically reinforcing parallel notions of ecological interconnection, human with more-than-human. I hoped that such a walk would also be a vehicle to facilitate conversations *about* energy – that which we purchase and use, but also which we possess and 'practice' as human individuals: the energy that allows us to care about anything, including how much energy we consume.

The 60-mile *Trans-missions* performance began on Hergest Ridge above Kington, on the western border with Wales on 16 June, and finished on Saturday 20 June atop the Herefordshire Beacon in the Malvern Hills on the eastern border with Worcestershire. The route took me across the rivers Arrow, Lugg and Wye, along sections of Offa's Dyke and Marcle Ridge and over the Iron Age hill forts of Dinedor, Kilbury and British Camp. It passed through the towns, villages and hamlets of Kington, Almeley, Kinnersley, Mansell Gamage, Bridge Sollers, Madley, Clehonger, Dinedor, Holme Lacy, Mordiford, Woolhope, Putley, Aylton and Ledbury. The pylons hove in and out of view, as public rights of way drew me closer or further away. The pace of the walk was slow: at the height of the growing season and before the harvest, many of the routes that crossed arable land were nearly impassable. I waded through waist-high wheat, barley and oats, got tangled in tripwires of oilseed rape, and battled through field margins and wastes of head-high ruderal herbs. In doing so I was made scratchily aware of the conflicts of interest in rural landscapes – agriculture versus recreation, 'nature' versus human endeavour. As I passed the stench and squeal of intensive pig rearing units and the ominous silence and ammonia waft of broiler chicken sheds – vast hangars that

Figure 13.4 'Tangible power lines': electricity transmission lines running alongside a track running between Kilbury Camp and British Camp in east Herefordshire.

hide out here – I was daily conscious of the misery our consumption can cause, and how the 'intricacy' of these picturesque, patchwork landscapes can so conveniently provide the place for hiding that away.

But in complete contrast to the other pieces, *Trans-missions* was resolutely *not* about revealing or unearthing gritty rural dysfunction or discomfort. Rather it was intended to reinforce the vitality of human agency. This derived from my concern that didactic activism or environmental threat-mongering was ultimately pointless when, at the root of our inability to make even small behavioural changes in response to ecological crisis, is a general reluctance to make changes in our lives at all. I hoped that by asking recipients to return the bulbs I gave them, I was creating the opportunity to perform an achievable act,[2] a small commitment to doing something out of the quotidian ordinary. Those who made the leap of faith to attend – and be rewarded with food and conviviality – were also participating in a shared responsibility to provide sufficient light to illuminate the gathering. The ultimate installation in the orchard thus became an 'illumination' on many levels: a literal one of place and people, but also a lit display of co-operative power and distributive agency – an agency distributed by and between people, trees, lightbulbs. The latter underscores, to me, the decentring ecological message of Jane Bennett's vital materialism in that it posits that 'the power to make a difference' is not only shared between us as human actants but is 'a power possessed by nonhuman bodies too' (2010: Ch. 3).

In being a vehicle – a conductor – for transmitting the messages about personal 'power' that I elicited from person to person, the walk was also a very literal attempt to carry – or hold up – over the landscape a sense of its inhabitants' beliefs, hopes and desires. This required me to relinquish *my* 'power' as an artist, and hand over the idea of any kind of activist message to the Herefordshire people I would encounter. I began by simply seeding the opening exchange, asking the first lightbulb recipient in Kington car park to reflect on what this encounter signified to him and how that might translate to a positive message for a stranger. And so I found myself transmitting 41 subsequent messages across Herefordshire that had personal power and resonance for the respondents but over which I had no ownership. Some were, to me, genuinely unexpected and inspiring: 'Get to know your neighbours/Don't be too hasty to judge others/Be grateful for difficult people in your life because they teach you how not to be.' But often I found myself frustrated by their saccharine and generic predictability – 'Live life to the full!'/'Make the most of all opportunities!'/'Always look after your health!' – and feared I might be walking a series of trite motivational car sticker slogans across the countryside. But what gave the messages genuine power, and gave me faith in the score, were the conversations and personal stories that unfolded in the process: the invariably-shared motivation for the message itself which ranged from experiences of overcoming illness, to addiction or bereavement, living with disability, and connecting with family across the world. All spoke to the 'energy' inherent in being – and surviving being – human, an energy that we need to explore and nurture in order that we can effectively look outwards at our wider ecological (inter)relationships and future on a hotter planet.

During the performance, I met a greengrocer, a pharmacist, village shopkeepers, dog walkers, farmers, publicans, parents and children, recreational ramblers, a fruitpicker in a polytunnel ('Life is beautiful. USE it!'), a market stallholder, householders in their yards and gardens, and even an electrical contractor who'd coincidentally worked on burying the powerlines at Eastnor in the Malvern Hills AONB, 'because …', he explained hesitantly, unsure of the terminology, '… of outstanding beauty'. One man in Aylton had recently moved to the area and was rediscovering the beauty of the natural world: 'even on the dullest day, look around you … it's beautiful'. Sometimes the message was presciently matched to the placename of an encounter's location: a peripatetic fishmonger delivering salmon at Hope Springs near Woolhope offered the hopeful: 'even the smallest light can vanquish the darkest darkness'. And to complete the journey, the final message – my own – was shouted out from the top of the Herefordshire Beacon, back west over the county I had just crossed, into the full force of an oncoming summer rain storm raging towards me (Figure 13.5).

Figure 13.5 The Herefordshire Beacon on British Camp in the Malvern Hills which run down the Herefordshire/Worcestershire border.

Although this performance took place entirely outdoors in the 'countryside', the lightbulbs themselves came to be a totemic symbol: something both everyday and domestic, but defamiliarised and foregrounded in the extraordinary context of an encounter on a rural footpath. They rarely gave rise to conversations or messages about energy *use*, but to interactions that were nonetheless subtly infused with a sense of it. But what the bulbs did signify most strongly, in the invitation to return them, was a commitment to act, to change, or to *make* change by exerting personal agency. On the evening of the summer solstice, the night after I completed the walk, 15 of the bulbs were returned by 35 people who ate local food, drank local cider, talked to each other, forged unexpected connections and made sense of it all amongst the slowly burgeoning apple trees, so emblematic of this region. Metaphorically and literally, in coming together from across the county and adding their bulbs to the festoon string, they were completing an electrical circuit to bring about an 'illumination' – a wider metaphor for enlivening ecological awareness through commitment to change in everyday life. And the empowering realisation that even simple gestures can reveal or do something that is both subtle, and (collectively) powerful, hopeful and beautiful (Figure 13.6).

Of course, in the cross-county route of *Trans-missions*, beginning and ending on the high ground of each administrative border, was the offer of both literal and metaphoric perspective: the seductive possibility that I could seize a complete

Figure 13.6 'The Big Hug': the straw bale structure at Dragon Orchard, near Ledbury is partly illuminated with returned lightbulbs on the evening of the *Trans-missions* final gathering, summer solstice, June 2015.

understanding of this place that has been both home and 'studio'. Echoes of the previous pieces were present: in the crops I had difficulty walking through; in a consciousness of what I was eating while walking; in the inconvenience of locating means of crossing water, interfering with my ability to follow the pylons as directly as I might have liked; in the not un-yokelike burden of my unexpectedly unwieldy rucksack – even 50 'light'bulbs can be cumulatively heavy. In this final walk, I imagined myself as a small, rucksacked, line-drawn figure on a page, treading the line of a topographic cross-section of the county that had nurtured, contained, informed and challenged my arts practice, the peaks and troughs representative of the theoretical challenges I have encountered along the way, that have been as much a barrier or challenge to my practice as waist high wheat or slippery red clay soils.

Walking to Work

What I have begun to articulate above is, by necessity, only a limited view of the myriad reflections on region that have emerged – often quite unexpectedly, certainly tangentially – from the curious cartography of a pedestrian performance practice. Herefordshire became my muse by default: it is where I live and, determined to work locally and sustainably, it became the inevitable setting for my art. This practice of performance-making 'at home', which embraces or problematises the 'limitation' of working entirely with the materiality at our immediate (geographical, physical) disposal is becoming a significant trope amongst ecological performance makers (e.g. see Lavery and Whitehead, 2012; Joyner, 2015). Indeed, the etymological root of ecology lies in the Greek *oikos* or home. And performative 'home-making' has recently been posited as expressly eco-*ethical* in that making use of intimate or vernacular spaces, working with minority languages, challenging quotidian domestic routine, creating relations and celebrating (or subverting) local rituals and habitats are all practices that serve to foreground our ecological enmeshment with place (Andersen, 2015; Joyner, 2015). As such they can facilitate productive dialogue with a particular locale and allow a regional voice to emerge. Of course, performance itself is also a form of *place-making*, as well as being an inherently 'ecological' process, which in Giannachi et al.'s conception is characterised by an 'exchange between the subject and the living environment of which they are a part' (2012: 13).

This processual quality of live performance is an important component of tracktivism. While Herefordshire has of course been the muse of countless others – including Gilpin and Watkins, but also famously Wordsworth, and later the Dymock Poets, and more recently a host of contemporary visual artists whose work is showcased in the annual countywide h.Art festival (Brightstripe, 2015) – the inspiration they have drawn from this place is so often based on a visual apprehension of, or sublime response to, scenic or pastoral beauty. In contrast, my contemporary ecofeminist aesthetic practice is one that is embodied, ephemeral, determinedly non-visual and non-representational (Thrift, 2007). Indeed, my intention has been expressly to challenge or bypass representation and fixity in favour of a *relational* aesthetic (Bourriaud, 2002), but one that, in physically traversing rural landscape, 'relates' to place as much as its people, at the same time as attempting to draw them both into mutual co-relation. In this sense, the aesthetic component of my work is very much tied up in its symbology – the shape of the routes, how I choose to walk, the objects I choose to carry and the signifiers that might be attached to them, the exchange or 'offer' that characterises each encounter – and how this continuously unfolds and refolds in the 'doing' of it. No tracktivist work can be experienced as a totality, even by me (who has no sense of what it is to encounter *myself* as the artist, for example) and even the practice of performing it gives rise only to a partial understanding of place, which is itself 'in process', and with which one can only 'intersect' at any given point in time. As Doreen Massey writes:

> to walk across a landscape with any degree of awareness is to pick your way across the locations of a host of unfinished trajectories. Their unfinishedness addresses our today … [T]he stories we stumble across are often entangled with each other … but they are autonomous too and lead off in other, unrelated directions … there are always loose ends in space. (2008: n.p.)

Nonetheless, my practice has been informed *by* this place in that the scale, shape and pace of my walking have had to respond to the character of the landscape and people. Herefordshire has slowed down the speed of my walking – through hunger derived from the infrastructure that placed so much of its edible produce out of my pedestrian reach; or from the difficulties of negotiating geology (slippery clay soils in winter) or agricultural land use (ensaring crops in summer). In reflecting on the reciprocity of my relationship to the county, I often find myself returning to Watkins's leys, and his endearingly fallible, quixotic attempt to codify or legitimise the ultimately intangible magic of this particular place. As Macfarlane writes:

> Moving through that fecund landscape, it made perfect sense that Watkins should have dreamed his straight-track dream in Herefordshire. The county felt to him like a kingdom set apart, ringed around by mountains and woods … and geologically separatist with its Old Red Sandstone. What he lovingly called its 'fertile undulations' had about them the bosomy cradlings of an earth goddess …. He imaginatively configured Herefordshire to himself as a kind of Tolkienish Shire, … in which myth and vision might muster themselves as a mist gathers. It was to him a deep-time landscape, which guarded its secrets carefully. (2013: n. p)

My experience of performing here tells me that its people might be said to guard their 'secrets' – their contemporary environmental fears or concerns – carefully too, at least from a stranger appearing to them on a footpath. I have been deflected or defeated by a distinctive, canny wariness on more than one occasion, causing me early on to reconsider how I approach the 'way in' to the moment of performative encounter that sits at the heart of my practice. In this sense, Herefordshire has also sped me up, encouraged me to find something more immediate to 'offer' – the wish, the lightbulb – that might be sufficiently attention-grabbing to become a talking point because it is both reassuring and familiar – the action, the object – but also precisely because it *deflects* attention or removes the *obligation* to talk. As such, these encounters might just as often remain simply a fleeting exchange without much language at all, in which case my challenge as performer has been to conjure into being what Eliot has called 'the unattended/Moment, the moment in and out of time' (1944: 44). As one encountee later wrote to me about her experience of being a 'wisher':

> In an intense week it was a moment of calm - of reflection and connection [...] both to the global issues embodied and expressed by water but also to myself – especially in that intensely personal moment of making a wish and dropping the stone into the bucket of water [...] next to the river – where I happened to meet you. That moment of stopping and being with you and taking a moment to be still and gather myself into a wish was very special. (Kate Gathercole, 2013: pers. comm.)

Perhaps then, rather than being rooted in the 'externalised' language-driven world of conversation that defines Heim's slow activism, tracktivism might actually be about opening up an internal perceptual space – which of course artist interventions in vernacular spaces often do – but one with a loosely-constructed activist frame in which participants are 'held'. And as such they become free to explore and contemplate a wider message of their own making, guided by whatever the symbology of the performance evokes.

The Parochial is Political

Operating as it does on this particular, small, intimate scale – one expressly dictated by the pace of rural walking in lowland Britain, the habitat in which it has evolved – tracktivism could invite immediate, alliterative criticism for being both parochial and pastoral. These formerly benign adjectives have, over the past century, increasingly become fixed in our lexicon as negative terms. The former is so often used to signify short-sightedness or selfish disinterestedness in wider politics, when it is simply the adjectival form of parish: a spatial, 'platial' signifier. More recently the term has been revisited – and championed – by Macfarlane and others, frequently citing Irish poet Patrick Kavanagh for whom 'the parish was not a perimeter, but an aperture: a space through which the world could be seen' (Macfarlane, 2003: n.p.).

What Kavanagh knew innately – and the participant's reflection above confirms – is that our scales of perception, local and global, can slide together more readily than we might think: performing and travelling exclusively on foot has meant that all my work has been played out at the scale of the parish, but in the performative imbrication of local (community) concerns with global (ecological) ones is perhaps an important reminder that the latter still exist legitimately in our own backyards in some form, and learning to care about what and who we *can* see is a necessary step in cultivating and practising 'ethical imagination' (Moore, 2013) toward that and those we can't. In this sense, walking here has proven to be a literal means of pacing out the perceived pettiness of parochialism. Though of course I remain conscious of Timothy Morton's argument that to have any hope of responding to ecological crises as large as the 'hyperobject' of climate change – his term for phenomena which exist on a scale imperceptible to humans – requires a gross expanding-outwards of our consciousness; a 'think[ing] bigger than totality itself' (2010: Introduction).

I am also aware of similar dangers that in so deliberately focusing on ecological 'loss' in first-world, rural contexts, one is reinforcing conservative pastoralism or overinflated nostalgia: 'let's pretend we had a land. Then we 'lost' it. Now fondly describe it. That is pastoral' (Clarke, 2006: 88). This type of thinking encourages a dysfunctional relationship with rural landscape in which it becomes reduced to a romantic *mise en scène*, a place that exists for our entertainment rather than one that is materially enmeshed in our own existence. But tracktivism's strength may ultimately lie in its rural camouflage: using a recognisable recreational form – walking – to unsettle the pastoral from within and politely foreground or worry at the invisible issues that hide in seemingly idyllic locations.

Certainly I feel that change can still be achieved by practices that work *inside* the settings and systems that they are seeking to critique and that employ what progenitor walking artist Richard Long so famously described as 'vocabular[ies] of universal and common means' (cited in Andrews, 1999) – i.e. familiar, quotidian practices, like walking and talking – as devices for deconstructing the present and reconceptualising the future. Because developing a politically infused walking art practice in Herefordshire has demonstrated to me that there is subtly provocative potential inherent in letting '… our ruralist yearnings, our collective desires for simple archaic pleasures, come together to celebrate a place, not simply of pastiche but [as] a landscape for political futures' (Clarke, 2006: 88).

Notes

1 Here I focus on my experience of the walking performance, but documentation and details of the installation are available on the website dropintheocean.org.uk.

2 I spent some time pondering and agonising over the ethics and cost of rural transport, especially people's access to it and how this might bias attendance in favour of those with 'means' to this kind of autonomy.

References

Andersen MF (2015) Temporary home: an ethical investigation into the ecologies of a home-making 'between wheat and pine'. *Performing Ethos* 5(1/2): 65–78.

Andrews M (1999) *Landscape and Western Art*. Oxford: Oxford University Press.

Bourriaud N (2002) *Relational Aesthetics*. Dijon: Presses du réel.

Brightstripe (2015) h.Art Herefordshire Art Week [Online]. Available at: https://www.h-art.herefordshire.brightstripe.co.uk (Accessed 12 December 2015).

Clarke P (2006) 'Pastoral' in 'Lexicon: P-S'. *Performance Research* 11(3): 87–126.

Crane N (2007/2008) *Great British Journeys*. London: Phoenix.

Eliot TS (1944) Four Quartets. New York: Harcourt.

Giannachi G, Kaye N and Shanks M (2012) *Archaeology of Presence: Art, Performance and the Persistence of Being*. Abingdon: Routledge.

Hanisch C (1969/2006) *The Personal Is Political: The Women's Liberation Movement Classic with a New Explanatory Introduction* [Online] Available at: http://www.carolhanisch.org/CHwritings/PIP.html (Accessed 14 December 2014).

Heim W (2003) Slow activism: homelands, love and the lightbulb, in B Szerszynski, W Heim and C Waterton (eds) *Nature Performed: Environment, Culture and Performance*. Oxford: Blackwell, 183–202.

Heddon D and Turner C (2010) Walking women: interviews with women on the move. *Performance Research* 15(4): 14–22.

Herefordshire Walking Festival (2015) About us [Online]. Available at: http://www.walkingfestival.com/5052.html. (Accessed 15 January 2015).

Ingold T (2007) *Lines: A Brief History*. London: Routledge.

Joyner S (2015) Ystum Brodorol: a score for indigenous gestures. *Performing Ethos* 5(1/2): 31–35.

Lavery C and Whitehead S (2012) Bringing it all back home: towards an ecology of place. *Performance Research* 17(4): 111–119.

Macfarlane R (2003) Call of the wild. *The Guardian*, 6 December [Online]. Available at: http://www.theguardian.com/books/2003/dec/06/featuresreviews.guardianreview34 (Accessed 10 November 2015).

Macfarlane R (2013) The truth behind Alfred Watkins's ley lines. *The Telegraph*, 31 May [Online]. Available at: http://www.telegraph.co.uk/culture/hay-festival/10076220/Hay-Festival-2013-The-truth-behind-Alfred-Watkinss-ley-lines.html (Accessed 14 July 2013).

Massey D (2008) Landscape/space/politics: an essay. *The Future of the Landscape Blog*. Available at: http://thefutureoflandscape.wordpress.com/landscapespacepolitics-an-essay/ (Accessed 23 January 2013).

Moore H (2013) *Encountering Others*. Presentation at TEDxOxbridge, Said Business School, Oxford, 1 June 2013 [Online]. Available at: http://www.henriettalmoore.com/2013/08/encountering-others-henrietta-l-moore-at-tedxoxbridge/ (Accessed 2 December 2013).

Nicholson G (2011) *The Lost Art of Walking*. New York: Riverhead Books.

O'Shaughnessy S and Kennedy EH (2010) Relational activism: reimagining women's environmental work as cultural change. *Canadian Journal of Sociology* 35(4): 551–571.

Rackham O (1986/2000) *The History of the Countryside*. London: Phoenix

Snyder G (1990) *The Practice of the Wild*. San Francisco: North Point Press.

Thrift N (2007) *Non-representational Theory: Space, Politics, Affect*. London: Routledge.

Weiner JF (1991) The Empty Place: Poetry, Space, and Being among the Foi of Papua New Guinea. Bloomington: Indiana University Press.

14 Animating *Terroir* in the French Alps

Rory Hill

> Terroir is territory linked to practices. Each place has its own *savoir-faire*. There are customs and practices that persist.
>
> (Interview with Mrs S [Reblochon producer, Haute-Savoie],[1] 11 June 2013)

> The countryside itself is largely an aesthetic construction, one that reflects the variety of aesthetic criteria that diverse social and economic actors and institutions bring to bear.
>
> (Miele and Murdoch, 2002: 325)

For us it began after lunch. For the two farmers, and their cattle, it had all started before sunrise. Three thousand feet up in the French Alps, in the picturesque village of La Giettaz, Susanne and Jean-Claude tended to their herd; they washed, fed and ensured each cow was ready for their annual climb to the high pastures. This late springtime movement of cattle from the valley up to the treeless grass meadows, or *alpages*, is an activity that has taken place for centuries in mountainous parts of Europe. It was an activity that I, and a few others, were lucky enough to take part in one sunny afternoon in June 2013. At heart, it is an activity that forms an essential, and more than ever visible, part of the *terroir* of the cheeses that are made in this mountainous, challenging region of France (Figure 14.1).

What do we mean by terroir? The short answer is territorial character. The long answer is what I have been trying to discern through research in and on France over the past four years. In essence, terroir refers to the constellation of elements, from soil and stones to stories and *savoir-faire*, which combine in a territory and impart character and quality to the food and drink that come from there. The terroirs of the wine regions (Burgundy, Bordeaux, Champagne …) are perhaps the most famous, but France is a land of terroirs: numerous, diverse, meaningful, political. Terroir lies at the base of applications made to the French government, and approved by the European Commission, for products to receive labels of geographic protection – mostly *Appellation d'Origine Protégée* (AOP) and *Indication Géographique Protégée* (IGP) – because it is incumbent upon those soliciting such a label to explain how the product is related to the place it comes from. Terroir is a well-known term with a wide-ranging evocative power in France, and it is often used in the making of a persuasive case for the authenticity and uniqueness of a product coming from a particular part of the

Figure 14.1 Climbing together.

country. In this chapter, I want to recount my participation in a practice that explicitly mobilises this concept, and show how visual and affective encounters with landscapes animated by particular practices allow the stories of a region to be narrated in persuasive ways.

We know that cows have been kept and cheeses made in this region for hundreds of years. Savoy's landscape [2] is marked by chalets, rough tracks, picket fences and endless sweeps of grass in valleys and on mountainsides, which explode in bright floral colour in the spring and summer months. It is a landscape that makes one think of *Heïdi*, or *The Sound of Music*, and it is a landscape that is home to a set of practices which result in cheeses that are famous around the world (see Ricard, 1998; Delfosse, 1998; Frayssignes, 2008; cf. Fumey and Bérion, 2010). The main output of Jean-Claude and Susanne, and of dozens of other dairy farmers in La Giettaz and neighbouring parts of Haute-Savoie,[3] is the soft, cow's milk cheese known as Reblochon. This is an invention with a long backstory. During the middle ages, farmers in this region often paid their feudal dues in quantities of milk. Some came to adopt a canny trick whereby, after having milked the landlord's share from their cows, they would milk them again (*re-blocher* in the language of the time), and obtain a dense, fatty second helping. With this extra milk, they would make a soft cheese for their own consumption, or to gift or barter with as a form of currency. The extensive grazing opportunities afforded by the mountain pastures meant that dairying has been a long-running pursuit, though the practices and economy of its performance have changed over time. Given the hard winters where snow covers those pastures for months at a time, and long before the fodder revolution allowed more predictable supplies of feed, farmers adopted the seasonal rhythm of *transhumance* – walking with the cattle up to the mountains in the spring to benefit from the rich grass and flora, and descending in late autumn to spend the winter in the valley. This movement is a highly visible means of understanding the geographical basis of the special character of Reblochon, and of other alpine cheeses. This transhumance is an annual rhythm, with farmers and cattle climbing in concert, one that is considered a major part of the region's agricultural traditions, and finds itself listed amongst the defining characteristics of Reblochon in its official production manual (*cahier des charges*) (INAO, 2015). It is a rhythm that has in general declined in importance in modern French agriculture, even though the '*sensibilité au pastoralisme*' or 'pastoral sensibility' on the part of consumers and tourists in France has never been stronger (Aubron et al., 2014; cf. Cleary, 1986; Lambert, 2006). And indeed it is a rhythm that I discovered being opened for volunteers to participate in by *Saveurs des Aravis*, a tourism organisation which seeks to connect landscape and local foods in these mountains. For somebody investigating the spaces and practices that make up terroir, and for somebody whose jaw drops at the sight of mountains, it was an opportunity not to miss.

So it was that I found myself mustering on a farm in the village after lunch. Driving up from the pretty lakeside town of Annecy, I had passed a mountain bike race taking place around the Col des Aravis, the mountain that separates La Giettaz from La Clusaz, and a location that offers breathtaking views over the Alps. Already I had seen cows and chalets, already I had seen, through binoculars, two daredevils racing down a tongue of snow on seal-skin skis, and all around me bodies were in motion contending with the steep slopes of this region. I was ready to tackle this landscape too. The walkers who arrived bit by bit at Susanne and Jean-Claude's farm were a mixed bunch: families, individuals young and old, the seasoned and the débutants, and they had come from all over. I talked to a lady who had moved down to the region from Paris some years before, and now, given its beauty and its active possibilities, had no intention of moving back. I also chatted to a mother who had dropped off her little boy – 'un futur agriculteur' ('a future farmer') – who, like many of the others, had his walking stick by his side. This was to be his first climb up the mountain alongside the cows. It was, his mother hoped, to be the first of many.

Carole, the lady from *Saveurs des Aravis* who had organised the climb, offered round some coffee and biscuits, and told us a little of what to expect. She had already been up one mountainside that morning with a herd of cattle; this was the second of the day, but not something unusual as, at this moment of the year, dairy farmers all around were climbing. Jean-Claude and Susanne, who ran the farm where we had assembled, and had been up since four in the morning, were already way up ahead of us – the plan was to walk up and join them en route. We piled into a bus for a short drive up to the highest point of the village and there began walking. We were in woods, climbing constantly, and I used this time to look for a stick like the others all had in their possession. Eventually I found one that was just right, and used it for extra propulsion as the trail began to steepen.

When we emerged from the tree cover, I saw the valley plunging off to the right. The pitched roofs of La Giettaz were below us, and my eye followed the bends of the Arly River, down the valley to the town of Flumet. I switched on my camera and began taking photos. After walking a short while longer, we met up with Susanne, Jean-Claude and their handful of assistants. The cows were with them, grazing excitedly on the side of the track, waiting expectantly for more exercise. Now fully assembled, we all started making our way up together. To begin with, we stayed ahead of the cows, always looking back curiously, pointing and taking photos, but bit by bit the group lengthened out and people and cows mingled together. The process of walking with cows was a constantly interesting one. In general, they were docile, not too much trouble; but an eye had to be kept on them all the way. Carole had explained to us that because they had been penned in for months, they had been exercised outside daily for two weeks before making the journey "pour qu'elles puissent refaire les muscles" ("so that they could build up their strength again"). Now, out in the mountain air, smelling the lush grass on the side of the track, and enjoying that soft terrain under their hooves, every now and then some of these pretty brown and white heifers would err onto the slopes, and would have to be encouraged back onto the track before all their friends followed suit (see Figure 14.2).

Figure 14.2 Sometimes the cows couldn't resist the smell of grass on the side of the track.

Each cow wore a bell, and the endless chiming was the background score to the entire journey. Over the clamour, I struck up a conversation with a man from the local agricultural office and carried on talking to him for much of the way. My questions about terroir had found an ideal respondent. He told me about his work on the management of the territory in the region, of biodiversity and his work with farmers, and promised I would hear more once we arrived at the top. A more pressing matter had to be dealt with first: crossing a stream where snow-melt was racing down into the valley. These became more and more frequent as we climbed. Some were easier than others. Most of us got at least our feet wet. Children had to be carried, and sticks were used to test the stability of rocks in the channel before using them as stepping-stones. The cows were a lot like us, in that they would happily cross a narrow or shallow stream, but when the going was more difficult they proceeded in conference with each other, searching out the best place to cross and encouraging one another, with noise, nudges and gestures, over to the other side (Figure 14.3).

It would be possible to read the whole experience of the transhumance in a sense developed by Tim Ingold and by several cultural geographers, i.e. that it was a chance to observe *and* participate, to appreciate the landscape as a cultural image but also to see, and to some extent share, its dwelling and fashioning through a series of tasks (Ingold, 1993, 2000; Cloke and Jones, 2001; Wylie, 2005; Duncan and Duncan, 2010). The idea of terroir emerging or at least being

Figure 14.3 Cattle and people finding their way across the stream.

better understood through this experience depends on visual and haptic processes. Olsson's (2007: 89) 'primitive epistemological tools' of eyes and index fingers were certainly the first to encounter and be guided in the encountering of the terroir of this region. But whilst they were the tools of immediate knowledge creation on the walk up to the high pastures, the mobile heuristics of the transhumance also led many to attempt to capture the experience using a camera, to mobilise the very human desire to record events and images on a more permanent substrate (Ingold, 2012; Cosgrove, 1984; Derrida, 1996). I have highlighted these actions in Figures 14.4 and 14.5.

Such photography allowed participants to frame their own visions of terroir, and to make sense of the events around them by grouping things together. In Figure 14.5 I have indicated in blue some of the possible frames the photographer may have used for her images. She could have focussed on the cattle in close-up, she might have chosen to include the farmer and the chalet, or she might have included all of the above along with the pastures and mountains in the distance. The important point is that, whichever of these she chose, the elements included could all represent the terroir of the product that results from their interaction. This June expedition presented participants, including me, with the opportunity to see and be shown, to make sense of and be guided to sense, the terroir of Reblochon and other alpine cheeses. The memories stored and the images created could enter the circulation of similar montane images used in the commercial promotion of the product by its producers. In short, we were all producing images of terroir just as we were walking through it.

Figure 14.4 Recording images with a camera.

Figure 14.5 Recording images with a camera.

Like the cows, we also got tired and hungry. Watching the cycle race earlier on the other side of the Col, I had noticed the refreshment stands, where volunteers were handing out orange segments and words of encouragement to the tiring participants. We were lucky enough to also enjoy refreshment en route, with tables being set up in front of chalets, ever more isolated, as we climbed higher and higher. At one, a bearded fellow cheerfully offered drinks to the walkers. 'What's on offer?' I asked, stopping and wiping my brow. 'Apple juice, orange juice,' replied the man, then after an instant, moving his hand to the right of the table, 'Some white wine, some red …' This piqued my interest. I had just been discussing the relative merits of the traditional French diet with a fellow walker, and I felt moved to ask for just, 'A little drop of red.' Happily, the man filled the glass with a generous hand. As I chugged it down, I thought of those tired workers in the past who desired wine simply for its refreshment or for its calories, and not solely as a luxury to be poked and pondered. Here was local wine, being consumed to slake a thirst created by local work. Revitalised, I thanked the bearded fellow sincerely and continued up the mountain.

Indeed, as we climbed, we came across other chalets, places that looked like they had weathered the storms and snowfall of many years, and from time to time people would come out from them to greet us. One couple emerged with warm smiles and a bottle of wine, and talked with us for a moment. I guessed that these must be other dairy farmers who had already made the journey up, and were now settled in for the summer. Delighted to see the latest arrivals, there was a real sense of welcome, of togetherness, of repeating a long-held tradition of journeying up into the mountains. On the banks, our cows conferred cheerfully with theirs. Our particular journey was in the middle of the season. The long winter that lasted well into 2013 had already postponed our departure by a week. Each farmer has to study the conditions for him or herself and make the decision of when to go and spend their time in the high pastures. Unlike in Burgundy, there was no central, official 'banns' to announce the start of a regional period of activity like harvesting or climbing.

In the distance we could see remnants of that long winter, and its now dormant sporting activities. There in the distance, their summits shrouded in cloud, were the Mont Blanc and its surrounding peaks. The slopes of the Col des Aravis to our left had been, and were destined to become, the ski pistes of La Clusaz each winter, and there were more ski lifts and electricity pylons off to the right, amongst the trees. By the late 1930s, the village of La Clusaz was already well-equipped to host ski activity in the winter months, and this was part of a pattern that became established of the summer's high pastures being used for winter skiing. Many visitors would discover Reblochon for the first time in these holiday circumstances in the decades that followed the Second World War, and this form of tourism was a means by which its terroir was appreciated first hand by consumers with disposable incomes from outside the region (cf. Roybin, 1991; Delfosse, 1998). I was told that the annual arrival of thousands of winter sports enthusiasts to this particular mountain playground shifts Reblochon like nothing else. Indeed, it was mentioned to me that a sizeable proportion of all Reblochons made today are used in the preparation of *tartiflette*, a hearty dish of cheese, bacon and potatoes which, although based on a traditional Savoyard idea, is itself a 1980s invention of the ski resorts. Like us walkers, those skiers would get hungry, and could also be incited to 'eat the view'. So it was not surprising to discover that in the winter of 1979, a newspaper entitled *L'Echo des Alpages* ('Echo of' or 'Gossip from' the Alpine Pastures)[4] was established in La Clusaz to serve a readership of the small number of permanent village inhabitants and the much larger number of temporary visitors. The newspaper was at pains to make the reader aware of the Reblochon-producing heritage of the valley they were in. On the one hand, this involved advertising where Reblochon could be bought, and on the other, it involved extensive stories where a reporter named Marie would undertake interviews with Reblochon producers and other farmers and people of the village, such as Mr Bétemps (see Figure 14.6), a Reblochon producer and president of the local agricultural association, pictured holding a stick in a summer pasture with his cows around him. This was an image that was reproduced around me as I walked (see Figure 14.7). But in the newspaper, it was as if the terroir of the valley's pastures, which lay under snow and bore the weight of winter sports enthusiasts at the time of printing, needed to be rhetorically unearthed. To this end, actors, practices and *le temps passé* which may have been unfamiliar to the visiting reader were described in great detail, celebrated and to some degree romanticised.

Figure 14.6 Mr Bétemps, Reblochon Producer.

Source: Echo des Alpages, 1979; Archives Départementales de la Haute-Savoie. Used with permission.

Figure 14.7 With stick and cattle.

This buoyant winter sports economy still ensures a market for alpine cheeses such as Reblochon, and it is an association of food, place and tourism that has meant dairy farmers in Savoy often receive a more sustainable income for their product than dairy farmers in other, less visited regions of France. This is not to say that mountain dairy farming is *inherently* more lucrative than its counterparts in the valleys and plains – there is ample evidence from elsewhere attesting to its difficulties (e.g. Duruz, 2013; Squires, 2014) – but it is to say that today's producers of Reblochon enjoy the returns of the reputation of their product which has been built up over many years (cf. Bowen, 2010; Fumey and Bérion, 2010) and central to which is a notion of terroir whose authenticity is constantly associated with landscapes encountered and anteriority evoked.

As we continued to climb, now being told we were about half-way towards our destination, the landscape became more and more austere, and I was presented with images that transported me back to the physical geography textbooks of my school days. Streams gushed down the valley and scree littered the slopes of the snow-capped mountains towering above us. Up close, as we walked, we also came across pockets of snow, on the slopes that didn't receive much sunlight. I poked a patch with my stick, and pressed some in my hands. The cool slush was a novel thing to pick up in the month of June; the children in our group enjoyed playing with it. On the slopes, the trees thinned out, and in the end disappeared, though grass and flowers were everywhere abundant. At times, people remarked upon their beauty, and some produced pocket books of alpine flora to try to identify them. This biodiversity would also please the cattle when they would finally settle into their grazing. The alpine flora supposedly enriches the flavour and colour of the cows' milk and some can pick up the difference in the delicate taste of the Reblochon. In other parts of Savoy where hard cheeses are made, such as the Beaufort region, the flavour of this rich summer milk is more pronounced, and Beauforts 'from the alpage' or 'from the summer' are especially sought after, and command a premium price (Figure 14.8).

Figure 14.8 Snow and scree on the slopes above us.

What had started as a closely-packed group had by now extended to a long line up the mountain path, with cows and people interspersed, and two off-road vehicles moving at a snail's pace at the rear. Throughout the ascent, we had to move at the cows' pace. The several stops on the way were as much for their benefit as for ours because, as Carole explained, the cows do not regulate their walking pace like we do. They give one hundred percent and then run out of breath. For all of us, the mountains wouldn't give respite until the course reached its end. But these creatures could manage the terrain and the efforts required, and generations of their predecessors had made journeys of this kind. From the mid-19th century onwards, there was an acceleration of interest in the selective breeding of milking cattle in this region and more widely in France, with genealogies recorded and herd books maintained (de Planhol, 1994),[5] and this figures within the 'long and distinguished history of bovine biotechnology through which the bodies, ethologies and ecologies of cattle have been modernised' (Lorimer and Driessen, 2013: 251–52). In place of the adventitious admixture of cattle that had long prevailed – the 'bastardised' cows that slipped through the herd book classifications (Cholley, 1925:511) – improving farmers in the region had managed to double, even triple milk production by concentrated selective breeding of Abondance and Tarine in the late 19th and early 20th centuries and, furthermore, the cows were bred to get fatter. Arbos (1921: 213) recounts that in 1840 the average Tarine weighed 400kg, but by the beginning of the 20th century, it was 530kg. He also notes a 20% increase in the average weight of Abondance cattle over this period. Part of the reason for this was that farmers were adopting more 'rational' modern ideas concerning feeding practices (cf. Delfosse, 1994). And as Arbos puts it (ibid.: 232), this had effects elsewhere in the ecology of the production chain:

> In winter, the cattle were only given just enough that they wouldn't die of starvation. Wastage in the feed was not the only bad side-effect of this. In the spring, the animals threw themselves voraciously onto the grass, not without damage to their own health and to the state of the pasture.[6]

Those processes of modernisation were not visible to us; the land and cattle of our intensely present-tense experience did not communicate history in the same way archives can, but they could prompt further investigation (Dodgshon, 2008; Lorimer, 2010). We pressed on, passing what appeared to be the last of the chalets until in the end we passed over a crest and began a slight descent. A cirque opened up before us, and we saw in the distance the highest chalet in the valley – ours – was waiting. We walked down in a more relaxed, and tired, pace, and about a hundred yards before we reached the chalet, Jean-Claude passed, announcing our arrival, and the cows trotted instinctively off the track and onto the steep mountain pasture. They, and the two farmers, had returned to their highland home for the summer (Figure 14.9).

We assembled, red-cheeked and satisfied, in front of the chalet, where a table was set up and leaflets, pictures and plates full of cheese were laid out. Carole gathered us round and introduced Susanne and Jean-Claude, who thanked us for

Figure 14.9 The cows finally enter their summer pasture.

coming up and said a few words. Then she introduced our man from the agricultural office, who talked to us about the dairy industry, the terroir, and the geography and biodiversity of the region. He explained the origins of many of the things we saw in the landscape around us, and talked about his work on sustainability with the region's farmers. At every turn, the link between product and territory was made clear to us; at every opportunity, we were encouraged to appreciate what was unique about this region, about the agriculture that takes place here, and how these things might be worth protecting. And in these beautiful surroundings, the story was a convincing one. Høyrup and Munk (2007: 7) have made the point that the value of terroir can be 'hard to contest' when it is presented or recounted in a persuasive way, and we may note that such opportunities to encounter terroir, to make 'specific associations between product, history and the natural and social qualities of place' (MacDonald, 2013: 96), have spread far and wide in France, and indeed elsewhere, happening both virtually and in the field. My argument is that terroir is entered into a circulation of images and practices by actors who wish to promote, defend or profit from it. Several of the farmers I interviewed, in the Reblochon and other food chains, referred me to television programmes in which they had themselves appeared; one even gave me a memory stick bearing an episode of a programme in which he featured as something to view as part of my fieldwork. Organic farmers are profiled in the regular magazines of the French organic store *Sato'Riz*, farmers feature prominently in the long-running France 3 television series *Les Carnets de Julie*, in which the eponymous host travels throughout the country and discovers, then cooks, local specialities; and it would appear that farmers are particularly susceptible to appearing in tourist literature throughout France's regions. Given the almost country-wide coverage of geographically protected products, and the importance of gastronomy in tourist promotion (Lignon-Darmaillac, 2010; MacDonald, 2013; Aubron et al., 2014), we can imagine that terroir and those who produce things from it would be evoked in discourse and image throughout France's regions. In addition to this, tourist boards, trade associations and bridging organisations such as *Saveurs des Aravis* stage events at which interested visitors, and local people, can touch and taste, as well as see terroir.

Our man from the agricultural office told us that the region was in an 'équilibre délicat', a 'delicate balance'; those who worked in the dairy industry in the summer often took jobs in the ski resorts in the winter (as David, 1973, attested some years ago, and as was mentioned in some of the farmer profiles in *Les Echos des Alpages*). The cows grazing in the pastures today were maintaining those areas for their use as ski pistes in the winter; the continued activity in the mountains in the summer made economic and environmental preparation for their use in the winter. Ultimately, the extensive use of the relatively poor soils for cattle grazing was a level of agricultural activity that appeared sustainable. The fact that farmers made a reasonable return on the sale of their product, with a constant market based on winter sports, allowed this form of agriculture to continue in the face of pressures of property speculation here, the temptation of less geographically challenging farming conditions elsewhere, and competition from other cheeses everywhere. But the timeless appearance of the Reblochon-producing landscape, and the impression of practices being 'local, loyal and constant' that tales of terroir often perpetuate (see Pitte, 2001), can belie a history of dramatic change. Though narratives of tradition and authenticity have today largely replaced the narratives of progress and innovation that worked to transform the economy and ecology of rural regions in centuries past – and most spectacularly in the 19th century – it is still possible to sense today's sustainability as being an achievement relative to an economy of struggle in the past. Historical geographical work can serve to elucidate these changes. Clout (2003, 2004), for instance, has shown how although the pasturing landscape of the Pays de Bray in Normandy appears *natural*, attracts tourists and is celebrated in terms of regional tradition, this image in fact masks the many controversies, conflicts and transformations that it underwent over time. Farming in Savoy also underwent profound changes as processes of modernisation wove dairying activity more and more tightly into the economic life of the nation. For a long time Savoy was a poor region, a region of emigration, as imagined in Hippolyte Bellangé's picture *Le départ de petits Savoyards* and other 19th-century media. French geographer André Cholley (1925: 489) wrote that in the 18th century,

> This was a region of arable farming, and a poor region; the land was divided between fallows and wheat fields; connections to the outside world were very restricted – the region simply looked in on itself.[7]

But emigration of Savoyards throughout the 19th century facilitated the efforts towards modernisation undertaken in the last decades of that century by virtue of fewer people needing to live from the land. Archival sources show that by the time that Reblochon producers in the Thônes valley were forming a union and seeking a label of geographical protection for their *produit de terroir* in the 1930s, the population of their villages had significantly declined from what it was in the mid-19th century (see Table 14.1).

Like other parts of France, both agricultural improvement and economic integration accelerated in this region as the 19th century progressed, with farmers increasingly concentrating their efforts on those products that would sell in the network of national markets rather than for themselves or the radial lifeworld of local markets (Weber, 1976; Clout, 1980; Plessis, 1985; Braudel, 1988). By the late 19th century, in common with several other Alpine cheese production chains, Reblochon had found powerful external actors who valued it and whose money supported concentration upon quality; 'Reblochon went from the table of the mountain-dweller to the table of the bourgeois consumer' ('*Le reblochon passait de la table du montagnard sur celle du bourgeois*') (Roybin, 1991: 4). Moreover, the geographic facts of its production became ever more predominant in the region, as documented by Perpillou (1977a, 1977b): more land was dedicated to pasturing as the need to produce grain for the local population fell and, following legal changes, more of this land was in private hands. The potential supply of quantities of cheese to large urban markets was, as Clout found in the pays de Bray, 'better realised from individual pastures than from rough grazing' (Clout, 2004: 61). In their regional accounts, the French geographers Arbos (1921) and Cholley (1925) also argued that the rapid growth in the number of *fruitières* (central cheese production units) and professional *fromagers* (cheesemakers) throughout the 19th century changed the dairying landscape of Savoy, and this has been corroborated by more recent scholarship (Roybin, 1991; Delfosse, 1994; Micoud, 1998).

Ultimately, the old agricultural order of this region was irremediably transformed by improvements and specialisation; and, as de Planhol (1994) has argued,

Table 14.1 Population change in the Thônes Valley, 1848–1936.

Village	*1848 Population*	*1936 Population*	*% Change*
Thônes	2,919	2,563	–15%
La Baume de Thuy	341	181	–47%
Saint-Jean-de-Sixt	642	507	–29%
Le Grand Bornand	2,332	1,702	–27%
La Clusaz	1,202	1,005	–16%
Manigod	1,898	895	–56%
Les Clefs	756	443	–42%
Serraval	1685	418	–77%

the economic differentiation of national space led to what we might describe (after Muniesa et al., 2007) as agricultural goods *becoming* economic in new ways. Thus, by the time of Cholley's regional survey in 1925, instead of the 'nonsense' of wheat production in the Alps dictated by remoteness and necessity (de Planhol, 1994: 353), this region had become a '*pays herbagé*', ('grass country') wherein, 'Cattle have taken the leading role and the production of milk for *fruitières* has become the principal concern of all the farmers [*paysans*]' (Cholley, 1925). As well as the changes to the practices of pasturing and the nature of the cattle themselves, the improvement of methods of cheese production provided for a more efficient monetisation of the aptitude of the territory for raising dairy cattle. Economic adaptation fed back into territorial aptitude, and the changes that were wrought under conditions of modernisation (cf. Plessis, 1985; Harris, 1991; Oakes, 1997; Swyngedouw, 1999) contributed to the landscape dominated by permanent pasture which exists throughout the region today. Over time, Reblochon became part of the system of geographical protection in which the agricultural capacities and aptitudes of regions were appreciated at the national level and privileged within a national economy of goods. These modernising efforts began in the region of Savoy in the 19th century were so fruitful that in his 1925 regional survey, Cholley (1925: 1) argued:

> In the Thônes valley and on the surrounding plateaux, the adaptation to modern conditions has been very simple and very swift, thanks to specialisation in the production of a soft cheese: Reblochon, a real gourmet product.[8]

Hungry again, and now aware of some of the story behind the Reblochon produced through this seasonal movement up the mountain, Susanne invited us all to sample it. We ate, drank and chatted contentedly. An accordion struck up and some of the group started singing. I was informed that these were songs from the region, and there was an extra note of local terroir about the bandleaders, with their fulsome beards and feathered hats. I sampled the Reblochon and the Chevrotin cheese, which had been calling to me whilst I listened to the story of their production. They were delicious, and partnered beautifully with some of the local white wine we were offered. Whether it was the elation of the climb, the lack of oxygen at altitude, or the spirit of the company, I fancied that here and now I was savouring the elements of terroir in their most stunning alignment: the life of the cattle, the abundance of their food, the fragile beauty of the landscape, the annual rhythms through which it is put to use, and the tang of the fruits of that same land. This final act of tasting employed one final epistemological tool, that of the mouth. In some ways this was the most important act of the day. It was the chance for people to be rewarded for their labour in climbing, and for them to encounter terroir in a way that, whilst also stimulating nerve-endings and conjuring memories, would go beyond the work of the hand and eye in apprehending place and allow the product to be ingested, to establish an 'intimate biomaterial connection' with it (Roe, 2006: 118). If good food in France draws upon local knowledge, and 'embodies the traditions and rhythms of a particular place' (Whatmore and Clark, 2008: 403), the participatory transhumance ultimately provided both the food for thought and the food itself (Figure 14.10).

Figure 14.10 The group listening to a talk about sustainability and biodiversity in the region, before tasting cheese, wine and other local products.

After everyone had eaten, drunk and rested, Susanne and Carole manned a cheese stall on the table, which did a brisk trade (I myself acquired some to bring home), and then after saying our goodbyes we turned and headed off back down the mountain. I travelled back down at a gentle walking pace and chatted to some of the other participants. One of them thought I was a journalist. I explained that he wasn't far wrong. The transhumance we participated in was a mediatised event. I participated in its mediatisation, as did many of the other participants. I took pictures and was in pictures, I am writing about it now just as others have written about it. But terroir *has to be* mediatised, it has to be communicated outside its geographic origin, whether by word of mouth or more modern means. Buller (1996: 173) has argued that in France, 'agricultural heritage remains economically and socially rooted in national culture, notwithstanding the relative decline in numbers within the farming profession',[9] just as Frayssignes (2008) has argued that modern French society is 'in search of its roots',[10] and as Le Figaro (2012) has showcased what it describes as a national 'Comeback of Terroir'.[11] Visual, literary and tactile experiences are all necessary to allow France's majority urban population to appreciate the terroir they have inherited from previous generations both in its cultural value and its rural territorial materiality. However, as I have argued, a too delectable history can dissimulate some quite grounded discontinuities in the region's history *and* geography. Furthermore, whilst what I witnessed in taking part in the transhumance was, without doubt, an expression of long-established *savoir-faire* in the landscape, I cannot escape the fact that my participation involved a particular set of actions and images that were used as part of the promotion of terroir of the Reblochon food chain. Indeed, I featured in an image that was posted on the *Saveurs des Aravis* website and which thereby entered into the promotion of the product. Terroir lives through the circulation of images, products, practices and people. The animation of the transhumance, opened to a fascinated public, was a means to promote interest in landscape, product and region, as well as a means for me to attune to and be affected by the living elements of my fieldwork (after Whatmore, 2003; Wylie, 2005; Lorimer, 2010; Mol, 2010).

On the way down, we saw the Mont Blanc, and this time free of clouds. It was beautiful, majestic, and invited discovery and adventure. We continued our descent at our relaxed pace and eventually, eventually, I threw my new stick back into the forest and we came upon the rest of the group, waiting for us at the trail-head where we had been dropped off. A few others, the last few, came down, and then we covered the last couple of kilometres by bus to the village and the farm where we had started. Tired and happy, my feet damp inside my boots where the streams had overcome them, I climbed into my car and was ready to begin my motorised descent through the beautiful peaks of the Aravis towards home. I noticed the young farmer's mother had arrived to pick him up. He still had his stick, with which he had now completed his first transhumance. In light of what I had learnt on the way up the mountain about the sustainability of this annual practice, and the active desire to keep it as part of a living agricultural landscape, I reckoned it would not be his last.

Notes

1 In what follows, my own translations will be provided of text and speech originally in French. Some names of participants have been changed.

2 Some clarification may be helpful on the use of terms here. Savoy refers historically to the House of Savoy and the duchy and later kingdom under its control which covered parts of present-day France, Italy and Switzerland. In 1860, the western part of this territory, bordering France, came under French control and was entered into the French administrative system of *départements* as *Haute-Savoie* (the northern section, with the principal town of Annecy) and *Savoie* (with the principal town of Chambéry).

3 Concentrated especially in the Thônes valley.

4 Issues 1–11 are to be found in Dossier PER 640 at the Archives Départementales de la Haute-Savoie, Annecy, France.

5 See dossiers 7M 13 (Statistiques des bestiaux, 1879–1901); 7M 109–113 (Abondance Cow - Herd-Book, Concours, etc); 7M 124 (Inspections sanitaires des vaches, 1872–1914); cf. 7M 37 (Syndicats d'elevage des races Tarine, Abondance et Mulassiere, 1936–1938); ▲ 3432 (card index) (Rapport sur la nécessité et la possibilité des améliorations à apporter à la production du Bétail en Chablais, 1889) – Archives Départementales de la Haute-Savoie.

6 Tr: 'En hiver, le bétail ne recevait guère que juste de quoi de pas mourir de faim. La déperdition de produit n'en était pas le seul mauvais résultat. Au printemps, les animaux se jetaient avec voracité sur les gazons, non sans dommage et pour leur propre sante et pour le bon état des pelouses.'

7 Tr: 'C'était une région de cultures et une région pauvre; le sol se partageait entre les jachères et les terres a "bled"; les relations avec le dehors étaient fort restreintes, le pays vivait replie sur lui-même.'

8 Tr: 'Dans la vallée de Thônes et sur les plateaux voisins, l'adaptation aux conditions modernes a été très simple et très rapide, grâce à la spécialisation dans la fabrication d'un fromage à pâte molle: le reblochon, vrai fromage de gourmet.'
9 Tr: 'l'héritage agrarien reste économiquement et socialement enraciné dans la culture nationale malgré la diminution relative du poids démographique de la profession agricole.'
10 Tr: 'à la recherche de ses racines.'
11 Tr: 'Revanche du Terroir.'

References

Arbos P (1921) *La vie pastorale dans les Alpes françaises: étude de géographie humaine*. Paris: Armand Colin.

Aubron C, Peglion M, Nozières M-O and Boutonnet J-P (2014) Démarches qualité et pastoralisme en France. *Revue de Géographie Alpine* 102: 2–14.

Bowen S (2010) Embedding local places in global spaces: geographical indications as a territorial development strategy. *Rural Sociology* 75: 209–43.

Braudel F (1988) *La Dynamique du Capitalisme*. Paris: Flammarion.

Buller H (1996) Regards croisés: Angleterre, Irlande, France. *Etudes Rurales* 141: 171–74.

Cholley A (1925) *Les Préalpes de Savoie: Genevois, Bauges et leur avant-pays: étude de géographie régionale*. Paris: Armand Colin.

Cleary MC (1986) Patterns of transhumance in Languedoc (France). *Geography* 71: 25–33.

Cloke P and Jones O (2001) Dwelling, place and landscape: an orchard in Somerset *Environmental and Planning A* 33: 649–66.

Clout H (1980) *Agriculture in France on the Eve of the Railway Age*. London: Croom Helm.

Clout H (2003) The Pays de Bray; a vale of dairies in northern France. *Agricultural History Review* 51: 190–208.

Clout H (2004) The contested commonlands of the Pays de Bray. *Rural History* 15: 47–67.

Cosgrove D (1984) *Social Formation and Symbolic Landscape*. London: Croom Helm.

David J (1973) Les agriculteurs à double activité en Savoie et en Haute-Savoie: survivance ou renouveau. *Revue de Géographie Alpine* 61: 285–94.

de Planhol X (1994) *An Historical Geography of France (Translated by Janet Lloyd)*. Cambridge: Cambridge University Press.

Delfosse C (1994) Le savoir-faire des fromagers suisses de la France de l'Est (1850-1950) *Études rurales* 135: 133–44.

Delfosse C (1998) De l'illustration du genre de vie pastoral au produit patrimonial: Le statut du fromage chez les géographes alpins depuis 1920. *Revue de Géographie Alpine* 86: 15–33.

Derrida J (1996) *Archive Fever*. Chicago: University of Chicago Press.

Dodgshon RA (2008) In what way is the world really flat? Debates over geographies of the moment. *Environment and Planning D* 26: 300–14.

Duncan N and Duncan J (2010) Doing landscape interpretation, in D DeLyser, S Herbert, S Aitken, M Crang and L McDowell (eds) *The Sage Handbook of Qualitative Geography*. Thousand Oaks, CA: Sage, 225–47.

Duruz C (2013) Marché impitoyable: un agriculteur vend ses vaches aux enchères. *Tribune de Genève*, 20 March 2013.

Frayssignes J (2008) Démarches de qualité et développement territorial: quels apports pour la géographie rurale? L'exemple des AOC fromagères françaises. *Géocarrefour* 83: 295–305.

Fumey G and Bérion P (2010) Dynamiques contemporaines d'un terroir et d'un territoire: le cas du gruyère de Comté. *Annales de Géographie* 674: 384–403.

Harris C (1991) Power, modernity, and historical geography. *Annals of the Association of American Geographers* 81: 671–83.

Høyrup JF and Munk AK (2007) Translating terroir: Sociomaterial potentials in ethnography and wine-growing. *Ethnologia Scandinavica* 37: 5–20.
INAO (2015) *Cahier des charges de l'appellation d'origine « Reblochon» ou « Reblochon de Savoie »*. Available at: https://info.agriculture.gouv.fr/gedei/site/boagri/document_administratif-cadf8434-ef21-4e02-b107-206a7c561c06/telechargement (accessed 22 October 2016).
Ingold T (1993) The temporality of landscape. *World Archaeology* 25: 152–74.
Ingold T (2000) *The Perception of the Environment: Essays on Livelihood, Dwelling and Skill*. London: Routledge.
Ingold T (2012) Introduction, in M Janowski and T Ingold (eds) *Imagining Landscapes*. Farnham: Ashgate, 1–18.
Lambert D (2006) *Bergers et transhumance: pâtures, des plaines aux alpages*. Haute-Savoie: Neva Editions.
Le Figaro (2012) *La Revanche du Terroir* (Special supplement), 28 December 2012.
Lignon-Darmaillac S (2010) Les terroirs viticoles, quels enjeux pour l'œnotourisme?, in J-R Pitte (ed) *Le bon vin: entre terroir, savoir-faire et savoir-boire*. Paris: CNRS Editions, 331–38.
Lorimer H (2010) Caught in the nick of time: archives and fieldwork, in D DeLyser, S Herbert, S Aitken, M Crang and L McDowell (eds) *The Sage Handbook of Qualitative Geography*. Thousand Oaks, CA: Sage, 248–72.
Lorimer J and Driessen C (2013) Bovine biopolitics and the promise of monsters in the rewilding of Heck cattle. *Geoforum* 48: 249–59.
MacDonald KI (2013) The morality of cheese: a paradox of defensive localism in a transnational cultural economy. *Geoforum* 44: 93–102.
Micoud A (1998) Le reblochon de Savoie, ou comment mettre toute la montagne dans votre assiette. *Revue de Géographie Alpine* 86: 71–80.
Miele M and Murdoch J (2002) The practical aesthetics of traditional cuisines: slow food in Tuscany. *Sociologia Ruralis* 42: 312–28.
Mol A (2010) Actor-network theory: sensitive terms and enduring tensions. *Kölner Zeitschrift für Soziologie und Sozialpsychologie* 50: 253–69. Available at: http://dare.uva.nl/record/374993.
Muniesa F, Millo Y and Callon M (2007) An introduction to market devices, in M Callon, Y Millo and F Muniesa (eds) *Market Devices*. Oxford: Blackwell, 1–11.
Oakes T (1997) Place and the paradox of modernity. *Annals of the Association of American Geographers* 87: 509–31.
Olsson G (2007) *Abysmal: A Critique of Cartographic Reason*. Chicago: University of Chicago Press.
Perpillou A (1977a) *Utilisation agricole du sol en France: Première moitié du XIXème siècle*. Paris: (Map) CNRS.
Perpillou A (1977b) *Utilisation agricole du sol en France: Première moitié du XXème siècle*. Paris: (Map) CNRS.
Pitte J-R (2001) La géographie du goût: entre mondialisation et enracinement local. *Annales de Géographie* 110: 487–508.
Plessis A (1985) *The Rise and Fall of the Second Empire, 1852–1871 (Translated by Jonathan Mandelbaum)*. Cambridge: Cambridge University Press.
Ricard D (1998) Produits de terroir et normes de fabrication Les fromages d'AOC face aux nouvelles exigences sanitaires. *Revue de Géographie Alpine* 86: 103–14.
Roe E (2006) Things becoming food and the embodied, material practices of an organic food consumer. *Sociologia Ruralis* 46: 104–21.
Roybin D (1991) Typologie fonctionnelle des exploitations et evolutions de la production de Reblochon fermier en Haute-Savoie, in B Vissac (ed) *Milieux, Société et Pratiques Fromagères*. Paris: Société d'Ethnozootechnie, 3–17.
Squires N (2014) Rapid rise of forests changes the landscape for Italians. *Daily Telegraph*, 13 May 2014.

Swyngedouw E (1999) Modernity and hybridity: nature, regeneracionismo, and the production of the Spanish waterscape, 1890–1930. *Annals of the Association of American Geographers* 89: 443–65.

Weber E (1976) *Peasants into Frenchmen: The Modernization of Rural France, 1870–1914*. Stanford, CA: Stanford University Press.

Whatmore S (2003) Generating materials, in M Pryke, G Rose and S Whatmore (eds) *Using Social Theory*. London: Sage, 90–105.

Whatmore S and Clark N (2008) Good food: ethical consumption and global change, in N Clark, D Massey and P Sarre (eds) *Material Geographies: A World in the Making*. London: Sage, 366–416.

Wylie J (2005) A single day's walking: narrating self and landscape on the South West Coast Path. *Transactions of the Institute of British Geographers* 30: 234–47.

15 Performing Landscape Using a Locative Media Deep Map App

A Cornish Case Study

Lucy Frears, Erik Geelhoed and Misha Myers

In this chapter we explore whether locative media can develop a deeper connection with a region and its landscape. In the context of our research, locative media is defined as multimedia content delivered through users' mobile phones dependent on their geographical location. The chapter draws on the analysis of and reflection on data collected from users of the *Hayle Churks* app (2013) created by Lucy Frears using app-making software *AppFurnace* by *Calvium*. The development of the app was partly funded by a *Heritage Lottery Fund* (HLF) grant and created as part of inter-disciplinary practice-based research supported by the *European Social Fund* (ESF) and *Falmouth University*. *Hayle Churks* was published on *iTunes* in December 2013 and won a national *Collections Trust* award in June 2014. The app can be downloaded over Wi-Fi onto an *iPhone* and contains over an hour of audio content that plays automatically, triggered by GPS as the participant walks (walking includes wheelchair movement in this document) around the Hayle landscape. The audio content is accompanied by images such as archive photographs, old maps and a painting. In addition, there is an on-screen map that geo-locates the 'listener-walker-participant' (Myers, 2010: 70) at all times.

The audio content itself includes oral histories from the archive of the *Hayle Oral History Project* (coordinated by Lucy Frears, 2008-10), in addition to recordings made specifically for the app: a seven-part narrative called *Minnie's Story*, a layered field recording loop (with sounds recorded around Hayle), a musical loop (also containing Hayle field recordings) and three original songs. The binaural background loops open up a hyper-real three-dimensional aural sphere (Cardiff and Miller, 2012) around the participant's body pitching the senses out into the landscape to aid embodiment and the intertwining and interaction of human and landscape. The loop also performs the function of confirming the app is still working, but most of all it provides texture by mixing ambient environmental sounds (such as seabirds calling and waves) that bleed in past the headphones to mix with the recorded digital sound to create what George Bures Miller refers to as 'a third reality' (Cardiff and Miller, 2012). Reid and Hull describe the 'synaesthetic confusion caused when you are not sure if a sound is real or virtual' (2011: 197) as a 'magic moment' (2011: 197).

Walking with the app, the participant experiences an overlap between the landscape: the physical present and the digital past, pre-recorded oral histories, sound effects and archive images. The participant slides through levels of immersion between physical and digital realities, both experienced simultaneously (Figure 15.1).

Figure 15.1 After looking at the mobile phone interface with located map, archive images and instructions, audio memories and photographs lead the senses and imagination out into the landscape mixing digital content with physical reality.

Three-dimensional *Merz* collages by Kurt Schwitters (1887-1948) are a methodological inspiration. The artist, sound poet and sometime Dadaist used *Merz* to juxtapose, overlap and layer diverse elements and materials creating a textured, sculptural object to which others could add (Dietrich, 2006). As a methodological tool, *Merz* reaches through the practice into data gathering. On two of the three occasions data were gathered, qualitative and quantitative data were layered, overlapped and juxtaposed to compare, complement and draw out meaning.

Locative media, emerging as a mobile art form in the late 20th century, is still evolving rapidly and has yet not reached its potential (Stenton, 2011). Wireless invisible computing, locatedness and GPS technology behind locative media can be traced back to Mark Weiser, who imagined ubiquitous calm computing – quietly active out of sight enhancing our peripheral or sensory reach and available, or visible, when needed (Weiser, 1994; Weiser and Seely Brown, 1995). Invisible computing and the portable technology containing it – in this context, the mobile phone – combine to create the potential for an embodied locative media experience.

Although more recently associated with social and commercial apps, it is the more poetic and creative locative media experiences that this chapter concentrates on. There are claims that those experiencing locative media can 'gain a deep connection' (Farman, 2014: 6) with location. These claims, made by artists working in this field, those experiencing the artworks and recently theorist Jason Farman (2014), are more anecdotal in nature. The primary contribution of this chapter is to provide empirical evidence in this area. The practice and research around the *Hayle Churks* app uses systematic analysis, unusual in the arts and therefore distinct. Experimenting through practice and building on insights from others' artwork, experienced live or through documentation, includes revisiting empirical research on locative media containing audio narrative such as in *Riot! 1831*, made in 2004 (Reid et al., 2005; Blythe et al., 2006; Geelhoed et al., 2008; Reid and Hull, 2011). Since GPS technology was incorporated into smart mobile phones in 2008, what Goggin refers to as the '*iPhone moment*' (Wilken, 2012: 244), locative media has changed significantly, highlighting the need for new research at the confluence of regional landscape, locative media and art.

New embodied explorations in landscape by geographers (see Lorimer and Wylie, 2010; Cresswell, 2014; Hawkins, 2015), urged on by Crang (2003: 501), have bridged the gap, however temporarily, between human and landscape, a gap which has been articulated as a tension (Pearson and Shanks, 2001: 151; Wylie, 2006: 1, 2007: 475). Since the 1990s, embodied engagements with landscape using audio and walking have proved rewarding for artists and performers such as Janet Cardiff, Teri Rueb, Duncan Speakman, Graeme Miller and Mike Pearson. Historians and geographers are also making artful MP3 audio walks using gathered field recordings and oral histories. Toby Butler's *memoryscapes* (2005), memory walks along the banks of the River Thames, London, and *Kilmahew Audio Drift* (2012), a wander or drift around a ruinous site near Glasgow by volunteers and geographer Michael Gallagher, are two notable MP3 examples. The *Hayle Churks* app, using audio and image, is the first multimedia locative media research in geography's investigation of regions and intends to inform not only current dialogues in geography, performance and locative media, but other disciplines with an interest in region and its reanimation through the articulation of its histories, for example, history, archaeology, anthropology, heritage and tourism.

The *Hayle Churks* app aims to reanimate a deteriorating post-industrial regional landscape undergoing rapid transformation through rebuilding. In addition to reviewing memory archives, diverse sources were explored enabling community members and experts to share local knowledge, myths, personal stories, gossip, photographs and documents. Gathering, selecting and layering mixed and sometimes unexpected materials and media can be described as 'deep mapping', a notion developed and articulated by performer Mike Pearson and archaeologist Michael Shanks (2001: 162) and experimented with further during the project *Stalking the San Andreas Fault* (2001) by their friend and colleague Clifford McLucas (1945-2002).

Deep map content appears in the app as strata: layered multivocal histories of a region. App participants hear personal memories through headphones that bring voices into intimate proximity with the listener, right into the ear, words as close as a lover's breath touching the ear (Myers, 2011: 75). After the second test, a female writer wrote:

> *These are the human real stories and I felt privileged that they wanted to share them with me. The drunken father and the shame over a half-Italian baby were extra moving because of this closeness that having them in my ears affords – more than written text.*

Locative media can juxtapose varied deep mapping content, layering contested and non-hegemonic histories with a region's dominant narrative revealing new perspectives. Within the app, memories from different decades, from past and present, come and go as hauntings without introduction or contextualisation. Often, location is the only link between voices speaking of different decades and themes. Having no need to press a button to start the stories, the participant can control the audio by tapping the screen to replay, skip or pause stories. An archive image or occasionally a sequence of images can be viewed on the phone as each track plays. A participant can tap the screen at any time to switch to the map (appearing as a human shape on the map) to check navigation. The large number of archive images and historical map details can be viewed on site during the experience and/or afterwards at home.

Cornwall has been voted *Best UK Holiday Destination* 2009-2014 in the *British Travel Awards*. St Ives, an ex-artists' colony of around 11,000 residents, with cobbled streets surrounded by attractive beaches, is a top attraction and received over 750,000 visits in 2012 (The South West Research Company Ltd., 2012). Hayle, located on the other side of the bay, is different. The three-mile beach is hidden from view and still has fragments of World War II defences littering the easiest access point from the town. Once an industrial town with two foundries whose inventions spurred on the Industrial Revolution, it lacks the chocolate-box quaintness and scale of its popular neighbour. Most of its historic buildings have been demolished, although debris was left for decades before the surge of rebuilding in recent years. An Asda supermarket opened on the prominent South Quay in late 2014 blocking the view along the estuary (Hayle, or *heyl*, is Cornish for estuary) and dwarfing the terraced houses, viaduct and surviving historical buildings. The supermarket's placement nearly displaced the *Devon and Cornwall Mining World Heritage Site* status for the town and whole region (Smith, 2014). The derelict North Quay has been raised up on flood defences: promenades on different levels have been created between the working quay and large gravelled waterside real estate plots. Discovered heritage artefacts have been re-positioned and decontextualised, concreted in and left without explanation for passing strollers (Figure 15.2).

During Hayle's regeneration, Lucy Frears tagged North Quay with GPS and invisible aural graffiti. Just as ghosts are described as haunting sites, walking through walls built since they died, wading waist-deep through the road they walked on before it was re-laid, disembodied audio memories now appear like revenants. By placing the memories in relevant locations, oral histories are returned to the community and escape archive opening-hours restrictions and permissions. Improving community access could increase understanding of the historical significance of neglected areas, perhaps encouraging more sensitive local planning decisions, soon to be devolved to Hayle Town Council once its Neighbourhood Plan is approved.

Unlike an MP3 tour, the app does not follow a linear narrative. Neither does it stick to the town's standard narrative: the warring between two foundries at either end of the town in the early 19th century still tangible today. Participants instead overhear traces of the fraternisation between residents and US soldiers stationed in Hayle during World War II. Between happy tales of love, friendship and childhood pranks other stories rise up to be heard: racism against African-American

Figure 15.2 A new supermarket overshadows the start of the *Hayle Churks* app walk set in Hayle, a post-industrial Cornish landscape experiencing rapid change.

servicemen by their white countrymen that shocked the town, women's experience of inequality at work, what the most respected and powerful employer in town was really like to work for, plus murder, illegitimate children, betrayal and cruelty. Could hearing the past and present encourage a listener to reflect on the future and their legacy in the town and community?

App Evaluation Process

This chapter focuses upon what the 108 participants drew from the locative media experience in the app's evaluation, especially in relation to a connection with the region and its landscape. This will be addressed here in detail via three evaluations conducted between 2012 and 2015.

The First Evaluation

For the first evaluation the app was a work in progress. The area for the drift (no set route) started on an old bridge. Once over the bridge, the road forked, and one way led to North Quay. In derelict neglect during the evaluation, the quay once was extremely busy, with large ships loading and unloading cargo and many different industries based along it. The right fork followed a speed-controlled road with ornamental tropical gardens to one side and Copperhouse Pool on the other – once the location of Hayle's biggest day, the Regatta, and still a popular promenade.

The app was evaluated against a control measure, a professionally produced and scripted MP3 historical walk (Audiotrails, 2012). Although the app was developed for use on a smart phone, we decided to carry out the evaluation of both audio walks on the same device, a larger *iPad*. In addition to the app content – oral histories, narrative, live located map and field-recording background loop that played between clips – questions appeared on the screen that the user could reply to by text within the app. There were 'guerrilla interruptions'. Sounding like an incoming telephone call, the participant rejected or accepted the caller, *Counter Tourist* (Smith, 2012), an alter ego of performer Crab Man (Phil Smith), by pressing a button on the screen. The *Counter Tourist* encouraged alternative approaches to the heritage site through interactions and imagination.

For the first evaluation, during an unseasonably cold March in 2012, there were 25 participants. On the first day, eight students (two male) and a female lecturer from a second-year site-specific theatre module at *Falmouth University* participated. On the second day, 15 students, nine female and six male plus their female lecturer, came from a *University of Exeter* heritage site geography module. Three of the female participants were 37 or older, and the others were all 18 to 25. Each group walked both the app and the control measure (the MP3) on the same day, with lunch in between. Users were split into groups at the beginning of the day, order 1 (app first then MP3) and order 2 (MP3 first then app).

Although all students studied modules that included investigation of different sites, none had previously downloaded an MP3 walk onto their device or investigated a site using an app. All evaluators completed a pre-visit questionnaire (two sides of A4) and one immediately after the evaluation or MP3 walk (four sides of A4). Drift direction and button usage were logged within the app and we observed the students at intervals during the app walk, noting comments and behaviours. Text boxes eliciting qualitative responses were embedded into the questionnaire but the majority of questions were in a graphic rating scale (Stone et al., 1974) format. The advantage of graphic rating scales is to attenuate cognitive interference. In other words, it records more immediate, spontaneous responses by marking a line between two extremes rather than choosing a number or phrase that matches respondents' experience. Below is an example of a graphic rating scale question (Figure 15.3):

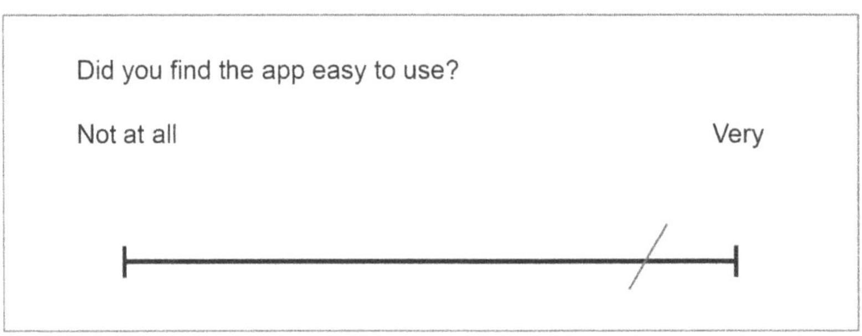

Figure 15.3 Graphic rating scale example: the mark on the line indicates this respondent found the app easy to use.

The questionnaire data was analysed using SPSS (Statistical Package for the Social Sciences, IBM) to identify statistical descriptions. Analysis of variance (ANOVA) was used to explore differences while correlations analyse similarities. Geelhoed used this type of questionnaire and analysis successfully in the empirical research on locative media narrative *Riot! 1831* (Reid et al., 2005; Blythe et al., 2006; Geelhoed et al., 2008). Key findings from the first evaluated app: a high and close agreement that it was easy to use; that it was good (although unfinished); and it received a significantly higher enjoyment rating than the published MP3 walk, which from qualitative feedback relates to the magical hands-off appearance of stories and enjoyment of the memories. App users felt less lost than they did walking with the MP3, although the app had no set route or directions. Participants using the app and MP3 noticed more than walking around without a gadget, but the MP3 scored higher because it informed users where to stop and look while explaining why they should do so. Of significance is that participants felt they had learned more with the app despite directions, context and facts scripted into an over-arching narrative in the MP3 experience, against traces of stories in the app that often had no connection between each other except place.

To summarise the correlations: those who felt more deeply immersed in the oral histories felt they learned more; those who learned more liked the app experience more; and those who felt they learned from the app also noticed more using the app. Some found the sudden appearance of media uncanny or disconcerting. Those who found the app disconcerting liked the overall app experience and felt deeply immersed in the app's oral histories. Theatre students linked stories to the location and were more immersed in them than geography students.

Themes emerged from the first app evaluation analysis, of which embodiment and levels of immersion will be discussed here. The experience of walking in landscape with a portable gadget and open app (computing and process invisible to the user) encourages an embodied and sensory experience of the physical world. Listening to the pre-recorded app content, mostly memories, some walkers simultaneously embody the physical landscape and the digital space – the space within the story being listened to. Smart phone and app use have become integrated into many users' lives. Experiencing and embodying two places at once is common with a mobile phone, of being *there* – with the person speaking at the other end of the phone or while viewing online content – as well as *here*. Straddling digital and physical worlds to enhance both is becoming the norm. This research adds a nuance, that contained within the '*hybrid space*' (de Souza e Silva, 2006) of '*being aware of two places at once*' (Hight, 2006: 5) or '*doubling-of-place*' (Moores, 2012: 14) are levels of immersion between physical and digital ends of the scale rather than staying equally immersed in both. What is in the foreground or background shifts; for example, a person speaking on the phone or speaking next to you while one is on the phone changes the level of engagement with the digital conversation or physical presence (Meyrowitz in Moores, 2012: 5). If one is too deeply immersed in the app's digital content, for example, an oral history, one can lose the connection with the physical present, as this participant in the second evaluation describes:

> *Because it was so good and immersive I felt disorientated and separated from the here and now.*

Stories encouraged some participants to look around, although immersed in both the digital memories and the physical landscape, as this theatre student explains:

> *Enjoyable matching stories to the landscape and seeing change.*

In 2004 a panel of practitioners, researchers and theorists[1] who gathered in Bristol defined locative media immersion as, '*that quality of the experience which held them in an imaginary or imaginative world, and left them feeling removed from the everyday surroundings of the experience*' (see Dovey and Fleuriot, 2011: 101). Immersion occurs more readily in art experiences that separate a participant from others physically or by using headphones, for example, during sound walks pioneered by artist Janet Cardiff (Christov-Bakargiev in Cardiff and Miller, 2012). One of the male geography students became separated from his friends during the first evaluation and enthused that it is 'Amazing, when you're on your own you get really involved in it'.

App participants were asked if they experienced a feeling of solitude, as it can be an indication of immersion, as Mauer describes '*isolation is a state of separateness while solitude is a state of intimacy with oneself and the universe*' (2010: 103). When asked if solitude was experienced, a geography student scribbled next to the rating scale, 'Very much but in a good way'. Reid and Hull's research illustrates that users flick in and out of immersion regularly during locative media experiences (Reid et al., 2005: 1736; Reid and Hull, 2011: 202). Reasons they identified are supported in our evaluation and broadened, including different modes of address and narrative, experimented with in *Hayle Churks*. Who is speaking and in what way they address the listener affect immersion, connection to landscape, enjoyment, and whether the participant is inspired enough to want to pass on the stories. Rather than feeling solitude, but still connected with immersion, a conviviality or companionship is felt by participants due to the close-up and intimate nature of some of the stories. Two theatre students explain: 'Feeling like I had company with the app stories, I enjoyed the company of the tracks *and* felt I was part of a group.'

Whether the evaluators felt *connected* to the landscape of this region is of importance. Interested in whether connection to landscape emerged as a theme without prompting, participants were not asked about it explicitly in the first evaluation questionnaire. Evaluators certainly connected with the *stories* from the landscape, which was the most liked aspect of the app and one many wanted to share with others. Some felt an increased connection to the landscape as these theatre students describe:

> *I felt more connected to the place and people and I felt a part of the history. Allowed me to understand presence and structure of older buildings as well as appreciating what is no longer there.*

Eighty percent of app evaluators said they would come to Hayle again and see it with different eyes, compared to only 53% after the MP3 walk. After using the app, 56% would think about the future of the area, while 48% would pay more attention to planning proposals in the area.

The Second Evaluation

In 2013, from the opening day of the *Hayle Heritage Centre*, 29 August, through 22 September, members of the public were invited to evaluate the app using *iPhone* or *Android* devices during a long looped walk of approximately two hours wearing headphones. Participants were self-selecting and invited via a *Facebook* page (reach of 2,000), local press (newspaper and radio), posters around town, requests forwarded through friends and organisations, and some of the *Heritage Centre* opening publicity. Sixty evaluators, 33 women and 27 men between ages 13 to 69 (87% over were over 36), completed questionnaires that once again required users to both mark the graphic rating scale and write reflective answers, to provide quantitative and qualitative data that could be layered and compared. There was only one strongly significant result involving gender. Responses to the question 'Do you feel more connected to the landscape now?' showed a variation between male and female responses. Women were in close agreement about feeling more connected to the landscape. Only a quarter of the evaluators (15 people) lived in Hayle.

The app now started at the entrance of the *Hayle Heritage Centre*, based in the old office of one of the town's two powerful, long-closed foundries. Participants walked along the harbour and edge of town to reach North Quay and Copperhouse Pool, experienced in the first evaluation, and onto the Towans (the Cornish word for *dunes*) and coast. A shopping street became part of the route in order to pass the location of the rival foundry. Here, participants strained to hear the recordings, and some struggled with being conspicuous by wearing headphones and walking slowly. A Hayle resident felt embarrassed by the 'She's listening to music on one of those "new-fangled gadgets" looks from the general public', and a local couple, retired teachers, told me of their amusement when someone stopped in front of them, wearing their headphones, and shouted, 'Rock n roll!'

In this app version, the changes included new interviews with younger voices to draw in contemporary Hayle, audio marked by dots, and a home page with a button called 'listen at home'. Once published, this 'armchair mode' would enable stories and images to be experienced at home (but it was not yet functioning). Findings from the second evaluation follow. First, the story from the quantitative feedback will be told, focusing on the differences between the answers and then the similarities between pairs of answers and what they reveal. Examples of quotes and findings from the qualitative data will then follow.

Quantitative Data: Differences

The bar chart (Figure 15.4) shows the means in descending order. In addition, Table 15.1 shows the standard deviation.

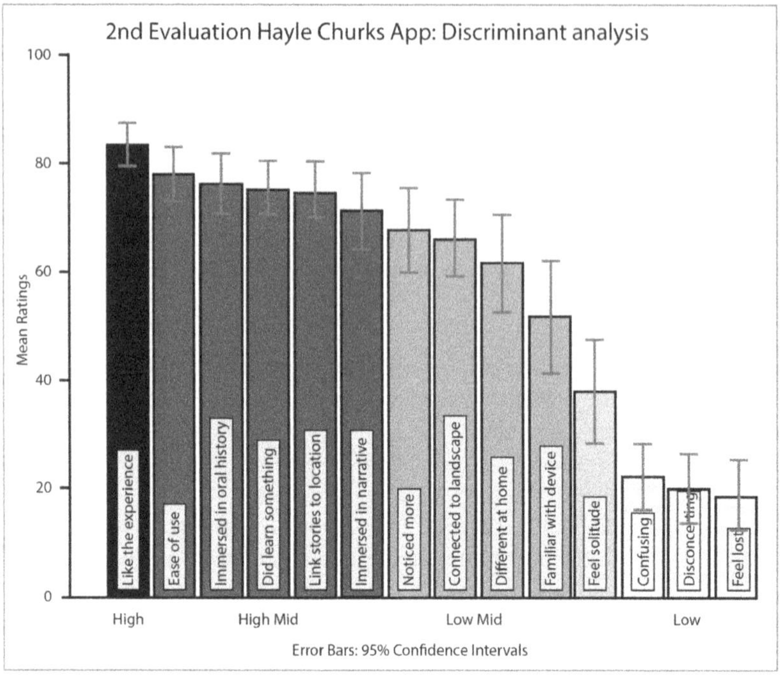

Figure 15.4 Mean ratings, second evaluation, *Hayle Churks* app.

Table 15.1 Descriptive statistics of the second evaluation of Hayle Churks.

Band	*Item*	*Mean*	*Standard Deviation (SD)*
	Like Experience	83.8041	14.27053
	Ease of Use	78.2558	17.83731
	Immersed in History	76.3188	19.52584
	Learn	75.7278	17.63785
	Link to Location	75.3250	17.99512
	Immersed in Narrative	71.3847	24.71554
	Noticed More	67.9309	28.11735
	Connected to Landscape	66.4015	25.21415
	Different at Home	61.6913	31.06762
	Familiar with Device	51.7451	36.65427
	Feel Solitude	37.9503	33.53204

Band	*Item*	*Mean*	*Standard Deviation (SD)*
	Feel Confused	22.2027	21.59264
	Disconcerted	19.9091	22.57037
	Feel Lost	18.7442	22.74821

We were able to delineate five significantly different bands of scores (indicated by the different grey shades, from black to light grey). For details of how these bands were delineated, please contact the authors.

High Ratings (Mean 83.80)

Liking the experience was rated highly by participants. In addition to the high mean 83.80, there is a low spread of the ratings (standard deviation = 14.27), indicating a high concordance amongst the participants. Enjoyment was rated significantly higher than all other ratings. In other words, it is not an exaggeration to say that the app was enjoyed tremendously.

High Mid Ratings (Means 78.26–71.38)

This band of high mid ratings (around the 75% mark) is made up of five items: *ease of use* of the app, being *immersed in oral history*, feeling that they have *learnt something*, feeling a strong *link between the stories and the location*, and being highly *immersed in the narrative*. Usability-wise, the app is very easy to use (mean = 78.23, SD – 17.84). Given the nature of a prototype this was very positive feedback. The ease of use helped participants engage with the content without the technology being a barrier. The spread of the ratings around the means was mostly narrow (most SDs are below 20), which means high agreement amongst participants. The high ratings in this band relate mostly to being highly engaged with the app and deeply immersed with the narrative situated in the location where the story takes place. However, this connectedness to story and location does not necessarily translate into feeling connected to the landscape. As we shall see next, the ratings for feeling connected to the landscape were significantly lower than this band of high mid ratings.

Low Mid Ratings (Means 67.93–51.75)

The next band of ratings, consisting of four items, is significantly lower than the previous band (high mid). There were relatively lower ratings for the app making one *notice more* in their environment and feeling a *connection to the landscape.* However, the ratings were, on average, still above the 65% mark. In this band we also see a higher spread around the mean with SDs ranging from 25 to 36, indicating less agreement amongst the participants. The participants did rate that experiencing the app in situ would be *different from* experiencing the application *at home*, but the mean was lower than one might expect and in addition there was low agreement amongst the participants; some rated it much higher (than the mean rating of 61.69) and some much lower. This is an odd finding, since one would expect a greater difference between being seated at home and roaming around with a mobile device during an embodied experience. As discussed later, some participants were so immersed and unaccustomed to hearing the spoken voice while walking that they kept their head down rather than looking around, which could have connected the content and themselves to the environment.

Comparing the high mid versus the low mid rating, we could speculate that the immersion in the oral accounts strongly linked to its location produces an experience more akin to those of experiencing a site-specific theatrical performance, that it deepens the connection to the *people* and *their stories* that are grounded in that location rather than being able to describe it as a deepening of connectedness to the landscape. Finally, participants rated *familiarity with the device* significantly lower than ease of use of the app. Almost half the evaluators (26) borrowed an *iPhone*. In spite of the appliance being unfamiliar, the app was still very easy to use, with very positive feedback about its design.

Low Ratings (Means 20.20–18.74)

We received more positive feedback about the app, as there were very low ratings for possible negative aspects, such as *feeling lost, disconnected* and *confused* by the experience. Interestingly, *feeling solitude* took up a statistically significant intermediary position between the low and low mid ratings. In addition, the SD was over 30, indicating a relatively wider spread around the mean. Maybe the notion of solitude has different ramifications for different participants? It could be a more meditative state for some, whereas for others it could be more related to a more negative feeling of being isolated: loneliness.

Quantitative Data: Similarities

In the previous section, we looked at where ratings differed and delineated five separate bands of ratings. It is equally insightful to analyse where responses to questions are similar, i.e. how pairs of questions co-vary, calculating 91 correlations between pairs of questions. Such a large correlation matrix is difficult to describe and interpret, so we used Multi-Dimensional Scaling (MDS), a technique that allows the depiction of a large correlation matrix as a two-dimensional plot. Figure 15.5 shows how close (or not) questions relate to each other. For consistency reasons, we use the same grey-scales as in the bar chart showing the differences (Figure 15.4). The size of the circles relates to the strengths of the correlations. For those questions where there were five or more significant correlations, we entered the number of correlations in each circle.

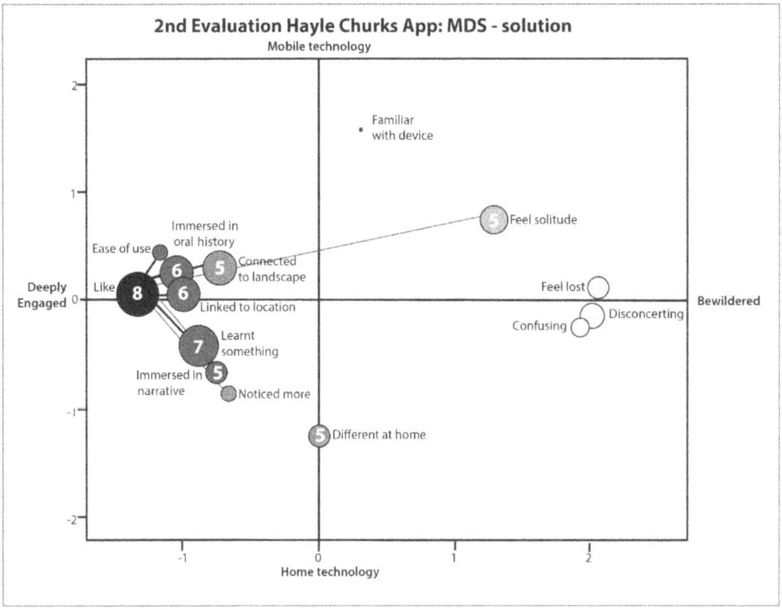

Figure 15.5 Multidimensional scaling, second evaluation, *Hayle Churks* app.

The question that correlated strongest with other questions was '*Liking the experience'*. There were five significant correlations at $p<.01$ (depicted as thick lines) between *Liking the experience* with *Ease of use, Immersed in oral history, Connected to the landscape*, stories being *Linked to location* and having *Learnt something*. There were three (slightly less) significant correlations at $p<.05$ (depicted as thin lines) with *Immersed in narrative, Noticing more* and (oddly enough) *Feelings of solitude*. Although correlations only show how responses co-vary and are not necessarily indicative of a causal relationship, it seems that those who gave high ratings for ease of use, being immersed and connected to the landscape as well as for the, possibly, more meditative feeling of solitude, find their culmination in expressing a high level of enjoyment.

We have interpreted the MDS scaling, the *Hayle Churks* design space, as follows. Most of the items are positioned relatively close to the x-axis. On the left, we find all those items that relate to being immersed in the audio app and connected to the geographical location, i.e. deeply engaged with the app (including ease of use). On the right-hand side, we see items that indicate a level of bewilderment, even though this level was low, signified by feeling lost, confused, disconcerted and, slightly separate, a feeling of solitude. As such, the x-axis runs from 'Deeply Engaged' to 'Bewildered'. For the y-axis we have not much to go on. At a stretch and only based on the location of 'familiar with the mobile device' near the top of the y-axis and 'different at home', we tentatively describe the Y-axis as one that relates to (experiencing) the technology.

Qualitative Comments

As illustrated in the quantitative data above, liking the app scored highly with all ages and genders. 'Liking' was unaffected by people walking alone or with others:

> *It added a depth and colour that I was not aware of.*
>
> *Feeling a different kind of connection with the familiar landscape through the stories.*
>
> *The app added another layer onto my encounter/experience of the place.*
>
> *I felt part of it, the place, the history, the people.*

The stories were, again, well liked; 42 out of 60 mentioned them favourably:

> *Range of stories: detail, personal, scientific and all the lovely Cornish accents.*
>
> *[It's like] going through a living museum – almost an abstraction, it becomes poetic, removed from reality* […] *Unusual because you used your imagination and intelligence to make sense of it. We think we want facts but they are quickly forgotten.*

More facts and context were requested by some participants:

> *The stories were good: I think we felt some contextualising e.g. direction of attention, place, dates, relationships etc. would help relate the stories to what is there now.*

Images viewed while listening to the stories helped some participants make the link between past memories and the contemporary landscape:

> *I liked how the images overlapped with what you saw.*
>
> *It allowed me to see the landscape in a completely different way and create pictures in my mind of how it was and visualise the detail of what went on there in the past. This would not have happened having not had the images in front of me on the phone and listening to the details in the stories at the same time.*

The disjuncture between the past – brought to life through memories – and the present became more of an issue as the area underwent change through building projects. Seventy-one percent of walkers reported that after the experience they would think about the future of the area as well as reflect on the past.

> *The experience made you concentrate on the surroundings and the history of the area and its future.*

> *Being here, hearing the voices and walking made me aware of the dangers implicit in managing change.*
>
> *It [...] makes me more inclined to preserve what we can and avoid developments that will change how Hayle looks and feels.*

The app exposed participants to long-term effects of local and personal decisions, which encouraged some participants to think about their own legacy and could encourage land stewardship:

> *It was curious to think that where I was standing/walking, people had stood before and will do again (with many similar themes e.g. family life), and it was great to have an insight into what happened in the past, and made me think about what memories I would leave to future generations of today's time.*

The Third Evaluation

The app was published on *iTunes* in late 2013. In addition to new clips and mixes, the dots marking audio points on the walk disappeared when played so that the map detail would become clearer. The route was adapted. The last section, through Copperhouse, the shopping area, was dropped, which forced participants to double back along the tropical gardens by the Pool instead of completing a loop. As an artist academic pointed out, it should have been made clearer that, 'It's what people in Hayle do, they promenade along this,' to make retracing steps more acceptable.

From May 2014 to April 2015, 25 people (8 male, 17 female) agreed to semi-structured recorded interviews after evaluating the app. Two female teenagers emailed their comments. From a group of 19 walking artists who evaluated the app, some of them makers of MP3 audio or filmed walks, eight returned additional comments about their connection to landscape after a six-month interval of reflection. Six of those questioned evaluated the first version of the app and 19 evaluated the second edition, which included small changes: code change to make the fades smoother and a second background soundscape loop. This multitrack soundscape of field recordings – birds in the air, cave acoustics under the earth and under the surface of the sea, for example – was layered with overlapped fragments of stories. Influenced by Glenn Gould's (1932-1982) counterpoint experiments with multiple voices played simultaneously in *The Idea of North* (1967), the collage of voices attuned the participant to an unfamiliar way of listening while transmitting the ghostliness of the disembodied voice. The *Merz* audio collage reminds listeners of many unheard stories and voices and the intangible nature of memories, which were noticed by this male geographer:

> *I quite liked the voices fading in and out – it was a bit like the past was there and it was gone – it didn't give you that false sense of I'm really knowing this. It was still that thing that you couldn't quite grasp, just given a glimpse of.*

In this app version, the walker encounters ('*the voices came to me*') 38 sound clips. The sound clips last from between 11 seconds to more than 4 minutes, containing one voice or multiple voices, some with sound effects or music.

Qualitative Data from Third Evaluation

The initial interview topic was left to the evaluators. Many mentioned technology and its functionality first. The qualities unique to locative media, the appearance and disappearance of audio and being able to locate oneself on the map at all times, were especially liked:

> *The freedom and accidental meeting feeling.*
>
> *The fact that I could walk and it could locate me and allow me to tap into the story of that site was really wonderful and I've not had that experience before so in that sense it was a really user-friendly application actually.*

Various modes of address were still being evaluated in the published app. Traces of oral histories were still well liked. *Minnie's Story* was pre-recorded and scripted to drive the walker towards the next episode. Minnie's 'black steps' episode often resonated because they could be seen, touched and stood on, though it also raised the issue as to whether some participants realised it was a scripted story:

> *There is an extra power when you think that in this very spot these people stood and this was happening [...] a bit uncanny [...]. You've also got that distance from it as well – talking about the ICI and power station, all that stuff that's not here anymore, so you've also got that slightly weird feeling of, my god, this was a really industrial landscape.*

The '*most immediate link to the present*' was through the voice of factual interviews. Human effects on the immediate environment, such as water pollution, dune erosion and climate change, were described, and more recent oral histories, such as with a younger fisherman, received a mixed response:

> *I liked those more contemporary things [...] could definitely have had more of those factual things in.*
>
> *Contemporary heritage of the fisherman that couldn't wait to go out and see his basking sharks. There was something really nice about that in the mix with the history that was very ... that resonated.*
>
> *The woman talking about the dredging and the* Surfers Against Sewage *[SAS] they were fine but they were so different that it was jarring as well [...] The other voices are sort of more intimate or something. They're not talking at you, they're just [...] going inwards to give you the memory whereas the SAS guy he was just telling you some stuff.*

In addition to the different voices within the app, Lucy Frears introduced Hayle to the *Walking Artists Network* (2007-) group and the town's contemporary themes (such as the Asda build controversy) before walking the app. Although it added another layer to their experience, the preamble exposed participants to the gap between the recent transformation of Hayle and the app content and initiated reflection on the difference between recorded and live voices:

> *I was actually enamoured by being shown by a person who lives and breathes and knows the stories of Hayle. So I had this kind of dilemma all the way through about the lived experience and the live voice and the mediated voice.*
>
> *[We experienced] your whole pre-narrative [...]and then we've got these kind of sepia voices – where's that voice going 'oh they built that and that went wrong' [...] If you could find the voices that linked bits of it maybe that would bridge that gap from the sepia into the now.*

Hayle inhabitants' daily activities passed by the walkers mirrored those in the oral histories and linked the past to the present for many participants:

> *...Bathing and having fun and being with their families. That was all happening around me.*

For participants looking for physical reference points to match the voices, Hayle locals became part of the app experience:

> *I had this kind of overlapping of the voice in my head and the people I met on the way.*

Engagement with Hayle's residents involved conversation and other acknowledgements. 'I smiled at him because I thought he was the one telling me the story,' said a performer who passed an old man on the quay:

> *I sensed my own person-ness in doing this and also the other people who spoke and it made me more inclined to engage with other people that we randomly met, like the children who were catching crabs on the side of the quay. They were great and I think if I hadn't had this kind of immersive sense of being part of a performance – it felt they were actually choreographed into it – I would never have engaged with them.*

Headphones made some walkers feel they 'couldn't properly say hello' but the effect of removing headphones surprised this participant:

> *I felt kind of lonely [...] I felt like I'd had a companion with me and my companion had left me [...] It was a much richer set of experiences that were going on while I was listening than when I just took them off and was walking.*

As in all evaluations, immersion was frequently commented on. 'There is something really nice about the solitude of it,' said a performer academic. Others, all women, found parts of the route isolated. Discomfort experienced by female walkers has been written about by Heddon and Turner (2012; see also Solnit, 2001) and was compounded during the *Hayle Churks* experience by ambient live sound being distorted and reduced by audio played into headphones. Women spoke of listening to their surroundings when alone in an outlying location in order to detect danger. Headphones immediately made them more vulnerable. In response to hearing about a reaction close to a panic attack, a male performer empathised:

> *The whole thing asks you to be hyper-sensitised so that's what will kick in. If you make that invitation you're going to get that response.*

Walking while listening to an individual's stories in headphones opened up the landscape and community to some participants rather than cut them off from it. An artist academic reflected on the experience six months after walking with the app:

> *I certainly think more warmly of Hayle because of using the app. I walked alone and the combination of solitude and the companionship of the voices made for a very intense, sensory experience of the place – the experience was intensified by the collaging of material.*

The embodied sensory experience and app content forged a connection between the participant and landscape as this female geographer explains:

> *I was also getting a connection to landscape by really looking deep into it [...] I was trying to look at the pictures and compare them to what I was seeing. I felt connected to the landscape, I feel much more connected to the landscape than if I hadn't done this.*

To encourage and enhance a more embodied exploration or sensing of place, strong stimulation of hearing through app audio content aimed to reduce the dominant sense of sight. Using the body to hear but also move, balance and experience different temperatures, weather and textured surfaces heightened senses. Sound – invisible, immaterial but affective – creates atmosphere and animates the landscape that moves past the walker like frames of a film. Composer and sound artist David Prior compares the binary of passive *listening* and 'active engagement' during *hearing* (2010: 95) to the increasing scale of attention in the sight descriptive terms 'seeing', 'looking' and 'watching' (2010: 95). Concentration or effort to understand (*entendre* means to listen *and* to understand in French [Iddon, 2010:7]) implies cognition during *hearing*. With '*no separable, disengaged and disembodied "mind"*' (Moores, 2012: 40) in the phenomenological experience, mind and body act together during the app, described as 'mindscape landscape bodyscape', extending a geopoetic notion of 'mindscape landscape' (White, 2004: 63; Legendre, 2011) by inserting the corporeal.

Active listening is needed to catch and process a live layered mix while moving – fleeting traces of external sounds, recorded sound effects, recorded narrative and sometimes internal narrative, although this was silenced for one female geographer:

> *The experience of listening to the voices, it throws you out of yourself into the landscape because you're trying, you're listening to someone and not listening to yourself [...] you don't have that little white noise of your own narrative going on.*

Unfamiliarity with listening cognition, the immersive quality of the work combined with the 'newness' of the locative media experience, were given as reasons behind those that experienced '*the head down listening thing*' rather than looking about them to connect with the landscape, a primary aim of the app. 'I suspect I listened and didn't look,' said a female artist academic. A male artist described why he enjoyed sitting down and listening to the tracks rather than walking:

> *I [...] was able to listen to them properly rather than listen to the contradiction between them and the environment I was in, or trying not to be in two places at once [...] but that's possibly my dyspraxia [...] having to really concentrate on what I'm hearing to be able to hear it properly.*

The sensation of being in two places at once, physical and digital, is part of the locative media app experience – but, as the comment above indicates, this is disconcerting and difficult to process for some people. The contradiction between the embodied physical reality and the (sometimes embodied) digital storied place was also hard to process. From a tourist's perspective, a participant commented, Hayle looks '*twee and peaceful*' so that it is:

> *A bit weird thinking of it as a really industrial landscape because that's not what you're sensing.*

There is a clash between the busy industrial or wartime Hayle in the app and the transformation of Hayle through new buildings, popping up late in the app-making process.

Conclusion

After collecting different media and content that can be described as deep mapping, an original layered multimedia app (rather than solely audio, the usual focus of audio walks research) was created during practice-based research. Locative media research is most usually found in urban environments with good Wi-Fi and mobile phone network connections. Instead the *Hayle Churks* app was developed in a challenging site off the main tourist trail: a marginal coastal area on the edge of a post-industrial town from which many visible historical traces, which could have linked past and present, had been removed. During the evaluations the participants walked into GPS zones triggering multimedia content. The combination of the physical experience in landscape and a digital layer, stories and archive images, shifted participants between physical and digital worlds simultaneously:

> *[The] app certainly introduced me to the landscape and stories of Hayle in an embodied way.*

As a unique contribution to research in this inter-disciplinary field, a deeper connection to landscape using locative media has been explored through three evaluations from a total of 108 participants. The app experience was quantified and supported with quotes from which these conclusions have been made. Located oral history traces produce a very enjoyable immersive experience. Nostalgic experiences make participants feel good and have deep effects on well-being, according to evidence cited by Robinson et al. (2015: 185). The more nebulous notion of feeling connected to the landscape definitely contributes to the enjoyment. Interestingly, being immersed in oral history and narrative, the performative aspect of the app, as well as feeling a (close) link between a particular story and its location, is rated significantly higher than feeling connected to the landscape. The app has a stronger (possibly temporary) effect around the performance and deepens the connection with the landscape, a more longitudinal philosophical effect, to a lesser extent:

> *Not so much 'more connected'... as differently connected ... connected to a landscape that is historical as well as present; connected to a landscape that is storied and narrated and animated ... connected to a landscape that is layered with meaning.*

There is intensity in the response to the oral histories and their connection to specific locations. Therefore the main connectedness was to the stories of Hayle grounded in the landscape:

> *There was definitely a grounding or rooting (in history) going on.*

Access to and participation with stories of place using locative media extends the potential of deep mapping and its exhibition and dissemination through rich media *Merz* layers and textures accessible on a mobile phone as demonstrated in the *Hayle Churks* app. The '*narrative archaeology*' (Hight, 2006: 2) of people's memories and place are played through the app in layered, sometimes binaural three-dimensional sound:

> *The landscape feels so dense when you're doing it. When I took my headphones off it sort of flattened.*

The performative aspects of the work, which kept participants listening and walking for around two hours or more, outweighed the deeper connection with the landscape. Participants felt connected to the location through the voices and stories of its community; digital (pre-recorded residents) and physical passers-by became companions along the route:

> *It is incredibly potent. From my previous visit to Hayle I found it a run-of-the-mill, standard Cornish town. During (and after) the experience I feel as though I have discovered my own familiar connections. The town feels three-dimensional, or somehow more solid, now I have heard these stories, memories and seen the photos. I wasn't expecting such a strong reaction but walking back once the app had finished I told my friend 'I feel at home here now'.*

To increase the connection to landscape for others, a stronger link with the location that encourages associating the story with the present could be trialled. Many mentioned the 'black steps' scene in *Minnie's Story* because it placed them in the same spot as Minnie's grandmother:

> *The really interesting parts were where the audio directly related to the location you were in.*

Using oral history recordings from an archive created before an app was dreamed of meant that the detail needed for exact locatedness, of mentioning something still visible that could link the story to the present, was not recorded. Without viewpoints, one relies more heavily on 'earpoints' (Myers, 2010: 59; Myers, 2011: 70). From feedback it can be said that deep listening cuts off the physical world for some participants, which results in a more passive immersion such as that experienced while watching a film, reading a book or listening to a radio play – a disconnection from location. Until mobile phone development allows more mobility while physically moving, rather than needing to 'stop and interact' (Marshall and Tennent in Robinson et al., 2015:98), verbal cues that draw participant's attention to 'viewpoints' are needed to bring the present physical world into focus. With faces up, eyes looking around, women might feel safer. Reid (2013) encourages interviews done on location so that description of place is included.

The recent landscape change in Hayle and the controversies around it were not articulated in the app but were appreciated by those introduced to the site before trying the app. More content that bridges the gap between past and present could pull faces up away from the screen or users out of deep thought to look for clues. Expert voices in the app could have been encouraged (more) to speak from a personal perspective. Being spoken *to* rather than chatted *with* disrupted an intimate immersive experience for some. Interactivity might increase a connection to landscape. By uploading their own stories (unfortunately, not yet possible in Hayle due to network connections), participants place themselves within the experience and landscape. Co-authoring from those familiar with the landscape would build on the original work deepening the layers of the *Merz* app.

Comparing how the app stands up to an initial aim, increasing awareness of history to encourage more careful town planning and land stewardship, it could be useful to review Hayle-area residents' words:

> *Thinking about the past, particularly North Quay and how busy it was, gave me goose bumps.*
>
> *Hayle is an area that needs developing, hopefully this can be done sympathetically incorporating its historical industrial past.*
>
> *I grew to appreciate more what Hayle represented to people long ago [and it] meant more to me than before.*
>
> *The walk has made me feel closer to the area having walked those places before but without the stories.*
>
> *Made me appreciate more about where I live [Hayle].*
>
> *Reaffirmed my love of Hayle.*

Many spoke of feeling connected to *here, Hayle*, its people and histories. As this wasn't always supported by the quantitative data, we reviewed the language used in the questionnaire. We hypothesise that the term 'landscape' could have been an issue. There is more understanding of the term 'location' used in one of the questions, compared to 'landscape'. Perhaps unaware of academic debates on 'landscape' articulated in, for example, Wylie's *Landscape* (2007), the word for many participants could conjure up a distant view rather than the environment or location around them, whether urban or rural, causing some confusion. Participants said they would be more likely to come back to Hayle, so there is a further opportunity of deepening the connection or attachment to landscape sparked by the app through what Tuan identifies as 'repetition and return' (Tuan cited in Moores, 2012: 30).

*With thanks to Phil Stenton, Calvium/Jo Reid, Caitlin DeSilvey, Donna Anton, Heritage Lottery Fund, and all those who took part in the *Hayle Churks* evaluations.

Note

1 Constance Fleuriot, Phil Stenton, Jo Reid, Richard Hull, Jon Dovey, Martin Rieser, Teresa Dillon, Clodagh Miskelly and Mark Jacobs.

References

Audiotrails (2012) *Audio Trail: Hayle*, Hayle: audiotrails. Available at: http://www.cornish-mining.org.uk/areas-places-activities/audio-trail-hayle#overlay-context= [Accessed 15 July 2016].

Blythe M et al. (2006) Interdisciplinary criticism: analysing the experience of riot!, a location-sensitive digital narrative. *Computer and Information Science Behaviour Information Technology* 25(2): 127–39.

Butler T (2005) *Memoryscape: Drifting and Dockers*, River Thames, London. Available at: http://www.memoryscape.org.uk/ [Accessed 15 July 2016].

Cardiff J and Miller GB (2012) *Works from the Goetz Collection*. Berlin: Hatje Cantz.

Crang M (2003) Qualitative methods, touchy, feely, look-see? *Progress in Human Geography*, 27(4), 494–504.

Cresswell T (2014) The fence furthest north. In *Geopoetics II*. AAG Annual Meeting. Tampa, Florida.

de Souza e Silva A (2006) From cyber to hybrid: mobile technologies as interfaces of hybrid space. *Space and Culture* 9(3): 261–78.

Dietrich D (2006) Hannover, in *Dada: Zurich, Berlin, Hannover, Cologne, New York, Paris*. Landover: National Gallery of Art, 519.

Dovey J and Fleuriot C (2011) Towards a language of mobile media, in M Rieser (ed) *The Mobile Audience: Media Art and Mobile Technologies*. Amsterdam, Netherlands; New York, USA: Rodopi, 97–108.

Farman J (2014) *The Mobile Story: Narrative Practices with Locative Technologies*. NY, Oxon: Routledge.

Frears L (2013) *Hayle Churks*. Available at: https://itunes.apple.com/gb/app/hayle-churks/id777596532?mt=8 [Accessed 15 July 2016].

Gallagher M (2012) *Kilmahew Audio Drift No. 1*, Kilmahew. Available at: http://www.theinvisiblecollege.org.uk/AudioDrifts [Accessed 15 July 2016].

Geelhoed E et al. (2008) Probing experiences: logs, traces, self-report and a sense of wonder, in F Toolenaar et al. (eds) *Probing Experience from Assessment of User Emotions and Behaviour to Development of Products*. Philips Research. Netherlands: Springer Verlag, 57-68.

Hawkins H (2015) Creative geographic methods: knowing, representing, intervening. On composing place and page. *Cultural Geographies* 22(2): 1–22.

Heddon D and Turner C (2012) Walking women: shifting the tales and scales of mobility. *Contemporary Theatre Review* 22(2): 224–36.

Hight J (2006) Views from above: locative narrative and the landscape. *Leonardo Electronic Almanac* 14(7): 1-10.

Iddon M (2010) Plato's Chamber of Secrets: on eavesdropping and truth(s). *Performance Research* 15: 3.

Legendre T (2011) Landscape-mindscape: writing in Scotland's prehistoric future. *Scottish Literary Review* 3(2): 121–32. Available at: http://thomaslegendre.com/landscape-mindscape/ [Accessed 18 February 2012].

Lorimer H and Wylie J (2010) LOOP (a geography). *Performance Research* 15(4): 6-13.

Mauer B (2010) Glenn Gould and the new listener. *Performance Research* 15(3): 103-08

McLucas C (2000–2001) *Stalking the San Andreas Fault*. Available at: http://metamedia.stanford.edu/~mshanks/threelandscapes/Map-on-a-wall-video.html [Accessed 15 July 2016].

Mobile Bristol (2004) *Riot! 1831* (Audio installation). Bristol: Roaring Girl Productions.

Moores S (2012) *Media, Place and Mobility*. Hampshire, UK; New York, USA: Palgrave Macmillan.

Myers M (2010) Walk with me, talk with me: the art of conversive wayfinding. *Visual Studies* 25(1): 59–68.

Myers M (2011) Vocal landscaping: the theatre of sound in audiowalks, in L Kendrick and D Roesner (eds) *Theatre Noise: The Sound of Performance*. Cambridge: Cambridge Scholars Publishing, 70–81.

Pearson M and Shanks M (2001) *Theatre/Archaeology*. London: Routledge.

Pearson M and Shanks M (2007) Performing a visit: archaeologies of the contemporary past. *Performance Research* 2(2): 41–53.

Prior D (2010) The cochlea unwound: a case study for a listening aid using a sonic crystal array. *Performance Research* 15(3): 95–103.

Reid J (2013) Keynote, in *Expanding Narratives*. Plymouth: University of Plymouth. Available at: http://www.expandednarrative.org/symposium/ [Accessed 15 July 2016].

Reid J et al. (2005) Parallel worlds: immersion in location-based experiences, in G van der Veer (ed) *Late Breaking Results: Posters*. CHI 2005: Conference on Human Factors In Computing Systems. Portland, Oregon, USA: CHI 2005, 1733-36.

Reid J and Hull R (2011) What makes mediascapes compelling?, in M Rieser (ed) *The Mobile Audience: Media Art and Mobile Technologies*. Amsterdam; New York, NY: Rodopi, 193–204.

Robinson S, Marsden G and Jones M (2015) *There's Not an App for That*, Amsterdam, Netherlands; Boston, USA: Elsevier/Morgan Kaufmann.

Smith (CrabMan) P (2012) *Counter-Tourism: A Pocketbook – 50 Odd Things to Do in a Heritage Site (and Other Places)*. Devon, UK: Triarchy Press.

Smith G (2014) Supermarket 'poses no risk to Hayle heritage' says UNESCO. *The Cornishman*. Available at: http://www.cornishman.co.uk/Supermarket-poses-risk-Hayle-heritage-says-UNESCO/story-21450216-detail/story.html [Accessed 15 July 2016].

Solnit R (2001) *Wanderlust*. London: Verso.

Stenton P (2011) Fusing the physical and the digital: the art and technology of pervasive media. Available at: http://www.falmouth.ac.uk/ [Accessed 15 July 2016].

Stone H et al. (1974) Sensory evaluation by quantitative descriptive analysis. *Food Technology* 28(11): 24–34.

The South West Research Company Ltd (2012) *Cornwall Towns 2012: Tourism Volume and Value Estimates*. Cornwall: Visit Cornwall. Available at: https://www.visitcornwall.com/sites/default/files/generic_files/Cornwall%20Towns%20impact%20of%20tourism%20research%202012.pdf [Accessed 15 July 2016].

Weiser M (1994) The world is not a desktop. *Interactions* 1(1): 7–8.

Weiser M and Seely Brown J (1995) *Designing Calm Technology*. Available at: http://www.ubiq.com/weiser/WeiserPapers.html [Accessed 15 July 2016].

White K (2004) *The Wanderer and His Charts: Exploring the Fields of Vagrant Thought and Vagabond Beauty*. Edinburgh: Birlinn Polygon.

Wilken R (2012) Locative media: from specialised preoccupation to mainstream fascination. *Convergence: The International Journal of Research into New Media Technologies* 18(3): 243–47.

Wylie J (2006) Depths and folds: on landscape and the gazing subject. *Environment and Planning D: Society and Space* 24(4): 519–535.

Wylie J (2007) *Landscape*. London: Routledge.

16 Extractive Geographies, Immersive Lives

Performative Explorations of Labour and Materialities in the Southern Peak District

George Jaramillo

On this early winter morning, the constant murmur of machinery is heard from the road and the thick morning fog does not seem likely to let up, hindering our drive to the quarry site from the administrative office.[1] Along the way, grey stone dust masks the surrounding woodland, including the shoulders of the road, creating a grey-white ribbon through the narrow dale. I am accompanied by Rick, the quarry manager, who will take me on a guided tour of the Longcliffe Quarries on the edge of Bonsall Moor. Nearing the site, I see the machinery ahead – four pairs of massive steel cylindrical tanks towering over the lorries. The thick fog slowly fades out to reveal an expansive opening, a vast and wide chasm, with vertical edges over twenty metres high. The multi-coloured upper strata change into layers of cream, followed by golden hues of orange with hints of deep red iron oxides. We are at the heart of the quarry, with the earth as its supplier. Noise emanates from all around us: the clank of diesel engines from lorries charging along the sides of the quarry banks, their tyres clipping the muddy road; chains rattle and conveyor belts hum as rock is carried from the floor of the quarry into giant hoppers and crushers; the sound of crushing and falling stone is heard throughout, echoing off the walls. The cream-coloured exposed rock displays the compressed eras of the ancient seabed that the region once was, millions of years ago. Thousands of fossils are embedded within the rock layers, each piece of calcium chemically combining to form the rock removed for transformation into the items of our modern life.

'Alternate Tellings'

As I am taken through this quarry, I realise that the southern Peak District is more than the romantic travel posters or nineteenth century paintings which so commonly portray this region. This quarry tour presents me with an alternate 'way of seeing' the landscape that moves beyond the Romantic spectacle of the landscape towards a more enacted one (Berger, 1972) – 'one whose being is constituted in the unfolding practices that surround it' (Rose, 2002). The landscape is alive with activity of humans at work, but also the activity of farm animals, trees, machines, and minerals from the earth. To understand it, I will need a different way to approach it, and argue that this rural landscape is enacted through socio-technical entanglements between the practices of human labour and the agency of human and more-than-human materialities (DeSilvey, 2006). These entanglements are presented through the laborious practices of extracting, walling, milking, and transporting that make and remake the landscape, holding it together and tearing it apart (Swanton, 2013). Therefore, the landscape is constructed, not only as a final product, but also as flowing through a constantly 'becoming' landscape. I am able to identify the difficult and considerable labour required to 'hold together' (Swanton, 2013) the landscape, by 'attuning' (Stewart, 2011) myself to these practices with the aim of recovering the actions describing how a landscape is performed (Butler, 2010). In turn, I argue that these entangled practices holding the landscape together expose a political economy of power, exclusion, and exploitation (Matless, 1997). Such relationships are exemplified by rural gentrification where extractive industries are removed for middle class recreational industries, the exploitative nature of agri-business on farm animals, and the loss of social housing and services (Howkins, 2003).

I focus on three common practices of this landscape, quarrying, milking, and walling, exploring its material and human entanglements to understand the 'alternate tellings' that go beyond the rural idyll commonly portrayed through art as well as through the preservation policies and practises of local councils and heritage agencies (Peak Park, 2005, 2012; Drennig, 2013). In my ethnographic study of the region, I gathered stories from villagers and from my own experiences within the landscape; an 'alternate telling' of these stories is presented in this chapter, divided between theoretical sections and my empirical narratives of quarrying, milking, and walling. Each narrative explores a theme of materialities and external relations of stone in the quarry, human–animal power entanglements in milking, and the continued exclusionary practices of land ownership in walling. I go about these 'alternate tellings' by approaching the historic mining landscape as an assemblage of practices and materials, rather than as a mere entity or set of representations.

Assemblage

Assemblage concerns the rethinking of relations between parts and their whole, understood as an emergent system in a state of 'becoming' that emphasises multiplicity and exteriority and connects a vast array of socio-spatial 'components' (Anderson et al., 2012; Dittmer, 2014).[2] In societal terms, it reconceptualises society from an 'organismic' totality to a 'rhizomal' collection of components that focuses on emergence, gathering, and dispersal (DeLanda, 2006) through their relations of exteriority, meaning that 'component parts of a whole cannot be reduced to their function within that whole, and indeed they can be parts of multiple wholes at any given moment' (Dittmer, 2014). Therefore, the important aspects of assemblage are the *capacities* of components rather than their *properties* (Dittmer, 2014) because of the infinite possibilities of relationships made, not just by people, but from materials, events, ideas, words, and signs. This theoretical device is useful in that it emphasises the emergent nature of the relational exteriority and the relative autonomy of each part (Anderson et al., 2012), allowing each component to connect with a variety of other components. Assemblage in landscapes is an ongoing study (Stewart, 2014) that liberates the viewer/object relationship and opens the understanding of landscapes to an emphasis on processes of practices, actions, materials, and ideas, rather than the landscape as the ultimate achievement.

Assemblage allows the landscape to be explored, not by *what* it is, but by *how* it is, focusing my thinking of landscape as a process and practice, constituted through the interacting 'forces' of things and the labour required to hold these forces in sympathy. Rather than viewing a laboured landscape as the outcome of work, assemblage sees it as the 'effects of socio-material processes' (Swanton, 2013). Therefore, assemblage thinking blurs the distinction between object and viewer that is present in the 'spectacle' of the landscape, exploring elements like provenance, gentrification, capital, and labour which are brought into being through the practices and materials of the landscape (Mules, 2008). This performative approach to the landscape allows it to be experienced corporeally through the actions of its dwellers and material interactions with the things we make, held in tension and 'created in the face of all those working to transform it' (D. Mitchell, 2003a). These attunements to landscape making (Stewart, 2011) are explored through an *unforgetting* of landscape in the relationships between narratives, materialities, and practices. I will demonstrate how these gazed upon and restored landscapes are constantly made, manipulated, and altered, acknowledging the 'workings' of their past and present assemblages without a nostalgic view of that past, but rather by exploring the power and material relations created in the making of landscapes (D. Mitchell, 2008) where a different kind of remembering is performed.

Quarrying

The Longcliffe Quarry remains one of the last family-run quarries within the region. It forms part of the major holdings of Longcliffe Calcium Carbonates Limited, employing about 150 people from the local region. Founded by the Shields family of Isley Walton, it opened in 1920 as a small quarry in what then would have been the hamlet of Grangemill and is currently co-directed by Robert John Gillies Shields, whose grandfather operated the initial opening and whose family now resides in Parwich Hall. The quarry is roughly triangular in plan, with the eastern end of the site plunging into the Via Gellia valley below, and sits on the immediate edge of the Peak District National Park, across the road from a caravan park (Figure 16.1).[3]

Tap tap tap tap tap tap tap … thump. TAP tap tap tap TAP tap tap tap … thump. Rumble. TAP tap tap tap tap tap … thump … … hum.

The stone is crushed, monitored, sorted, weighed, and chemically analysed for use in variety of products, including aggregate for road building, industrial mastics and fillers, animal feed, fertilisers for fields, and countless others. The

Figure 16.1 A view of the interior of the Longcliffe Quarry site in Grangemill on the edge of the Peak District National Park.

influence of the stone from this one hillside is everywhere; at the same time, the land is being extracted of its physical creation. The millions of years that it took to create the rock, its solid form, is instantly decimated into a fine powder for our consumption.[4]

An air raid siren wails and is followed by a pause, announcing the imminent blasting of the rock. The blast goes off, yet nothing is immediately felt, as modern blasting is so controlled that most of the energy goes into splitting the rock and not much else; the siren, and its call, is thus only sound warning of the danger and destruction about to happen. Once the second set of sirens resonates, production continues in a ceaseless cycle. Although the quarry workers work only in daytime to remove the rock, the processors work non-stop at crushing and sorting, monitoring and analysing. The quarry is a living assemblage, continuous and ever changing, where the stone, conveyor belt, and weather can affect the way the quarry functions from one moment to the next. Today, the caller from the main office requests a half tonne of stone for construction; tomorrow, perhaps a need for limestone fertiliser will emerge. The quarry feeds the land and the people who work it. It is not just an assemblage enclosed within, but open to the systems of regional and national economies.

The 'Material' Landscape

In this, the first of three stories, I focused on the entanglement of the machine, humans, and stone in how the extraction processes not only alter the landscape, but how the landscape enacts upon the population. This 'vital materialism' recognises that all types of things exert a kind of agency in the world (Butler, 2010). Used here, agency is more than the idea of free will or the socially-determined capability to act and make a difference (Barker, 2003: 435); rather, it is 'the property of complex hybrids comprised of various strands of human and non-human materials (McMaster and Wastell, 2005: 175). Things are not just dead matter, but engage in the world where the 'materiality of things' is an exercise in agency, matter, signifiers, and the philosophical applications of what make things, 'things'.

Vital materialism sees things as actants with a differential agency towards each other (Bennett, 2009). They are active constituents in an assemblage where people, electricity, animals, rivers, wooden posts, and love come together to make the landscape (Bennett, 2009). This 'vital materialism' is key to understanding how materials are concerned with processes rather than with only the inert object. DeSilvey (2013) has explored this concept through her work on the 'thingness' of things, suggesting that objects embody our labour and the efforts of their places and understanding artefacts as a process rather than as stable entities (DeSilvey, 2006). This is exemplified by the deserted Montana homestead where remaining artefacts are as much engaged in a type of making as they were when in use by the people who left them behind.

This approach to materialities thus acknowledges that the landscape is a verb rather than a noun, and is much more than an aesthetic or visual representation but is instead a performance of materials and humans. In this exploration of things, I can reconstruct how the landscape is made; how materials, be they stone, milk, or cows, create the assemblage of landscape; form discrete assemblages within it, like a quarry; or form larger regional assemblages of human-animal-mineral entanglements. The landscape is such that these components engage one another to create a dynamic and living landscape; it calls out the way that the people of the rural landscape truly are a 'people of things', more about an insistence of the material basis of economic activities that shape landscape. They create the things for living, for making and engaging life. Through my exploration of things, I encounter how they slip from a final material to a raw material and to a new thing, or become waste moving through the land. Therefore, things are performing components within a landscape assemblage. In the following section, I explore a more intimate role of how mineral components become transformed within animals and milk.

Milking

I don my boiler suit, ready to take on the beasts, and approach the newly constructed milking shed, manure-spattered on the outside but clean within. A small anteroom, separated from the milking area by a sliding door, holds a sink and a large stainless steel tank of approximately 10,000 litres. Stepping into the space, an acrid mixture of bleach, manure, and milk permeates the crisp dark December afternoon air. Down the centre of a long concrete shed with fluorescent lights overhead runs a large depressed floor, approximately half a metre below the main level of the room. Overhead, a metal structure of pipes holds a network of tubes and hoses waiting to come to life, reminiscent of a science-fiction scene. Ten milking stations in a row have their dangling udders at the ready. The room is empty; a faint sound of cows mooing comes from the back. The farmer and his daughter come in, wearing identical boiler suits that fit them easily and well. At once, the farmer begins to input a series of numbers into a control panel and a loud tumbling sound like pouring rice reverberates through the large pipes and into the hoppers below. At the same time, the herd – each one a sentient beast –appears at the far end of the room, their breaths as white puffs quickly warming up the space.[5]

Every day of the year, the dairy farmer must wake up and milk his herd. Every afternoon, he must do the same thing. There can be no rest, no holiday, and no time out. If a cow is not milked, she instinctively halts her production of milk until she delivers another calf, thereby halting the farmer's livelihood until she gives birth. Our desire for milk places these animals, people, feed, and gates into a milk assemblage.

Ten at a time, the cows file into their stalls, rears facing the centre of the room and ready to be milked. Industrialisation and modernisation transformed the hand process into a mechanised hydraulic system of hoses and pumps. Once each teat of the cow's udder has been sterilised and prepped, a mechanical arm drops down with a tangle of hoses and four receiving cups. Approaching the beast from behind requires a certain type of finesse and composure. Too timid and the cow will not respect you, too forceful and she will resist. A certain gentle yet sturdy approach assures the cow of your intention, not to harm, but to extract her milk. And so, with the whooshing sound of a vacuum pump in the background, each cup is raised to its teat, and with a slight upward pull, latches on by suction (Figure 16.2).

Thump, thump, thump, thump … the pumps suck on the cows' teats.

Milk begins to flow through the hoses up and over into the large holding tank in the anteroom. A constant pumping, sucking sound emanates from each machine attached to a cow, as if the entire shed has come alive – one milking giant. Each cow can provide from 8 to 11 litres of milk per milking. At two milkings a day,

Figure 16.2 A collection of nine screenshots from a video of milking at a local farmer's milking barn in Bonsall Village.

365 days per year, that's about 7,500 litres per year, per cow. The process is repeated seventy times, ten cows at a time. Prep teats, attach, pump, and remove. One is constantly active, aware of the risk of excrement from the cows' rears or a kick from their hooves. As the final cow from the herd gets pushed through, the process does not end: the entire shed must be doused with water hoses to clean and prep for the next morning. This milking session lasted only an hour and a half; sometimes it's longer, sometimes shorter, depending on the size of the herd entering the shed. The action is played out day after day, morning after morning. A natural process transformed into an ever-growing need for food and nutrition, animal turned into a machine for milk with its life altered to fit the needs of humans.

Dairy farming is an industry, like mining, or quarrying, although the perception of agriculture varies from pastoral to industrial. In the modern world, the industrialisation and mechanisation of farming creates a million pound industry with regulations, quotas, and subsidies. There are stresses in maintaining a farm: rearing animals, keeping them healthy, and maintaining the required product standards (Alpass et al., 2004). The farmer is a connector, a labourer, part of the landscape assemblage. Milking cows is one of many jobs here at the Slater Farm. There are fences and stone walls to be mended, fields to be tended and fertilised, a tractor to repair, and milk to deliver. Farmers face the hardships of modern life and struggle to maintain relevance in today's society. Either they are too small or too big. Rural groups are established to provide assistance by supporting the networks of agricultural activity. Farming creates a particular landscape, one of sheds, barns, and muddied pathway drives. The landscape assemblage is therefore maintained and held together by these everyday practices. They reinforce the actions of a proactive and highly maintained system, one that people expect but never see. The 'natural' placement of the cows is thus the outcome of a larger industrial process of milk.

A 'Laboured' Landscape

The idea of a socially-produced landscape, one that speaks to the groundwork of justice and labour (D. Mitchell, 2003b), implies that a working landscape incorporates labour relations in its making and unmaking. I frame my argument of a laboured landscape through this understanding of social relationships and capitalist production, embedded within a cultural political economy (T. Mitchell, 2008). I propose that, with the assistance of assemblage thinking, I can bridge the social justice work of Don Mitchell with the cultural economic thinking of Tim Mitchell. Much of this stems from the work of Don Mitchell (1996, 2003a, 2003b, 2008) as well as other work on power and landscape (W.J.T. Mitchell, 2002) and political landscapes, particularly the views of landscape and social justice, which are useful in uncovering hidden dimensions of labour within landscapes.[6]

According to Don Mitchell (2003a: 245), landscapes are a 'social product, made and remade' by the people who live within them and the desire of other social actors to present them in their own view; therefore, a landscape is a social struggle between different actors who vie over the way that it is produced and represented. This is exemplified by the Central Valley of California (D. Mitchell, 1996), which from afar, is a landscape of verdant agricultural cornucopia brimming with fruits and promise. Within the landscape, however, are migrant workers, trees, labour dealers, landowners, and their social struggles that created that verdant valley (D. Mitchell 1996). The landscape is therefore 'dead labour', representative of these relations as 'an outcome and the medium of social relations' (D. Mitchell, 2003a), or the 'true' nature of the landscape where the landscape relations are typically 'a struggle, as well as one that impedes struggle' (D. Mitchell, 2003a: 246). For example, landscapes produced through migrant movements not only are representative of a struggle (between worker and owner), but also conceal that struggle through technological innovations, agricultural subsidies, and labour supply from distant places. Therefore, a landscape of production is one where the processes of labour and power create the material objects of our modern world as well as the social relations of those processes, meaning who owns the means of that production, who sells and controls the prices of those materials, and what happens to surplus. Thus, what is useful about these socially contested relationships is that landscape represents the injustice in these systems and the recovery of the struggles within.

These relations of struggle and dominance between the people who make the landscape (proletariat) and the people who control it (bourgeoisie) express the power and control present throughout much of the capitalist landscape. This power, however, is not necessarily a dualistic idea of coercion and persuasion between a dominant and subordinate group. By engaging power and domination as 'working through novel methods of creating and recreating a world' (T. Mitchell, 1990: 573), power can be understood as a set of practices, complicating the struggles of capitalistic exploitation. This approach to power can be construed by 'enframing' (T. Mitchell, 1990), where a 'projectness' of capitalism is emphasised, represented by work that produces or stabilises particular capitalist social relations and evaluating how well they endure. Therefore, a capitalist society engages in a means of power and measures of administration to control efficiency and growth, transfer commodities, and support an ever-flowing network of goods; those processes involved in power also ensure exclusion and exploitation by physically creating topological barriers like walls and fences as well as politically creating abstract divisions within labour. Tension is inherent, not only what is produced, but in where it is produced, understanding forgotten or missed power relations. These can include the relations between builder and tool, familial structures, or the transformation of village dynamics.

Today, the landscape is contested and fought over by people who challenge, not only the existing extractive industries, but also the newer 'green' industries. A voice exists in the community which strives to maintain a 'dominant' narrative within the landscape and is decidedly against the extraction of further minerals. Critics of the dairy industry cite its abusive use of animals as mere milk makers by forcing cows to produce endless amounts of milk and raising calves to serve the same purpose. Fields are maintained for the sole purpose of feeding cattle and sheep, as the artificial nature of the fertilisation process keeps fields as monocultures and limits ecological diversity. These critics also view small farmsteads as antiquated and in need of efficiency and modernisation. Quarries are contested as they are too large and destructive to the overall landscape. Yet, over the last few pages, I have managed to show how interactively connected the quarries and the livelihoods of the farmers are to each other. Individual assemblages are linked through multi-scalar components, be it fertiliser from the quarry or the sustenance of milk to the quarry workers. In the following section, I explore a final narrative on walling to see how the stone not only becomes entangled within the human system, but plays a role in the practices of ownership and exclusion.

Walling

Stone walls are rarely rebuilt, but in the hill country – where it is known as a 'farm for stones' – a stonewall is the physical embodiment of enclosure, the division of ownership and usefulness, and physically represents the abstract lines of property that land owners create on their property deeds. Easier ways exist, however, of dividing a property, so many walls are nowadays in various states of ruin.[7]

The basic reconstruction of a wall is relatively straightforward. The existing wall is disassembled down to its foundation stones, which usually have moss on their surfaces, expressing the length of time that they've lain exposed. One side shows its age, whereas within the stone itself the creamy white limestone colour is on display. In dry stone walls, each stone is of a different size and shape, situated according to its place in the wall. No single stone is the same as another, and each takes a rough form: large ones, flat ones, round ones, jagged ones, and ones that need two people to lift. Each stone is representative of where it came from and how it got here, taken from the earth and placed with its brethren. Once sorted by type, however, each stone takes on a purpose in the assembly which creates the strength of the wall. Walls built without mortar are held together by the stones' weight and friction, and a particular arrangement that locks the stones together in an intricate three-dimensional puzzle, running along the moor.

The wall is about 60 cm at its base and 15 cm at the top. The battered form confers stability and extra reinforcing if animals or people collide with it. A wall can be built to almost 160 cm in height, although this one is no more than 92 cm tall. The stones are laid in an interlocking fashion, larger ones at the bottom and slowly diminishing in size towards the top. At particular intervals, the level and plumpness of the wall is evaluated. Misalignment can cause collapse or simply a deviation from its proper course. It is also maintained to minimise material use. After laying stones all day, the efficient and effective use of the stones allows for maximum hold with minimal material use. Slowly the wall takes shape, with each stone laid, moved, re-laid, shifted, and finally set in place. Even then, it is not set, since there is no mortar to permanently bind the stones together; you can, theoretically, reconstruct the wall into whatever new form is desired. Perfectionism is not required, the end result is what matters. The construction of stone walls is an ancient tradition and form, stemming from Neolithic times, although their prevalence did not come into full effect until the early medieval period when fields closest to villages were enclosed to keep cattle and other livestock contained.

Over time, many of these walls ossified with the ridge and furrow system within, creating long and narrow fields near the village centres. Today, ancient and early modern walls are defining features of the landscape. Construction of dry stone walls is nowadays a labour intensive process, limited to a set of skilled craftspeople. Studies in the Yorkshire Dales show the influence of dry stone wall repair on local industries, craft skills, and the conservation of the environment (Courtney et al., 2007).

These walls are significant structures, ruined, moss covered at one end, or bright white in colour and marching across fields; they tell of the physical pieces of the earth, of the human hands that manipulated it. Stone walling is normally not used as a modern technique of livestock control, having been replaced by wood posts and barbed wire fencing. Entire fields have edges of stone with a barbed wire fence enclosure within, providing the means to protect and keep the animals within their fields. The ruined nature of the walls shows that many are not used and are simply allowed to collapse under their own disrepair. Groups exist who restore and reconstruct many of the walls; however, in reconstructing the walls, the image of the landscape is retained but their purpose is lost. As walls have become redundant due to changes in agricultural policy, the enclosures no longer represent any abstract thought of land ownership, as several people own the land parcels, negating the need for a large number of walls. I am reminded of Robert Frost's (1914: 3) poem, *Mending Wall*, where two men on a spring day set about repairing the wall that separates their properties. The narrator explains why walls (or fences) make good neighbours, adding further:

> Before I built a wall I'd ask to know
> What I was walling in or walling out,
> And to whom I was like to give offense.
> Something there is that doesn't love a wall,
> That wants it down.

In reply, the neighbour, reiterates that 'Good fences make good neighbours' (Frost, 1914). If the wall is maintained, its use is maintained; yet, when restored for the sake of restoration, the wall is merely an artifice of the picturesque and pastoral image.

A New Political Economy of the Landscape

The relationship between dairy farmer, quarry, and waller may not be apparent, but in reviewing the processes and practices involved in the making of these activities, a new political economy in the landscape is encountered. This new relational approach to the landscape affords me a way to understand the mining landscape beyond class struggle, economic quantities, and historical materialist thinking towards an inclusive social awareness and socio-technical system of landscape making. I have illustrated how Don Mitchell's work considers

Marxist social relations of landscape, while Tim Mitchell's work addresses the socio-technical relations of its production. These authors attune me to the landscape by allowing me to see and recount particular stories while analysing the formation of landscapes through labour, production, and the collaboration of diverse actants/materialities.

Although Don Mitchell's work encourages a relational approach to landscape production (2008: 34), where networks of production (and their maintenance) require our analysis, much of Mitchell's work lies in an interpretation of landscape at a purely economic foundation, where the landscape is a thing (e.g. dead labour) rather than something in process. Furthermore, this essentialist approach recognises a 'real basis' to the landscape (D. Mitchell, 2008), whereby uncovering the real relations of production and allows one to ascertain the true reason behind the struggle. Yet, these assertions may not always ring true. As assemblage thinking is about the relational acts, it is not limited to a confined idealisation of 'networks', incorporating not only the products and relations of labour and social and spatial politics, but the political and socio-technical potential of economics (D. Mitchell, 2008) or an understanding of how the politics of power endure (McCann and Ward, 2011). Thus, assemblage affords political and social justice a tool to expose the political 'becomings' of labour relations geography.

Therefore, this landscape is produced through its flow of capital, labour relations, supply of sites and technological improvements that influence its social interactions and struggles. A landscape of labour is generated through the creation and commodification of materials and products, as well as through the social justice of the women and men within the landscape (D. Mitchell, 2003a). These relationships are key to how and why a landscapes functions. This is the strength of Don Mitchell's work, a radical way of approaching the landscape; by diving deeply into the gritty and ugly side of social history and landscape, it focuses on laying the groundwork for social justice. Therefore, by bridging these two ideas of thinking of the landscape through a socially aware and materially relational aspect of production and consumption, I can take into account the performative aspect of the people, the material interactions, and the assemblages created within a political economy (Swanton, 2013).[8] I have described the farmer who tends to his cattle and milks them to supply milk to the market as well as the implications of subsidies, agricultural quotas, and animal welfare. There exist also the larger production assemblages, like quarry workers slowly removing the earth who supply the lorry drivers, who bring the stone to the builders, who build our homes. These assemblages engage in vast collective relationships producing commodities in a capitalist society.

'Unforgetting' Landscapes

From stone to fertiliser and cattle, to a bottle of milk and a stone wall connected to enclosures and control, the regional landscape as assemblage affords the unpacking of relationships between things and people. I am reminded that the working landscape is fleeting, that the impermanence of labour is constantly pushed and contested. The landscape's labour is forced to reconcile with itself and the needs of a greater society. The landscape is an assemblage, a social entity growing and changing – heterogeneous pieces each, a composite to act upon it. Yet, these constant movements find their stable entities, performed in the everyday practices that create routine (Butler, 2010) and stabilise the landscape assemblage. As Mitchell (2003b) has suggested, the landscape is not constantly in flux, it is trying to find its 'structured permanence', practised through the relationships of the landscape. The walling that is a type of *unforgetting* is now a part of the spectacle and making of the landscape. Customs and practices remain constant after hundreds of years, while certain ones die and others are introduced. The labour practices of extracting, taking, and removing are now transformed to other practices of rebuilding, service, and recreation. The landscape actively seeks its balance. Things change, yet this structured permanence of places that remain the same are what makes the landscape. Thus, we return to the assemblage of the landscape. This ever-working place, connected and being connected, strives for permanence yet does not quite reach it.

In this chapter, I explored the entanglements of human and animal labour, exclusion, through enclosures and walls, commodities, through milk, and production from quarrying. I have shown how stone can be transformed from a block in the earth to fertiliser for fields, to be fed to cows that are manipulated for their milk, that is used to drink and make foodstuffs – a constant connection made across the landscape. It is a landscape connected to a larger network of regional and national development. The landscape is an interconnected place where goods and products are transferred and the exclusionary actions of enclosures and the abstract concept of land ownership are represented in dry-laid stone walls, enduring through its practice. Each stone, unearthed from the ground, is placed, altered, and changed into a piece of power and control. It says, 'Do not cross!', and keeps the commodities of cattle and sheep from infringing upon the rights of others' land, the same cattle who come every day to be milked in order to supply our desire for dairy products. Milk is used to make hundreds of products, yet keeps the cattle living a life where they are forced to produce every day and the farmers' livelihood is threatened by development and ever-increasing regulation. The laws that maintain and manage the quarry are, at the same time, supplying the aggregate and fertiliser needed to maintain fields for the cows to feed on and produce milk for our consumption.

Each assemblage changes accordingly as regional places grow and shrink their connections across the landscape which transforms with them. Their paths or lines (Hodder, 2012) are engaging in different relations, at times 'gathering' in nodes (Ingold, 2007) to pass the materials along, as is the case of the fields where the stone, cows, people, and fertiliser all are bound together in the practise of farming, walling, and lamping, making this particular landscape endure. This landscape works by showing how intricately connected seemingly separate thoughts and stories are to the functioning of society. It also demonstrates how a landscape works, and how its interconnectedness processes products from a block of stone to the builders, the quarry, and the manager. These players are constantly working to make the landscape.

There is the siren in the background, like a beacon in the distance, reminding me that the landscape is laboured and is not a sanitised pastoral place or spectacle to be viewed from afar. It signifies an active and destructive place – it is extraction at its purest form. The siren calls out in defiance against the rural idyll it must fight. As I have shown, the land is connected through the constant pressures of the spectacle and production at odds with each other. The rural landscape is contested, and within this contested element there exists a desire to see it develop into one form or another. The working landscape also strives to remain permanent in an idealised set of agricultural processes, yet is altered to a modern service-based society. As I have shown, the landscape is vibrant and alive with the practice of landscape making; however, in that making, there exist growing tensions, exclusionary and exploitative practices in the commodification of materials, and social inequality. Through comprehension of how those tensions are held together, we can begin to seek the interconnected nature that labour and material practices have on the landscape with vastly different outcomes.

Notes

1 The sound of the works from the immediate vicinity is monitored, and the local caravan park maintains that it does not have any noise concerns, but on Bonsall Moor the workings can be heard from almost two kilometres away on a clear and quiet day or evening.

2 Examples of assemblages include systems like power grids (Bennett, 2005), steel plants (Swanton, 2013), as well as abstract networks like neoliberalism (Collier, 2013) and geopolitics (Dittmer, 2014).

3 The many quarries of the region lie just outside the boundaries of the Peak Park, including the larger examples on the outskirts of Buxton. Many of these quarries, including Hope Quarry in Castleton and Birchover, were founded before the creation of the National Park. Their regulation is mired in a hazy assemblage of planning laws, ancient mining customs, land policies, and financial kickbacks.

4 The exploitation of the earth is expressed here, and assumed to be a part of the expected order of things. People want, and perhaps need, the stone to construct buildings, feed their cattle, and fertilise their fields; this is the best result and use of the land.

5 The cow is bred to constantly produce milk. To do so requires it to be in a reproductive state, or in a feeding state to its young. Her udder can contain a limited volume of milk and, since the calf is not there to suckle, it must be drained to make room for more milk. The cow is a component of a human–animal assemblage of breeding, killing, and feeding, set within a larger system of economic policy, agricultural subsidies, and traditional animal husbandry techniques.

6 His work on Johnstown (Mitchell, 1992) was a critique of the sanitation of labour struggles via the creation of heritage museums, which in course has occluded much of the contestation of the town. His review, however, drew much critique from the heritage sector (Miner and Burkett, 1992).

7 Research on dry stone walling is limited, yet some ecological benefits to the surrounding environment by the niche that dry stone wall creates have been demonstrated (Collier, 2013).

8 Swanton's work is inspired by the ethnographic work of Burawoy (1989) in his Lenin Steel Works of Hungary.

References

Alpass F, Flett R, Humphries S, Massey C, Morriss S and Long N (2004) Stress in dairy farming and the adoption of new technology. *International Journal of Stress Management* 11(3): 270–81.

Anderson B, Kearnes M, McFarlane C and Swanton D (2012) On assemblages and geography. *Dialogues in Human Geography* 2(2): 171–89.

Barker C (2003) *Cultural Studies: Theory and Practice*. London: Sage.

Bennett J (2005) The agency of assemblages and the North American Blackout. *Public Culture* 17(3): 445–65.

Bennett J (2009) *Vibrant Matter: A Political Ecology of Things*. Durham: Duke University Press.

Berger J (1972) *Ways of Seeing*. London, British Broadcasting Corporation; Harmondsworth: Penguin.

Burawoy M (1989) Reflections on the class consciousness of Hungarian steelworkers. *Politics and Society* 17(1): 1–34.

Butler J (2010) Performative agency. *Journal of Cultural Economy* 3(2): 147–61.

Collier MJ (2013) Field boundary stone walls as exemplars of 'novel' ecosystems. *Landscape Research* 38(1): 141–50.

Courtney P, Gaskell P, Mills J, and Edwards R (2007) A study of the social and economic impacts and benefits of traditional farm building and drystone wall repairs in the Yorkshire Dales National Park. *Valuing the Historic Environment 3*, English Heritage.

DeLanda M (2006) *A New Philosophy of Society: Assemblage Theory and Social Complexity*. London: Bloomsbury Publishing.

DeSilvey C (2006) Observed decay: telling stories with mutable things. *Journal of Material Culture* 11(3): 318–38.

DeSilvey C (2013) Object lessons: from batholith to bookend, in *The Wiley-Blackwell Companion to Cultural Geography*. London: John Wiley and Sons, 146–58.

Dittmer J (2014) Geopolitical assemblages and complexity. *Progress in Human Geography* 38(3): 385–401.

Drennig G (2013) Taking a hike and hucking the stout: the troublesome legacy of the sublime in outdoor recreation. *Culture Unbound: Journal of Current Cultural Research* 5: 551–68.

Frost R (1914) *North of Boston*. Boston: David Nutt.

Hodder I (2012) *Entangled: An Archaeology of the Relationships between Humans and Things*. Malden, MA: Wiley-Blackwell.

Howkins A (2003) Qualifying the evidence: perceptions of rural change in Britain in the second half of the Twentieth Century, in D Gilbert, D Matless and B Short (eds) *Geographies of British Modernity: Space and Society in the Twentieth Century*. Oxford: Blackwell Publishing, 97–111.

Ingold T (2007) Materials against materiality. *Archaeological Dialogues* 14(1): 1–16.

Matless D (1997) Moral geographies of English landscape. *Landscape Research* 22(2): 141–55.

McCann E and Ward K (2011) Introduction. Urban assemblages: territories, relations, practices, and power, in *Mobile Urbanism. Cities and Policy-Making in the Global Age*. Minneapolis: University of Minneapolis Press.

McMaster T and Wastell D (2005) The agency of hybrids: overcoming the symmetrophobic block. *Scandinavian Journal of Information Systems* 17(1): 175–82.

Miner C and Burkert R (1992) The myth of demythification: a response to Don Mitchell's 'Heritage, Landscape and the Production of Community'. *Pennsylvania History*, 227–32.

Mitchell D (1992) Heritage, landscape, and the production of community: consensus history and its alternatives in Johnstown, Pennsylvania. *Pennsylvania History*, 198–226.

Mitchell D (1996) *The Lie of the Land: Migrant Workers and the California Landscape*, Minneapolis: University of Minnesota Press.

Mitchell D (2003a) Dead labor and the political economy of landscape-California living, California dying, in *Handbook of Cultural Geography*. London: Sage, 233–48.
Mitchell D (2003b) Cultural landscapes: just landscapes or landscapes of justice? *Progress in Human Geography* 27(6): 787–96.
Mitchell D (2008) New axioms for reading the landscape: paying attention to political economy and social justice, in D Johnston and J Wescoat (eds) *Political Economies of Landscape Change*. Netherlands: Springer, 29–50.
Mitchell T (1990) Everyday metaphors of power. *Theory and society* 19(5): 545–77.
Mitchell T (1998) Fixing the economy. *Cultural Studies* 12(1): 82–101.
Mitchell WJT (ed) (2002) *Landscape and Power*. Chicago: University of Chicago Press.
Mules W (2008) Open country: towards a material environmental aesthetics. *Continuum* 22(2): 201–12.
Peak District National Park Authority (2005) *Peak Through Time*. Bakewell: Peak Park Authority.
Peak District National Park Authority (2012) *Peak District National Park Management Plan*. Bakewell: Peak Park Authority.
Rose M (2002) Landscape and labyrinths. *Geoforum* 33(4): 455–67.
Stewart K (2011) Atmospheric attunements. *Environment and Planning D: Society and Space* 29(3): 445–53.
Stewart K (2014) Road registers. *Cultural Geographies* 21(4): 549–563.
Swanton D (2013) The steel plant as assemblage. *Geoforum* 44: 282–91.
Wylie J (2007) *Landscape*. Abingdon; New York: Routledge.

Afterword

What's Next for Regional Geography?

John Agnew

Studies advertised under the sign of 'regional geography' have had a long and tortuous history. Until the 1960s the term described what was widely seen as the highest form of the geographer's art. But to the ascendant advocates of spatial analysis it was seen as a descriptive endeavor antithetical to their attempts at turning Geography (as a university discipline) into a science modeled on nineteenth century physics. To focus on regions was to emphasise uniqueness over generality. The pathway to scientific reputation was paved with empirical generalisations. Thus, regional geography was best consigned to the history of the field as a mere curiosity. The future led elsewhere.

Of course, this was not the end of regional geography at all. Since the 1980s numerous efforts at reviving regional studies have attempted to either incorporate regional analysis into research questions from abstract theoretical frameworks or develop approaches that play up precisely the particular as valuable in itself as illustrative of human agency or the interplay of the human and the natural. In my understanding, what's next for regional geography cannot be reduced to just one or another of these efforts even though they can represent very different views of what constitutes regional geography. It also cannot be restricted to a narrow disciplinary sphere. Scholars in a wide range of fields have discovered 'the region' as a context for their studies.

The first typically will involve using regional geographies to answer theoretical questions of a broad social or physical science nature. The second takes the form of using personal experiences or fieldwork in areas identified as regions to raise broad questions about the sources and consequences of different cultural practices and socio-political identities. These broad perspectives need not be mutually exclusive. Following an overview of what I would call the fall and rise of regional geography, I will say something about each of the current framings and what I think they can do. My main concern is that within Geography room must be found for both. Currently there is much interest in many fields in the possibilities of regional analysis particularly under the first label. It would be strange if geographers, presumably those most invested in thinking regionally, were to underemphasise its potential at precisely the moment when others are finally taking regional geographies seriously.

The Fall and Rise of Regional Geography

The idea of the region typically goes against that of the nation-state as the fundamental geographical unit of account that has been at the heart of much academic scholarship as a whole since the late nineteenth century. Yet, the 'view from below', or that of social groups marginalised in orthodox political history and often associated with, for example, social history and anthropology as fields of study, rests on the premise that the national scale typically represents the privileging of attention to the institutions associated with the interests and outlooks of modern political élites more than the reality of an homogeneous and enclosed society conforming to the political boundaries imposed by the modern system of territorial states. Moreover, not only have the world's political boundaries been unstable over even relatively short periods of time (consider how 'Poland' has moved across the map of Europe in this century), but the geographical patterning of social life is by no means successfully captured by a singular focus on the national scale. Social networks, cultural influences, and economic linkages often transcend borders as well as cluster regionally inside them.

Regional geography, as a label for a certain type of geography, always tended to privilege meso-scale or sub-national regions irrespective of whether the focus was on the physical landscape or the socio-cultural character of places. So, even figures such as Carl Sauer and Richard Hartshorne writing in the 1940s and 1950s, and divided over whether culture produced regional divisions or regional divisions produced socio-economic differences, could agree on limiting the geographic scope of regions to the meso-scale. This limitation was perhaps one of the reasons why regional geography became passé in the context of a historic period when 'methodologically nationalist' views (privileging the state as the primary unit for making generalisations) became hegemonic. In the course of the March of History the regional distinctions to which regional geography drew attention were supposedly destined to disappear.

Some 'schools' of history, particularly that associated with the *Annales* in inter-war and immediate post-World War II France, have been explicitly devoted to avoiding the privileging of the state as the primary unit of geographical context. Perhaps the close link between the academic fields of geography and history in France led to a greater recognition by social and economic historians of the importance of assumptions about the spatial units used in research that is largely missing in the English-speaking world where an abstract sounding but usually nationally-oriented sociology has tended to be more influential than geography among historians. Fernand Braudel's classic study, *The Mediterranean* (first published in 1949), is an excellent example of the use of an alternative geographical frame of reference, in this case an ocean basin, to the nation-states that had dominated historical research during the nineteenth and for much of the twentieth century. For Braudel's long-term total history using a macro-region, the relatively short histories of European states posed a significant barrier to the historical understanding that only a larger regional entity, such as the Mediterranean world, could adequately convey.

Of course, even Braudel eventually turned into an afficionado of national history in his *L'identité de la France* (1986), though this work remains more sensitive than the typical national history to the physical geography and regional distinctions of the territory that later became France as we know it today. In addition, according to the historian Lynn Hunt (1986), this sort of work also succumbed to the allure of thinking entirely in terms of states or of isolated sub-national regions as exemplars of statewide processes.

Thus the usage of regional geography in the sense of large macro-regions such as the Mediterranean or Europe also went into eclipse as anything other than a clumsy teaching device to simplify an otherwise too complex world. They were historical relics. Cold War geopolitics also conspired to produce a global regional framework reflecting the main spheres of influence of the US and the Soviet Union with a Third World of competition between them. This did produce an intellectual division of labour between specialists on the different Worlds. But it operated at such a high level of geopolitical abstraction that it rapidly disintegrated once the Cold War came to an end.

It was as this was happening in the 1980s and 1990s that revival of thinking about regional geography began to emerge. Initially this was as much in the public as in the academic sphere. Terms such as region and regionalism became keywords in academic discourse, practical governance, and politics at various geographic scales from the sub-national to the world regional. In particular, one of the most important examples was the discussion of the contemporary and future roles of the 'Europe of Regions', but debate about the role of regions (at various spatial scales) and cross-border regions became significant worldwide following the collapse of the Cold War East-West divide. This resurgence has, therefore, taken place in both academic research and in the world of practical politics. Indeed, this rediscovery has been not restricted to disciplinary Geography but also characterises such fields as international relations, political science, history, and sociology. Across these fields the question of geographic scale matters. Whereas to many geographers the region most typically means sub-national geographic units, for specialists in international relations, for example, it is often continent-related institutional arrangements (for example, the EU, NAFTA, MERCOSUR) that are of prime concern.

Framing Regional Geography Today

Usage of the term 'region' in many fields today is often without much conscious motivation other than to either group together countries that are apparently similar and thus to simplify a greater complexity, or to ground local studies within a larger meso-regional/sub-national field of reference. The drawing of regional differences above and below the national scale also frequently involves deploying such familiar, and often theoretically unexamined, conceptual oppositions as modern-backward, capitalist-feudal, and core-periphery, depending upon the theoretical orientation of the author in question. In this light, regions often serve as geographical units in narratives in which they are merely incidental to more fundamental processes operating across space and time.

Regions at a sub-national level and regions at a supra-national level are often invoked by social scientists, depending on the phenomenon in question, to provide more appropriate territorial units than the putative nation-state upon which to base their empirical investigations. The historian Otto Dann (1989: 117) sees the region as a methodological necessity for detailed studies in social history. This is the predominant significance that 'the region' has acquired in many fields. But it has also recently inspired a rather different type of scholarship.

For some geographers, anthropologists, and literary scholars, bringing together region, landscape, and culture has become a renewed aspiration following partly in the footsteps of older traditions (such as those established by Carl Sauer and Yi-Fu Tuan) but also striking out in novel directions as well. In this vein, the mention of Patrick Geddes by David Matless in his chapter is instructive. Here is a figure from the past who contradicts the 'dry descriptive' image of ancient regime regional geography and who speaks to many concerns of the present day, from regional ecology to regionalist political attachments. Yet, the evocation of Geddes can only be the beginning of a re-exploration of the benefits of thinking regionally about ecologies and attachments, as Matless also makes clear. It is not a question of simply going Back to the Future.

The region, then, whatever its precise geographical and social parameters, is increasingly important in a range of fields, even when it is not rigorously defined as an inherent feature of a particular study. In recent years, however, there has been a resurgence of studies explicitly engaging with sub-national regions, not least because of the regional-ethnic revivals going on around Europe, from Spain and the British Isles to the former Yugoslavia and the Soviet Union. Regions as geographical units with which to define the *contexts* of study of a wide range of social structures and processes are therefore important both implicitly and explicitly in the contemporary humanities and social sciences. This book contains a number of chapters devoted to the processes of political regionalism/separatism.

More recently, world systems frameworks, such as that of Immanuel Wallerstein (1974), based on distinguishing dynamic economic-geographical core macro-regions, such as northwest Europe after 1700, from relatively peripheral or exploited ones, such as eastern and southern Europe, theoretical frameworks such as that of E.W. Fox (1971) posing an opposition between 'commercial' and 'feudal' regions within countries such as France, and internal-colonial or mode of production arguments (such as those of Michael Hechter (1976) and William Brustein (1988)) identifying different types of regions within states with respect to political and social characteristics, represent different ways of explicitly incorporating regions into social-historical or economic analysis.

Even greater emphasis on the role of regions as contexts for social invention, economic development, and political affiliation can be found in the work of the economic historians Sidney Pollard (1981) and Gary Herrigel (1996), of economic sociologists such as Arnaldo Bagnasco (1988) on local economic development and the social construction of the market, and economic geographers such as Michael Storper (1995) and Allen Scott (2001) on the importance of regionalised agglomeration economies in big cities to the overall global geography of economic growth. Nicholas James's chapter in this book is a very good example of the possibilities implicit in this genre of regional geography. Much research, however, still tends to operate on an implicit rather than an explicit conception of region. Even as they adopt regional frameworks in their research, scholars are often not very self-conscious about the nature and role of the geographical divisions that they use.

The region has been a significant but often vague category in recent debates but as in previous eras it is still understood in many different ways depending on the purpose at hand. One important overall trend, however, is to challenge conventional territorial-bounded approaches with so-called relational thinking, which suggests that regions should be seen as non-fixed and closed entities. In this way, regions 'stretch' across space so that their social contents and relations can be networked across borders. It is this networking that in fact constitutes region. Thus, regional boundaries and identities need not to be exclusive to one another. In terms of politics, and following the writing of Doreen Massey, for example, seeing regions as bounded can be viewed as 'regressive' while seeing them as open is 'progressive'. This relational thinking is also strongly implied in the ideas of scholars representing the so-called 'new mobility paradigm', emphasising how much people move around rather than tie themselves to places. The question arises to how far this type of thinking can be pushed before regions dissolve into webs of networks and the stories of those in them go ungrounded in any conception of territorial space.

Pushing Forward

What's next then? One direction would be to invest more energetically in sponsoring regionalist-type analysis of economic and political processes. What I have in mind are the sorts of studies I highlighted in Agnew (2000). As I noted there,

> regions have been resituated within global and continental as well as national contexts. Globalisation is increasingly seen as exacerbating more than attenuating regional differences. A *regional political economy*, accepting as a basic premise the intersection between a globalising world economy and uneven development, is making inroads into the intellectual hegemony exercised by conceptions of regions that see spatial difference as either a temporary aberration on an inevitable path to universal spatial equilibrium or as an independent variable that can be reduced to marginal significance if enough non-geographical independent variables are specified in its place. (Agnew, 2000: 102)

Some good examples of this approach come from recent studies in the 'sub-national analysis' of China's political economy. As political economist Meg

Rithmire (2014: 165, 167) points out in a recent review of recent book-length studies: 'China is not one place. … [the authors] are interested not only in variation in economic outcomes but also in variation in local economic *orders*, or the very logic of economic decision making and patterns of behavior.' The work of Guy Herrigel (1996) mentioned earlier is a direct inspiration for this latest round of regional geographies as a way of understanding economic development.

A second direction is to build on the merging between the more idiographic stories and broader theoretical themes highlighted in a number of the chapters in this book. This is illustrated forcefully in James Riding's writings (e.g. 2015, as well as in this book) about the politics of Bosnia as he brings together his personal memories and reading about a discrete part of the country long before he set foot in it with his subsequent travel and fieldwork in the aftermath of the Yugoslav wars of the early 1990s. On one reading this is a memoir about one person's experiences. But on another reading it also engages with the collective memories of the combatants in the atrocities of the Bosnian war and connections they draw back to the liberation from the Nazis toward the close of the Second World War. In openly situating his own 'voice', Riding (2015: 385) hopes to avoid 'an unreflective, distantiated, and voyeuristic account of the Balkans'. All told, then, regional geographies cannot and should not strike only one note. What they all do, however, is to offer routes out of the impasse of a world that can no longer, if in fact it ever could, be adequately understood solely in terms of the bordered spaces of the world geopolitical map.

References

Agnew J (2000) From the political economy of regions to regional political economy. *Progress in Human Geography* 24: 101–10.

Bagnasco A (1988) *La costruzione sociale del mercato*. Bologna: Il Mulino.

Braudel F (1949) *La Mediteranee et Le Monde Mediteraneen au l'epoque de Philippe II*. Paris: Armand Colin. English translation Reynolds S (1972) *The Mediterranean and the Mediterranean World in the Age of Philip I*. New York: Harper Collins.

Braudel F (1986) *L'identite de la France*. Paris: Les Editions Arthaud. English translation Reynolds S (1989) *The Identity of France. Volume I: History and Environment*, New York: Harper and Row.

Brustein W (1988) *The Social Origins of Political Regionalism: France, 1849–1981*. Berkeley: University of California Press.

Dann O (1989) La regione. Una cornice elastica per la nuova storia sociale, in F Andreucci and A Pescarolo (eds) *Gli spazi del potere*. Florence: Usher.

Fox EW (1971) *History in Geographic Perspective: The Other France*. New York: Norton.

Hechter M (1976) *Internal Colonialism: The Celtic Fringe in British National Development*. Berkeley: University of California Press.

Herrigel G (1996) *Industrial Constructions: The Sources of German Industrial Power*. New York: Basic Books.

Hunt L (1986) French history in the last twenty years: the rise and fall of the *Annales* paradigm. *Journal of Contemporary History* 21: 209–24.

Pollard S (1981) *Peaceful Conquest: The Industrialisation of Europe, 1760–1970*. New York: Oxford University Press.

Riding J (2015) Landscape, memory, and the shifting regional geographies of Northwest Bosnia-Herzegovina. *GeoHumanities* 1(2): 378–97.

Rithmire ME (2014) China's 'new regionalism': subnational analysis in Chinese political economy. *World Politics* 66(1): 165–94.

Scott AJ (ed) (2001) *Global City-Regions*. Oxford: Oxford University Press.

Storper M (1995) The resurgence of regional economies, ten years later: the region as a nexus of untraded interdependencies. *European Urban and Regional Studies* 2: 191–221.

Wallerstein I (1974) *The Modern World-System. Volume I: Capitalist Agriculture and the Origins of the European World-Economy in the Sixteenth Century*. New York: Academic Press.

Index

For Product Safety Concerns and Information please contact our EU representative GPSR@taylorandfrancis.com
Taylor & Francis Verlag GmbH, Kaufingerstraße 24, 80331 München, Germany

www.ingramcontent.com/pod-product-compliance
Ingram Content Group UK Ltd.
Pitfield, Milton Keynes, MK11 3LW, UK
UKHW022009180926
475701UK00003B/274
9780367874087